DESERT
REDLEG

AMERICAN WARRIORS

Throughout the nation's history, numerous men and women of all ranks and branches of the US military have served their country with honor and distinction. During times of war and peace, there are individuals whose exemplary achievements embody the highest standards of the US armed forces. The aim of the American Warriors series is to examine the unique historical contributions of these individuals, whose legacies serve as enduring examples for soldiers and citizens alike. The series will promote a deeper and more comprehensive understanding of the US armed forces.

SERIES EDITOR: Joseph Craig

An AUSA Book

DESERT REDLEG

ARTILLERY WARFARE IN THE FIRST GULF WAR

L. SCOTT LINGAMFELTER

UNIVERSITY PRESS OF KENTUCKY

Part of the Robert R. McCormick Foundations

FIRST DIVISION
MUSEUM
— at CANTIGNY PARK —

The First Division Museum at Cantigny Park in Wheaton, Illinois, is proud to partner with the Association of the US Army and the University Press of Kentucky in the publication of this important account of the Persian Gulf War. We believe that familiarity with our military past fosters responsible citizenship and the military and civic leadership that will help ensure our democracy for the future. The museum is part of the Robert R. McCormick Foundation, Chicago, Illinois.

www.fdmuseum.org

This book is dedicated to all the soldiers who gave or were willing to give the last full measure of devotion to the United States of America while serving in our armed forces. It is also dedicated to their families and mine, especially to my children and grandchildren, so they will know.

Editorial and Sales Offices: The University Press of Kentucky
663 South Limestone Street, Lexington, Kentucky 40508–4008
www.kentuckypress.com

Cataloging-in-Publication data available from the Library of Congress

ISBN 978-0-8131-7920-9 (hardcover)
ISBN 978-0-8131-7922-3 (pdf)
ISBN 978-0-8131-7923-0 (epub)

This book is printed on acid-free paper meeting
the requirements of the American National Standard
for Permanence in Paper for Printed Library Materials.

Manufactured in the United States of America.

 Member of the Association
of University Presses

Contents

Photos follow page 150

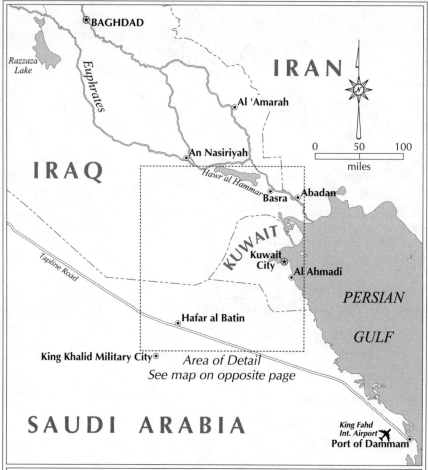

MAJOR OPERATIONAL PHASES
(depicted on opposite page)

•*Phase I:* Occupation of TAA Roosevelt (28 Dec 1990 – 13 Feb 1991).

•*Phase II:* Movement from TAA Roosevelt to occupation of forward attack position in the vicinity of AA Manhattan; then ground counter reconnaissance and artillery raids on the enemy forces (14 – 23 Feb 1991).

•*Phase III:* Attack of Iraqi 26th Infantry Division from PL Kansas to PL New Jersey (24 – 25 Feb 1991).

•*Phase IV:* Movement to contact and attack of the Iraqi Republican Guards on OBJ Norfolk (26 – 27 Feb 1991).

•*Phase V:* Movement to contact and attack of Iraqi forces vicinity OBJ Denver (27 – 28 Feb 1991).

•*Phase VI:* Attack to eject Iraq Forces and secure Safwan Airfield for peace negotiations (1 Mar 1991).

•*Phase VII:* Reoccupation of southern Iraq vicinity of AA Allen (21 Mar – 15 Apr 1991).

•*Phase VIII:* Redeployment to Saudi Arabia vicinity RAA Huebner (15 – 16 Apr 1991).

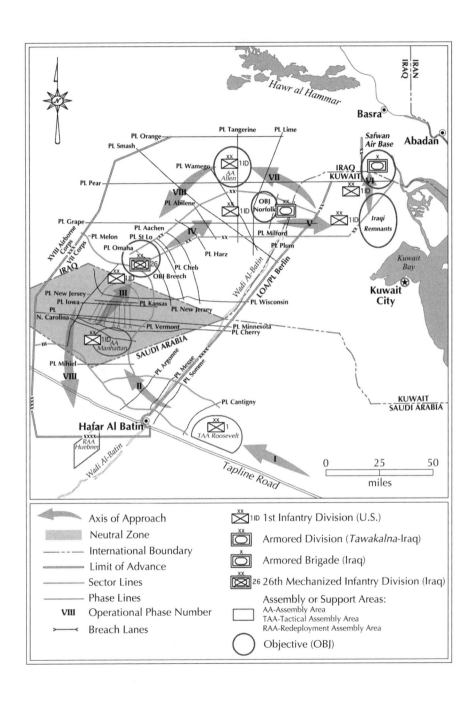

Movements of the 1st Infantry Division from January to April 1991

Introduction

This book is not designed to be a history. That's left to others. It is one man's view of a war he never thought he would fight. My view. An artilleryman's view.

When I entered the US Army in 1973 as a freshly minted second lieutenant from the Virginia Military Institute in Lexington, Virginia, America was in the waning years of the Vietnam conflict. When the selective service draft that recruited soldiers for the war ended on January 27, 1973, America committed to a volunteer Army, even as the Cold War still loomed before us. I was a member of that Army, deployed to the Federal Republic of Germany (FRG) standing opposite the armed forces of the Russian-led Warsaw Pact. Then, as now, the politico-military rivalry between the US and the former Soviet Union (USSR) was fraught with danger. One simple miscalculation by either superpower might result in World War III, a sobering reality for a young second lieutenant newly assigned to a heavy artillery, nuclear-capable battalion in the US V Corps Artillery.

Despite conflicts between the Arabs and Israelis in the Middle East at the time, which had flared badly during the 1973 Arab-Israeli War, the idea of fighting a future war in the deserts of Kuwait and Iraq was far from the minds of the soldiers and officers of my unit, the 2nd Battalion, 92nd Field Artillery. Garrisoned in the Hessian town of Giessen, north of Frankfurt, we riveted our attention on the Fulda Gap, the historic high-speed avenue of approach in upper Hesse that ran northeast to southwest of our position, offering two enticing avenues of advance to the Soviets. These two lowland corridors combined to form "the gap," as we called it, which was a certain pathway for the tank-heavy forces of the USSR. If they chose to, they could launch a massive assault on North Atlantic Treaty Organization (NATO) forces stationed in the FRG. It was a real threat, one that gripped our attention. We had the clear mission to block any Soviet incursion into Central Europe, and frankly, for those of us in the "Red Devil" battalion equipped with powerful and accurate 203mm

1

(8-inch) self-propelled howitzers, the Middle East was someone else's problem. We had enough to worry about in Central Europe.

Indeed, the Army had just emerged from war-torn Vietnam and was demoralized and struggling to recover. That effort was made no easier by major budget cuts and downsizing measures to the entire force during the administration of President Jimmy Carter (1977–1981). What resulted was what we termed the "hollow" Army. Despite the weakened state of America's Army then, we quickly pivoted from our preoccupation with Vietnam to focus more keenly on the Soviet threat. Prosecuting war in the Middle East simply wasn't in the cards for those of us worried about Soviet tanks descending on the plains of Germany.

In time, things would improve for the Army. In 1981 President Ronald Reagan made a major commitment to rebuild American military strength. Ironically, while the improved weapons, newly focused war-fighting doctrine, and quality soldiers resulting from that military buildup rescued the Army from its "hollowed-out" condition, we would never engage the Soviets in direct combat. Rather, in 1991, that enhanced Army would encounter Moscow's well-armed surrogates, the Iraqis, on the desert plains of Iraq and Kuwait and, in the process, defeat that proxy force in detail. Indeed, the improved Army of Operations Desert Shield and Desert Storm—the operational title given to what has been generally referred to as the "First Gulf War"—would engage in a conflict that was unanticipated and improbable in our estimation. Any American involvement in a Middle Eastern war would surely be one of "stand-off support," providing help from afar. This was how we thought we would assist our close ally Israel if Arab armies attacked it. Indeed, this is precisely how we assisted Israel in 1973. Any war in the Middle East, we reasoned, directly involving the US would certainly be one on Israel's side, not fighting as we did to liberate one Arab nation from another in Desert Storm.

US involvement otherwise was both unlikely and improbable for two reasons. First, the suggested presence of Western military forces on Arab soil raised the specter of Crusader occupations of old. Would that not be the case again? In the run-up to the Gulf War, politicians, the press, and pundits everywhere warned that putting US ground forces in the Middle East would create a certain quagmire, and further enflame Arab sentiment against the US. There was a basis for that resentment. Arab hatred of the Jewish state and the Arab states' deep misgivings about America's role in the Middle East had intensified in the decades since Israel reemerged as a nation in 1948. When conflict flared between Iraq and Kuwait in 1990, the idea that the US—Israel's best friend—would come to the aid of an Arab nation brutally invaded by an Arab neighbor was the stuff of fictional Hollywood scripts. How could it be that Israel's chief ally would have the trust of Arabs in an endeavor like that? Never in our wildest dreams would we have predicted the development of a huge US-led coalition of Arabs and Western allies riding to the rescue of Kuwait. After all, in the eyes of many Arabs, the prospect of US forces based in the Middle East would amount to the latest rendition of the Crusaders eager to occupy and conquer their lands. Remarkably, under the leadership of President George H. W. Bush, Saudi Arabia extended an invitation for the US to form an international coalition to come to the Middle East. That huge military coalition indeed emerged. When it did, it stood with tiny Kuwait, no larger than New Jersey, against an assault from a Soviet client state led by a diabolical and self-absorbed dictator, Saddam Hussein. In the strictest sense of the word, these new crusaders would, in fact, be liberators.

Second, the same pundits who warned of quagmires also predicted that war in the Middle East would wind up being a bloodbath. Indeed, I had seen this personally during a tour of duty as an analyst with the Defense Intelligence Agency (DIA) in the mid-1980s during the Iran-Iraq War. From 1980 to 1988, both sides suffered horrendous losses as they struggled violently for dominance in the region, stretching from the mouth of the Shutt al-Arab, located at the head of the Persian Gulf, to the northern mountains of Kurdistan. The enormous carnage of that war was fueled by the palpable hatred between Iraq's Saddam Hussein and Iran's Grand Ayatollah Sayyid Ruhollah Mūsavi Khomeini. The Iran-Iraq War was a bloodletting horror. In suicidal fashion, armed soldiers were hurled at one another, just as they had been in the trenches of World War I. Anyone who had studied the Iran-Iraq War, cynics would say, had to know that if US forces were ever engaged in a conventional war in the Middle East, our losses would be similarly severe. Many Washington politicians at the time worried that casualties would be significant. Even as President Bush worked to build an impressive international coalition, skeptics on Capitol Hill sounded ominous warnings about potential losses. Our own military war planners predicted and anticipated thousands of casualties, not only from conventional weapons, but possibly weapons of mass destruction (WMD), including chemical warfare. Despite these profound concerns—quagmires and sanguinary ones alike—a Western coalition sprang to life to come to the aid of Kuwait, along with the deployment of thousands of US military personnel sent to combat in a region of the world where few of us expected to fight in 1990 or in any other year.

It was against that backdrop that I deployed with the Division Artillery (DIVARTY) of the 1st Infantry Division (1ID) from Fort Riley, Kansas, to Saudi Arabia in January of 1991. The stage was set. I was to be part of the storied "Big Red One" (BRO), a nickname patterned after the bold red numeral "1" that sat amid the olive-drab patch we wore on the left shoulder of our battle dress uniforms (BDU). It would be a remarkable experience for us—indeed a very personal experience for me.

This book details the exploits of the 1ID and, in particular, the contribution of the DIVARTY in the role the BRO played in prosecuting that war. This story is about what we did: the difficulty, the uncertainty, the smells and sounds of battle. It's also about the camaraderie, both good and bad, the serious and the humorous, and the brilliant as well as the idiotic, as all of us pulled together to do our best to get the mission done. It wasn't easy. And sometimes in combat you wind up wondering who is pulling with as well as against you, even on your own side of the battlefield.

I have also endeavored to tell a story not addressed in other works of this nature, specifically, the performance of the field artillery in Desert Storm and, in this case, that of our DIVARTY in supporting the BRO. That contribution has been obscured, some would say ignored, by a characterization of the Gulf War as 100 hours long, a blitzkrieg of sorts, largely involving the audacity of armored and infantry soldiers bounding unhampered across the desert to defeat a feckless opponent. The ground maneuver brigades, battalions, companies, and platoons of our great division performed superbly. But there is more to that story. Likewise, while the contribution of the US Air Force in gaining air superiority in the early stages of the Gulf War to facilitate the destruction of many Iraqi targets deep behind enemy lines is both true and significant, that too is not the whole story.

Since the days of Napoleon, the artillery has been known as the "King of Battle." It earned that title because of the violent and effective contribution made by past "Redlegs"—a traditional term of endearment among the field artillerymen that reaches back to the days when cannoneers wore red stripes on the sides of their pant legs to distinguish them in battle. The same dominance would be true of the Desert Redlegs in the First Gulf War. But in a world of cable television and inflight cameras to record and reveal the high-tech destruction of enemy forces, the actions of artillerymen did not garner the attention or coverage that would give a more fulsome and accurate picture of their combat achievements. This book will address that gap in knowledge. Moreover, for anyone whose son, daughter, father, mother, husband, or wife went to war in the Middle

East in the last two decades—or may in the future—this chronicle will leave them with a broader appreciation of what their soldiers experienced, or could, and how it may have impacted their lives then, or possibly later. It's important to know.

In telling this story, I relied on the personal daily diary I kept throughout the conflict, along with my original battle map. I was also fortunate to have access to after-action reports about the war along with the journal notes of my wartime colleagues. No less useful was my academic and professional experience as a Middle East Foreign Area Officer (FAO), my alternate specialty in the Army when I wasn't assigned to field artillery units. Hopefully, that perspective, training, and experience will help the reader better understand the complexities we faced in fighting in the Middle East. Nothing was easy there, and that will come across "loud and clear."

While this book is largely about the role of the field artillery in support of the 1ID during Operation Desert Shield/Desert Storm, as a student of both military science and Middle East foreign policy, I have crafted my own assessment of this conflict to resolve a central question: "Did we get the job done?" In the final chapter of this book, I assess this conflict at the tactical, strategic, and geopolitical level. Tactically, I examine what we did well and what we didn't. Strategically, I address our approach to the conflict and what resulted from it. And finally, geopolitically, I provide my own verdict concerning whether we truly achieved our goal to secure peace and our national interests in a region torn by unrelenting conflict.

Specifically, I want to offer my special thanks to the DIVARTY commander during the war, Lieutenant General (Retired) Michael L. Dodson (then a Colonel), and the DIVARTY S-3, Colonel (Retired) Ed Cardenas (then a Major), along with my subordinate battery and company commanders in the DIVARTY, Captains Murv Hymel, Rick Nichols, Larry Seefeldt, and Phil Visser, who reported directly to me throughout the conflict. I found the written recollections of Mike Dodson, Ed Cardenas, and my subordinates very closely matched my own as I recreated the events of the war in this book. Using their remembrances and mine, I have attempted to paint a picture of how the BRO and its DIVARTY prepared for combat, deployed to the Middle East, fought the war, and then redeployed back to the US. Throughout it all, these soldiers were superb Redlegs and contributed distinctly to the artillery's reputation as the King of Battle. This book honors their service. I also want to thank Lieutenant Colonel (Retired) Douglas F. Slater, who was an armor officer in the 1ID G-3 (Operations and Plans) section, who provided me with a copy of the original battle graphics we used during the war. I applied them to my personal battle map to help me shape this narrative.[1] A rendering is included in this book, so the reader will have a better appreciation of our maneuvers throughout the war.

I also want to offer my gratitude to my proofreaders for their help, criticism, and suggested editorial revisions. First, to my wife, Shelley, who for the first time in reading the manuscript learned a level of detail about the war I had never shared with her. Many years of hearing me casually relating what we did is not nearly as comprehensive as reading a firsthand account. She was every bit a part of this war, at home, wondering, waiting, praying, and caring for our family throughout the conflict. She is a rock of a woman. To my former legislative aide from my time as a legislator in the Virginia House of Delegates, Terry Durkin, I am deeply grateful for his edits and observations. While not a soldier by profession, he is an inveterate reader of military history, so his clarifying suggestions were most helpful to me. I especially want to thank Lieutenant Colonel (Retired) Dean A. Phillips, who is an accomplished field artilleryman and Vietnam veteran. Dean was one of my first battery commanders when I was a "wet behind the ears" lieutenant. His observations and edits as a soldier and seasoned leader were indispensable in this work. I am grateful to him for that and much more in developing me as a future leader. He had the patience of Job.

Finally, this is a story about the men and women of the finest fighting force in the world, the 1st Infantry Division, the "Big Red One," whose motto says it all: "No Mission Too Difficult, No Sacrifice Too Great, Duty First!" They are the ones—infantrymen, tankers, artillerymen, engineers, aviators, and a plethora of support personnel—who gave or were willing to give their last full measure of devotion in armed service to our nation. I will always remain in awe of them.

To be certain, in 28 years of military service, I never served with finer soldiers. And when the final 24 notes of the bugler's taps drift over my remains, let it be said, "He fought with the 1st Infantry Division."

Duty First!

1

The Big Red One

For a Virginian, the panorama of the resplendent Blue Ridge Mountains or the vast and placid waters of a calm day on the Chesapeake Bay count as two of the most beautiful sights God created. But on a sunny winter day in January 1989, this US Army major first beheld the endless plains of Kansas, another masterpiece of His hands. Their expanse seemed to go on forever, inviting my eye to survey the enormous blue sky above and ahead. Even when the horizon was broken by the Flint Hills east of Fort Riley, home of the 1st Infantry Division (1ID) situated between the towns of Manhattan and Junction City, you could not avoid marveling at the vastness of "The Sunflower State." It was simply big. I suppose it was fitting that the division I was joining as a field artillery (FA) officer was known as "The Big Red One" (BRO).

As we drove west on Interstate 70 (I-70), I struggled to pay attention to the road, even while responding to determined and periodic "When will we get there?" queries from the back of our minivan. My wife, Shelley, and I and our three kids, Amy, John, and Paul, were headed for a new home and an assignment that would change my life and theirs forever.

The 1ID is a storied outfit, and now I would be part of it. It was constituted in the Regular Army on May 24, 1917, beginning as the First Expeditionary Division, composed of Army units on the Mexican border and various Army posts throughout the US. Officially organized on June 8 of that year and further redesignated as Headquarters, 1st Division, it shortly embarked on its new mission to Europe, and the war that awaited. Its history and record in World War I, World War II, the Cold War, and Vietnam were the stuff of Medals of Honor, heroic actions in battle, and even Hollywood movies.

My personnel assignments officer in Alexandria, Virginia, then Lieutenant Colonel (LTC) Joe Monko, was one of my best mentors from my early years in Germany. When he advised me that I was being assigned to the BRO, he said, "Hey, it's a great division. They throw around a lot of crap about how great they are, but it's good crap." To be sure, there's plenty of blarney in any unit. Bragging rights, special bravado, bovine scatology (BS), call it what you want, but it all reflected and built unit pride. And the 1ID had many reasons to be proud.

In one of the last major battles of World War I at the Meuse-Argonne Forest, the division advanced seven kilometers and defeated, in whole or in part, eight German divisions. One of its regiments, the 28th Infantry, was even christened by the Germans as "the Lions of Cantigny" for its ferocity in battle. To this day the 28th Infantry is known as "The Black Lions," and its soldiers proudly wear a regimental crest that bears the creature's image in honor of their battlefield ferocity.

In World War II, the division's performance in North Africa and the invasion of Sicily were alone enough to sustain its reputation for bravery and achievement in combat. But D-Day, June 6, 1944, will forever guarantee the division's place in history. Despite withering fire from German positions above that raked soldiers, noncommissioned officers, and officers of the division's 16th Infantry Regiment with equal prejudice, Colonel (COL) George Taylor, commander of the regiment, rallied his men, saying, "Two kinds of people are staying on this beach! The dead, and those who are going to die! Now, let's get the hell out of here!" His troops rose to the occasion and slugged it out on the beach—ironically labeled "Easy Red" on the battle maps—to seize the German positions on the high ground in front of them. Nothing would be "easy" that day. When they took the heights, they established the 1ID's forward command post (CP) in a German bunker from which, minutes earlier, murderous fire had poured down on the young men of the BRO. The CP was appropriately named "Danger Forward," and since then, from that bloody day to now, the division's forward CP, wherever it may be in the world, is called "Danger Forward." The division's performance in World War II would ultimately result in 16 Congressional Medals of Honor for its members.

As the chill of the Cold War descended on a post–World War II world, the division remained in Europe as an occupation force, returning home in 1955 to the plains of Kansas, its new posting at Fort Riley. From there, it would send forces to fight in Vietnam, where its record was in keeping with its history. The division suffered 20,770 casualties in Vietnam and added 11 more Medals of Honor for the heroic actions of its members.

For a new member of the division like me, its impressive campaign credits said it all. In World War I: Montdidier-Noyon, Aisne-Marne, St. Mihiel, Meuse-Argonne, Lorraine 1917, Lorraine 1918, Picardy 1918. In World War II: Algeria-French Morocco (led invasion), Tunisia, Sicily (led invasion), Normandy (led invasion), Northern France, Rhineland, Ardennes-Alsace, Central Europe. In Vietnam: Defense, Counteroffensive, Counteroffensive Phase II, Counteroffensive Phase III, Tet Counteroffensive, Counteroffensive Phase IV, Counteroffensive Phase V, Counteroffensive Phase VI, Tet 69 Counteroffensive, Summer–Fall 1969, and Winter–Spring 1970. You would be hard pressed to find a division that better lived up to its motto: "No Mission Too Difficult, No Sacrifice Too Great, Duty First!"

So there was plenty to be proud of when I displayed the emblem of BRO on my uniform. That patch, an olive-drab shield of 2 ½ inches in width and 2 ¾ inches in height, flat at the top and with a 90-degree angle at the base pointing downward, sported a bright red Arabic numeral "1" at its center. It was worn on the left shoulder by soldiers assigned to the division. Those who had been in combat with the division were entitled to wear it on their right shoulder sleeve. A few proud soldiers stationed at Fort Riley in 1989 were privileged to display one on each shoulder. They would jokingly say of their service in the Army, "Hey, if you're gonna be one, be a Big Red One." They had bragging rights, and it was imprudent, provocative, and sometimes dangerous to tell them about the accomplishments of other divisions, particularly in a bar after a few drinks. I suppose you could say that was "good crap." But I found myself embracing the reputation and battle focus of the division, subscribing readily to its motto's shorthand: "Duty First!" That about said it all. And it was the mission environment I raced toward in January of 1989 in a van full of precious cargo, my family.

I wasn't supposed to be going to Fort Riley. Joe Monko had arranged for me to interview with a three-star general on the promotion list to take command of Central Command (CENTCOM). CENTCOM is a major combatant organization headquartered at Tampa, Florida, with a mission area covering Southwest Asia and the Middle East. The general wanted an aide-de-camp, who was both a combat branch officer (infantry, armor, or field artillery) and a Middle East Foreign Area Officer (FAO). I satisfied both requirements, as an artilleryman and as a FAO having earned a master's degree in 1981 from the University of Virginia in Comparative Governments of the Middle East and Soviet Foreign Policy. That general officer, H. Norman Schwarzkopf Jr., would go on to be the Commander-in-Chief (CINC) in Operation Desert Shield/Desert Storm (ODS/DS), and his interview of me was, in a word, memorable.

He was impressive in stature and manner. Even seated, he had a commanding presence. I had been briefed that he was imposing, demanding, and self-assured. I sat in the center of a couch next to his easy chair for the interview. My heart was in my throat, and I struggled to project confidence, but not boastfully. Calmly he asked me about my background as a combat officer. I had just completed a tour of duty with the 3rd Infantry Division (3ID) in Germany. He also was interested in my first assignment to the Middle East as an observer for the United Nations Truce Supervision Organization (UNTSO), responsible for keeping the Arabs and Israelis apart along the Golan Heights bordering Syria as well as Israel's northern boundary with Lebanon. I had also written my master's thesis on US arms sales to Iran and how those transactions enabled Iran to expand its influence over US prerogatives in the region, putting Tehran in the driver's seat. General (GEN) Schwarzkopf was interested, and we talked about Iran in some depth. I could tell this was no ordinary man. He was clearly an accomplished combat officer. But he was also an intellectual and knew the Middle East. As the interview proceeded, I sensed I was what he was looking for, both combat-trained and knowledgeable in the region that would be his responsibility as the CENTCOM CINC, including war-planning and potential combat operations.

After we had spoken for a while he leaned forward and said abruptly "So, do you want the job?" I was startled, but managed to respond calmly, "Yes, sir, I do." A few days later, I was advised by the colonel who was his executive officer that I had the job, but there was a catch. I had to leave my current assignment as a student at the career-enhancing Armed Forces Staff College (AFSC) in Norfolk, Virginia, a month before graduation to accompany Schwarzkopf on a tour of the Middle East and Southwest Asia. "He'll need his aide," I was told. I was more than willing to escape the clutches of military academia but was severely disappointed when I was told that if I left the AFSC before graduation, the commanding general there would not grant me a diploma. Schwarzkopf had to go with his second pick. For weeks afterward, I wondered if my most important professional opportunity had slipped through my fingers. Monko wasn't happy with AFSC's decision to hold me in place. In fact, he was thoroughly steamed.

I had known Joe since 1974 when I was a second lieutenant during my first assignment as a Redleg to the 2nd Battalion, 92nd Field Artillery (2–92 FA). As the Battalion S-3 (Operations Officer) in the 2–92 FA, Monko, then a captain, had taken me under his wing and taught me more about soldiering and shooting artillery than I had learned in all the years I had trained at VMI and Fort Sill, Oklahoma, home of the Field Artillery School. I wasn't always a cooperative student. I was headstrong and "knew everything." You only had to ask me to verify that. Yet Joe was patient, as were my first two superb battery commanders, Captains (CPT) Dick Sherwood and Dean Phillips, in recognizing that I was clearly a "live round" needing focus and "special" handling. They did their best to point me in the right direction, and occasionally I cooperated. But Monko saw me as his special project. When I screwed things up, and I did frequently, he would pull me aside and address me in an avuncular manner, saying, "Son, that was truly the stupidest thing I've ever seen a lieutenant do!" I took his counsel—sometimes it was painful—and would snap back, "Thanks, Dad." So when Monko learned that the AFSC scotched my assignment as aide-de-camp to "Stormin' Norman," Schwarzkopf's nickname, "Dad" Monko went to work finding me an assignment with a combat outfit. He slated me for the 1ID DIVARTY.

My disappointment over the Schwarzkopf opportunity still swirled in my gut as I made the turn north from I-70 into the southern gate of Fort Riley, Kansas. But in short order, I found that my new job as the DIVARTY S-3 Operations Officer would be one of the most satisfying I would ever have. What I did not know then, what I could not have imagined, was that I would soon find myself on the desert plains of the Middle East, not the grassy plains of Kansas under the commanding influence of the same Schwarzkopf, who would lead one of the most remarkable combat campaigns in modern history. But in that fight, I would be with the best, a Redleg with "The Big Red One."

Yep, Monko picked a winner, as I would soon learn.

2

Fort Riley

To most soldiers in the US Army in 1989, Fort Riley, Kansas, located 125 miles west of Kansas City, was a place in the middle of nowhere. Indeed, it sits about two and a half hours southeast of the geographical middle of the US at Lebanon, Kansas. But "nowhere" was "somewhere" for the people of the two great communities of Junction City, on the western boundary of Fort Riley, and Manhattan, just east of the fort and the home of Kansas State University. One economic brochure boasted of the positive impact Fort Riley had on the surrounding region, contributing $568,722,015 in payroll and $88,436,808 of purchases from local businesses annually.[1] Economics aside, these communities—and Kansans in general—loved Fort Riley and took pride in those who soldiered there. It was affectionately said of the 1ID by residents of Kansas, "The Big Red One is Kansas's Division, but we'll loan it to the US in a pinch."

Young soldiers looking for nightlife and other attractions had a slightly different view of the once-frontier outpost founded in 1853. It was from the rolling hills of Fort Riley that George Armstrong Custer, who served there after the Civil War, led the 7th Cavalry to its "last stand" against the Indian warrior Crazy Horse at the Battle of the Little Bighorn in Montana. Certain to provoke laughter among young soldiers who found Fort Riley lacking the fun they sought, was a well-worn joke that finds one of Custer's officers galloping up to him at the Little Bighorn to render a report. "General, I have good news and bad news," the officer declares.

"Good grief," Custer remarks, "What's the bad news?"

The officer responds, "The bad news is soon thousands of hostile Indians will ride down upon us, attack us, fill us with their arrows, take our scalps, and leave our bodies to bake in the Montana sun."

Custer then asks anxiously, "Well then, what's the good news!?"

The officer responds, "We're not going back to Fort Riley!"

Actually, Fort Riley was a great assignment if you were one of the over 35,000 soldiers assigned there, particularly if you wanted to experience cutting-edge training with a great combat unit. It was also a wonderful family post. From the post exchange (PX) that sold just about anything you needed, to the commissary where families purchased groceries, to the schools where we sent our children, Fort Riley was a great place to raise a family. And if you liked to fish or hunt, there was no shortage of opportunities for either in neighboring lakes or on the grassy plains set aside by the post commander for upland bird or deer hunting.

When Shelley, the kids, and I settled into our new two-story home, an early-20th-century 1,200-square-foot brick duplex on the Main Post located on a street appropriately named Riley Place, we were content. The quarters were small and even tighter once we crammed in our oversized furniture, but for us, it was home. Our daughter, Amy, had her own room surrounded by dolls and dress-up clothes, and our two young sons, John and Paul, fit snugly in a room so small that a single bed and a crib took up most of the floor space. Shelley and I had the largest of three bedrooms, which doubled as a romper room when the kids came in to play before heading off to bed. It was the place our kids grew up with other military kids in a safe and parklike neighborhood. Amy, John, and Paul adapted to this idyllic setting and its customs quickly. When the kids frolicked near our house at a community playground and heard the evening "Retreat" bugle call at 1700 hours sharp, followed by a lone round fired from the ceremonial cannon signifying the lowering of the post flag for the day, they knew what to do. Without adult supervision, they all would pause, face the direction of the post flag, place their hands over their hearts, and stand quietly as the nation's colors were lowered to the sound of "To the Colors." In the shadow of the house where they now lived at Fort Riley, the kids knew it was a special place.

Our little house also had a dusty basement that was a convenient shelter from tornadoes, a weather event we saw more than a few times a year. Invariably, when I went to the field with my troops to train, a tornado would manage to spin its way toward Fort Riley, usually from the southwest. When the warning sirens warbled their mournful and unmistakable alarm, those of us in the field would seek shelter in ravines and secure ourselves to small stubbornly rooted saplings. This was better than seeking shelter under a large native cottonwood tree that could end up being your immediate cause of death instead of your salvation. At home, Shelley would respond to the warning sound by quickly grabbing the kids and huddling in the basement under a spare mattress. This drill became a routine experience in the spring and summer months. And one day when I announced I was going "to the field to train," our then four-year-old son John dryly remarked, "Well, Mom, let's get in the basement. Dad's going to the field, and a tornado is coming," evoking chords of laughter from both of us. The brick dwelling at 535A Riley Place was our home, and even though we were shoehorned in, it was our "Little House on the Prairie."

While married officers, noncommissioned officers (NCOs), and young soldiers lived on the post or in nearby towns, single soldiers lived in the barracks located on Custer Hill, a plateau uphill from the division's headquarters. Custer Hill was home to the division's infantry, armor, artillery, and combat-support brigades and battalions. Arranged in a large semicircle, unit mess halls and motor pools were just a short walk from where most of the soldiers slept. Beyond this crescent of unit headquarters and billets sat the lion's share of Fort Riley's 100,656 acres where our units trained and fired weapons, from small arms to artillery. In this vast training area, we also conducted complex maneuvers often involving the combined arms of the infantry, armor, artillery, and combat aviation units assigned to the division.

A typical training day would find a unit conducting its daily physical training (PT) after rendering honors at the raising of the post flag as "Reveille" sounded. After PT, soldiers would head to the mess hall for what was frequently a high-protein breakfast. Then to the billets to shower up, clean the barracks, and conduct "police call" to pick up litter in the unit's area of responsibility. Without a doubt, "order" on an Army post is the order of the day. Following those routine activities, units would conduct a morning formation and roll call to account for all the soldiers, and then prepare for training or equipment-maintenance activities for that day.

That training might include a trip to the rifle range where a unit could focus on marksmanship, or possibly gas-mask skills where soldiers would rehearse how to properly employ their chemical-defense gear in a tear-gas environment, the nonlethal training substitute we used to simulate nerve, blood, or blister chemical agents we might one day face on the battlefield. A unit might also conduct driver training on its combat vehicles or go with its armor and mechanized infantry combat systems to the Multi-Purpose Range Complex (MPRC). This field-training facility provided both infantry and tank units with a realistic environment to perfect their maneuver and direct fire proficiency, consisting of maneuver lanes and simulated targets for live-fire training. An artillery unit, like those in the DIVARTY, might go to the field to conduct live-fire training at targets arrayed in the huge impact area at the center of the expansive post.

Meanwhile, higher headquarters organizations that provided tactical command and control, like the DIVARTY or brigades and battalion headquarters, orchestrated lots of the daily company- and battery-size training. Sometimes they focused on tactical decision-making training in the form of battle-simulation command-post exercises (CPXs). Equally important were the host of administrative and logistical activities and meetings that would involve brigade- and battalion-level senior command and support staff. There were countless support activities and routine tasks involving soldiers who "trained" by doing their actual support jobs. Those who trained daily in their specialties included medics, mechanics, supply personnel, mail clerks, personnel administrators, armorers who maintained our weapon inventories, and cooks who kept us fed three meals a day. Every day was a busy day when it came to training.

As the DIVARTY S-3, I oversaw much of the training that took place in the artillery world. My S-3 shop, as we called it, would dispatch observers to the field to review the training of DIVARTY subordinate battalions and batteries and then report our findings to the DIVARTY commander. And when we weren't inspecting training, we were planning future training and operations. We were also kept busy updating our war plans—primarily our reinforcing mission to NATO and US forces on the ground in Germany—since orders to deploy overseas could come with little warning.

When not training on combat skills, units also focused on the maintenance and care of their equipment. This included our monstrously large combat systems, tanks, armored infantry vehicles, artillery, radar systems, fleets of trucks and command-and-control vehicles, radios, firearms, and related individual combat gear. Everything, from our pistols, rifles, gas masks, first aid items, even down to the knives, forks, and spoons in our aluminum field mess kits, had to be kept clean, operational, and combat ready.

Our days were long and packed from morning reveille to taps each evening. Duty was 24 hours a day and 7 days a week, which meant that even after a long duty day, a soldier could find himself or herself on guard duty somewhere on the vast post or at the unit barracks or headquarters. Officers were on duty also, supervising the guard force or preparing for the next day's training. It was a busy time for everyone.

As training areas went, Fort Riley was well equipped and gave units the opportunity to hone their skills, precisely the ones that would be needed in war. The war we were training for, however, would be fought on the northern plains of Germany, not the sands of the Middle East. Yet in an ironic twist of fate, the place where we would conduct our most challenging training for our NATO mission would not be on the grassy and cottonwood-strewn plains of Fort Riley; rather, we would train on the desert sands of Fort Irwin, California, home to the National Training Center (NTC).

While Fort Riley provided the place where we sharpened our warfighting skills, it was the high desert of the NTC where we put those skills to the test in a highly realistic environment to train our brigades and their subordinate battalions together as a combined arms team. There, infantry, armor, artillery, engineers, air defense, aviation, and support units trained in unison to execute complex maneuvers and focus their collective combat power on enemy formations and positions just as they would in actual combat. The "enemy" we fought against at the NTC was a well-trained opposition force (OPFOR) composed of US soldiers who were permanently stationed there and equipped with Soviet military equipment. Moreover, they were skilled in executing the same Russian and Warsaw Pact tactics we might encounter in the Fulda Gap or on other European battlefields.

The NTC offered the toughest conditions a US soldier could expect—short of war—and posed a real challenge mentally and physically. There we faced heat, cold, wind, dust, fatigue, and the confusion of battlefield scenarios. We encountered what the brilliant German military strategist Carl von Clausewitz termed "the fog of war." The NTC was not a place to show up unprepared to do battle. That's why our training at Fort Riley was so important. We did our best to replicate the NTC conditions at Fort Riley, including the rigorous after-action reviews (AAR) the observer controllers (OC)—who supervised the exercise scenarios—would conduct after every mission. These AARs were brutally honest and exposed the good, the bad, and the ugly of a unit's performance. I recall one seasoned and weatherworn field artillery OC saying before each AAR that he conducted, "Look, it ain't good, it ain't bad, it's just what happened." His words were intended to settle us down and focus us on the lessons we needed to learn after an operation, so we would do it better the next time. But it was frequently painful to embrace the findings of a mission poorly executed. Compliments were rare. The thin-skinned did not fare well in these reviews, only those wearing "big boy pants" and willing to learn, focus on the fixes, and improve with each mission.

Most of us embraced the lessons learned, and in the end, we were better for having looked honestly at our actual results. In combat, you must see things as they are, not as you would wish them to be, because self-delusion, never a good thing, is certainly not a virtue in war. The AARs at the NTC were a dose of reality and created the right venue to see things as they were in the wake of our actual performance. That desert training proved indispensable to our combat readiness, even when a fight with Iraq was the last combat scenario we had in mind.

To adequately prepare for our rotations to and through the NTC, we found ourselves in the field at Fort Riley a lot. These long hours of training on the plains of Kansas also had unintended consequences for our families. While they worked to keep daily life in order on the home front as we endured extended training regimens in the field, our spouses and children were also unwittingly preparing themselves for their own version of "the fog of war": the uncertainty, the doubt, the icy fear that would descend on them when it would become clear that the division would deploy for combat to the Middle East. Such is the life of soldiers and their families; they must always be prepared for the possibility of combat deployment.

The questions are always the same. Will my loved one come home safely? Will I be raising children by myself? Did I really sign up for this? These questions and more have haunted soldiers' families, particularly as they lovingly whisper what might be their last goodbyes. In a strange convergence of circumstances, both the soldiers and families of Fort Riley were nonetheless preparing for the uncertainty that combat brings to the lives affected by it. What we didn't know, or foresee, was how quickly the clouds of war would gather and call on all of us to do our part in ways we did not imagine.

A tornado, to be sure, was coming to Fort Riley. It would be in the form of a great and violent desert storm, a *shamal* as the Arabs say, and no one would have the luxury of waiting it out in the basement, not even at placid 535A Riley Place where we lived in peace.

3

The Convergence of Leaders

On June 6, 1944, when COL George Taylor of the 16th Infantry Regiment bravely rallied his soldiers off Omaha Beach to destroy German positions entrenched above the surf and sand where many young 1ID soldiers lay dead or dying, you might say he exemplified the motto of the division: "No Mission Too Difficult, No Sacrifice Too Great, Duty First." He was not the last "Big Red One" leader since World War II to inspire his men ahead of a fight. There would be others in the months to come.

In 1989, the first time I met the commanding general of the 1ID, Major General (MG) Gordon R. Sullivan, I was a major and newly assigned as the S-3 of the DIVARTY, whose motto, "Drumfire," harkened back to the thunderous staccato of artillery as its cannoneers provided rapid and continuous fire in previous wars. Sullivan, an armor officer, was stately and plain spoken. He carried himself with the certainty of a man on a mission. That mission was to infuse every soldier of the division with a warrior's spirit. A Norwich University graduate, he was fond of reminding all of us that the message we should be communicating to our would-be enemies was clear and simple: "If you're looking for a fight, you've come to the right place." It was his way of saying, "Be fit and ready to fight." All the time. That meant training—lots of training.

Sullivan connected with troops. Great leaders do; they must. Soldiers yearn for leaders who stand with them. Soldiers understand, from the initial moment they meet their first drill instructor, that they need and want leaders who inspire, guide, encourage, and admonish them, sometimes nose-to-nose. And like nature, "leadership abhors a vacuum." If that void isn't filled, things fall apart rapidly, both in peace and in war. The rule of thumb for leaders in the 1ID was simple: when in charge, be in charge and live out your leader role robustly. Sullivan was good at this, and his connection was genuine. He also had a great sense of humor. Once when soldiers in the division had a spate of rowdy behavior in nearby Junction City, known for its bars, discos, and other distractions just beyond the post's limits, Sullivan had a take-charge message for them. Speaking before a large assembly of troops, he said with great certitude, "Nothing good will happen to you in Junction City after 11 p.m. at night, men. You won't find the girl of your dreams, you won't win the lottery, and no one will give you the keys to a new Cadillac." Whether these words did the trick is anyone's guess, but we had fewer incidents after his encouragement. I think the troops got the message, and I frequently repeated it to my soldiers. Sullivan also knew how to impart wisdom through a well-turned phrase. One of his favorites was "Hope is not a method." That was his way of suggesting, through an oblique reference to birth control and the insufficiency of hope in preventing conception, that when it comes to leadership, you don't "hope to lead," you do it with determination, confidence, and commitment.

In July 1989, only six months after I arrived, Sullivan would leave the division to be promoted to lieutenant general (LTG) as Deputy Chief of Operations of the US Army, a key position in the Pentagon. A short time later, the division he admired so much would be called up for deployment to the Middle East, and while he would not lead it in battle, his positive influence on us carried over in our execution of duty when we had to take the division into combat. No one could see the gathering clouds over the Middle East from our vantage point on the plains of Kansas in the summer of 1989 when Sullivan handed the reins of command to a lean, sharp-edged infantryman from Winnfield, Louisiana. But that new general was ready for the challenge.

Sullivan's replacement was MG Thomas G. Rhame, an infantryman with a no-nonsense demeanor and the frank rhetoric to accompany it. If Sullivan spoke of enemies looking for a fight, Rhame gave the impression he was eagerly seeking them out. Sullivan infused the warrior's spirit in all of us. Rhame embodied it and expected others around him to do likewise. Indeed, Rhame was a perfect fit to follow Sullivan in command of the BRO. Rhame was keenly aware of the need for the division to be able to fight as a combined arms team. He put his focus there almost straightaway through the Battle Command Training Program (BCTP). This simulation-based combat-training program, based out of Fort Leavenworth, Kansas, was designed to help command and staff leaders learn and improve their war-fighting skills in applying and synchronizing a division's combat power. It served us well in putting us through our paces.

My first, and not-so-gentle, encounter with Rhame was during my tenure as the DIVARTY S-3 and smack in the middle of one of these BCTP training exercises at Fort Riley. I was responsible for synchronizing the indirect fire support of the DIVARTY for this field exercise, and things had not gone well. My job was to ensure we stayed in step to support the "scheme of maneuver," the tactics that the infantry and armor units would employ in a battle. However, unlike the direct fire of the infantry and armor—who can observe what they're shooting—artillery indirect fire originates miles from the intended target. That required a forward observer with "eyes on the target" or reliable intelligence about the target location to ensure our deadly ordnance fell on the enemy, not on friendly units nearby. Unfortunately, for me, during this BCTP exercise, we were not in our finest form. The fire plans were not properly executed, the tactical fire-control computer system had malfunctioned, and the notional enemy units were poorly targeted. The list of mistakes was long.

During the AAR, when we evaluated our performance, I attempted to explain to Rhame and others why a particular fire support procedure was not working properly within the artillery. That's when Rhame, seated at the front of the briefing room packed with the division's leadership, quickly wheeled his chair around and pointedly addressed me. With a steely cold look that easily could have frozen boiling water, he made clear to me in an instant that he had no interest in my flimsy and inane explanations. He wanted the problem fixed and fixed immediately. For Rhame, even a BCTP, while just a simulation, was serious business, and his expectation was that within our areas of responsibility we would resolve issues, not whine about them. I got the message.

The next time I surfaced a problem to Rhame concerning artillery fire support operations was on the desert floor of the NTC at Fort Irwin, California. In this particular "rotation," the term we used to describe a visit to the NTC, our DIVARTY units were in support of the division's 1st Brigade. As we conducted training at the brigade, battalion, company, and battery levels, Rhame pulled into my position in his High Mobility Multi-Purpose Wheeled Vehicle (HMMWV, or Humvee) equipped with several command radios, further evidenced by the long whiplike antennas for the four FM (frequency modulation) radios he used to monitor operations. When he emerged from his vehicle, I had no idea why he was visiting my headquarters, but thinking about my first encounter with him gave me pause at this latest visit.

I greeted him with a sharp salute accompanied by our traditional "Duty First" salutation. He wasn't pleased with the performance of our fire support officers (FSO), asking, "Scott, what's up with the FSOs?" These officers were responsible for the fire planning to support the maneuver units. Rhame wanted to know why their planning in a just-completed training battle had gone badly. Recalling my last encounter with him and doing my best not to impart a complaining tone, I told him concisely what the problem was and how I would address the issue promptly. To my surprise and relief, he agreed with my assessment and left satisfied that I'd fix it. It was at that point, the moment when I took ownership of the problem, that I had gained his confidence. Rhame was looking for "take charge" leaders because he knew those were the ones who would get things done when the chips were on the table. As we said in the division, "When in charge, be in charge." That's what Rhame would instill in all of us as we inched toward an imperceptible fight, not in the mountainous high desert of California, but the near featureless deserts of Iraq and Kuwait in the months to come.

In the spring of 1990, I assumed a new position as the executive officer (XO), the number two position in the DIVARTY. By then my replacement as S-3, Major (MAJ) Ed Cardenas, a West Point graduate, had arrived. Shortly thereafter, our new DIVARTY commander, COL Michael L. Dodson, took command on May 30. Dodson attended the University of Washington and held a Master of Science degree in Operations Research/Systems Analysis from nearby Kansas State University. He had entered the Army as an aviation warrant officer. However, while on a subsequent deployment to Vietnam in 1968, his leadership identified him as someone with great potential and recommended that he be given a direct commission as a second lieutenant in the field artillery. From that point until he arrived as our DIVARTY commander, he had accumulated a very impressive record, not only as an experienced helicopter pilot in combat, but as a commander of Redleg outfits from the battery to battalion levels. Most importantly, he had been an S-3 at the battalion and brigade levels. When he wasn't in a combat unit or some sort of military professional school, he had either been with soldier units or commanding them.[1] He was a perfect fit for the job. While Dodson and Cardenas had worked together in a previous assignment and knew how each other operated, I was an unknown to my new boss.

Dodson insisted on precision and accountability. This suited me fine, and we quickly established a close working relationship. As his XO, I soon learned that the serious-minded Dodson, while occasionally affable, was also a very good listener. He wanted details to fully understand problems brought to him, but he expected that when his staff surfaced issues, they would also offer solutions. He was not impressed with excuses, a trait he shared with Rhame, his new boss.

Dodson brought a high level of precision from his training as an aviator and an engineer, an attribute he would emphasize as our commander.

He kept meticulous notes in a small green memo pad, penning a box symbol at the front of each lined entry he made. When action on that item was started, he would put a single diagonal slash through the box. When completed, he would place a second diagonal, forming an "X" in the box, signifying accomplishment. An "X" was a good thing. But a single slash meant work was ahead and not easily swept under the carpet. With Dodson, there were lots of boxes, and they never just disappeared. Those memo pads held the status of things in DIVARTY like genes hold one's genetic information. If anyone thought he would simply forget about something, there was a box to account for any failures in memory. Dodson was the ideal pick to command this brigade-sized unit and tackle the tough mission that lay ahead of us. He was a truly competent and focused Redleg and expected us to be the same.

My duties as Dodson's XO meant that I was his right arm in many activities. That included being the de facto commander of the four battery-sized units that existed separately from the two 24-gun M109A2 self-propelled (SP) 155mm howitzer battalions under Dodson's command. These smaller "separates," as we called them, included four battery- company-sized units; our Multiple Launch Rocket System (MLRS) unit, Bravo Battery, 6th Field Artillery (B-6 FA); our target acquisition battery (TAB), D Battery, 25th Field Artillery (D-25 TAB); the 12th Chemical Company (12th Chemical); and the DIVARTY Headquarters and Headquarters Battery (HHB).

The MLRS battery, B-6 FA, was composed of nine M270 Self-Propelled Loader Launchers (SPLL), and all the soldiers needed to load and fire them. It was commanded by CPT Allen West, who would go on in later years to be a congressman from Florida. West was a dynamic officer who was keenly mission focused. A few months after I became the XO, West was followed in command by one of my top lieutenants from my 3ID days, CPT Rick Nichols. D-25 TAB was commanded by CPT Larry Seefeldt, a South Dakota native with a wry sense of humor and a solid work ethic. With its three Q-36 counterbattery/countermortar radars and two Q-37 long-range counterbattery/counterrocket radars manned with highly technical crews, D-25 TAB was capable of detecting enemy fire targeting our friendly units and plotting the enemy's location for our return fire. The 12th Chemical dealt with threats from chemical, biological, or radiation weapons. It was led by CPT Phil Visser, a gung-ho Chemical Corps professional, and contained a host of gear and soldiers to provide chemical detection, defense, and decontamination. CPT Murv Hymel, commander of the HHB, supported the staff and soldiers of the

DIVARTY headquarters. He was very talented at juggling several balls in the air at one time, a skill that would serve us well in the months to come. All of them were top-notch officers.

Dodson placed all four units under me for supervision and command duties. Collectively, the separates were quite a handful in addition to my primary responsibility of coordinating the daily activities of the DIVARTY staff. That large staff included the S-1 (Personnel), the S-2 (Intelligence), my old S-3 shop (Operations, Plans, and Training), the S-4 (Logistics), and special staff activities including the division's Fire Support Element (FSE) responsible for fire support planning between DIVARTY units and the division headquarters.

The DIVARTY was fortunate to have a first-rate staff. MAJ Don Mathews was the S-1, and he was very focused on keeping personnel and administrative matters in good shape. Nothing got past him concerning personnel manning. Our S-4, MAJ Barry Brooks, was an armor officer with a can-do attitude that ensured our logistics were in order. He was ably assisted by CPT Gary Rahmeyer. If we needed something, we could count on Brooks to pull a rabbit out of the hat and get us what we required. Our Communications and Electronic Signals Officer (CESO) was CPT Tom Martin, who would receive significant assistance from MAJ Luis Rodrigues who eventually linked up with us in Saudi Arabia. Both were technically superb, and we needed that expertise because the field artillery is very dependent on reliable radio communications, both for our voice capability as well as tactical fire direction, which used digital signals over the same radio systems. The S-2 team, which developed intelligence and enemy targeting, was staffed with the very able and cerebral CPT Sandy Artman and his superb deputy, First Lieutenant (1LT) Cherie Wallace. With Cardenas in the S-3 position and his several vigorous, talented, and seasoned field-grade officers, including MAJs Tom Conneran, Mike Madden, and Jim Stoverink, we had a dynamite operations section. Cardenas also had a stable of hard-charging junior company-grade officers including CPTs Jeff Bruno, Jim Fain, Rick Hanson, Ralph Nieves, Phil Thurston, Bill Turner, Joe Willis, who was our staff chemical officer, and 1LT Tim Bizoukas. At the division's FSE, the DIVARTY team that worked directly with division planners, we had LTC Bob Hill, MAJs Mike Cuff, Don Birdseye, Lon Borjas, Pete O'Hara, and Joe Ramos, along with CPTs Jeff Bruno and Mike Kirklin. While there were many staff functions and personnel to supervise as XO, I found these officers to be vital partners in getting our day-to-day mission accomplished. Later, when we arrived in Saudi Arabia, we were augmented with more outstanding officers who were deployed across our staff sections, including LTC Guy Berry (FSE); MAJs David Denhnel (S-3), Oscar Judd (S-3), Richard Kirsch (FSE), David Petrey (FSE), John Smith (Civil Affairs), and Charlie Wise (S-4); and CPT Chris Hubbard (S-3). Their contributions were invaluable.

Additionally, we were really blessed to have as the top enlisted soldier in the DIVARTY Command Sergeant Major (CSM) Curtis E. Manning. He was Dodson's other "right arm" in all matters dealing with our noncommissioned officers (NCOs) and enlisted members (EMs). Manning was a steady rock and a mentor to officers, NCOs, and EMs alike. Our competent and effective Operations Sergeant Major (SGM), Theo Vann, was Cardenas's right arm in the S-3 shop. He was there when I came to the S-3 job in 1989, and there was no task, no problem, no controversy that Vann was not capable of resolving. He was a "fixer" to be sure and an indispensable member of our tactical operations center (TOC).

In addition to all of this, as Dodson's XO, I worked to assist his two subordinate battalion commanders and their M109A2 155mm self-propelled howitzer battalions, including their three firing batteries (A, B, and C²), their Headquarters and Headquarters Battery (HHB), and their Service Battery (SVC), which were the battalion's subordinate units. With a crew of six including a section chief, driver, gunner, assistant gunner, and two ammunition handlers, the M109A2 was the "workhorse" of the field artillery. A self-propelled, lightly armored cannon first produced in the early 1960s, this system had gone through several upgrades, and in the 1990s we were on the "A2" version, which had a range of 18 kilometers, or about 11 miles.

Command of these M109A2 battalions went to the most highly capable artillerymen in the Army. LTC Harry M. Emerson, a 1971 graduate of the University of Idaho, commanded the 1st Battalion, 5th Field Artillery (1–5 FA), which traces its lineage to the Revolutionary War battery commanded by none other than Alexander Hamilton. LTC John R. Gingrich, a 1970 graduate of Texas A&M, commanded the 4th Battalion, 5th Field Artillery (4–5 FA) and had preceded me as the DIVARTY S-3. Both officers were accomplished artillerymen, technically and tactically sound and singularly focused on their commands. They modeled the "take charge" leadership style that both Sullivan and Rhame exemplified.

But they could be a challenge, often when dealing with the plethora of tasks and other distractions we handed down to them as their higher headquarters. Justifiably, they sometimes "pushed back," since they also were focused on the fire support needs of the division's maneuver brigades, primarily the 1st and 2nd Brigades. They saw the DIVARTY as competing for the time and energy that they needed to devote to the infantry and armor brigades and battalions they supported. Our demands for their personnel to meet operational and training assignments were occasionally requirements passed down to us by the division headquarters. That was a distinction that failed to impress either Emerson or Gingrich, and often—both as the S-3 and later as the XO—I received an earful from them when they argued, sometimes vociferously, that the DIVARTY was overreaching. "You guys need to ease up and back off!" would be their frequent complaint. The DIVARTY's rejoinder, normally from me, was, "Look, this needs to be done, and complaining about it won't make the task go away."

At times the relationship was contentious, if not outright heated. This is the nature of the give and take between higher and subordinate commands, where a commander's first obligation is to his unit's mission and his troops, not the distractions passed down by the "lug heads" in the higher headquarters. I learned to live with the inevitable pushback and genuinely respected them for their tenacity. They were fighters, and I liked that. Nonetheless, I wondered, sometimes out loud to Dodson, if they had a clue about how to deal diplomatically, much less amicably, with anything. When discussions would escalate, Dodson would calmly intervene and resolve matters, either using me as an intermediary to carry "the message," or directly himself, often in the quiet of his office situated next to mine. In either case, things would settle down, and these two superb battalion commanders would get back to business. They were warriors to the bone, and that is what we would need in the months ahead. To be sure, my life was busy and at times taxing. But Dodson provided the right leadership climate that allowed all of us to work together productively, a skill that would pay huge dividends on the battlefield.

I saw Dodson's aplomb clearly in the summer of 1990 when he sent me on a mission to Fort McCoy, Wisconsin, famous for pesky tiny chiggers the locals refer to as "no-see-ums." There I would have two weeks of temporary duty (TDY) as the chief evaluator of a National Guard field artillery battalion undergoing a rigorous annual training test. Dodson, having only recently arrived, was still getting his feet on the ground and sent me on TDY to do a task he would have readily kept to himself as the senior Redleg in the division. When he dispatched me, I knew going to Wisconsin was also a test for me as his XO. He managed to carve a few days out of his schedule to get to Fort McCoy, in part to observe me observing this National Guard artillery unit in action. That was Dodson's style: observe, learn, and act. In short order, he was satisfied that I had pulled things together on the evaluative side of the house and was impressed that I also had managed to adopt his "box technique" to track the details of my work.

Being a chief evaluator of an artillery battalion is something that requires comprehensive knowledge of how the fire support system works. This outing for me showed Dodson I knew my stuff, and for him that was critical in our professional relationship. When you earned his trust and confidence, Dodson would be willing to give you much leeway, and this TDY trip was a confidence builder for him to trust me with important assignments. I would see that in many ways in the months to come when what we did was not an exercise, a simulation, a drill, or a test, but real combat with all its consequences. The confidence and trust we built then would be vital in doing things we could not foresee in the months ahead.

The leadership that I served with in the 1ID, both commanders and staff, was a unique convergence of warrior spirit with the tactical and technical precision to form the foundation of our future operations in combat. As Sullivan had declared, "If you're looking for a fight, you've come to the right place!" That fight was ever closer. But in July 1990, as the plains of Kansas dried to dust under a hot summer sky, the tiny, oil-rich country of Kuwait was not on my mind. Even as I attentively evaluated artillery rounds as they fell into the impact area of Fort McCoy, Wisconsin, with the observant Dodson looking quietly over my shoulder, we did not see the coming fight for Kuwait.

However, soon—very soon—the precision of DIVARTY "rounds on target," like we said in the artillery, would demand our constant attention. As the warriors of ancient Rome admonished soldiers of their epoch, *Si vis pacem, para bellum,* or "If you want peace, prepare for war," and as the division's leaders converged, preparing for war was what we were about.

4

The Approaching Storm

Like those we routinely witnessed over Fort Riley, a foreboding tornadic sky gathered—uneventfully—over the Middle East in the early months of 1990. Then tensions escalated sharply into the year. As I was recovering from my battle with the annoying "no-see-ums" of Fort McCoy, Fort Riley was abuzz that summer with talk of US Army deployments to Saudi Arabia.

In February of 1990, Saddam Hussein's saber rattling included demands that US warships leave the region.[1] But few of us detected the approaching storm. After all, I had watched Saddam closely during my time as a Middle East analyst in the DIA, and this was the kind of blowhard rhetoric for which he was well known. I had learned a lot about him as the Iran-Iraq War raged on from 1982 to 1985 when I worked hand-in-glove with other intelligence agencies, including the Central Intelligence Agency, to report daily on the conflict to our senior leadership of the Pentagon. That included the political-military developments that swirled in and around that war. The Pentagon brass was keenly interested in the war, particularly its impact on our geopolitical and national interests. While I assessed that daily, my primary focus was learning as much as I could about how the Iraqis and Iranians fought tactically on the ground and reporting that to our leadership.

My assignment to the DIA followed a tour of duty with the UNTSO headquarters in Jerusalem. As a UN peacekeeper in 1981, I was initially posted to Damascus, Syria, as part of the US contingent to Observer Group Damascus (OGD) that was responsible for maintaining calm on the Golan Heights between Israel and Syria. Living in Damascus was a window into the Arab psyche, and that insight and understanding broadened further when I found myself on an unarmed UN observation post (OP) in southern Lebanon during the second half of that year. By then, I was assigned to the UNTSO headquarters in Israel, and "home" was the UN operations center in Jerusalem. The contrast between how Arabs and Israelis in that ancient city saw the world could not have been more pronounced. From my graduate studies, I understood the chasm between them was wide. But not even a degree in regional studies could prepare me for the complexity and contradictions of the Middle East. Lebanon was the "Wild West" without a good saloon. Everybody had a gun—and a blood feud to go with it.

A year later when I found myself staring into the face of the Iran-Iraq War from safely behind my desk in the basement of the Pentagon, reviewing raw intelligence, I was not surprised to be looking at the mother of all blood feuds. To say that Saddam Hussein and the Grand Ayatollah Sayyid Ruhollah Mūsavi Khomeini of Iran despised each other is to understate the extent of their mutual hatred. The Iran-Iraq War was the ultimate expression of that hostility, dominated by human wave attacks, chemical warfare, and death. Lots of death. It was costly, particularly to Iraq, which felt it was doing the rest of the Arab world a favor by fighting Iran—at least that's what Saddam asserted. In fact, with the overthrow of Iran's shah in 1979 and the rise of Khomeini and his Revolutionary Guards, Saddam's real concern was the threat to his ruling Sunni Muslim dictatorship posed by a radical Shia Muslim regime in Tehran, particularly one that could stir up discontent with Iraq's Shia population in the south. In an effort to win Arab financial backing for the war, Saddam argued that a radical Iranian regime in Tehran was dangerous to the Arab world and decided it was his task to address it. The war was, in fact, both provocative and unnecessary. But the Iraqi dictator fancied himself the preeminent Arab at the time, and on September 22, 1980, he blundered into a very costly and deadly fight.

Saddam ran up quite a bill in the wake of that conflict, including a large stipend he had promised his troops. He sought debt forgiveness from Arab states that had loaned money to Baghdad to foot some of the bill. By some accounts, Saddam's debt to Arab nations was $130 billion, of which $67 billion was loaned by Kuwait, Saudi Arabia, Qatar, the United Arab Emirates, and Jordan. Getting back in the oil business was an important postwar objective for Saddam and was essential in resolving Iraq's debilitating debt. However, the oil market within the Organization of Petroleum Exporting Countries (OPEC) was unsteady in 1990. Saddam blamed other OPEC states for causing that instability. That included his tiny neighbor Kuwait, who Saddam thought was trying to undermine the oil market figuratively and literally, accusing Kuwait of absconding with Iraqi oil by drilling slanted well shafts under the Iraqi border. It was in that context that Iraq began to openly threaten Kuwait with invasion.

By the time I had returned from Fort McCoy to Fort Riley in July, Iraq had put 30,000 troops on its border with Kuwait. Within weeks, that number had grown to 100,000, including 300 tanks.[2] On August 2, Iraq invaded Kuwait, a sheikdom about the size of New Jersey. Those who shared my background in the Middle East wondered how the US would respond. That answer came soon enough. On August 8, Saddam Hussein announced that he was annexing Kuwait, and President George H. W. Bush announced the deployment of elements of the 82nd Airborne Division (82ABD) to the region. Over the next few weeks, rumors abounded that the BRO would deploy to the Persian Gulf region as part of a larger coalition military deployment.

Despite heightened tensions, MG Rhame was skeptical that the division would be called up. He didn't believe that the 1ID was "a logical candidate" for deployment.[3] After all, our standing mission was to deploy to Europe in the event of a crisis there, and it was easy to speculate that the Pentagon wouldn't want to send us to the Middle East and create a hole in NATO's contingency plan. But Rhame wasn't one to risk unpreparedness. He ordered the division to get busy preparing to be called up.[4] And we did. Rhame's instructions were prescient because, had we waited, we would have risked showing up in Saudi Arabia less ready for combat. It wasn't the last time that this steely-eyed general's warfighter intuition would cause us to prepare for action that was not otherwise apparent.

As we "leaned forward in the foxhole"—Army-speak for preparing for action—many of us watched intently as the situation unfolded in the Middle East. In August, we received a new version of the five-ton trucks we used to transport everything from ammunition to command-post equipment. New HMMWVs, pronounced "Humvees," arrived to replace the older command-and-control vehicles that leaders and smaller operational elements would use to get around the battlefield, dramatically improving our maneuverability. Other new items of equipment began to flow to us ahead of schedule. This windfall of updated equipment was evidence that something big was afoot, indicating it was just a matter of weeks before we would be ordered to deploy.

When the Kansas summer turned to fall, we began receiving written "lessons learned" from US forces, like the 82ABD on the ground in Saudi Arabia: what and what not to bring, how to deal with soft sand and heavy vehicles, and soldier care, including how to make life tolerable in the harsh desert environment. By now it was clear that Rhame's preparatory insight was validated. As an added benefit to our efforts, many of the units in the DIVARTY had spent much of the summer in preparing for their Annual General Inspection (AGI) that evaluated every aspect of unit readiness. It was perfect timing, and the AGI feedback was fortuitous. As we worked to improve and hone our skills and procedures for the inspection, we were also polishing up many areas that made us better and ready to deploy.

In September, we were notified that the division was placed under "stop-loss," an administrative action designed to halt the reassignment of personnel to other units. In other words, if you thought you were escaping Fort Riley and heading to that dream assignment in Hawaii, you weren't. It was unambiguous confirmation that we were headed to the desert. Late in October, the month I was promoted to lieutenant colonel, COL Dodson and I shared thoughts and agreed that it looked as if we would go. All the signs were clearly there. As US military activities on the Saudi peninsula began to unfold, along with the brutality Iraq was inflicting on Kuwait, our higher headquarters at Fort Hood, Texas, the III Corps, sponsored several BCTP simulation exercises. Our division and the DIVARTY staff, led by Dodson, participated in those events, which were focused on desert scenarios.

Further reinforcing our belief that deployment was imminent was the bevy of rumors and second-hand indicators that took the form of hints from "friends" on the Army staff in the Pentagon. These indicators provided more certainty that we were bound for the Middle East. There were also unexpected actions, like getting equipment that you didn't anticipate, receiving new maps of Iraq, or getting authorization to take specific classified readiness and logistical actions we were previously not cleared to do. Those things and others signaled we would be going to the desert soon.[5] Sure enough, on Thursday, November 8, the official announcement came down that we would deploy to Saudi Arabia as part of Operation Desert Shield. Shortly thereafter, the first written confirmation of our alert to deploy to Saudi Arabia was delivered to me by my staff.[6]

The words of OPORD (Operation Order) LEXICON DANGER jumped off the page with a reality that was unavoidable. "THE 1 ID (M) IS ALERTED TO DEPLOY TO SAUDI ARABIA. A-HOUR IS 130600SNOV90."[7] I held the "A-Hour"—or "Alert Hour"—order in my hand for a moment, noting that the historic directive bore the signature of my Riley Place neighbor, MAJ Mike Barefield, as the authenticating officer at division. I then walked to my office window on the third floor of the DIVARTY headquarters building and looked out. The troops to the rear of our headquarters were moving about the area with a business-as-usual pace. But I knew a lot of work remained in front of us as I noted schedules for issuing supplies, painting vehicles, and moving equipment to the Middle East would soon be forthcoming from the Deployment Control Center (DCC) at division headquarters. It was official now. We were going to war.

Despite the warning signs, rumors, and hints, it was nonetheless electrifying and sobering for officers and soldiers of the BRO to receive this OPORD. Events accelerated rapidly as we moved expeditiously toward deployment. We modified existing deployment plans, continued getting our combat vehicles and equipment into top shape, received more modernized equipment, and fine-tuned intensive soldier skills.[8] The following day, we began a massive repainting operation of our combat vehicles from camouflage forest green to desert sand, which continued throughout November. Dodson tasked me, along with the DIVARTY S-4, to push vehicles through in an assembly-line fashion that would have rivaled a Detroit automobile factory. It was a 24-hour operation that required our soldiers to work in shifts to meet an aggressive timeline. This elaborate repainting operation turned out newly painted combat vehicles to a fighting force happy to have equipment that would not stick out like a sore thumb in the desert.

Additionally, our more complex combat systems, like the technology-laden M270 MLRS rocket launchers of B-6 FA, were mechanically overhauled to ensure they were in tip-top shape. These launchers were capable of ripple-firing 12 rockets at a time, each loaded with 644 individual bomblets that could destroy both personnel and armored vehicles. With a range of 32 kilometers, they would be deadly in combat. Our launchers, however, happened to be the oldest in the Army's inventory, and many modifications—electronic, technological, and automotive—had to be applied to them to get these aging systems combat ready. That task was bigger than we could accomplish on our own. Recognizing that we didn't have much time to spare, the US Army Materiel Command (AMC) sent a fully equipped maintenance team of civilians and military experts north from the Red River Army Depot in Texas, where launchers are normally sent for detailed overhaul. Given the immediacy of the situation, however, sending this team to us was a very wise move by the Army to speed up our preparations.

The AMC teams had the skills, parts, and equipment used at the depot level that far outstripped our division's organic and maintenance-support capability. Composed largely of skilled civilians, they worked day and night to get these MLRS launchers into flawless condition. After the modifications to the launchers were completed, we moved B-6 FA to the field to conduct a live-fire exercise and fired 54 rockets to validate the upgrades AMC had installed. Every launcher performed perfectly, and afterward, we had a thank-you barbeque to show our gratitude for AMC's superb work. AMC, in turn, gave us a framed photo of one of the refurbished launchers test-firing, inscribed with "Good Luck and Good Hunting." B-6 FA's troops loved it, and I was greatly relieved that our aging systems had a new lease on life. They needed it, and had we not been going to war, it's unlikely we would have gotten such favorable treatment.

Meanwhile, the howitzers of our battalions were borescoped, a procedure to detect wear and metal fatigue inside the cannon tube, to ensure they were in good order. An in-bore explosion due to structural weakness and excessive use is not something anyone ever wants to experience. Making sure these cannon tubes were in good shape was vital. The AMC teams checked each of the howitzers and pronounced them ready to go. No detail was overlooked.

Our highly technical and somewhat fragile counterbattery radars were brought up to top condition. We also received additional spare parts in the form of telewave tubes (TWT) that were essential to the operation of the radars. These TWTs were often damaged when radars encountered particularly rough terrain, so any extras could be especially valuable. Additionally, our Tactical Fire Direction System (TACFIRE), the computers we used to calculate firing data, and associated subsystems at the DIVARTY, battalion, and battery levels, all received the latest software updates.

We were also introduced to a new technology called GPS, geopositioning systems. These devices, made by civilian manufacturer Magellan, were very early prototypes, and their reliability was questionable. For artillerymen like Dodson and me, who had been trained in manual procedures, our skepticism of this new technology resulted in dispatching the DIVARTY S-4, MAJ Barry Brooks, to a marine-supply store in Lawrence, Kansas. There he purchased fully gimballed marine compasses, which we mounted on the dashboards of our Humvees. Just like a ship at sea, we could then find our direction magnetically while using our vehicles' odometers and speedometers to determine accurate direction and distance as we navigated the desert. Besides, our standard practice in computing artillery firing data was to also have a backup solution. We reasoned that having one for navigation would be wise since we were not enthralled with the idea of newfangled technologies that would "magically" tell us where we were. We knew better. We were artillerymen and quite capable of locating where we were on the ground by using a good old-fashioned map. Now, equipped with the ancient pathfinder of the seas and a wristwatch, we were ready to navigate the featureless deserts that awaited our arrival. It proved an astute purchase.

While an abundance of logistical and maintenance activities demanded our attention, Dodson was concerned about fundamental combat tasks, primarily individual soldiering skills as well as battalion- and battery-level cannon and rocket live-fire proficiency. Individual training focused on survival techniques, especially with our gas masks, anticipating the enemy's use of chemical weapons. Saddam Hussein had used chemical weapons on the Iranians, as well as on Iraqi civilians. Our soldiers also spent considerable time with small-arms training, mostly with their M16A2 combat rifles, which could be fired in either a semiautomatic or fully automatic mode. Officers like me, whose primary weapon was the 9mm Beretta 92FS Centurion—known to us as the M9 semiautomatic pistol—also spent time on practice ranges. Without a doubt, our training was comprehensive, right down to the proper digging of a fighting position or "foxhole" for personal protection from enemy fire.[9]

Fortuitously, the division's training cycle that summer prior to our alert was designed to prepare for another deployment to NTC at Fort Irwin. The home-based training activities, called "Gauntlets," were battalion- and company-level training exercises. However, even with this focused training, the orchestration of artillery live-fire above the company or battery level still needed work. Dodson made a determined effort to concentrate on battalion-level fire support. He knew this would be vital in the desert, where the entire division and all its maneuver brigades would be moving simultaneously in a real fight.[10] Fortunately, our separate units, B-6 FA, D-25 TAB, and the 12th Chemical, also participated in the live-fire and Gauntlet exercises, training for the supporting role they would have in combat. These Gauntlet exercises gave Dodson an opportunity to emphasize the importance of live-fire training for our rocket and cannons units. He assessed that at the battery level, live-fire proficiency was good. But at the battalion level, he wanted more focus on massing battalion fires by bringing the fire of their batteries together on a single target to maximize their impact on the battlefield. He felt that accurately massing artillery would be vital in the desert. Therefore, he had the battalions focus on fire support planning and execution—the development of detailed and coordinated firing plans—and the accompanying maneuvers that guns and launchers would employ to occupy positions quickly and fire their ordnance.

This required the involvement of operators—S-3s and supporting fire planners—of the battalions, the DIVARTY, and the Division FSE to better coordinate the overall artillery support. Dodson knew that in the desert, where we would encounter large enemy units arrayed in classic Soviet-style formations, those targets would be susceptible to massed fires. So his focus at Fort Riley was designed to get us ready to deliver such overwhelming firepower. Without a doubt, he had the "eye of the tiger," and for those of us who watched him at work, we knew he was focused on the right things.

One of the more interesting aspects of preparing to deploy was acquainting the troops with the Soviet-style equipment we might face. This included the appearance of Soviet-style helicopters that the US had obtained from Afghanistan in the wake of the Soviet invasion there. Suddenly, we saw them flying in the skies above Fort Riley. Soldiers were treated to this sight so that they would recognize the types of aircraft in the Iraqi inventory. It brought home to us that this was reality, not American soldiers playing the role of OPFOR at the NTC, and further spurred our desire to prepare.

Yet amid the painting, the refitting, and the almost carnival atmosphere of Soviet aircraft soaring above us, there was the dark horizon of the danger ahead. The around-the-clock activity had a beneficial effect: it diverted our minds from the thought that many of us might not come back alive. Officers and soldiers alike wondered if we too would see the human wave attacks, the employment of chemical munitions mounted atop Iraqi SCUD missiles, or worse. How would the Iraqis fight? For years, our focus in the post-Vietnam era had been on countering Soviet-style tactics that would be employed on the plains of northern Germany. That's how I trained there in the 1970s and 1980s. Air-Land Battle (ALB) was the doctrine we practiced that envisioned the synchronized employment of ground combat power and air support at a point on the ground to overwhelm the enemy and his rear echelon forces that supported his frontline troops. The Iraqi-style of warfare had been quite different during the Iran-Iraq War, which I observed while at the DIA. Would our ALB approach work, or was it too cumbersome for a static defense that the Iraqis might mount?

Three months earlier, I had already rendered an opinion on this to division planners. After the Iraqis invaded Kuwait on August 2, I visited the division headquarters on the main post, where I had occasion to speak to the Division G-2 (Intelligence), LTC Terry Ford. As the senior intelligence officer in the BRO, he was already evaluating how the Iraqis would fight. Through the grapevine, Ford had learned that I had been a Middle East specialist who had watched the Iran-Iraq War closely. The subject of how the Iraqis would fight came up, and I shared my observations about their tactics. After discussing their use of fortified triangular revetments—essentially earthen defensive positions that the Iraqis employed against Iran—he said he'd like to talk further when we had more time.

That weekend our friends on Riley Place, along with our collected tribe of children running about, had a neighborhood cookout. Everyone was abuzz with anticipation about whether we would be alerted to deploy. We speculated about our involvement and the nature of warfare with the Iraqis. As we enjoyed our cookout, downing a few beers in the process, I shared with the group my experience in tracking the Iran-Iraq War, offering my unsolicited opinion on how the war might play out. I didn't think much about it afterward and frankly didn't expect anyone paid much attention to my observations. Besides, the division had plenty of experts, including Ford. I was wrong.

The opportunity to share my opinion showed up on Monday, August 6 in a most unusual manner when I received a call from the 1st Brigade S-1, MAJ Bo Barber, one of my neighbors who had been at the cookout the previous weekend. "Hey, Scott, just wanted to call and tell you that Rhame just visited our brigade headquarters," he said cheerily.

"Oh really, what about?" I asked.

"Well, he wanted to talk to us about the current crisis in Kuwait, and, well, I told him you were a Middle East expert. I knew you wouldn't mind," he said playfully. "Oh, by the way," he added, "he should be at your headquarters any minute now. See you later!"

I thanked him painfully and hung up the phone, rather stunned by the call. I then popped into Dodson's office next to mine to give him a "heads up," when suddenly I heard the duty orderly at the entrance of our headquarters call out, "Headquarters, tench-hutt!" bringing all of us to "attention." As he strode past my office, Rhame looked in and, casting aside his general officer's ceremonial belt on a chair outside Dodson's door, said to me directly, "So, an old Mideast guy, huh?"

I responded, "Yes, sir, once upon a time I was," hoping he wasn't entertaining any idea of pulling me up to the division intelligence shop. I followed Rhame into Dodson's office, where the commanding general had already taken a seat in one of the red vinyl armchairs next to a couch where I sat down. Dodson joined us around the coffee table that was at the center of this arrangement.

Rhame wasted no time in getting to the point. "So, Lingamfelter," he asked, "what's this Saddam guy gonna do anyway? Are these Iraqis gonna fight?" Before I could respond, he injected, "Is he gonna invade Saudi Arabia too?" with a hint of Louisiana skepticism in his voice. They were blunt questions that caught me a bit off guard.

I glanced at Dodson, who gave me an approving look. Then I turned to Rhame and told him, "First, sir, Saddam is not insane, but he can be irrational. It's unlikely that he'll invade Saudi particularly if the US shows up," I said. "They will fight," I continued, "but not with Soviet-style maneuver tactics, at least not the regular Iraqi Army forces." I related that the regulars, whose training was not as comprehensive as the elite Iraqi Republican Guards, had largely depended on defensive operations against the Iranians to fend off human wave attacks.

"Will they come out of the triangular positions to fight us?" Rhame inquired, referring to the shape of the defensive structures the Iraqis had used against the Iranians. I said that the regulars probably would "stand fast" inside their revetments, the outwardly sloped defensive positions they would occupy, particularly since the fire and maneuver tactics the US and the Soviets employed were skills the Iraqis did not generally possess. At least they did not exhibit any such skills during the Iran-Iraq War.

Then he asked, "What should we prepare for?"

I paused a moment, feeling the weight of the question, and then said, "POWs, General, lots of POWs." I explained that the Iraqi regulars were not the battle-tested soldiers some were saying they were. In the Iran-Iraq War, large numbers of prisoners of war (POWs) from the regular ranks were a common occurrence on both sides. I told him that we really needed to think hard about how we were going to handle large groups of prisoners. This could develop rapidly, outstripping the capability of our lone divisional military police (MP) company to handle the problem.

He then asked me about the vaunted Republican Guards, how they would fight and how we should prepare for them. I told him that the Republican Guards were, in fact, "the best" that Saddam had in his army. They were the "ones most loyal to him and better equipped than the regular forces." These units would comprise the strategic reserve behind the regulars, just as they had in the war with Iran. And, indeed, they would fight. I asserted that I was confident our firepower and skills could overpower them, particularly the massed fires Dodson had in mind, but that we would take casualties. I believed then—and told Rhame what he probably already thought was the case—that the Republican Guards would pose the most determined threat we would see, even exceeding the land mines and imposing defensive revetments of the regular forces we would initially face.

Rhame's final question was as pointed as the first ones he shot at me. "Will Saddam leave Kuwait?" he asked, leaning forward in his seat toward me.

"No, sir," I responded, "not unless we push him out at gunpoint."

Satisfied, Rhame made some small talk about getting ready to deploy and then was out the door as quickly as he had arrived minutes earlier. It was clear to both Dodson and me that the warrior spirit in Rhame was alive and well. After he left, I turned to Dodson, somewhat overwhelmed by the abruptness of this interview, and was assured by him that "all was good." When I went to bed that night, this encounter kept my brain active. Was I right? Would what I had witnessed in the Iran-Iraq War bear out in a war we might fight with the rebuilt 1990 forces Saddam would array against us? I did not regret what I had told Rhame, but I sure hoped that I was right as I struggled to fall asleep. One thing was for sure. I'd find out soon enough; we all would.

As we continued to make our preparations for deployment that fall, many soldiers were excited with the prospect of doing what they were trained to do, fight in combat. It's common, I suppose, for a soldier to express enthusiasm to "get in the fight" yet recoil somewhat from the visions of violence one might encounter, even one's death. I found this to be the case with me as I sailed on our 22-foot Catalina sloop—ironically named "Peace and Plenty"—on Lake Milford west of Fort Riley with our children that summer and early fall. As we glided carefree on a placid lake in central Kansas, I watched them move playfully about the boat, unaware of the turmoil that lay ahead and the violence that was being visited on Kuwait. I wondered, if something happened to me, how they would get along without a father. Would Shelley remarry and their memory of me be resigned to a sad, yet ever increasingly distant chapter in their lives? My son John had mentioned to his babysitter shortly after I deployed, "My Daddy is going to die, but I'll just say a magic word and get a new one." Our S-3, MAJ Cardenas's two-year-old daughter, Annie, invented two imaginary fathers to take the place of hers: two farmers, Rossi Hill and Jossi Hill, who, like her daddy, "worked in the field." The idea that fathers might not come back was clearly on the minds of these tender children as both were trying, in their own way, to cope. John knew, even at four years old, that war can mean death, but unlike him, I knew no magic word would bring me back to his loving arms and those of his older sister, Amy, and little brother, Paul. I found my warrior enthusiasm waning in the chilly wind of reality as fall turned to winter that year. The call to arms was calling me away from the arms I feared to leave behind. Yet this was my duty, and I embraced it.

When Thanksgiving arrived, the division was preparing to dispatch advance forces to the region, and the flow of our equipment to the Middle East via rail and ship began four days later. The rail yard at Camps Funston and Whitside, southeast of Fort Riley's main post, was a hub of activity around the clock. Every day between November 26 and the end of the first week of December, over 6,000 combat systems, including M1 Abrams tanks, M2 Infantry Fighting Vehicles (IFV), artillery, and every manner of combat transport from tractor trailers to small tactical vehicles, were moved south by rail to Gulf of Mexico seaports in Texas for onward shipment to Saudi Arabia.[11]

Some high-priority equipment went on large US Air Force cargo aircraft, like the division's tactical headquarters vehicles, but most of our combat systems went by sea. It was a surprisingly orderly process that required vehicles to be staged and ready to go when the railcars were spotted for loading at the railhead. Delays were unacceptable if we were to meet the tight timelines to transport vehicles to the port, so they would arrive by the time our troops landed by aircraft a few weeks later. Many of us, previously assigned overseas, were experienced in moving heavy combat equipment by rail from our German garrisons to the remote combat training areas of Grafenwöhr and Hohenfels, giving us an advantage in meeting tight shipping schedules. It was, nonetheless, a remarkable feat in a very short span of time. As it turned out, the first of 13 ships bearing the division's combat vehicles docked in Saudi Arabia on January 7, after about a 29-day voyage, and just days before our soldiers arrived by aircraft. The last vessel would arrive 20 days after the first had, completing a tremendous effort by the soldiers of the 1ID.[12]

My Humvee was one of those vehicles, and my driver, Private First Class (PFC) Roger Lee McGary, and I had meticulously prepared it for combat operations. One evening, in the most surreal setting, McGary brought the vehicle down to our family quarters on Riley Place. There, during a family cookout on our back porch, Shelley and the kids watched us use the same rotary saw that had belonged to my dad to install a ¾-inch slab of plywood in the back of the truck, effectively splitting the rear compartment of the vehicle horizontally into two even halves. We would store our equipment and other gear in the lower half, and at night—when we were unable to deploy a tent—we would sleep in the vehicle on the top half of the plywood slab. There was virtually no headroom in this arrangement, but given that we expected to be on the move frequently, this seemed like a good idea.

In a moment, I caught myself wondering, would this be the way my kids would remember me if I didn't come back? Would they say that one of their last memories of me was "struggling with Roger" as we attempted to turn our Humvee into a desert mobile home? It evoked a chuckle as I recall, but later that night, in the quiet of our bed as Shelley slept soundly, I lay awake wondering where all of this would lead. I knew how brutal Saddam could be. I was sure, though, that if he fought us as he had fought the Iranians, we would prevail. The question that tugged at me was "At what cost?" I had told Rhame that we would win. But we had not talked about the human costs. I had said there would be lots of Iraqi POWs. But what if Saddam used chemicals? How many thousands of us would be killed or incapacitated for the rest of our lives? In the press we read that expected casualties would be in the thousands. We quietly and soberly accepted the notion of heavy losses. That's what soldiers are trained to expect, and do.

Soon we were issued our desert camouflage uniforms (DCU), another poignant reminder that deployment and combat were ever closer. As we conducted our predeployment planning, we began a process called Preparation for Overseas Movement (POM). It's a comprehensive procedure that includes personnel and medical records reviews, immunizations, "dog tag" verifications, life insurance arrangements, and wills, the latter punctuating the persistent thought that some of us might not return. Unquestionably, there was real apprehension over our impending deployment. But as CPT Seefeldt, my D-25 TAB commander, observed as we readied ourselves, "The soldiers were calm and professional," knowing that they were better prepared, equipped, and led than any Army in modern history.[13]

That night I returned home from the POM with my DCUs and my newly minted dog tags, two metal rectangular plates rounded at the corners with my name, identification number, blood type, and religion stamped on them, and placed on a small 24-inch beaded chain to be worn around my neck to identify me if I were wounded or killed in action (WIA/KIA). When I placed them on my bedroom dresser that night, there was a lot to think about as I went in to quietly kiss my sleeping children goodnight. I reminded myself that Seefeldt's observation was right, of course. Our troops, training, doctrine, and equipment were second to none. But Saddam was a brutal character. Evil. As I crawled into bed, I did my best to fall asleep. It took a while that night.

As Christmas approached, it was eerie to drive past the empty motor pools in the semicircle arrangement of units on Custer Hill. Once filled with combat vehicles, they now were empty lots and reminders of what was to come. Even stranger was the slow disappearance of unit personnel, as we began our deployments in the days before Christmas and around the New Year. To soften the impact on families being separated by our rapidly approaching deployment to the Middle East, the DIVARTY family-support leadership team planned a farewell potluck in the days prior to our deployment. At the event, besides the wonderful food, there was a US map displayed where everyone marked their hometowns. That backdrop served as a festive setting for family pictures. Yet a somber cloud hung over everyone. Could this be the last family picture taken of loved ones together? All of us did our best to chase that painful thought away, but like a well-thrown boomerang, it kept coming back as many of us exchanged knowing looks among ourselves.

On December 15, the Division's Tactical Assault Center (DTAC)—or "Danger Forward" as it has been known since D-Day in 1944—departed Fort Riley to coordinate logistics and act as a forward area liaison for the division's leadership. Accompanying the DTAC were eight DIVARTY troops along with MAJ Tom Conneran, our Assistant S-3, who would lead our advance party. On December 29, I bid Dodson farewell early on a bitterly cold day as he headed out with our fire support team, LTC Bob Hill and MAJs Mike Cuff and Don Birdseye of the Division FSE, along with the entire 1–5 FA. All of them were now headed to Saudi Arabia to establish the DIVARTY's forward operations and continue the early planning of combat operations, something Dodson was very eager to do.[14] On January 5, our second cannon outfit, the 4–5 FA, deployed. Soon the DIVARTY TOC and the separate batteries would be heading out. But I still had things to do.

Just before Christmas, I went to Manhattan, east of Fort Riley, to purchase a little yellow cocker spaniel we named Gunner, another term of endearment for artillerymen. He was cute beyond description, and I thought he would be a nice distraction from the stress that lay ahead for Shelley and the children. As it turned out, he probably caused more stress for Shelley than comfort for the kids as she struggled to housebreak him. But it was my sincere effort, possibly a miscalculation, to comfort the family I was leaving behind.

Soon, it was time for many of our DIVARTY families to say goodbye. After sad farewells by soldiers and families at the huge hangar facility at Marshall Army Airfield (MAAF), the realities of deployment began to sink in for our families. When we left, they would busy themselves in the days, weeks, and months ahead with the challenges of family life, many with kids at home. For those DIVARTY spouses in family-support leadership positions like Diane Dodson, Mary Cardenas, and my wife, Shelley, time would be split between planning gatherings, sharing information with the unit's spouses, troubleshooting crisis situations that might arise among families, and keeping family life at work and home as normal as possible. On many days, "normal" could be a variant of "chaotic." Nevertheless, the friendships forged under these circumstances were another form of combat readiness. Just as their soldiers were "joined at the hip," DIVARTY spouses knew their survival depended on working together. This shared experience was the binding factor that quickly made these relationships more like those of family than friends or neighbors.

Then the day came to say my goodbyes. I recall vividly standing on the back porch of 535A Riley Place, holding Shelley in my arms. The words we shared are forever ours, and I refused to think then that I would not be back. It was Thursday, January 10, 1991, and I was headed into combat with the 1ID and the warriors of the DIVARTY. The previous August it had been hard to imagine a war that wouldn't include the BRO. It was fitting we should be there—as we had in World War I, World War II, and Vietnam. Many of us had speculated that our former division commander, now GEN Gordon Sullivan, who was then at the center of major force-deployment decisions in the Pentagon, would insist that the BRO be included.

Whether true or not, that day as I turned away from my bride and the mother of my children—seven-year-old Amy, four-year-old John, and two-year-old Paul—Sullivan's words reverberated in my mind: "If you're looking for a fight, you've come to the right place." We were now ready for that fight, and we were headed there, leaving our most precious treasure behind and in the hands of God.

5

A First-Class Ride to Confusion

It was January 10, 1991. "Ironic" was the word that came to mind as I boarded a commercial Boeing 747 with several hundred of my troops and took my seat as the aircraft commander in the first-class section. It was a duty that fell on the senior officer aboard, and I was that person.

It had been a relatively short ride—a bit over an hour—on I-70 from our assembly point at the MAAF on Fort Riley to Forbes Field in Topeka, Kansas. When we arrived, we gathered in a large hangar where we waited to board the aircraft. Our personal items and combat gear had preceded us in cargo trucks and were already loaded. We kept our weapons with us, mostly the M16A2 rifles that each soldier carried and the M9 9mm pistols that were the typical sidearm for officers. We would receive ammunition once we had arrived in country, which was fine by me. Getting everyone quickly onboard and accounted for was enough to worry about without the potential for an accidental discharge of a weapon inside a 747. Moreover, it was a cold day, and the hangar had given us little comfort from the Kansas wind. We were glad to finally board the aircraft and head to warmer weather, even if it was in a combat zone.

After the aircraft started down the runway, accelerated to takeoff speed, and became airborne, there was a firm and certain thump when the aircraft's landing gear lodged in its wheel wells, leaving no doubt in anyone's mind that we were surely headed to Saudi Arabia. After reaching cruising altitude, I unbuckled my seatbelt and went to the cabin deck below to chat with the soldiers. There was an air of cautious ease among the troops. They were glad that at last we were on our way, but to what? I wondered too, and after some light conversation with a few soldiers, I returned to my seat in the upper deck. There I sat, thinking to myself, "Ain't this something. I'm headed to my first war in a first-class seat on a 747." I wondered if the return trip would be as good, or whether I would be alive to experience it? The flight seemed to go on forever. But we were treated to three good meals and snacks by the flight crew, who were unmistakably motivated to make it a pleasurable trip. They were certainly moved by the youthful faces of the soldiers who were now headed to war. They must have wondered, as I did, "Will they all come home?"

Day turned to night, and I slept fitfully. Most everyone else did as well. We made a stopover in Germany, and then it was back in the air late on January 11. As dawn arose ahead of our speeding aircraft, I knew that we would soon be arriving in the Kingdom of Saudi Arabia. I had never been there. Indeed, my only tour of duty in the Middle East had been with the UNTSO as a military observer. There I had gained valuable experience in the Golan Heights in Syria bordering Israel, the Sinai Peninsula in Egypt, the hills of southern Lebanon, and the Jordanian desert. All these areas were good geographical and cultural proxies for what was ahead for me and my troops once we arrived in Saudi Arabia. My years of graduate study also gave me a sound working knowledge of the Saudi culture, government, and history of this vast desert kingdom. And, of course, I had a unique insight into the politico-military and diplomatic challenges the Saudis faced in the Middle East from my days at the DIA where I had access to intelligence information many people never see. Nonetheless, like everyone else on the flight, this would be a new experience for me too.

As our 747 winged its way east from the continental United States (CONUS) and then over Europe and the Mediterranean Sea, I had time to think about the Middle East. My graduate studies had focused on the governmental structure of Middle Eastern nations and US and Soviet policy in the region. None of the Arab nations in 1990 could be termed a democracy. They ran the spectrum from monarchies like Saudi Arabia, Jordan, Kuwait, Qatar, and the United Arab Emirates, to dictatorships like that in Syria and Saddam Hussein's Iraq. Most of these nations had had their borders drawn by European powers in the wake of past world wars. This mandated array of governments and borders was artificially rooted in Western Europe's desire to create a "stable" and "delineated" Middle East. The Western powers wanted order and governments that would behave nicely, predictably, and within the paternal and economic expectations of European powers. In other words, governments that could be controlled and aligned to meet Western political objectives and vital national interests as envisioned by Europeans.

While the borders in the region were largely accepted among the state actors after World War I as a fait accompli, order and peace were rare. Indeed, following World War II, the politics of the Middle East became chiefly defined by Arab-Israeli animosity. That troubled—and innately hostile—relationship between Arabs and Jews would find full expression in several major conflicts in 1948, 1956, 1967, 1973, and 1982. The last conflict—largely between Israel and the Palestine Liberation Organization (PLO) as well as Syrian and Lebanese forces—began only months after I left UNTSO for the Pentagon. At DIA, I witnessed from afar how that violent conflict played out, making it clear to me that any future war in the Middle East could be a bloody affair. Poignantly, in 1983, the US witnessed just how costly military involvement in the Middle East could be. In October two terrorist truck bombs struck separate buildings housing US Marine Corps and French military forces, who were in Beirut as part of a multinational force in Lebanon. In one horrific act, 241 Marines and 58 French servicemen lost their lives. Add to all this the carnage of the Iran-Iraq War from 1980 to 1988, where casualties were at least 600,000, and it's easy to understand why the Middle East is one of the most dangerous regions on earth. Moreover, the intervention of Israeli Defense Forces (IDF) against Iranian-backed militia and Syrian forces in the Lebanese War from 1982 to 1985 posed a serious threat to the nascent peace between Tel Aviv and Cairo following the Egyptian-Israeli Peace Treaty of 1979. So by 1990, all was not well in the neighborhood where we were headed to fight Saddam Hussein's Iraq.

The invasion of Kuwait by another Arab state had created a significant shift in the geopolitical situation. The US would now be allied militarily—not just diplomatically—with other Arab states. This situation—and direct US and coalition involvement originating outside of the Arab world—was an unprecedented conflict scenario not witnessed in modern times. We were now sitting atop a powder keg.

Before the invasion of Kuwait, Arabs kept their distance from the US, having had their fill of Western intervention. To be sure, they did not need our financial aid. Nor did they want our culture. They were sitting on billions of dollars in oil revenue. What they did want was for the US to help keep Iran in check through our sea power. To that end, our naval presence there, accompanied by arms sales to the Arabs from the US, was thought to help stabilize the region. Otherwise, Saudi Arabia and its neighbors were happy to stand apart from America. All of that changed, however, with Iraq's military occupation of Kuwait. The Iraqi invasion resulted in a US-led coalition, including Western and Arab forces, working together toward a common goal. We had broken new ground. Nowhere was that groundbreaking more evident than the formation of the coalition—a remarkable accomplishment—and one that I found hard to believe could have come to fruition so quickly. It seemingly rose out of the desert sands like a great *shamal,* the notorious hot and dry northwesterly wind that blew across the Arab and Persian deserts. This 35-nation coalition would eventually include 737,000 soldiers, sailors, airmen, and Marines, 190 ships, and 1,700 combat aircraft. Indeed, the coalition ranged in size from our closest ally, the United Kingdom, to Bangladesh.[1]

As I winged toward a combat zone in my first-class seat, I thought about all that had transpired in the Middle East historically, even in recent years. Many questions raced through my mind. First, would these Arabs actually fight other Arabs? Despite the turmoil in the Arab world, they rarely took up arms against one another. Indeed, would they fight at all? The Saudi military was not particularly professional. Their officers, far from the "take charge" tradition of US and NATO officers, were well known for standing back and doing little. Unlike their enlisted soldiers, the officers enjoyed privileged status at the top of the Saudi moneyed hierarchy. The "dirty work" of soldiering was left to the lower echelons of society who occupied the enlisted ranks of the military.

My second question was, would Israel agree to stay out of the conflict, especially if attacked by Iraq? While the Arab states knew they needed the US to turn the tables on Saddam, could the coalition withstand implosion if Israel got into the act? I knew the IDF from my time with UNTSO. Standing by quietly while being attacked was not something Israeli military leaders were likely to do. If provoked to take military action, a counterattack by Israel against Iraq would almost certainly destroy the coalition's legitimacy with Arab states. The coalition could never be seen as "allied" with Israel, something Saddam would surely use to hasten the disintegration of Arab support for this unusual military alliance.

Third, what would the Russian response be to all of this and to the coalition? Moscow was Iraq's patron and chief supplier of arms. Saddam Hussein's overt and unjustified aggression had put the Soviet Union's Mikhail Gorbachev in a bad position, virtually incapable of stopping the US-led juggernaut racing toward the Middle East. This was a major setback for Soviet influence in the region. All politics in the Middle East was a zero-sum game for Moscow, where US ascendency meant Soviet decline, and vice versa. If things went badly for Iraq, would Russia feel compelled to enter the fight to reassert its position in the region?

The irony was inescapable. Here we were, an Army trained to fight the Soviets on the plains of Western Europe, headed to the Middle East where—if things soured—we might wind up fighting the Soviets alongside untested and, frankly, unreliable Arab allies. It was more than I could think about. Frankly, it was hard to imagine even as I was about to land in Saudi Arabia with a planeload of BRO soldiers.

As we prepared to touch down in the Kingdom of Saudi Arabia, I contemplated how all of this had come together. The Saudis' cultural and religious traditions, like an acacia tree found in the Saudi desert, were deeply rooted in the sands of a nomadic Bedouin and Islamic life. I wondered how this diverse coalition would stay together when the going got tough and the fighting began. We, the West, and the Arabs simply approached life from such different directions. Could we really work together, much less fight alongside one another? I wondered. It seemed to me that Desert Shield, the name given to the first phase of this operation, had all the risk of a back-alley crapshoot in which dice produce both winners and losers. I thought we would win, but could this coalition hang together? I had my doubts.

Exhausted from the flight, I dozed off for a few minutes. But when our aircraft made its final turn, a momentary glint of morning sunlight through my cabin window skipped across my face and snapped me back to reality as we approached King Fahd International Airport (KFIA) on the eastern side of Saudi Arabia near the Persian Gulf port city of Dammam. We would soon be reunited with our combat vehicles and equipment and be able to get on with our mission.

On January 12 my first-class ride to the Middle East ended as the aircraft descended quickly and touched down. When we had taxied to our stopping point and the doors swung open, we were greeted by a blast of warm air laced with the familiar smell of aviation fuel. I went down the steps to the tarmac, where I was greeted by MAJ Tom Conneran, our Assistant S-3 who had arrived two weeks earlier. "Welcome to Saudi Arabia, sir," Conneran said with a smart salute and a faint grin.

Returning a salute of my own, I said, "I want to get to the port ASAP."

COL Dodson had deployed days after Conneran and was already situated with the division's FSE colocated with the DTAC in the desert 465 kilometers (289 miles) west of the port. There he was busy working on our fire support operations, sorting out logistics, and trying to determine what additional artillery would be assigned to us in the days ahead, all requiring detailed planning. Anticipating our arrival, Dodson had dispatched Conneran to meet us so that we could quickly—as soon as humanly possible—begin operations to get our combat vehicles out of the port.

"Sir, this place is a frigging mess," Conneran said, shaking his head in marked disgust as MAJ Cardenas and I got into the Humvee that would speed us first to our billets at Khobar Towers. Khobar was an abandoned civilian high-rise neighborhood that would serve as our temporary home while we wrested our vehicles and equipment from the clutches of the port.

"What's the biggest challenge?" I asked Conneran.

"Everything, everything is hard, sir. Everything. Vehicles are spread out all over the port, and just finding yours among several other divisions' is a nightmare," Conneran complained. "Oh, and the food service here sucks too," he added. The food was provided by civilian contract services, and Conneran's assessment was validated after we had our first meal later that day. It sucked.

As we rolled up to Khobar, we wove through a security labyrinth of sandbag structures and vertical concrete culverts filled with sand linked with concertina barbed wire. Armed guards motioned us through quickly, and we soon found ourselves on a narrow street leading up to the highrise building designated for us. It was of concrete construction without a single stick of furniture in it. When we reconnected with our personal equipment from the aircraft, we spread out our sleeping bags on the floor and, to the extent possible, made an effort to bring some order to the space that was now our new home. Shortly, we were joined by busloads of our troops, and for several hours, officers, noncommissioned officers (NCOs), and soldiers all worked to settle in.

Unfortunately, two of my separate batteries, including half of the HHB and all of B-6 FA, our MLRS unit, were sent to "Cement City," a camp next to KFIA that was the launch point for US F-15E Strike Eagles and F-16 Fighting Falcons. Cement City—an apt description, if not also an understatement—was little more than a cement factory where tents had been erected to house soldiers not fortunate enough to find space in Khobar. This dismal place was about 19 kilometers (12 miles) and 30 minutes in traffic away from the majority of the other DIVARTY soldiers. When I visited it a few days later, I was appalled by its inadequacy, even for a field army familiar with harsh conditions. The tents that were erected by support personnel were scattered in ponds of cement-colored mud and water. Those conditions would serve as an inspiration for me to work harder than ever to get our troops out of the port and into the desert, where at least we could live as soldiers were accustomed to in the field.

In that regard, from the moment I arrived, I was anxious to get to the port 26 kilometers (16 miles) from Khobar to assess what we needed to do to get to the desert. As Cardenas and I made our way to the Port of Dammam, I was struck by how the roads were filled with civilian cars and trucks not unlike what I had experienced while driving in Damascus,

Amman, and Cairo a decade earlier. Looking around, it sure didn't feel as if we were headed to war. But when we arrived at the port, the description Conneran had given us at the airfield was accurate. My immediate "war" would be a bureaucratic one to deal with mass confusion. I noted as much in my diary: "We arrived in country. The port is the picture of mass confusion. Everyone is serious. The ADC-S, BG Rutherford, is glad to see the DIVARTY leadership get control. He tells me every effort here is like 'pushing a boulder up a hill.'"

Brigadier General (BG) Jerry R. Rutherford had been our Assistant Division Commander for Maneuver (ADC-M) at Fort Riley until he left to take command of a forward-deployed armored division in Germany. But with the deployment of his 2nd Armored Division-Forward (2AD-F) to the desert to be the BRO's third maneuver brigade, Rutherford assumed responsibility for the coordination of our division's logistical operations and duty as our Assistant Division Commander-Support (ADS-S). A short, plain-talking, soldier's soldier, Rutherford had a bias for action. When I found him encamped in a large hangar at the port, he resembled a football coach pacing the sidelines, frustrated with the state of play. "Lingamfelter, 'bout time you got your ass here," he barked. Then he said confidingly, "I am glad you're on the ground, and I'm counting on you to get the DIVARTY out of this damn place."

He was right. A huge part of the challenge was the lack of leadership on the ground to take charge of the many tasks, including the bureaucracy, that needed to be done to locate, organize, and move our tactical vehicles to the field. Even in the military, bureaucracy—like the invasive kudzu vine that grows unrestrained in America's deep South—can be depended upon to take root anywhere, including in a war zone. And like kudzu, bureaucracy is hard as hell to kill.

Our wheeled and tracked vehicles were dispersed all over the port, which was an enormously disorganized concrete parking area of about 280 acres. When vehicles were off-loaded from the ships that had borne them from Texas, the East Coast of the US, or ports in Europe, there was no guarantee that they would be parked in such a manner that the owning unit could readily find what was theirs, even with unit designations stenciled on vehicle bumpers. Moreover, 1st Infantry Division equipment was intermingled with equipment from other divisions, and having a 1st Armored Division and a 1st Cavalry Division also in the port with us made sorting things out all that more difficult. Whose "1st" was it?

Finding our vehicles parked haphazardly throughout the port, so they could be loaded with troops and equipment and put on the road to our desert positions, was like untying a Gordian knot with one hand while playing with a Rubik's Cube with the other. Additionally, movement to the field required a convoy movement order. Getting that cherished permission, the clearance to get on the road westward to our positions in the desert, was not easy. To make matters worse, there was only one road west, the infamous Trans-Arabian Pipeline (Tapline) Road, which was barely paved, swept with sand at places, and desperately dangerous. Putting vehicles on that road required strict and precise movement control to ensure the safety of our soldiers driving and riding on what we called the most dangerous road east or west of the Mississippi River. Despite that peril, the competition between our division and other units to get on that road to our area of operations (AO) was keen. We soon found out that divisions could care less about other divisions. It was "my division first." Comradery took a backseat to getting your vehicles out of the port. And in keeping with the spirit of the occasion, as far as we were concerned, the rest of the Army could get in line behind us.

Further complicating our movement to the desert was the fact that our heavy, tracked vehicles (M1 Abrams tanks, M2 Bradley Infantry Fighting Vehicles (IFV), and artillery systems) needed flatbed 18-wheel tractor trailer transporters, which was a very limited commodity. Our eventual position near Wadi al-Batin, 465 kilometers west of the port, required a full day's drive to a tactical assembly area (TAA). A road trip that long would put unnecessary wear and tear on our critical tracked combat systems. As a result, not only was our division competing for convoy clearances, we also had to contend for truck transport for our heavy equipment. Rutherford was right. Pushing that boulder uphill would be a Sisyphean task.

After this introduction to mass confusion, we returned to Khobar Towers to check on the arrival of the rest of our troops from the airfield. In the front of my mind was the immediate need to ensure we hit the ground running in the morning to find our vehicles and organize ourselves for movement to our desert positions. When I finally had some time to think, I made this entry in my diary about our new digs at Khobar Towers: "It takes all night to get our soldiers down to bed in a large abandoned, albeit, modern apartment complex. It's 0300 before we sleep." We awoke at dawn the next day, January 13, and after breakfast organized ourselves to move to the port and begin working. One of my initial diary entries after we arrived describes the situation in the port: "We work hard [to] locate all of our equipment. We have no transport, no hand-held radios, no nothing to orchestrate our efforts. We are reduced to using every officer, NCO, and soldier to fan out, locate equipment and move it from the A & B holding areas to the E holding area. The maneuver brigades have priority on lift, radios, etc. The King of Battle is but a pawn in the port. Everything is hard."

To get soldiers to the port, we depended on contracted buses, which ran unreliably and frequently behind schedule. There was no formality and little organization in getting vehicles positioned from assembly areas, designated "A" and "B" near the docks, into assembly area "E" that was our assigned area in the port where we would stage vehicles for departure to the desert. Rank was meaningless when it came to searching for vehicles. My driver, PFC McGary, and I would walk the huge assembly areas in search of DIVARTY's vehicles. When we found one, we hopped in, cranked it up, and moved it to our assembly area. Our lack of hand-held radios put us at a disadvantage in trying to coordinate actions in the port. The tactical radios we used for field operations, that we eventually would mount in our wheeled and tracked vehicles, were of no value at the time because they were secured in large 20-foot shipping-container vans called MILVANS (military container vans). These large aluminum boxes were also hard to locate in a port filled with them, because ours looked like everyone else's. And there was no guarantee that when you found yours and opened it, the radios you needed would not be packed deep in the rear of the MILVAN. Hand-held radios would have been very useful in the absence of our tactical ones. Unfortunately, we had none.

Fierce competition for vehicle transport, or "lift," was not confined to contending divisions anxious to leave the port. The "me-first" attitudes also showed up between infantry, armor, artillery, and support units within our own division. The field artillery may have been known as "The King of Battle," but in the eyes of our maneuver brethren, our battle heritage was a secondary factor when it came to movement to the desert. Even among division colleagues, tempers flared as some units felt pushed aside when given lower movement priority. We all wanted to get to the field and out of the port. Despite the importance of the artillery in the past wars, for now the exalted infantry and armor maneuver units held sway. On the chessboard called "escape the port," we were indeed the pawns.

When day three of our "assault on the port" arrived, I began taking things in stride, the frustration notwithstanding. On January 14 I chronicled life at Khobar Towers, which we nicknamed the "MGM" after the Metro-Goldwyn-Mayer hotel chain. While it was a far cry from the MGM in Las Vegas, it seemed an appropriate expression of soldierly sarcasm, especially considering the hard floors that were our beds each night after exhausting work at the port: "Life at the 'MGM,' our apartment complex, is not bad when the water runs and is warm. The food for breakfast is from a contract firm. It's awful. The ride to the port is 30 minutes. We get [sic] lost the first 3 trips. Getting better with each effort. I found my vehicle and the CDR's [commander's]. Transport at last. Our days are long and frustrating. I wonder if we'll ever get out of the port." Occasionally, Dodson and I had the opportunity to discuss our slow progress in the port over a tactical radio-telephone system our signal battalion had managed to install. These communications had been put in place to link us to the division headquarters in the desert where Dodson was located. He sensed my frustration and lobbied the division's leadership on his end to get the artillery some movement priority.

Meanwhile, Dodson had his own worries, and they were largely operational. In the week prior to our arrival, he and the rest of the leadership of the division had been engaged in high-level military planning at King Khalid Military City (KKMC), about a two-hour drive from his position in the desert and a full day's drive west of us in the port. There he got a glimpse into the operational planning of our new higher headquarters, the VII Corps from Germany, and their higher headquarters, ARCENT (Army Central Command), the Army component of GEN Schwarzkopf's CENT-COM. Most of what he learned then was not released below brigade or DIVARTY commander level. Therefore, he wasn't able to share much with me at the time about what was ahead since the leadership did not want to inadvertently disclose the location of our future operations.[2] While he was faithful to the secrecy involved in this planning, there was no mistaking his urgency in wanting to get our troops and equipment to the field as soon as we could. War was coming, and fast.

In that regard, Dodson and I knew it was vitally important for us to get the artillery, along with the counterbattery radars, to the desert to deal with potential enemy artillery and mortar attacks the Iraqis might preemptively mount against us. We didn't want to be caught short. The artillery may not have been an important movement priority in the eyes of our maneuver comrades, like their technologically advanced M1 Abrams tanks or the versatile M2 Bradley IFVs—"Tanks and Brads" as we would call them—but our cannons, rocket launchers, and counterbattery radars would be essential in setting the conditions for any success, particularly in softening up the enemy prior to any attack the division might eventually mount. Getting that message across to our movement-control decision-makers in the port, most of whom were partial to infantry and armor

units, was tough. Many times, it fell on me to carry the message, sometimes with an efficacious degree of soldierly vulgarity.

The news we were getting on January 14 further fueled my determination to get us out of the port. National Public Radio (NPR) in the US
was reporting that after UN Secretary-General Javier Pérez de Cuéllar of
Peru met with French President François Mitterrand, the UN chief
declared there was no hope for a peaceful solution.[3] That same day, the
Washington Post reported that the European Community had thrown in
the towel on a peaceful solution.[4] The next day, we were fairly confident
that war was coming, and my diary entry on January 15 reflected as
much:

> Today is the day of decision. Will Saddam leave Kuwait? I have
> been on record as certain he won't. War will come. We must be
> what we say we are (free people) and do what we say we will
> (defend freedom). I'm beginning to hate the port. DIVARTY is
> last in every regard. I resent this. No one will help us. Talking to
> the G-4 to get help in locating an ambulance sent to us from Fort
> Hood is like talking to a brick wall. Impotent! We work as
> friendly as our short tempers permit. MAJ (P) [promotable]
> Mike Cuff and I move equipment and generators ourselves out
> of desperation to make progress. We are becoming friends. We
> wait for hostilities.

Given the rumors of imminent hostilities, the confused environment, and
short tempers, the frustration of life in the port was unavoidable and
inescapable. It stuck to us like flypaper. We struggled with everything,
including the identification of critical equipment we would need in combat to transport our wounded. Before we left Fort Riley, we were told by
the division's G-4 (Logistics) that some key equipment we lacked would
be waiting for us in the port. A combat ambulance was one such item.
But finding it was like finding a needle in a haystack.

As we struggled to pull together and get things done, rank meant little
when it came to the dirty work of getting vehicles and equipment staged
for movement to the desert. My new friend, MAJ Mike Cuff, who was on
the promotion list for lieutenant colonel, had arrived at Fort Riley just
before we were alerted to deploy. He was the designated replacement for
LTC Gingrich, who was the battalion commander of the 4–5 FA. The
division's leadership thought it wise to leave our most experienced commanders in their positions with combat lying ahead of us. So the decision

was made for Cuff to work as a fire supporter in the Division FSE until hostilities ended, after which he would assume command from Gingrich. In the meantime, Cuff and I found ourselves developing a close working relationship as we teamed up to locate the wheeled 15KW generators used to power our TOC and then manhandle them into position in the areas designated in the port for the DIVARTY. Occasionally, we found ourselves acting like automobile mechanics as we applied jumper cables to vehicles that had dead batteries. At times, it seemed an impossible task to find any of our vehicles as all the equipment was painted a desert sand color, with the only identifying features being the small black unit stencils on the bumper of each vehicle. My Humvee was marked with "1-ID-FA" on one side of the bumper and "HQ-5" on the other, the numerical radio call sign and designation for the "XO." Dodson's Humvee was "HQ-6," the numerical reference to his position as "Commander." I was glad when McGary and I found good old HQ-5. It was in good order after a long trip across the sea, and the plywood modification we had made in the driveway at Riley Place had survived. We then put a priority on finding HQ-6 for Dodson since he needed his vehicle in the field as soon as possible. But when we found it, the entire front windshield had been shattered. I had McGary remove our windshield and put it on HQ-6, which then led to several days of work to find a replacement for ours. We did, and given the inclement weather we would see in the days ahead, I was glad we found one.

When January 16 rolled around, we were back at it, working feverishly to sort out what seemed like the world's largest pile of Legos. But unlike the small plastic cubes my kids loved to play with, snapping ours together in the port in a coherent manner to deploy to the desert was far more difficult. Complicating our challenge was the difficulty we encountered in getting our soldiers to the port each day to do our work. Unfortunately, there were few facilities to garrison our troops near the port, which resulted in having to transport shifts of soldiers to and from it all hours of the day and night. I noted this, among other things, in my journal that day: "No war yet. The confusion in the port has not improved. We have no transportation to get our soldiers from the MGM and 'Cement City,' an awful camp 1 hour away, to the port to move, position, and prepare vehicles for movement to the field. I pour out my guts to a TRADOC researcher, LTC John O'Bannion, on how poorly orchestrated the entire port effort is. We have no doctrine for this mess."

The Army, to its credit, recognized early in the process that Desert Shield was very much a departure from the doctrine that we had trained for and would employ during combat in Europe. When I learned that the Army's Training and Doctrine Command (TRADOC) had sent researchers to the port in the early stages of the conflict to capture lessons, I was impressed. "Lessons learned" are essential to warfighters as we look back on operations to better prepare for the future. The port offered a splendidly painful example of how the Army lacked a clear doctrine for uniting troops and equipment for onward movement to the field. To be sure, the Army had well-honed operational procedures and skills for Europe. There, US units like the 1ID planned to "fall in" on prepositioned, well-organized, and well-maintained POMCUS (Prepositioning of Materiel Configured in Unit Sets) equipment sites in the event we were to deploy to Europe in support of NATO. POMCUS sites were stocked with large amounts of ready-to-use US military equipment and combat vehicles in Germany, awaiting our arrival. Not so in the port of Dammam. There our doctrine could have employed an appropriate acronym "MESS," or "Military Equipment Scattered Senselessly." When TRADOC's O'Bannion sat down with me in a spare moment, I unloaded my frustration. But even a serious discussion about the lack of a port doctrine could not quickly fix any of what I was dealing with at Dammam. At the end of the interview, as O'Bannion closed his notebook, thanked me, and wheeled away, I was left with the pathetic realities of the port.

It's noteworthy that most tactical Army units, by design, are field units. Ports are not the field. Our Army was trained and equipped to live in the field where we work, eat, sleep, and fight. A port, with concrete pavement and thin-corrugated-steel buildings everywhere, is not a place you can dig a foxhole or construct an earthen berm for personal protection, techniques we routinely used in the field. Camouflaging vehicles in the port to confuse the enemy was pointless, since the camouflage nets stuck out like a sore thumb against the uniformity of built-up structures. Sanitation in the port was also very inadequate for an Army trained to dig latrines and provide field cleaning facilities to soldiers. We were adept at personal hygiene in a tactical environment, but the port facilities soon proved largely insufficient, and what was there in the form of temporary toilets were soon overwhelmed. Moreover, a common cold or case of the flu spread like wildfire in the port's close quarters where we labored day and night. At least in the field a soldier has the expectation of fresh air. For me, escaping the port quickly was as much for our physical health as it was for my mental health.

I made my way back to the "MGM" at Khobar Towers the night of January 16 after a long and exhausting day of dragging and positioning vehicles into our tactical holding area. I wondered and worried about being trapped in the port when hostilities broke out. We were sitting ducks. My first-class ride on a 747 just four days earlier had brought me and my troops to a place of utter confusion. Yet we were determined to get the work done despite the numerous obstacles in our way.

War was coming. We all knew it, and as I made my diary entry that night, I wondered what I would be writing next. Sleep did indeed come. But "next" would arrive very early in the morning.

6

War

"Sir, get up," a voice hovering above my head spoke urgently, prompting me to lift myself abruptly out of my sleeping bag. I squinted at my watch and saw it was just after 0230, January 17, 1991. MAJ Cardenas, the DIVARTY S-3, had just received notification to immediately get into our basic layer of chemical-defense clothing, or as we called it, our MOPP (Mission Oriented Protective Posture) gear. Almost right away, I reached for a transistor radio I had brought to tune in the US Armed Forces Network (AFN) radio station operating in Saudi Arabia. Maybe they knew what the hell was going on. My diary entry from that day said it all:

> We awake to orders to put on our MOPP gear. We know what is happening. I turn on AFN to hear the news of a massive air attack by the allies on Iraq. War has begun. No sooner than the news is announced, we are alerted to begin taking anti–nerve agent pills. Then a SCUD alert is sounded. I, as senior officer, ordered the key leadership to get to the port ASAP to get as much equipment ready to roll as possible. As we prepare to leave, we hear what sounds like a rocket directly overhead. We see the contrail of a Patriot missile jet skyward and a flash high above our heads. We see the first SCUD ever shot down by a Patriot. We are impressed and too fascinated to be scared. We hop in our vehicles and head to port. Before we leave the compound, we are notified to put on MOPP 4, full chemical gear. We ride to the port so equipped watching the northern skies for any signs of more SCUDS. Before I leave, I reassure those remaining at the MGM that we will be back to get them, to stay calm and confident in their training and equipment.

Something happens to soldiers when all hell breaks loose. Your ingrained instincts take over, and you get very focused and remarkably calm. You must. Leaders cannot panic. CPT Hymel, our HHB battery commander, took note of this and later reported, "The soldiers reacted well, and MOPP discipline was good."[1] That was a testament to our training, and ours was good, particularly since we had emphasized these procedures the previous autumn at Fort Riley. Fortunately, the Army had rigorously trained for years to prepare for chemical warfare. It was no secret that Saddam Hussein had and would use chemicals against his adversaries, a fact I reminded myself of as I swallowed a bitterly sour pyridostigmine bromide (PB) anti–nerve agent pill early that morning. Saddam had also deployed deadly mustard gas against his Iranian foes in 1985, and we would depend on our gas masks and MOPP gear to protect us from that terrible agent. He used a combination of toxic chemicals again in 1987 and 1988 in a brutal massacre to put down Kurdish insurgents in northeastern Iraq. So when we awoke to the sounds of air-raid sirens over Dammam, we knew this was not a drill. The threat was real and over our very heads.

Indeed, the back blast of a nearby Patriot missile battery left no doubt in anyone's mind that the war had begun. Its missile roared and streaked skyward to intercept an incoming Iraqi SCUD warhead. The SCUD was a tactical ballistic missile developed by the Soviet Union for use in the Cold War. Moscow had provided the system to Iraq. "SCUD" was the NATO term given to what were technically the R-11 and R-17 missiles, capable of carrying a chemical warhead great distances. On that morning, whatever it was carrying, a US Patriot missile blew it up. The Patriot was originally developed for high-altitude antiaircraft threats and adapted for an antimissile role for the Gulf War. On that day of reckoning, it validated itself as a premier antimissile system. We all were glad that it proved its worth, particularly our troops stuck in Cement City next to King Fahd Air Force Base (KFAFB) chock full of US F-15E Strike Eagles and F-16 Fighting Falcons jet fighters, a likely target for SCUD attacks by Iraq.

As Cardenas, his assistant MAJ Conneran, and I prepared to get to the port immediately to expedite movement to the field, I assembled our key leadership, including officers, noncommissioned officers, and enlisted troops. I told them we would assess the situation at the port and then call them forward as soon as we knew it was safe to resume our operations there. The expressions on their faces made it clear to me that no one wanted to stay where they were stationary targets, which added to my sense of urgency. As Cardenas and I conferred on which members of the DIVARTY team we would take with us, we realized we had just two Humvees, my HQ-5 and Cardenas's HQ-3, to transport people. Maybe we could take six or seven others. Cardenas took note of the mood among the team as we decided who would come with us and who would stay behind: "I had to make some decisions on who to take. The staff was all assembled on a first-floor patio waiting to see what we would decide. As I looked the staff over as Scott [Lingamfelter] and I made the decisions, it reminded me of looking at puppies at the pet store looking back at you with 'Take me! Take me!' expressions on their faces."[2]

Clearly, everyone wanted to get to the port to help us escape to our positions in the desert. We were now at war. As we were preparing to depart and keenly aware of the danger we faced, some of Cardenas's officers reminded him that they had yet to receive any ammunition for their weapons. The plan had been to issue ammunition once we were in the field and not while we were in the port. Conneran had brought a few magazines of 9mm pistol bullets with him from the desert for Cardenas and me, but that was all the ammunition we possessed. Cardenas, sensing the now double concern of leaving some of our team behind who were also unarmed, pulled out his magazine and issued exactly one bullet to each of his officers, reminiscent of the one round issued to the fictional deputy sheriff of the 1960s sitcom *The Andy Griffith Show*. He recalled the moment: "So, I said, 'come here' and proceeded to give each of the other officers one bullet apiece and told them 'Here is your Barney Fife bullet, so put it to good use only if you have to.' I thought to myself, that hopefully we would not need to here in the port."[3]

When all of us, including my driver PFC McGary, shoehorned ourselves into our Humvees, we found driving to the port in full MOPP gear wearing gas masks a challenging experience. First, it's very hard in a vehicle to communicate with one another with gas masks on without yelling at the top of your lungs to overcome the noise of the vehicle's diesel engine. Additionally, all of us were doing our best to scan the sky for more incoming SCUD missiles, while keeping our eyes on the road. When we pulled up to the entrance to the port, the Saudi gate guard announced to us that no one was permitted through. After a brief and not-so-diplomatic discussion, we blew past him and headed to our port operations center, a maneuver that may have set Saudi–American relations back a few centuries, at least with that one guard anyway. Upon arriving at our makeshift command post in the large corrugated-steel building we used to coordinate our vehicle-recovery operations, we found that everyone there was in full MOPP gear and seemingly unsure what to do next. It was evident to me that what was needed was to get our soldiers out of Khobar and Cement City, where we knew we were under attack, and to the port, where we could finish our "search and rescue" effort to find our vehicles and then "get the hell out of Dodge," as I recall making the point.

After a few hours passed since the first SCUD attack, the "all clear" came from our 12th Chemical personnel who had determined there was no contamination in the area. We then removed our gas masks, protective gloves, and rubber boot covers and began to function normally. It was then that we started getting the details of massive US and coalition airstrikes on Iraqi targets. That news created an enhanced sense of urgency and expectation among all of us. The air campaign was welcome news but served to highlight the importance of resuming our transition to the desert. This was not time to celebrate; it was time to accelerate.

In the port, and at Khobar and Cement City, we were like sitting ducks on a pond vulnerable to further SCUD attacks, including the high-explosive version of the weapon. That meant work faster, smarter, and more efficiently—a work ethos not readily found in the port. However, as we worked that day, things began to come together. We had located and moved many of our vehicles into our designated assembly area. Our cannon artillery units were beginning their movement to the field, and more transport assets were becoming available to move the DIVARTY separate units, including B-6 FA's deadly rocket launchers, and D-25 TAB's vital counter-battery radars. The firing and target acquisition capability these units possessed would be critical in locating and destroying enemy targets and I was anxious to move both batteries out of the port and into the field immediately.

I was, however, particularly comforted that I had the 12th Chemical's detection and decontamination capability and expertise in the port in the event we were hit by SCUD missiles loaded with chemical agents. Since it was under my supervision at Fort Riley, I had learned a lot about how to employ this specialized unit. Unfortunately, not every officer in the port understood how to use its capabilities effectively. Shortly after 12th Chemical's equipment arrived in the port, MAJ Walter Polly, the Division Chemical Officer (CHEMO), and 1LT Brad Byler, the Decontamination (Decon) Platoon Leader, met LTC Russell Honoré, who oversaw the division's port security. Honoré's staff had developed a completely unsupportable vehicle-decontamination plan that would have utilized three M12A1 decontamination apparatus to spray down contaminated vehicles in the port on a dock adjacent to the harbor. Their plan proposed using seawater for decontamination and then allowing the deactivated chemical agents and decontaminants to run off into the water of the Gulf! Polly wisely proffered an alternative course of action that, tactically, was more sound. He suggested establishing the decontamination site in a remote area of the port, since the docks were the most logical area to be targeted by the enemy in the first place. That way the decontamination area would be less likely to be destroyed during an attack and would be available to decontaminate personnel and equipment that weren't killed or destroyed. Second, using the briny salt water of the port, as opposed to fresh water to provide decontamination, would wreak havoc on the internal workings of the decontamination equipment, corroding it badly. Finally, pouring contaminated salt water back into the Persian Gulf was not only a bad idea environmentally, but one that could become a public relations nightmare. Honoré's staff thankfully agreed to change the plan, sparing us a potential news media fiasco, not to mention a platoon of corroded decontamination equipment.[4]

With hostilities now underway, the importance of getting our assets to the field took on a new level of criticality. Additionally, getting the command-and-control facilities out to the desert had moved up in priority for convoy clearances. Cardenas had been seriously ill in the recent days with "the port grunge," a flu-like illness that sucked the energy out of the victim. But he revived quickly when we learned that we would be pushing the DIVARTY TOC (tactical operations center) out to the field at 1700 hours that very evening. We rapidly staged our TOC equipment and determined that we didn't have sufficient transport vehicles to get all of our required personnel to the field. It was then that CPT Bill Turner, one of Cardenas's operations officers, reported, "Hey, Sir, I think we found a way to get everyone out of the port on the convoy. We have a bus that can accommodate all of us!" A wary Cardenas paused and thought momentarily about asking the 6-foot-3-inch Class of 1986 West Point football team quarterback where he had acquired the vehicle. But then he quickly decided not to explore the question too deeply with the enterprising Turner. Cardenas said this of his decision: "I really didn't want to know. I was just glad that we had a way to get everyone out of the port. However, I did ask if he was driving it and he said 'yes.' I then asked if he had ever driven a bus like this before and he said 'no.' I weighed the risk involved and the confusion that was going on trying to get out of the port and decided it was worth the risk. I just told him to keep in the middle of the convoy between our heavy wheeled vehicles and keep alert."[5]

After some "investigating" on my own I learned that some of D-25 TAB's resourceful troops had commandeered the bus earlier that day to get their troops to the port from the "MGM" at Khobar. That bus, now "requisitioned" for "combat duty," served us well in transporting soldiers to the desert who couldn't fit into the available tactical vehicles. To this day, I suspect that poor bus driver at Khobar still doesn't know what happened to his bus. Some would call it theft; others would call it "field expedient supply acquisition." Regardless, it would get our troops to the desert to begin combat operations.

As they formed up to roll out, I assembled the troops and mounted the hood of my Humvee to see all of them at once. I told them that they were the best, that they were trained and ready, and that we would defeat the Iraqis in battle. I warned them to be cautious and take care of one another, and concluded with this: "Some of us may not come home from this. But we are here to accomplish a great task. Focus your anger on the enemy, and whatever happens do not be fearful. It's fine to be scared. Being scared is normal. I'm scared, but fear is another matter. Fear will crush your heart, and you must not let that happen." The troops seemed to get it, and they moved quickly to their vehicles. Even if they thought I might have been a bit pompous, I was glad I could share my thoughts with them.

With that, our first DIVARTY convoy—hijacked bus packed to the gills—departed for the desert at 1830 hours that evening on a 465-kilometer road march. The destination was a position in TAA Roosevelt, named after BG Teddy Roosevelt Jr., who had served with the 26th Infantry Regiment of the 1st Division in World War I. There the DIVARTY TOC would join other BRO units that were concentrating to prepare for combat operations. As they disappeared from my sight, I prayed for their safety on the dangerous Tapline Road. This essential "highway" snaked north and westward through the Saudi desert and claimed at least one coalition death per day. Poorly paved and maintained, it had no road markings, no signals, no speed limits, no guard rails, just desert on either side and a fickle wind that unpredictably blew sand across the road, obscuring the pavement from a driver's view. Even when the road could be discerned by a cautious and observant driver, it could easily disappear in a matter of seconds. It was a highway that took lives as certain as an enemy bullet. As the TOC disappeared from my sight that evening, I shook my head, wondering what other dangerous vicissitudes lay ahead of us.

Meanwhile, MG Rhame issued a directive on his two-star notepaper addressing the commencement of hostile actions:

Soldiers of the First Infantry Division: Today the United States entered into a war with Iraq. The U. S. Air Force is currently preparing the battlefield and inflicting destruction on the Army of Iraq. In the near future, you and I like those great Big Red One soldiers who fought at Cantigny, Omaha Beach, and War Zone D will most likely be called upon to complete the destruction of an enemy of the United States. When called upon, we will do our duty. We don't want to hold anything back. Where the division moves, we are to ensure that the Iraqi Army has no military capability left. Prisoners are to be handled in strict accordance with international law. I have complete confidence in the soldiers of this division. I know you will do great. You are the best. Duty First! Thomas G. Rhame, MG, U. S. Army, Commanding.[6]

For those of us still in the port that night, our sleep was fitful despite Rhame's straightforward and inspiring call to arms that I neatly folded up and placed in my diary. We wondered if more SCUD attacks would occur, and they did in the early morning hours of January 18. My diary entry captured our quickened pace along with the activities of the previous night:

> More SCUD attacks. More success for the US Army Air Defense. I'm proud. News says our air strikes devastated Iraq's air force. We have the skies. The port is still a mess, but we make progress. I measure this vehicle by vehicle. No help on the ambulance. So, it seems insignificant problems dominate my time. Our quality of life in the port is the worst I've ever seen. At times I want to scream. We pushed the TOC out last night. It was "helter-skelter." An organized mess. Everyone was tired. I fear there will be an accident; one person dies on Tapline Road each day. I pray not these youngsters. Now my task is to get everyone else out.

With the TOC launched and in position in the early hours of the next day, I finally had a reliable point of contact in the desert to coordinate additional unit movements in that direction. Moreover, I was also glad to learn that Turner and his "combat bus" had arrived safely and—in the process—managed to redefine what it means to use "mass transit." That said, the young captain, true to his sense of honor, managed to get the bus returned to the port the following day, no doubt not wanting to go down in the annals of military history as a scofflaw. I would, however, call it "justified larceny in the defense of freedom."[7]

Meanwhile, coalition air forces were flying 2,000 sorties per day.[8] At that rate, we would soon have air superiority, and the threat of Iraqi air attacks would drop significantly. SCUDs remained a continuing threat, however, and more came in the early morning hours of January 18. Ominously, we also learned of a SCUD attack on Israel that same day.[9] This was a wildcard. If Israel were to become engaged in combat with Iraq, it would be a deal-breaker with our Arab allies in the coalition. Saudi Arabia and the Gulf states knew they needed the US, but to be pictured as fighting on the "side of the Zionists," as Iraq surely would have played it in the press, would have caused the coalition to fold like a lawn chair in a hurricane.

Most of us scrambling to get out of the port didn't give the Israeli attack a lot of attention, but as a former Middle East intelligence analyst, I was worried. Here we were astride a deployment of troops to the desert, soldiers scurrying about a port under daily SCUD attacks, while living under the threat that one false move by Israel, one miscalculation, and the entire endeavor could fall apart around us. Saddam knew the potential for this well, and it was for that reason he made the effort to draw the Israelis into the fight. The only thing that would keep Israel out of the war was the assurance of our Patriot batteries and the protection they could provide. Those air defense units would indeed deploy to the Jewish state and succeed—as they did at our port—in knocking down provocative Iraqi missile attacks designed to trigger an Israeli response. Their performance helped restrain Israeli involvement and kept the coalition from being shattered, an efficacious result that was in no way certain, at the same time SCUDs were falling around us. We were in a game of high-risk poker at the strategic level. But at the tactical level, where we could actually have an impact on events, we still had lots of work to do to get our troops out of the port and into the desert. That reality did not permit my mind to wander too far from the mission at hand.

By January 19, we were making real progress. I made this uncharacteristically optimistic entry in my journal: "We begin to see the light at the end of the tunnel. Maybe we can get the HHB, B/6, D/25, and 12 Chem on the road on 20 Jan. D/25 says he's not ready. I push everyone to get on the road ASAP. We must get out of the port. We find more vehicles. We are making progress. Another SCUD alert this AM. In MOPP 4 for three hours." The SCUD attacks continued that day, and indeed, three were directed at Israel. But I didn't have the time to worry about that. My focus was riveted on the impending deployment of my subordinate units. The HHB contained all the support activities for the DIVARTY TOC. This essential command center was now in the desert, lightly defended and operating on a logistical shoestring. The HHB was a necessary component to sustain the TOC. B-6 FA was a vital combat asset with its deadly MLRS rockets; and the counter-battery radars in D-25 TAB would be the eyes and ears for the MLRS. The 12th Chemical had already shown its worth in scanning the port for chemical agents in the wake of the SCUD attacks we had endured to that point. We needed all these critical assets in the field, not sitting exposed in the port.

I pressed everyone to "ruck it up," Army slang to get your rucksack or backpack on, and move out smartly. We needed to be ready to roll as soon as we received our convoy clearances. CPT Seefeldt, my D-25 TAB commander, worried that his equipment was not "up to snuff" for the movement, but I told him we were going and he "was coming with us, ready or not." Seefeldt was critical to our mission. I had no choice, and he understood that as well. I wasn't about to leave anyone in that port a minute beyond what was absolutely needed. That afternoon we finalized our road-march plans, briefed our troops, loaded equipment, and poised ourselves to launch. At long last, we were on the verge of escaping the clutches of the port and the possibility the next SCUD missile would fall on top of us.

When we returned to the "MGM" that night, most of us spent the evening packing and repacking our rucksacks and preparing to load out to the port in the morning. As I fell asleep that night, I was glad we would be moving out, not only for my sake, but to get the soldiers focused on the reason our nation sent us here: to fight a reprehensible tyrant with a history of vicious acts of violence and unpredictability.

My years of following the Iran-Iraq War in DIA, viewing the all-source intelligence and watching Saddam from a unique vantage point, gave me a clear picture of how evil this man really was. In a way, I felt that this was my war personally, my opportunity to strike a blow at a man who was without a doubt one of the most diabolical animals on the planet. I had come to know him for the despicable thug he was. My only worry, my only hesitation, was that good Americans would die fighting a man who was not worthy to untie the bootlaces of any of my troops. As I drifted off to sleep, I was nonetheless comforted that soon we would be where we could do something about this situation. Finally, in the desert, we would be fully armed, ready, trained, and focused on bringing every ounce of combat power we possessed in the BRO down on the heads of the Iraqi forces that had raped Kuwait. This was a war I was ready to fight, and indeed—as Rhame said his note of January 17—not "to hold anything back."[10]

When dawn broke on January 20, eight insufferably long days since we had landed in the Saudi kingdom, we were ready to roll. It was, for the several hundred troops under my command and the 90-plus combat vehicles we would deploy down the perilous Tapline Road, a day of liberation. We were all anxious to get on with the mission. Once again, I gave the troops a pep talk atop the hood of my Humvee about what fear does to a soldier's heart. They all seemed to appreciate the message. But it wasn't the last time I would need to remind them or myself of the need to focus on what we came to do: fight and win.

As we rolled out of the port, north-northwest from Dammam and onto Tapline Road, now dubbed "Suicide Alley" by the troops, we did so in good order. Soon it was clear to me that Tapline was as dangerous as I had been warned it was and that the trip to TAA Roosevelt would be perilous. Trucks of every size and type were flying east and west as if on the New Jersey Turnpike. Then this oddity occurred. When we approached a point on the route about 145 kilometers from the port of Dammam where we turned due northwest around noon, the Saudi transport drivers carrying our tracked vehicles abruptly stopped for Dhuhr (noon) prayers. No warning. They just stopped, got out, threw down their prayer rugs, and prayed. My driver, McGary, asked me, "Sir, what in the hell are these guys doing!?"

I remarked, "I think they don't share our sense of urgency, Roger," but then thought to myself, "This could turn out to be a very long road march and an equally lengthy war."

After dutifully observing their religious ritual, they would build a fire, cook a small meal, smoke their waterpipes, and then jump back in their trucks until the next time they chose to stop. The problem for us with this unanticipated prayer ritual—as well as others later in the day at 'Asr (afternoon), Maghrib (sunset), and yet again at 'Isha (evening)—was that the interruption considerably slowed our movement to the field while creating an accordion effect within the convoy. Combined with maniac drivers in other vehicles, wrecks along the route of march, potholes, soft shoulders, passing trucks cutting in and out of our formation, and a road that occasionally would be completely obscured with blowing sand, our convoy operations were difficult at best and life-threatening at worst.

Most of our trip was spent out of radio contact with the DIVARTY in the field. The range of our tactical FM radios in our vehicles was satisfactory for intra-convoy communications, but until we neared the end of our road march, the DIVARTY was largely in the dark concerning the status of our journey in their direction. They knew only that we were scheduled to depart the morning of January 20. Unfortunately, our tactical radios were incapable of ranging all the way to TAA Roosevelt located just east of the Wadi al Batin, a long dry riverbed running southwest to northeast through Saudi Arabia to the border that separated western Kuwait from Iraq.

As we rolled northwest on Tapline, I found the massive size of the desert captivating. Like the plains of Kansas, there seemed to be no end to it. That's where the similarity ended. Soon Bedouins on camels appeared on the horizon against a backdrop of blowing sand, and I was reminded that this was neither the high desert of the NTC in California nor the "amber waves of grain" in Kansas. It was Saudi Arabia, and the vast deserts of Iraq and Kuwait lay ahead of us. Occasionally, I referred to my map for our location on the route toward the Wadi al-Batin, but it was to little avail in the featureless desert. The Magellan GPS we had in HQ-5 seemed to be working as the distance to our rendezvous location steadily ticked lower. Nonetheless, I also referred to the marine compass I had bolted to my dashboard that showed us tracking reliably north-westwardly. The trip was long, and the bumps and potholes in the road took their toll on us. I learned to flex myself as I saw a hump or hole in the road ahead, but after 11 hours of this maneuver, I was worn out. To make things even more unpleasant, our convoys stirred up billowing clouds of dust that invaded our Humvee. Other than wearing a bandana over your nose, there was little you could do to avoid ingesting copious amounts of fine sand.

Fourteen hours after we departed the port, dusk had descended as we made our turn off Tapline to the rendezvous point south of TAA Roosevelt where I was to link up with Conneran. From there we would travel north 12 kilometers on Route Scorpion, no more than a well-traveled desert path, to our DIVARTY TOC position inside the TAA where 1ID units were initially prepositioned prior to launching into forward combat locations. Once again Conneran would be our guide as he had been nine days earlier when we had landed in Saudi Arabia. Unfortunately, our 90-vehicle convoy had been split up by the unanticipated stops our Saudi heavy-transport drivers—whom our S-4, MAJ Barry Brooks, had nick-named "Cowboy Bob," or "Bedouin Bob"—had made throughout the day. As a result, part of the convoy had become fragmented or lost. It would take the better part of the night to locate, reassemble, and redirect them into our final position.

When I arrived at the DIVARTY TOC location, McGary deployed our tent within the defensive positions the TOC had developed. I reported to the TOC to let Cardenas know our situation, but a long night of locating our remaining vehicles was ahead of us. As the remnants rolled into position throughout the night, exhausted troops did their best to get settled under the cover of darkness, but it would take until daylight the next day to establish proper order. As I collapsed in my sleeping bag that night, I made this entry: "We rolled today. I have 90+ vehicles in the convoy. Tapline Road is the most dangerous road I've ever seen. Trucks everywhere at excessive speed. No regard for safety on the part of the Iraqis [sic].[11] It takes 14 hours to make the trip. We are exhausted. Our 'low boy' drivers [Muslims] stop for prayer despite the convoy. I am resigned that such is the situation 'buk'rah, inshallah' (Tomorrow if God wills). We arrive after dark; half the convoy gets lost headed into position. Fighting at night will be hard." Aside from my mistaken entry of "Iraqis" instead of "Saudis," I don't think I could have more accurately recounted January 20 as one of the longest days of my life. But the port was at last behind us, and I was glad it was.

When morning broke on January 21, I saw for the first time the extensive work the DIVARTY TOC had accomplished in just a few days. The 1st Engineer Battalion (1-EN) of the division had bulldozed a huge two-meter-high (about six and a half feet) earthen berm around our entire position that would serve as a good defense against direct fire systems. While it was unlikely that we would get an attack from Iraqi ground forces that far inside Saudi Arabia, it was a comfort nonetheless that we were in a well-prepared position. We were now just east of the Wadi al-Batin, which could be used as a high-speed avenue of approach for Iraqi armored forces attacking southwest toward TAA Roosevelt. The thought of that kept us alert.

Shortly after I had shaved and had a cup of coffee, I encountered my boss, COL Dodson, whom I had not seen since he left Fort Riley the previous December. After exchanging sharp salutes, I said, "Damn, Boss, it's good to see you. I didn't ever think I would get out of that damn port!"

He remarked, "I'm glad you're here too, XO. We have a lot of work to do." Dodson was a detail man. He understood the complexities we faced, from fire support to the logistics we would need to sustain our operations. His immediate concern was the maintenance and logistical support the DIVARTY required. He was worried that maintenance for our equipment in the field and the ammunition supply system we would depend upon were "systemically broken," the term he used. He made clear that his man to fix this mess was now on the ground with him—and that man was me.

Dodson was very concerned that DIVARTY units were lacking some important pieces of equipment. Among them were night observation devices (NODs), which were essential for our nocturnal operations. While not a new technology to the Army, they were not standard issue; that is, not every soldier had one as part of his or her personal equipment. Nonetheless, NODs were essential to units as they maneuvered across the desert at night, and they were in high demand. Our standard procedure for operating vehicles during night operations was to drive them under "blackout" conditions to avoid enemy observation. That meant no use of headlights except for the small auxiliary night-lights mounted on the front and rear of our vehicles that emitted a low level of light through tiny slits instead of bright headlights. These slits were called "cat eyes" because they resembled the eyes of a feline. Unfortunately, "cat eyes" were designed to permit only enough light for a vehicle to be identified by other vehicles at very close range. They were almost useless as a navigation aid to the occupants of a vehicle depending on them to find their way in the dark.

The desert, while largely flat, was punctuated with ravines and dunes that dropped off suddenly, and at night, even a cautious driver could easily flip a vehicle. An accident like that could result in severe injury or death from being tossed around inside with lots of equipment flying about. Additionally, the NODs we needed were very helpful in seeing other vehicles at night to avoid collisions, and Dodson wanted key personnel, like battery commanders and first sergeants, to have them as they maneuvered their units. Additionally, there were personnel in specialized units, like MLRS launchers and counterbattery-radar drivers, who had to see where they were going at night so that they could get into position and operate their systems.

Dodson also worried, justifiably so, that maintenance support, particularly replacement parts for critical systems including our M270 MLRS rocket launchers, was inadequate. These weapons were intensively technological and dependent on sensitive electronic parts we called "black boxes." While we had rebuilt each of the launchers with the help of the depot team from Red River Arsenal, they could become inoperative in a demanding and harsh environment like the desert if these "black boxes" became "broken boxes."

Equally challenging was the maintenance of our counterbattery systems, the Q-36 and larger Q-37 radars that required very fragile glass telewave tubes (TWT)—like those in a television—to operate. If one of these TWTs broke while traveling over rough terrain, the radars would be useless. Our PADS (Position and Azimuth Determining System) were also essential to fire support operations to accurately determine positioning data for firing units. They were equipped with a very accurate gyroscopic positioning system to determine precise location, direction, and elevation (altitude above or below sea level) with an accuracy and speed quicker than a traditional manual survey team could produce. PADS were vital. Artillery units must have accurate information on where they are, within one meter, to shoot accurately. Generally, for a field artillery battalion, that meant establishing fifth-order survey, as we termed it. That level of survey would give firing units positioning data that was within 1-meter accuracy for every 1,000 meters of distance between established survey points. In most places where the Army operated in the modern world, there were established survey points that allowed us to "pick up and carry" survey data accurately from one established point to another, like newly occupied artillery firing positions. This wasn't so in the desert where there were no survey points to "pick up" data and "carry" it to the positions our artillery units would occupy. We had to establish "initial" survey, and the PADS, with their highly accurate gyroscopic system, could do that quickly. The problem was that, like our radars, our PADS were very fragile and frequently in need of maintenance and repair.

Radio maintenance had also bedeviled us. We used mostly FM systems that had been in the Army for decades. They often failed, and we were in a constant cycle of submitting our radios to our maintenance teams for repair. And, of course, there were our newly acquired GPS devices that we received at Fort Riley. They too were fragile, and the maintenance support system was not in place to properly fix the ones that weren't operating properly. Like NODs for our key personnel, Dodson was also keen to secure operational GPSs for his subordinate commanders who would control unit movements throughout our area of operations. Maintenance on these items was not easy. Nothing was easy.

Our logistics and unit-supply system back home were fairly responsive to needs like those we had in TAA Roosevelt, but that was Fort Riley. "Home" was now the desert. In the port, we created the system "on the fly" to link soldiers and weapons. But having to improvise and deal with an unresponsive supply system was more difficult. Logistical support in the desert, to be sure, was rooted in a sound doctrine that had been tested for years in Europe, Asia, and the US. Unfortunately, our supply system, unlike the adapted and sparse plant life in Saudi Arabia, had very shallow roots in the desert. Indeed, the challenge that confronted us was significant. Unlike the normal system at Fort Riley or at a post in Europe that functioned over modern infrastructure where logistical requisitions flowed logically by ground or air transportation from warehouses to the unit needing them, the desert had none of that. Reliable infrastructure, from roads to warehouses to fixed communications, was completely absent. Repair parts were aboard ships en route from the US and Europe across twó oceans (the Atlantic and Indian) to be off-loaded in the port. After that, they were stored in port supply centers for onward movement to catch up with units on the move as they dispersed rapidly across a vast and empty desert. They didn't catch up.

As a result, repair parts that combat and logistics units brought with them soon ran out. Once they did, the units were handicapped with a long logistics "tail." Moreover, that "tail" had yet to be properly config- ured and stocked with supplies to feed the "jaws" of a hungry combat force with a very large body. While there were plenty of mechanics every- where to work on vehicles and equipment in need of repair, they fre- quently had to repair broken things with the limited resources on hand. Supplies were rapidly depleted. "Field expedient repair," our shorthand for duct tape and baling wire, and even cannibalizing other equipment— the removal of a part from one broken vehicle to repair another—were the frequently employed techniques until proper repair parts arrived. Additionally, the inability to track where parts and equipment were in the desert logistics pipeline was a prescription for first-rate migraine head- aches, for which there was no easy cure. This vexed logisticians and war- fighters alike and often resulted in frustration, resentment, and outright anger. But through it all, everyone did their level best to get the mission accomplished. Clearly, we were in it together to get the system to operate so that we could do what we came to do: fight the bad guys.

Dodson's expectation for me was to get the system moving to be responsive and supportive of our units, so that we could prepare for operations. Daily he wrestled with the VII Corps Artillery and other planners to better determine the artillery organization that would be placed at his disposal. By then we knew that we would conduct the main attack. However, Dodson needed to know which additional units he would have to augment the DIVARTY in conducting future artillery raids and the preparatory artillery fires that would blast a way forward for our ground forces when the invasion began. None of that could happen, not a bit of it, without a logistics system to support the massive operation that was before us and would soon be placed squarely in our laps.

That was always on his mind, and as his XO, I was charged with untangling a lot of it. Sometimes it seemed more than I could wrap my mind around. I was grateful that I had Cardenas in the desert with us because he, as our S-3, was superb in discerning and defining the logisti- cal requirements—particularly artillery rounds and rockets—for the artillery organization that could emerge. The size of that force was potentially huge, maybe up to 20 battalions. It was a daunting task that had to be accomplished. I wondered from my first days in TAA Roosevelt if we had the wherewithal to do it. I hoped that we did. But in war, as GEN Sullivan frequently reminded us, "Hope is not a method." And we were at war now. As our operations chief, SGM Theo Vann, was fond of saying to excuse-making NCOs and EMs when they were foolish enough to offer one to him, "Excuses, even good ones, have a maximum effective range of zero meters." In other words, we needed to get the job done, no whining, no "hum-ma, hum-ma bullshit"—just get the right results.

The last sentence of my journal entry on January 21 summed it up: "We have much work to do."

7

Preparing for the Fight

The DIVARTY TOC, which was my base of operations, was positioned 60 kilometers east-southeast of the town of Hafar al-Batin in a central area of TAA Roosevelt. The TAA was a large, oval area shaped like the sideways letter "D" with its flat side parallel to the deadly Tapline Road that ran southeast to northwest just south of us (see map 7.1).[1]

It was a huge area, encompassing roughly 1,150 square kilometers of flat desert with sparse vegetation, and it was big enough to house the entirety of the BRO, providing ample separation between units in case of air strikes or missile attacks from the Iraqis. That separation would help survivability, but it also meant that traveling between units in the 1ID area consumed much time. Indeed, this massive assembly area contained three infantry and armor maneuver brigades, the DIVARTY, an aviation brigade with its attack helicopters, our combat support brigade, known as the Division Support Command (DISCOM), and numerous specialized units of the division including air defense, engineers, signal, intelligence battalions, and other smaller support units like our MP Company (see figure 7.1). Fortunately, most of the DIVARTY units under my control were nearby, and my priority was to visit them to assess their readiness, logistics, and operational posture.

My first concern was B-6 FA, our MLRS battery. With its nine rocket launchers, it possessed enormous firepower able to range out to 32 kilometers to the enemy's rear area of operations. A launcher was able to shoot 12 rockets in about 40 seconds. Each rocket contained 644 deadly anti-armor and antipersonnel submunitions, enough ordnance to cover an entire football field. Their operational readiness rate, or "ORR" as we would call it, was vital to the success of the fire missions we would conduct. Of the battery's nine launchers, a few were in repair after the long transit across the ocean, where salt air can take a toll on equipment. My first objective was to get those launchers fixed quickly. Keeping these launchers in top condition was a high priority. They were complex beasts that needed not only highly technical "black boxes," hydraulic actuators,

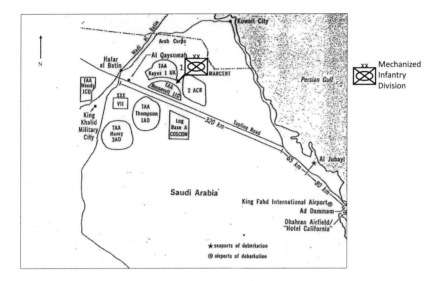

Map 7.1. Initial Tactical Assembly Area (TAA Roosevelt) for the 1st Infantry Division

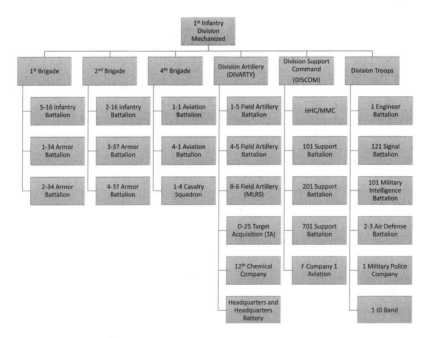

Figure 7.1. 1st Infantry Division Organization

electronic sensors, and mundane automotive parts, but highly skilled technicians to advise our mechanics on repair operations and diagnostics. Moreover, these launchers used the same engine and transmission as the M2 Bradley IFV. So we were in competition for available replacement engines with our infantry brethren. To help us with maintenance, the manufacturer of our MLRS launchers sent civilian technicians with the division to do much of this work in TAA Roosevelt, and these folks were a cherished asset. When all hope seemed to evaporate in trying to figure out how to fix one of these "mountains of technology," as we termed them, our "techie," the civilian from Lockheed Martin Missiles and Fire Control, would magically figure it out and conquer the problem. We had no alcoholic beverages in the desert, but if I had had a stock of fine scotch, I suspect I would have given all of it to our "techies" in appreciation for their work in keeping these launchers up and running. They were superb.

Logistically, we also had to ensure we had enough rockets to engage the enemy. The ones we had on hand—which constituted the basic, or standard, load of rockets for the battery—were stored in the ammunition holding areas (AHA) that the engineers had constructed by pushing up sand berms in a rectangular structure. They were all stacked safely and ready to move out whenever the order was given to load up for a mission. But many more rockets would be required to satisfy our fire plans in the future. To fire those rockets with precision, each launcher, which had an inertial navigation system (INS) on board, had to be calibrated for accuracy using the survey information brought to our location a day earlier. This required a "calibration run," in which the launcher's self-locating abilities were synchronized by using a survey control point (SCP) and its on-board computer. This entailed the operator's entering the coordinates from the SCP on the ground at the start point of the calibration run. Then the launcher would be driven straight as an arrow for 4 to 6 kilometers at a speed of about 40 kilometers per hour. The launcher would then return along the same straight route to the original survey point, where the operator would check the variance at the end of the run. If that variance was in tolerance, then the launcher could accurately determine its location. It was then ready to travel from a surveyed hiding position to a firing point several kilometers away to accurately launch its rockets. Afterward, the launcher would quickly return to its hiding position before the enemy could locate it and shoot back. The "calibration run" was an important procedure that enabled us to use what we called our "shoot and scoot" tactics that took advantage of the launcher's ability to "know where it was" after it left its hiding point, to launch its rockets from a firing point, and then to rapidly depart it before the enemy could shoot back. While we didn't give the Iraqis much credit for conducting effective and rapid counterbattery operations against our speedy MLRS launchers, we faithfully observed the "scoot and shoot" tactics.

B-6 FA wasn't my sole concern. My mission was to ensure that all our units in the DIVARTY were getting ready and had all the support they needed. On January 22 after I visited all the subordinate units in my direct care, the separates as we called them, including the HHB, B-6 FA, D-25 TAB, and the 12th Chemical, I then set out to find our logistical supporters with the DISCOM. They, like us, had just deployed to desert locations. From my diary that day: "Visited DISCOM. Saw Frank Rosebery and Kevin Gantt, both neighbors from Ft Riley. Both are well. We are now aware that the air war is behind schedule. A ground war is sure to come. Parts are hard to get. We continue to have fits getting our ambulance. The G-4 is no help." The DISCOM, commanded by COL Bob Shadley, had a very important mission, to say the least. It was responsible for delivering all classes of supply for every unit in the division, including themselves. That encompassed a lot. The Army uses a system to categorize ten "classes" of supply. Class I was food and drinking water. Class II included clothing, equipment like tents, and tools. Class III was petroleum, oil, and lubricants (POL). Class IV dealt with construction materiel to build protective bunkers in the field. Class V was ammunition of all types. Class VI covered personal health and hygiene products and creature comforts. Class VII included major assemblies, like engines and transmissions. Class VIII encompassed medical supplies. Class IX was the repair parts required to maintain our vehicles. Finally, Class X addressed materiel not included in other classes. To be sure, the DISCOM had a big task, and I wondered, as I prepared to head its way, if it could get it all done.

The location of the DISCOM was several kilometers from our DIVARTY's position, so PFC McGary and I had a chance to verify our newfangled GPS to see if it was reliable. We plugged in the map coordinates to the DISCOM east of us in the massive TAA Roosevelt. The GPS was convenient. Yet I couldn't help relying on the fully gimbaled marine compass we had installed in HQ-5. I calculated a direction to the DISCOM on my map, determined the distance, and told McGary to head 90 degrees for a determined distance, only turning where rough terrain made us veer one way or the other. After about 20 minutes on the "road," a euphemism when it comes to traveling over a featureless and bumpy desert, the DISCOM appeared on the horizon as a small city of sand-camouflaged trucks with a field of radio antennas reaching skyward. Sure enough, the compass method worked flawlessly. Happily, so did the GPS, but for this artillery-man, habits were hard to break, especially ones that had a few centuries of proven validity behind them. For that reason, I would continue using the compass as a fail-safe whenever possible.

When I dismounted my Humvee, I meandered through the maze of trucks. Many were the large five-ton variety with ten wheels, equipped with built-in sliding side panels and roofs that could be expanded to dou-ble the interior floor space of the truck van's working area. These "expand-o vans," as we called them, were the "office space" for TOCs like ours and in the DISCOM. Each had an air-conditioner to keep sensi-tive radio and computer equipment from overheating. This was a luxury in an otherwise austere environment. A visit to a TOC with "AC" on a hot day would let you catch your breath from the heat of the desert. And while it was January and the temperature was not yet terribly oppressive, all of us knew the AC would be critical later in the season.

I found the van for the DMMC (Division Materiel Management Center), where I linked up with MAJ Frank Rosebery and CPT Kevin Gantt, both very competent and engaged logisticians who shared my frustration with the support conditions in the desert. Frank's family lived down the street from us on Riley Place, and Kevin's wife, Machele, and their two kids, Brady and Becky, lived next door to Shelley and our kids. Our children played together, and our wives were friends. As I greeted them with a hearty handshake, it struck me that here we were at war in the desert of Saudi Arabia, even as our families were home together that moment. They must have been wondering where we were, what we were doing, and whether they would ever see us again. We all knew it. We didn't speak of it. There was too much work to do.

Kevin, in his Texas drawl, barked, "How the hell are you, Colonel? Don't come in here and tell me your dammed GPS doesn't work. I'm about to throw all of that crap in the trash bin!"

"Mine's fine for now, but I have a marine compass mounted in the Humvee," I responded with a hint of pride.

Gantt was impressed with the simple ingenuity of that idea and said, "Well, you're probably the only damn person who's gonna find his butt in this desert, 'cause these friggin' GPSs break all the time." I hoped he was wrong about that. The last thing anyone needed was to be "LID" (lost in desert) in Iraq. That was the term we used for people who had lost their way in the high desert of California's NTC. But no one at the NTC was looking to kill you if you were found wandering aimlessly in the California desert. Here, being LID could end badly.

Because Gantt was resourceful—a very good thing for a logistician—
he wound up as "Mr. GPS-fixer" in the DMMC, and it was turning out
to be a real headache for him. But my big headache for now was the availability of repair parts and supplies for just about everything. Gantt informed
me that one of the problems the division faced was that the ship carrying
many of our parts and major supply items, along with some of DIVARTY's
remaining vehicles, had flunked its sea trial not once but twice! After trying
to get the ship fixed and underway, the Army's MTMC (Military Traffic
Management Command) made the decision to send this deficient ship to
sea anyway, given the urgent situation. The ship did eventually arrive, but
the delay disrupted the supply chain for sure, causing a ripple effect from
the port to our positions in the desert. With that "great" news in my sails,
I left Gantt to his GPS woes and stopped at the DISCOM supply point to
see if any parts had arrived for DIVARTY units. There were a few items,
but as I looked around the supply area, I stumbled on piles and piles of
body bags, the heavy plastic containers used to store the remains of deceased
soldiers. It was a sobering moment as I wondered how many we would
wind up using—not a very uplifting thing to think about.

Pushing that morbid thought aside, I then made my way to the
expand-o van that housed our MLRS civilian maintenance technicians. I
coordinated with them concerning the status of our MLRS launchers and
convinced them to visit our position several kilometers away. They
agreed, but despite my most persuasive arguments, they resisted taking
up residence with our unit. I think it was possibly because some of the
creature comforts they had managed to ship to the desert, like a charcoal
grill, were already in operation next to their expand-o van. COL Dodson
and I would have forbidden that convenience, since it would surely have
violated operational security. The last thing we needed to do was to give
our position away with the smoke and fire of a charcoal grill, not to mention how the aroma could induce a profound case of homesickness in
everyone. Nevertheless, these techies were pure gold to us. They knew the
MLRS system thoroughly and had a direct line back to the states via satellite phones to get the right answer to a problem, if they didn't have it.
It made a lot of sense to me to have them forward deployed with us, but
the DMMC didn't like that idea, in part because the techies were civilians
and not protected as combatants under the rules of land warfare.

On the way back to DIVARTY, I swung by both of our cannon
battalions to check in with the battalion executive officers, 1–5 FA's MAJ
Paul Callahan and 4–5 FA's MAJ Jim Boyle. Both sang the same song
that haunted me concerning readiness. Like DIVARTY, Callahan had

problems with his survey PADS. Moreover, they had brought so much gear to the field with them, they could hardly transport it. At the time they were considering putting the equipment in a huge pit in the desert and setting it ablaze. That struck me as imprudent, to say nothing of possibly being deliberately destructive, and I concluded they couldn't possibly be serious. But it wasn't a problem I could devote much of my attention to at the time. Among the items they wanted to dispose of were large maintenance tents and the metal framework that supported them when erected. The tents were necessarily big so they could protect vehicles from the elements when repairing them. But they took up lots of space when loaded on transport vehicles. Months later, Dodson and I would come to learn they ultimately did burn much of it in a stunningly ill-advised act, particularly since someone was legally responsible for the property and would have to answer for its whereabouts. It was an odd way to deal with excess equipment.

When I got back to DIVARTY, I briefed Dodson on the state of logistics support. He did what he frequently did when hearing bad news. He just quietly shook his head in disbelief, pulled out his notebook, made one of his "boxes" with a brief note behind it, and patiently put it back in this upper shirt pocket. "XO, why is everything so damn hard?" he would ask. My response was usually, "Yes, sir, it's damn hard. But I'm on the case." As I thought about the difficulty and the "friction" it created in dealing with the port, logistics, and other problems that confronted us, I was reminded of the words of military strategist Carl von Clausewitz: "Everything is very simple in war, but the simplest thing is difficult. These difficulties accumulate and produce a friction, which no man can imagine exactly who has not seen war."[2] To be sure, there was no lack of friction in any direction we faced as we prepared to wage war with the Iraqi Army.

Dodson was slow to anger, very slow; but he was determined to get things fixed. Indeed, he was indefatigable when it came to resolving problems. So when I reported troubles to him, I instinctively knew that it was on me to continue to "work the fix." In that regard we were a good team. Unfortunately, so much of our time seemed to be fixing other people's problems. We had enough to worry about in trying to sort out the artillery fight that we were planning, without needing to fix logistical problems that were the job of the professional logisticians.

Meanwhile, I could see that Dodson was making the transition to more pressing operational concerns. He alternated from one problem to another, and there were lots of problems to alternate among. The VII Corps Support Command continued to struggle with ammunition supply, while the Division FSE, Dodson's team at the division level for planning artillery fires, was still getting organized. We were also challenged in attempting to coordinate with the VII Corps Artillery Commander, BG Creighton W. Abrams III, to get a clear picture of the field artillery organization that would materialize in support of the 1ID. Abrams had the misfortune of setting up meetings and then getting torn away to other matters. In a fast-paced environment, this was inevitable, I suppose, but it had a cascading effect on Dodson's busy agenda. I could see his frustration mounting. Unfortunately, aside from an encouraging word from me now and then, there was little I could do to fix that problem.

I knew Abrams. He had been my DIVARTY commander when I was assigned to the 3ID in Germany in 1985. Abrams was a very accomplished artilleryman, indeed technically and tactically brilliant. And like his four-star father namesake who had commanded forces in Vietnam and later served as Chief of Staff of the Army, Abrams had made his mark for sure. He had a very creative mind, was sharp as a tack, and frequently thought miles ahead of others. Sometimes, however, he was not ready to play his hand as quickly as folks might like to see it. He would think things over and over. But once he decided, he generally stuck with it, unless it was not working. I saw this in action—up close and personally—working with him in the 3ID, known as the Marne Division for its gallantry in World War I. The key to getting along with him was to be competent and patient. Dodson was both, which is why the two of them worked well together. But none of us had the time or inclination to bounce across the desert from one canceled meeting to another when there was so much to do.

Word soon filtered down from the VII Corps Artillery and division headquarters that we would see a huge augmentation of artillery units to the DIVARTY, maybe as many as 10–20 battalions, including a battalion of MLRS and separate MLRS batteries. In addition to our Fort Riley-based 1-5 FA and 4-5 FA, we added the 4th Battalion, 3rd Field Artillery (4-3 FA). It was the direct support battalion to the 2AD-F, the separate armored maneuver brigade stationed in Germany and commanded by BG Rutherford, that had received orders attaching it to the BRO. We were fortunate to have this particular outfit and its commanding general. Rutherford—who also worked like the devil to get us out of the port—had been the BRO's ADC-M just prior to his assignment to command the 2AD-F in Germany. Now our new ADC-S, focused on support, not maneuver, he knew the BRO inside and out. He had been sent to Germany to get this forward-deployed armored force trained and ready to receive more brigades from the US if war broke out in Europe. Desert

Figure 7.2.   2nd Armored Division-Forward Organization

Shield changed all of that as Rutherford's command would now consti-
tute the 1ID's 3rd Brigade. In a way, it was a homecoming, albeit an
unexpected one. This brigade brought with it two armored battalions,
one mechanized infantry battalion, its direct support field artillery battalion, 4–3 FA, as well as supporting units (see figure 7.2).

The 4–3 FA was commanded by my good friend LTC Lanny Smith,
a West Point graduate. We served together from 1986 to 1988 in the
DIVARTY of the 3ID in Würzburg, Germany. Smith came to command
of the 4–3 FA under rather odd circumstances. In November of 1990,
while serving as the S-3 Operations Officer of the Marne DIVARTY, he
was abruptly informed by his DIVARTY commander that he would be
activated for early battalion command of the Garlstedt-based 4–3 FA in
northern Germany. He was caught completely off guard by this announcement. Moreover, the battalion commander he would replace had been
relieved for poor performance. Further complicating that unfortunate situation was the fact that the subordinate battery commanders—four of
the five of them—had been in a near state of mutiny with their former
commander, a pestilential indiscipline Smith would have to resolve immediately. His no-nonsense West Point pedigree was immediately on display.
When he arrived at the battalion after a day-long drive with his family
north from Würzburg, it was near midnight. He proceeded directly to the
battalion headquarters, where he summoned the petulant officers. There
at 0100 in the morning he entered the unit conference room where the
officers had gathered. He then purposefully left everyone standing at a
position of attention for several minutes as he flipped through a briefing
book that had been prepared for him. When he was done, he looked up
coolly and succinctly ordered all of them to read Herman Wouk's *The
Caine Mutiny* and report to him by 0500 on the lessons to be learned.
Smith related to me later that—amazingly—none of them moved until he
barked, "Now get the HELL out of my conference room."[3]

After scurrying about to find a copy of the novel in the wee hours of the morning and digest it in a few hours, his officers came to see the error of their behavior and disloyalty in the overall command environment. Smith's dynamic leadership style had quickly galvanized these officers to their duty, and when they arrived in Saudi Arabia as a part of the BRO, they were ready to execute their mission. Smith was a superb officer, and his assumption of command of the 4–3 FA was—while abrupt—nonetheless fortuitous. Dodson now had a third 155mm battalion to work into the operational plan of the DIVARTY. He quickly realized, as I already knew from my service with Smith three years earlier, that he was a first-rate officer who would be an important member of our team.

With a full complement of battalions in the DIVARTY, Dodson and MAJ Cardenas would be responsible for the fire planning and maneuver of our three 155mm battalions as well as other field artillery brigades that would be placed under our control. The day I escaped the port, January 20, the VII Corps Artillery had just assigned the 75th Field Artillery Brigade (75th FA Brigade), commanded by COL Jerry L. "Gunner" Laws, to reinforce our DIVARTY. It brought with it one 155mm battalion, one 203mm (8-inch) battalion, two MLRS batteries—one capable of firing the deadly Army Tactical Missile System (ATACMS)—and a target acquisition battery (TAB) with the same counterfire radars we possessed. This brigade was an important addition to us with its considerable combat power.

Each of the subordinate battalions of the brigade would have one of four missions assigned to it. In the field artillery, a tenet of our doctrine is that the artillery is never held in reserve. This doctrine was rooted in the experience of previous wars. Owing to the deadly effect artillery has on ground units, it is simply unjustified to keep any gun out of action. Even if the maneuver units an artillery unit would normally support were in reserve, its artillery was committed to be in the fight somewhere. Thus, the field artillery developed four mission sets we called "Standard Tactical Missions." They are direct support (DS), in which an artillery unit directly supports a designated maneuver unit, normally a brigade or battalion; reinforcing (R), in which the artillery unit reinforces the fires of another DS unit; general support reinforcing (GSR), in which the artillery reinforces another artillery unit, but is available to a higher artillery headquarters to employ in other missions; and general support (GS), in which the artillery unit is at the call of a higher artillery headquarters, like a DIVARTY or a field artillery brigade.

So on January 20, our artillery combat power in the 1ID grew an astonishing 100 percent (see table 7.1). This was a challenging undertaking

Table 7.1.   1st Infantry Division Artillery Organization for Combat
(January 20, 1991)

1ID (Mechanized) DIVARTY: Force Artillery Headquarters (HQ)	
1-5 FA (155mm SP)	DS 1st Brigade
4-5 FA (155mm SP)	DS 2nd Brigade
4-3 FA (155mm SP)	DS 3rd Brigade (2nd Armored Division)
B-6 FA (MLRS)	GS
D-25 TAB	GS
75th Field Artillery Brigade: R 1ID (M) DIVARTY, Alternate FA HQ	
1-17 FA (155mm SP)	GS
5-18 FA (203mm SP)	GS
A-1-158 FA (MLRS)	GS
A-6-27 FA (ATACMS)	GS VII Corps Artillery
C-26 TAB	GS

Key: Direct Support (DS); Reinforcing (R); General Support Reinforcing (GSR); General
Support (GS)

for an organization like ours that typically might orchestrate, at most, five
battalions. The VII Corps, our higher headquarters, wanted the 1ID to create an initial breach in the enemy's defenses when we crossed the border
into Iraq. That plan would require a massive artillery preparation to blow
a hole so big in the Iraqi defenses that we could drive the entire division
through it. Dodson was making the case, however, that adding the 75th FA
Brigade alone—while helpful—was not enough.

Moreover, getting the VII Corps Artillery to finalize the artillery task
organization, the units Dodson would employ in both field artillery raids
and the preparation fires that would precede the attack by our maneuver
brigades, was like nailing Jell-O to a wall. Dodson was frustrated; so was
Cardenas, whose focus was on trying to develop fire plans; while I worked
to coordinate logistics and related support activities. Moreover, Dodson
had me keep a close eye on the operational planning to ensure that the
numerous units we had assigned to us worked cooperatively. He knew
that my position as his XO, and as a lieutenant colonel, would help provide support to the several majors, including Cardenas, in our DIVARTY
as they planned the operation. They would work throughout the day and
night to plan this massive undertaking and had to deal with many other
field-grade officers in our subordinate battalions, who often had their
own take on things. To be sure, everyone we worked with, including the
highly talented staff majors and lieutenant colonels, who commanded

battalions under our control, had a view of how best to execute the mission. But Cardenas was charged with pulling that plan together—not them—and it was my job to assist him by providing "top cover" from all the "helpful criticism" he would get from the circumambient field-grade artillerymen present, all experts in their own right. Several times I had to "throw the umpire's yellow flag" and separate the players. Dodson depended on me to keep order in the DIVARTY so that his guidance was what was executed, not someone else's interpretation of it.

In that regard, both Cardenas and I were as anxious as Dodson was to know which units we would have. The difficulty, as Dodson put it, was that unit assignment of field artillery brigades to the DIVARTY was a rotation of on-again, off-again possibilities. The organization for combat—the term we used to describe the composition of the units assigned to the force artillery Dodson would employ—was constantly changing. This led to significant difficulty in developing plans. In Dodson's mind, it was better to have a plan that you could execute, with units you knew you would have, than to develop a plan that included units that might not show up. But this revolving-door approach to sorting out the units we would have for our operations caused the DIVARTY's staff a lot of difficulty in planning anything. Moreover, the constant rewriting of plans as we went along had a direct impact on technical fire direction planning, which was the computation of actual fire mission data to engage targets.[4] In sum, being uncertain regarding the organization we would have to employ in combat made planning a persistent pain. Moreover, with the addition of the 75th FA Brigade, logistics also became a bigger challenge.

Ammunition supply for the massive artillery organization envisioned, but yet undetermined, would require a gargantuan effort. Fortunately, that would be handled by our S-4 supply team headed by MAJ Brooks, one of the most focused and "can-do" officers I knew. He and I started an early conversation on how we would tackle this huge mission. Not only would it take tons of ammunition, it would also require the trucking to move it long distances to our AHAs, where our battalions would assemble to pick up the projectiles and rockets they would eventually fire in combat. Moreover, the ammunition would have to be prepositioned on a battlefield 40 kilometers wide, yet in numerous locations to accommodate firing units that were, likewise, dispersed across a broad frontage. Several AHAs would be needed, and engineer units—as they had done for our MLRS battery and DIVARTY TOC—would need to dig the facilities to both store and secure this huge stockpile of ammunition. Additionally, we would need to come up with the forklifts and other mechanical handling equipment (MHE) to download the heavy pallets of ammunition onto the ground. Some of these projectiles—like those fired by the accurate M110A2 203mm howitzer that could shoot them 29 kilometers—weighed 200 pounds each. A pallet of six exceeded 1,253 pounds! More daunting yet was the weight of an MLRS pod containing six rockets, which topped 5,000 pounds, and we needed to move thousands of these. Manpower alone couldn't do it, not even a battalion of silverback gorillas.

On top of the several logistical challenges that occupied my immediate attention, from the availability of NODs to MLRS "black boxes," ammunition resupply for our firing units consumed my energy. Some of the ammunition estimates we were hearing called for tens of thousands of cannon rounds and rockets. I recall Brooks and I looking at each other astonishingly and wondering if there was that much ammunition in the entire theater of operations to meet our needs as well as those of adjacent Army and Marine Corps units stretching from the Persian Gulf east of us to another corps even farther west. Cardenas wondered too as he tried to scope the size of the fire plans he needed to develop for the preparatory fires to support the ground assault. We were also advised that there would be an extended period of artillery raids that the DIVARTY would conduct to destroy key enemy targets in advance of the preparation and ground assault into Iraq. That would require additional amounts of ammunition immediately, since the raids were being planned for the very near future.

My plate was full, and it would get fuller, just dealing with the day-to-day challenges. In the ensuing days, we began to build combat power. My stay-behind leader in the port, CPT Dan Murray, was doing a great job of finding our remaining vehicles and getting them on the road to us. It was welcome news, even as a period of cold rainy weather descended on us. Not only did this foul weather slow the air war with Iraq, but it chilled us to the bone. When you are tired, hungry, and overworked, a cold wet rain does not exactly brighten your spirits. For that I relied on a quiet time each morning when I got up to read morning prayer from my Episcopal serviceman's prayer book. I kept a picture of the kids nearby that I had brought with me and prayed each day that if I didn't survive, God would protect them as they grew. War tends to focus the mind on things spiritual. It did for me, and my constant prayer was that I would do my duty no matter what.

When January 27 rolled around, things were beginning to look better for us, as I noted: "Dan reports all of our vehicles are located but a few.

Next is to get to the field. Weather is better. The air war is back on. Indications are we won't attack until the enemy has taken a real thumping." A day earlier, I made a note that Murray, the 12th Chemical's XO, deserved an Army Commendation Medal (ARCOM) for his efforts at the port. In fact, Dodson agreed and pinned one on him when he finally made it out to us later in the week. He deserved it. On one occasion, I'm sure I taxed Murray's brain and patience with instructions concerning M2 Bradley IFVs sitting in the port that had been designated for Dodson and his battalion commanders, LTCs Emerson, Gingrich, and Smith to use when having to maneuver near the front lines during combat. They were armored, fast, and loaded with firepower and communications gear. My task was to get them to the field immediately. Murray reported that there were 19 of these in the port. Given the urgency, I told him to sign for all 19 to move things along. Murray, in stunned amazement, wondered if I thought he could move mountains "just like that!" as he later put it. I suppose he was a bit overwhelmed by my order, but he did in fact secure three of them for us.[5]

As the rain cleared out, coalition aircraft once again roared overhead, delivering punishing blows to Saddam's forces on the ground. Meanwhile, the last ship with our equipment arrived that day, and Murray quickly found everything, sending it all in our direction. Now with the air war back on, we began to focus on the ground phase that was to follow. Yet we were still short a medical ambulance. While that might have seemed to be a small matter compared to the massive ammunition mission, it was still important and could make the difference between a soldier's dying or living to see another day. The "We'll work on it" response I got from the logisticians had, by then, rubbed so thin that I was at my wit's end with the entire supply system.

The next day, however, one event put everything else in perspective. We had our first casualty in one of my subordinate units. I recorded the event in my diary on January 29: "Sadly, we had our first casualty today. PFC Kirk from D/25 TAB was crushed by a Saudi feed truck that tried to pass him while he was making a left hand turn off of Tapline Road. His BC [battery commander] was unharmed but shook-up. I spoke to the unit to comfort them. They are all shocked. Only this AM I spoke to all the units about our mission. I told them some of us would not come back, but nevertheless, never to lose sight of our purpose. Only a few minutes later, it came true." PFC Rueben Kirk was a very fine man as his commander, CPT Seefeldt, told me later that day. As the unit set about evacuating Kirk's remains, collecting his personal effects, and preparing a memorial service, Dodson pulled me aside and warned me that a death of this sort could negatively impact morale if the right leadership was not exerted. Dodson was no stranger to combat deaths. He had seen plenty in Vietnam. After the memorial service on January 30, Dodson expressed his concern to the chaplain who conducted the service, MAJ Tom Jones, that it needed to be more "positive and crisp." Later he expressed the same to me, noting that the unit faced the danger of "dragging around after a loss." I thought that sentiment was natural and somewhat unavoidable for those who had not seen combat before. However, both the chaplain and I took Dodson's point to heart concerning the negative impact a first death can have on unit morale. Later that evening, I assembled Seefeldt's unit as the sun set on our desert home and, once again, reminded them why we were in the desert: to fight the enemy, not mourn our dead. Our focus and resolve had to be on defeating the enemy that brought us to this god-awful place. Afterward, several soldiers came up and thanked me for "pumping them up" after this initial shock. They got it. Dodson knew they would, and I was glad they did. This was truly no time to "drag around." Dodson's counsel, as was often the case, was spot on.

In no time, we were back at work preparing for ground combat operations, and our pace quickened. Our mission was clear, as expressed in the doctrinaire language of a mission statement: "On order, 1st Infantry Division (Mechanized) attacks as the VII Corps main effort to penetrate Iraqi defenses; defeat enemy first echelon forces and conduct the forward passage of the VII (US) Corps forces. On order, follow VII (US) Corps' main attack in zone to destroy the Republican Guards."[6] A mission statement is a vital component of what the Army calls the five-paragraph field order. Paragraph 1 is the "Situation," both enemy forces and friendly forces. Paragraph 2 is the "Mission," a pithy "who, what, when, why, and how" of what we would do. Paragraph 3 covers the "Execution," how the mission would be accomplished. Paragraph 4 addresses the plan for "Service Support," how we would sustain the operation. Paragraph 5 is the conclusion and deals with "Command and Control," addressing who is in charge, where they would be on the battlefield, and how they would communicate with the troops. We planned everything in the field order format. But the mission component was vital, and this one reminded all of us of the seriousness of the task before us.

On January 31, the number of B-52 bomber sorties picked up. We could see the contrails—the line-shaped clouds produced by aircraft-engine exhaust—that these deadly bombers flying above us left behind. We could also hear and feel the thunderous impact of their bombs hitting Iraqi ground positions miles away. It was awesome power that, no doubt, terrorized the enemy. Meanwhile, we had linked up with the mighty 1st United Kingdom Armored Division (1(UK)AD) commanded by MG Rupert Smith, and it's Division Artillery (1(UK)FA) commanded by BG Ian Durie. The 1(UK)AD, Great Britain's ground contribution to the coalition effort, would take positions on the right flank of the 1ID in the days to come, while Durie's 1(UK)FA would reinforce our DIVARTY. As was customary, we exchanged liaison officers (LNO) to share information, and I made this entry that day about ours: "Working with the 1st UK is great. They are very interesting. Our movement forward with them must be worked out in every detail. Their LNO David Lime is a 'piece of work,' pedantic all the way, yet knowledgeable." MAJ Lime was an upbeat professional, and it was a comfort to know that such a well-trained NATO ally would be on our right flank. But one taste of the British equivalent of Meals Ready to Eat (MREs) made us abundantly thankful that we had our own version, even the tuna fish one I despised. Later, Lime would be replaced by CPT R. J. "Rick" Radice who was an equally superb LNO, one who would prove his worth in short order.

With the arrival of 1(UK)AD in our area of operations, things began to fall in place for the next phase of our operation, where we would take up positions closer to the Iraqi border to conduct a series of artillery raids to soften up our entrenched enemy. But our training in TAA Roosevelt continued. Our artillery battalions visited a firing range south of the TAA to conduct live-fire training, so our cannon crews were tuned up and ready to fight. Units conducted NBC (nuclear, biological, chemical) training to make certain that every soldier was prepared to respond to an attack. We conducted rehearsals of war plans, including communications exercises (Comm-X), battle drills, the routine actions our platoons and squads would take to apply fire and maneuver tactics to commonly encountered situations as well as the actions and decisions leaders would rapidly take in issuing oral orders. Operationally, we also conducted deep-strike missions on enemy positions with the ATACMS-capable MLRS battery from the 75th FA Brigade. The ATACMS of 1991 was an unguided missile that contained 950 M74 antipersonnel/antimateriel (APAM) submunitions, could achieve a considerable range of 128 kilometers (80 miles), and was very well suited to strike deep in the enemy's rear area of operations. Meanwhile, we continued to perform maintenance on our equipment to ensure we were prepared to roll on a moment's notice. We were ready to fight.

However, when it came to fighting, we wondered what the Iraqis were up to on their side of the border berm that separated them from us in Saudi Arabia. Just as I had predicted to MG Rhame in Dodson's office the previous fall, the Iraqis seemed quite happy to stay in their revetments, despite a few incidents when they came out to do a limited reconnaissance against BRO elements deployed in the forward area. If they did elect to remain in their defensive posture, we would devastate them with our accurate artillery fire and air attacks. Coalition bombs continued to fall day and night on February 1 and 2. A-10 Thunderbolt aircraft, with their air-to-ground aircraft munitions, also joined the fight. The A-10 was designed for close air support (CAS) of friendly ground troops, attacking armored vehicles and tanks and providing quick-action support against enemy forces. These "Warthogs," as they were affectionately known for their round bulky appearance as compared to fighter jets, could devastate the enemy. As I noted in my journal regarding the Iraqis, "They are ripe for the picking," and the A-10s were ready for the harvest.

There was no doubt that the air campaign was doing its job, and the ever-present roar of jets above was a comfort, except for the one that buzzed our TOC position like a screaming banshee at 0200 one morning and had all of us upright in our sleeping bags and ready to take cover in the closest foxhole! The ear-splitting roar sounded as if that fighter jockey was no more than 100 feet above us, and as he blasted by, many of us mistook him for an Iraqi aircraft on a strafing mission. In fact, one soldier started sounding an alarm, which was to bang on an empty metal projectile canister used to warn us of an impending chemical attack. It caused a great ruckus, but when we realized it wasn't an attack, we were all quickly back asleep, albeit unnerved by the interruption.

Meanwhile, Cardenas and I discerned that Dodson had a lot on his mind. While Cardenas worked daily to shape current and future operations and I ran around trying to slay the logistics dragon, Dodson was wrestling with the fluid events swirling around him. Among them was trying to make sense of the VII Corps Artillery commanding general's concept for the artillery raids and the preparation fires that would occur before our maneuver brigades would attack into Iraq. Typically, he found himself reacting to FRAGO's (fragmentary orders) and last-minute decisions that came down from the division. On top of this he had to make key decisions about which artillery units to launch first to the forward assembly area (FAA) to push our combat power forward for impending operations. When Dodson had to drive from one point to another to coordinate with other commanders and staff, it consumed his day. So when we were able to secure a helicopter flight for him, he was able to get a lot of coordination accomplished efficiently among the several field artillery brigades and battalions he was coordinating. Coincidentally, Dodson had maintained his status as a rated helicopter pilot since Vietnam, so some "stick time" flying the aircraft seemed to put him in a good mood. Given the frustration he dealt with around the clock, this was cathartic for the boss and, therefore, good for us as well.

FRAGOs were a way of life for much of what we did in the desert. An abbreviated form of the "five paragraph field order" used in virtually all levels of planning in the Army, it was composed of the same five key components, and we used it often. Whether planning a combat operation or digging a latrine, FRAGOs worked well. Like more complex operation orders, it contained the situation, both in terms of enemy and friendly forces, a mission statement, the plan of execution we would follow, the support requirements, and finally instructions on who was in command and how we would communicate among ourselves. FRAGOs were short, sweet, and to the point. And they were coming at us with greater frequency, as we found ourselves ever closer to jumping from our current position in TAA Roosevelt to positions farther northwest in the FAA from which we would launch an eventual attack.

Such a FRAGO popped up on February 2 when Dodson was told by Rhame that he wanted an artillery battalion to provide additional support to 1ID forces that had deployed west of the Wadi al-Batin, in the general area where the division would launch its eventual assault into Iraq. Rhame had dispatched an advance force—Combat Command Carter—named for our ADC-M, BG Bill Carter. Carter was ordered to conduct reconnaissance of and counterreconnaissance against Iraqi forces in the area of operations we would initially occupy in the FAA, 160 kilometers northwest of TAA Roosevelt. Dodson selected Emerson's 1–5 FA for the job. In Dodson's estimate, since 1-5 FA had preceded 4–5 FA and 4–3 FA into the desert, Emerson's battalion was better prepared for this operation since they had been in position longer.

When we awoke the morning of February 3, we experienced a rare winter *shamal*, a northwesterly desert windstorm that blew sand and dust into every crevice of our belongings. That same morning, we had been joined by the leadership of three brigades of artillery, the 42nd 75th, 142nd FA Brigades, and the DIVARTY from the 1(UK)FA, all of whom we expected would eventually be assigned to support our effort. Together these leaders represented 11 additional battalions of artillery, including two full MLRS battalions and two MLRS separate batteries. Coupled with our three DS battalions and MLRS battery, the force that was emerging was now equivalent to 17 battalions. That morning we gathered to conduct a council of war and work through how we would conduct raids, prepare for operations, and move forward to support our ground units. Moreover, we discussed how we would support the infantry and armor units that would make the breach in the face of up to two Iraqi regular infantry divisions. The *shamal* raged on throughout the entire endeavor and, while a bother, did not interrupt our planning conference. Now that the war had been named "Operation Desert Storm," the weather seemed appropriate.

The conference went well, but occasionally a subordinate commander would raise what seemed like superfluous issues, one after another, or "popped off" as Dodson would term it. Dodson's remedy for this was to scribble a short note of admonishment to the offending participant who was acting more agitated than necessary. After the note was passed, silence prevailed. Dodson had a convincing, albeit professional manner that was hard to resist. What this war council did reveal, however, was that much additional coordination would be required to make the details of the operation work effectively.

There were also numerous questions to be answered. Where would the AHAs with prepositioned ammunition be placed? Would we have enough ammunition on the ground to do all we were planning to shoot? What would be the scheme of maneuver for artillery units to move forward through the breach after the infantry and armor had completed their assault on Iraqi positions? What would be our follow-on mission once the breach operations concluded? The latter was in real doubt in the early days of February. What we didn't know then was that Rhame was doing a lot of thinking about this. Behind the scenes he was working the VII Corps staff in a determined manner to develop a follow-on mission for the division once the breach was accomplished. But that wasn't a topic addressed as our conference wrapped up that day.

VII Corps was resisting Rhame's insistence for a follow-on task because they were convinced that our division would take major losses and be combat ineffective after battling to open a breach in Iraqi lines. But in combat, a central tenet of doctrine is to "plan for success"—not failure—and Rhame wanted us ready to move and continue the division's attack against enemy forces well inside Iraq and onward to Kuwait. His G-3 Operations Officer, who was responsible for planning the attack, was LTC Terry Bullington. Like his name, he was truly a "Bulldog" in pressing the VII Corps staff for the specifics of a follow-on mission until their G-3 Operations Officer, COL Stan Cherrie, tossed him out of the headquarters.[7] However, both Bullington and Rhame persisted in their efforts to overcome VII Corps's hesitation.

Indeed, a follow-on mission after the breach made perfect sense to all of us in the BRO, particularly those of us planning the artillery fight. We knew that we would pound the Iraqis to death. I knew that when we did, the Iraqis on the front lines would likely collapse as they did in the Iran-Iraq War. The Republican Guards deeper inside Iraq were another matter. Until we knew what the follow-on mission would look like, it was difficult to prepare for both the initial assault and any follow-on fight. What we did know was that we needed to prepare for a lot of artillery raids ahead of us. Additionally, we had a huge preparation fire plan to develop and conduct. Those things alone gave Dodson, Cardenas, and me more than enough to do.

The following day, February 4, was a washday. The *shamal* had made a mess of everything, and many in the DIVARTY took time to shake the sand out of our possessions and clean clothes. Like others, I learned from the experience of units that had deployed to the desert ahead of us and brought laundry soap and a large Tupperware container to serve as a washtub. I also packed some clothespins and a clothesline that I strung up between my tent and Cardenas's canvas dwelling. While many of us were busy with these morning chores, imagine our surprise at being attacked by the US Air Force. From my diary that day: "A USAF aircraft dropped a Sidewinder missile on us today about 100M [meters] from D/25 TAB. I watched the thing happen and couldn't believe my eyes. Everyone reacted calmly. I went out to the crater to get markings off of the [missile] body. EOD blew it up later. This is a dangerous place." Apparently, a pilot jettisoned his AIM9 (Air Intercept Missile) by mistake. Dodson estimated the distance to be closer, at only 50 meters away. Others estimated it at 100 meters, still others 200 meters. Regardless, when your own air force "attacks" your position, it's too close by any measure. After the explosive ordnance detachment (EOD) team we summoned had disposed of the missile, the entire event served as a reminder that there are many ways to become a casualty of war—not to mention the motivation this event gave us to dig deeper foxholes for survival.

On February 5, we reconvened our war council to conduct a command post exercise (CPX). We walked through every step of the preparation we would fire, the movement of troops to and through the breach we would make in the Iraqi front lines, the assault on those enemy positions, and our onward movement and consolidation on the other side of the enemy's defenses. It was a lot to consider. This time we again included our British partners to test the fire and maneuver concept that we would employ during the breach operation. 1(UK)AD's Smith attended and was a very urbane gentleman. I made this note about our encounter and mutual love of recreational sailing: "We conduct a full CPX of our planned operation with the British. It was very productive. I have an opportunity to share sailing stories with the UK Division Commander, MG Smith. He waxes long about his adventures at sea. After 15 minutes of monologue, I begin to feel embarrassed for him. He was non-stop. I listened politely. Needless to say, this was correct on my part." The British were top-notch professionals. They knew their trade, and they had an unmistakable calm about them, always. "Yes, we were at war," they would admit, "but no need to get too excited about it."

That same day at that CPX, Dodson, Cardenas, and I witnessed a poignant example of British matter-of-fact calm. As we were going over the results of the CPX on a splendidly beautiful morning, a British M109 155mm howitzer and its ammunition carrier, an M548, positioned about a kilometer away from us, exploded, creating no less than a 200-foot-high fireball. Initially, we were mistakenly told it was due to an electrical issue. We learned later that, in fact, a young 1(UK)FA soldier was cooking his breakfast in the back of the ammunition carrier parked next to the howitzer when a fire broke out. It quickly spread and touched off an ammunition and powder conflagration. Amazingly, no one was killed, but the howitzer and ammunition carrier were history. Shortly after the incident, one of the senior British officers dryly remarked, "Right then; these sorts of things happen in war, wouldn't you say?" To the British, it was all just business as usual. I noted in my diary what a likely US response to such an incident would have been when I wrote, "We would have had a Congressional investigation with all the trappings!" We too would have our own near-catastrophic moments in the days to come, but likewise, we would take a less bureaucratic approach to bad things that can happen in combat.

On February 6, Dodson, Cardenas, and I attended an AAR of the previous day's CPX. One of the attending brigade commanders (as I recorded in my diary) didn't cover himself in glory as he protested—unnecessarily—over when his direct support artillery battalion would be reunited with him after the preparation fires concluded. Each infantry and armor brigade in the division had a field artillery battalion in "direct support," that is, directly responsive to the fire mission requests of that brigade. The artillery preparation plans we were developing would consume every single battalion we had, whether the field artillery unit was in a direct support (DS), reinforcing (R), general support reinforcing (GSR), or general support (GS) role. These four standard tactical missions were doctrinally designed to give us the flexibility we needed to task-organize the artillery force to keep everyone in the fight, since artillery units are never kept in reserve. But once the artillery battalions completed firing the preparation, those with a DS mission would promptly return to their supported brigade. Nevertheless, this one complainant at our CPX was not satisfied. He tossed barbs at the briefer, Cardenas, and even took a verbal shot at our British friends, protesting like a kid deprived of his marbles. It was uncommonly childish for a senior officer to act that way. In short order and after a stern look from Carter, our ADC-M, the worrisome fellow settled down. Even senior officers can get a bit jumpy, but it's never good form. Ever. Such uneasiness can be quickly picked up by subordinates. Beyond being poor form, it struck me as completely unnecessary. Dodson agreed.

As the desert sun rose on the early morning of February 7, I made time for some reflection: "Taking an easy morning. Normal day begins with reading my Bible and a morning devotion from the Episcopal Serviceman's Prayer Book. Keeping my faith must be a first priority. Only God will get me and the soldiers through all of this." Faith was not new to me. I was not a wartime convert, so to speak. I found my time in prayer and reflection an opportunity to focus on what mattered. To be sure I thought about my family and our friends. I desperately missed them and worried about what lay ahead of us. Wondering about the things that could happen—being shot or blown up, or choking to death in a chemical attack—was constant. No one talked about it. It was not manly, but we all knew what was on everyone's mind. I could see it in the eyes of folks as G-Day, ground day, approached. I also felt the pressure not to reveal my feelings. My job and the job of every leader was to inspire confidence in our troops, not "stampede the herd" by showing hesitancy. If we demonstrated doubt, if we expressed any anxiety about the days and weeks ahead, it could invoke the very fear I had told my soldiers would "crush their hearts." Being scared of something dangerous was one thing. Being fearful of it is being so scared that you freeze and become incapable of functioning as you must. In that regard, fear can crush a soldier's spirit as easily as stepping on a bug.

Most of the units we worked with, however, were confident and ready to fight, and the news we were receiving served to build our sense of focus and desire to get on with things. That same day we learned that the US Navy's USS *Wisconsin*, a World War II–vintage *Iowa*-class battleship that had been modernized, unleashed its firepower on coastal enemy positions. Coalition air forces flew 2,600 sorties against Iraqi targets, and the indications we received suggested that Iraqi ground forces were "waiting impatiently" for our ground assault. With reports that Iraqi jets were defecting to Iran, one began to understand the anxiety Iraqi soldiers were experiencing in their dug-in positions on the other side of the border.[8] To be sure, they had much to worry about.

We had our own worries too. Some of our attached artillery brigades remained concerned that their participation in our artillery preparation would delay their own onward movement to rejoin their respective brigades and divisions. Unfortunately, some of the brigade artillery commanders were picking up on the same concern that maneuver brigade commanders had about reconnecting with their DS artillery battalions after the preparatory fires were done. This too struck me as unnecessary whining. If we planned and executed the mission properly, as Dodson, Cardenas, and I were working hard to do, we would get the preparation fired on time and these units back on the road supporting their normal divisions or brigades. My diary entry went on to note this: "We had a rehearsal today with the D/A [DIVARTY], 75th BDE, 42 BDE, and 142 FA BDE. 42nd is getting cold feet. They fear if they support us, they won't get back to 3AD. I was not moved." Our plan was to unleash a devastating artillery barrage on Iraqi infantry divisions to our front and to support the armor and infantry who would then engage them in a direct firefight. The artillery preparation would not only kill the enemy but very possibly save the lives of our ground guys as well. The 42nd FA Brigade's perturbation about reconnecting to "parent units," like complaints from maneuver commanders, didn't strike me as very battle focused, much less representing team play. I recall being a bit disgusted by this attitude and expressed my sentiments to Dodson, who said I should take it all in stride. He understood, as the chief orchestrator of this grand artillery plan, that everyone would do their job. I wanted to agree but found the whole cacophony of grousing distasteful. "Do your damn job" was my attitude.

Juxtaposed to this nervousness was the eager 142nd FA Brigade of the Arkansas National Guard, commanded by COL Charles J. Linch. Activated for the war, the 142nd FA Brigade showed up in the desert on February 2 with two M110A2 203mm (8-inch) artillery battalions, an MLRS battery from Oklahoma, the brigade headquarters, and some other support activities. The 142nd didn't have the latest in tactical fire computers, so Dodson formed a liaison team to work inside their headquarters to transmit electronic fire plans developed by the DIVARTY TACFIRE computer in a timely and effective manner. On top of their lack of the up-to-date equipment that we had in the active US Army force, the

personnel of the 142nd FA Brigade, while motivated, were a bit unorthodox. In fact, they had a rather large contingent of down-home country
and farm boys who thought discipline and rules were for other people.
Dodson worried about this because he knew that discipline and attention
to detail would be essential in conducting the artillery raids and the preparation. He would not tolerate too much "freelancing" on the part of
these fellows, and on one occasion sent me to their headquarters to make
that point clear.

It was hard not to like their upbeat, bad-boy unit personality. When
I made my first visit to them, I respectfully made it clear that we were
counting on their "professionalism." In turn, they made clear to me,
"Don't worry, Kur-nel, we'll make yah proud." I was relieved, but Dodson was skeptical, and the 142nd FA Brigade—well, they remained just
"laid back." I knew they had their heart in it. They were proud and looking for a fight. I respected that. The BRO was all about "looking for a
fight," as our former division commander, Sullivan, was fond of saying,
and Rhame was equally fond of demonstrating. We shared that trait with
these Arkansas troops. And when it came to inventiveness, the 142nd FA
Brigade displayed a farmhand creativity that I found far surpassed that of
active duty units like ours.

On one of my Dodson-directed ambassadorial visits to them, my
driver, McGary, called out over the noise of our Humvee engine as we
bounded across the desert, "Hey, sir, what the hell is that?" I looked
ahead and saw a 142nd FA Brigade communication and wire team in an
M151A2 Jeep (the Humvee's predecessor) laying a field telephone connection between their headquarters and ours using a rather odd "home-
made" device. This contraption was essentially a plow making a trench
in the sand into which WD-1 telecommunications field wire was being
neatly inserted from a spool conveniently mounted on the back of the
jeep. The trench was then seamlessly covered over by a spoon-like attach-
ment behind the plow. The whole process was just like planting seeds in
a field. In all my years in the Army, I had never seen anything as efficient.
Given the difficult challenge of laying communications wire between
units across the large expanse of a desert, their homespun solution was
brilliant. They may have been a bit unorthodox in behavior, but they
were the height of American ingenuity. What they lacked in equipment,
they made up for in common sense and creativity. But when it came to
military discipline, they required lots of attention.

When February 8 arrived, I found myself once again in the middle of
logistical issues and other distractions. One of the perplexing problems

that confronted us was that we had so much ancillary equipment with us that we could not carry all of it into combat. Army units are equipped with all manner of things, from rifles for our soldiers to ice chests for our mobile kitchens. But some of this equipment, while convenient, took up a lot of space and needed to be set aside as we prepared for our upcoming battle. We needed a place to store the stuff until we could circle back after the war and collect it for the trip home. Burning it—like 1–5 FA contemplated and would go on to do—was not the best solution. The large storage containers we would eventually use for this excess equipment were 20-foot corrugated steel MILVANs that we had used to transport much of it to Saudi Arabia. These were hard to come by, and my frustration with our logisticians reached new heights when I was told that some MILVANs would be sent to the rear areas even if they hadn't been completely filled. Since they were hard to acquire, I didn't want to waste the space by not filling them to the brim. But given the short time window available to us to assemble the equipment we wanted to leave behind, we couldn't consolidate all the "stay behind equipment" for loading in the MILVANs as quickly as the logisticians demanded. So the storage units, we were told, would be sent to the rear area even if only partially filled. After visiting with the DISCOM XO, LTC Larry Githerman who was a superb logistician, we agreed this was a bad idea, but not without first pegging my frustration meter, as reflected in my diary on February 8: "Worked to get MILVANS to store excess equipment we can't haul into combat. Was told by the DISCOM XO that even if MIL-VANS are only partly full, they must be treated as full. This logic is beyond me. I twist arms." When I returned to the DIVARTY TOC that day, my focus shifted from the ridiculous to the sublime. I learned that one of our soldiers on guard duty had accidently discharged three M16A1 rifle rounds. Fortunately, no one was hurt. I entered this pithy comment in my diary afterward: "This is a dangerous place." It was not the last time I would write that.

On February 9 we continued to prepare amid another *shamal*. McGary and I loaded up in HQ-5 along with Brooks, the DIVARTY S-4, and drove in the reduced visibility to attend a meeting with the 159th Corps Support Group. Brooks and I were consumed with how we would obtain and preposition the thousands of artillery rounds and MLRS rockets we would need for the raids and preparation fires. That preoccupied our minds in addition to how we would support the battalions that would accompany the four artillery brigades supporting the DIVARTY. When I sat down along with the brigade commanders of both the 75th and the

142nd FA Brigades, who were present for the briefing, we waited with great anticipation to hear how the 159th Support Group commander, a colonel, would provide the needed supplies. When the meeting began, it soon became painfully clear to us that he considered our mission as a "bridge too far," the postbattle term used to describe the failed World War II allied airborne assault known as "Operation Market Garden" in Holland, when the British overextended their operation. The 159th commander had very little appreciation for our artillery plan, either in terms of the preparatory fires, the implications for ammunition supply, or the onward scheme of maneuver by the brigades and their many battalions. When we briefed him on the scope of the mission, the ammunition required, the maintenance, and the supply needs of the artillery brigades, he was visibly surprised. One of the brigade commanders then leaned forward and proceeded to characterize the support commander's lack of understanding with a chain of vulgarities that was assembled with such alacrity and pointedness that a bronze statue couldn't have missed the message. He was pissed.

When this same commander made a comment about "pistol whipping any dumb SOB" who failed to support him and his brigade in combat, that was the point at which I suggested we adjourn the meeting until an appropriate level of detail had been passed to the 159th staff. The last thing I needed to tell Dodson when we got back to the DIVARTY that day was that I had to break up a bloody fistfight among three colonels over beans and bullets. When it comes to supporting men in combat, emotions run high, even among professionals, and sometimes you must cool down and regroup. That was one of those days. After I briefed Dodson, he arranged for our DISCOM logisticians and the unit S-4s subordinate to us and the field artillery brigades to meet with the 159th and get things in order. Clearly, better mission awareness would be superior to a violent and vulgar brawl.

By February 10, we had been in Saudi Arabia for almost a month. It seemed like a lifetime in some respects. The Saudi culture was almost completely absent from where we were in the desert, with the exception of a few Bedouin shepherds doing their best to stay clear of us. It seemed strange to me, as someone who had studied the Middle East, to be smack in the middle of Saudi Arabia but to see little beyond an expansive desert to suggest we were in the Arab kingdom. But we were there, and that day we received news to get ready for a jump from our positions east of the Wadi al-Batin in TAA Roosevelt to the FAA farther northwest. Much had been made of this "wadi," but physically it was little more than an intermittent riverbed in Saudi Arabia and Kuwait. It ran for a length of 45 miles, or about 75 kilometers, southwest to northeast through what is known as the Al-Dibdibah plain. It was generally regarded as the boundary between western Kuwait and Iraq that then extended south into Saudi Arabia. Inside Saudi territory it divided TAA Roosevelt from the forward battle positions to the northwest, where we would eventually reposition. In that regard, our initial position east of this dry riverbed in TAA Roosevelt was designed in part by our war planners to convince the Iraqis that we would use this terrain feature to head north into Iraq because the wadi was a clear avenue of approach. We had no such intent.

At the same time, the Wadi al-Batin was a suitable high-speed approach that the Iraqis could use if they chose to launch a preemptive attack. Just a month earlier—on January 9, 1991, and prior to the arrival of the bulk of the BRO in TAA Roosevelt—the division received an "alert" that Iraqi tanks might be "on the move" down the Wadi al-Batin toward the BRO.[9] Rhame received the report over the radio even as he was standing with his boss, VII Corps Commander LTG Fred Franks, conferring on future operations. Rhame's aide-de-camp, CPT Steve Payne, recorded the incident. Noting his concern that the tanks—if true— would be "ripping through our area" at any moment, Payne was nervous but took note of Rhame's demeanor: "Rhame never batted an eye. He immediately asked how quickly one of our tank battalions could get something in that area. Franks didn't say a word. Then the two of them pulled out a map and went over the situation. Franks quietly made the comment, as he looked over the map spread out on the hood of the Humvee, 'Well, the first report isn't always accurate.' Rhame, quietly nodded, and smiled knowingly."[10] The report was wrong. There were no tanks and no surprise attack. But what Payne had personally witnessed was the professionalism of two seasoned warriors, the very kind of men who, in the wake of the Vietnam War, had rebuilt the Army that needed, so badly, to be regalvanized to greatness. This incident made a big impression on the young field artilleryman who observed their aplomb firsthand. As Payne noted of the incident, "To see these guys get this kind of report, and to slowly think, decide, and respond. Never an ounce of fear [or] panic. I wished all of our troops could have seen that demonstration of experience, confidence, and competence of our leaders."[11] In Payne's estimation, Rhame and Franks were "cool as cucumbers."[12] He saw what many of us knew to be the case. Rhame was that right man, at the right time, and in the right place to command the BRO. While the Iraqi threat didn't materialize, had they rolled down the Wadi al-Batin that day,

Rhame would have met them face-to-face. My money would have been on the sharply chiseled Louisiana guy.

Early on the morning of February 10, I received a short-notice FRAGO from Dodson to conduct a reconnaissance of an area north and west of the Wadi al-Batin in preparation for a movement even farther west to the FAA. That was where we would eventually begin our attack of Iraqi positions. I was glad to get the order to execute this reconnaissance, or "recon," and noted such in my diary: "It was nonetheless a welcomed change of scenery from the flat spaces we currently live in." I notified McGary to get HQ-5 ready, and we were soon joined by Cardenas, members of the TOC, the HHB's commander, CPT Hymel, and a survey section along with their PADS. When we were all assembled, I gave everyone a mission brief. Cardenas provided us with "waypoints", coordinates we would place in our GPS devices to guide us overland, and we departed. As we did, both Cardenas and I noted we were glad we had our marine compasses as backup. It wasn't that we were "old dogs who couldn't learn new tricks" as much as that we wanted to avoid having the technology tail wagging the "old dog."

The PADS we took with us would carry survey data forward from our current position, where we had survey control points (SCP) in place, to the area of operations (AO) we would occupy farther northwest where little if any established survey existed. Survey control is vital to the artillery because it provides precise positioning data to ensure firing units can accurately plot and engage their targets. The process we would use would have the PADS sections orient on the established SCP near the TOC. Then, along our route of march, we would stop to emplace a new SCP periodically as we headed west of the Wadi al-Batin and then northwest to our future locations. Once we arrived in the forward area, we would then return with the PADS to the DIVARTY TOC in TAA Roosevelt, by then many hours and 160 kilometers away, to "close" the survey. Once we "closed" on that SCP, the survey data would be verified. If it matched and was within tolerance, then it would be considered a "good survey." This tedious process, both going and returning, would slow our reconnaissance with frequent stops, making for a very long day. But it was important that we did this right so that firing units would have accurate and reliable survey data in the FAA.

When we departed on the designated MSR (main supply route), we soon discovered it was not well delineated. We struggled to follow a route marked Zone Green, crossing phase lines (PL) indicated on our map about every 20 to 30 kilometers named after famous battles the BRO had fought in during World War I: PL Cantigny, PL Somme, PL Meuse, PL Argonne, and PL St Mihiel. Along the way, using the PADS to record our locations, we marked key positions with wooden stakes and fluorescent paint, not unlike leaving "breadcrumbs," to guild other DIVARTY units in the days ahead.

After a long and bumpy trip over rugged terrain, we arrived late in the afternoon at "Danger Forward," the DTAC, which also served as the headquarters for Combat Command Carter. This organization—built around the DTAC and bearing the name of our ADC-M—was actively conducting screening operations opposite the Iraqi 26th Infantry Division (Iraqi 26ID). My friend MAJ Cuff, who weeks earlier had helped me manhandle equipment in the port and was now orchestrating the fire support functions in the DTAC, greeted me with a hearty handshake. "How you been, XO?" he asked.

"Pretty good, but my back is killing me," I said.

Cuff took me inside the DTAC, which was composed of several tracked M577 command post vehicles designed to move quickly. Huddled together in a large defensive revetment the division engineers dug for them, these lightly armored vehicles were chock-full of radios, maps, field tables, and a few chairs. I found one to sit in to take a load off my back, which felt as if I had been riding a pogo stick for the last 160 kilometers. "I'm just beat," I said, revealing my fatigue.

Cuff was then joined by MAJ Don Birdseye, another DIVARTY officer who served in the DTAC. "Hey, XO, having fun yet?" he asked, knowing damn well that I wasn't.

"I'll have more fun after I get some sleep," I joked. Fatigue was a constant companion in the desert. It affected everyone. When you are tired, you make mistakes, sometimes big ones.

Cuff leaned over to me after taking a seat in a rickety grey aluminum folding chair and said in a hushed and serious voice, "The maneuver guys are really trigger happy." The farther west and north we moved, the closer we got to the enemy, and the greater the jumpiness.

At night, things can make a soldier "jumpy," and the next thing you know, a round is fired, then another, and then a burst of rounds. Frequently, nothing was actually there, and hopefully no one was shot either. With that in mind, Cuff told me that no one moves at night "for fear of being shot." Needless to say, this revelation caused me to glance down at my watch. It was almost sundown at 1655 hours before McGary and I were back on the road with the recon team to our home base east of the Wadi al-Batin. Along the way, we stopped at the Division Support Area

(DSA) Junction City, named for the famed town adjacent to Fort Riley. After some food for the troops, we resumed our long and bumpy return trip. As the hours passed, we were slowed significantly while the PADS team sought out the last SCP we emplaced earlier in the day to "close" the loop on the survey we had begun some 19 hours earlier.

We finally found the elusive SCP at 0022 hours near the DIVARTY TOC. I then reported in, and Dodson was glad to learn we had returned safely. He knew we were worn out after traveling 320 kilometers round-trip over rough terrain. When I collapsed in my tent, I struggled to stay awake to make this diary entry: "Beat up and tired. My morale and back have had it. I feel 20 years older. But Duty First! I will take it easy in the AM." The "AM" I wrote of was February 11, a month since we had arrived in Saudi Arabia. With the confused port 465 kilometers behind us and new and dangerous positions 160 kilometers ahead of us, there would be little time to rest or take anything "easy."

8

A Fight to Remember

After the extended reconnaissance to our forward positions on February 10, we took some time on February 11 and 12 to recover. PFC McGary worked on our Humvee to keep it in top condition while I caught up on several staff actions that had gone unaddressed amid the activities of recent days. Staff work is omnipresent in the Army, even in a combat zone. But on February 12, my paperwork was interrupted when COL Dodson issued another FRAGO that we would be leaving the next morning for another reconnaissance of the forward area near where we would mount an eventual attack. I noted it in my diary: "We get the word to be prepared to move to the Forward Assembly Area (FAA). I will take the quartering party in the morning at 0700 along Tapline Road. I briefed them at 1700. We packed up most of our equipment tonight. The war has grown ever closer to us. We are into a new phase. We can only trust in God." A quartering party is a small reconnaissance team that goes ahead of the main body of an organization to reconnoiter or scout out an area prior to the main body's arrival. This way the main force does not wind up stumbling into a bad situation, either involving poor terrain or unexpected enemy activity. After using the day and evening to prepare for departure early in the morning, I settled in for some rest.

On the morning of February 13, I arose before dawn, shaved, got dressed, checked my personal gear, firearm, and ammunition, and headed to the mess hall for a quick breakfast and a cup of coffee to spur me to action. McGary broke camp and loaded our tent, cots, and related equipment neatly in the rear of HQ-5, which he cared for like a teenager with his first car. Dodson saw us off at 0707 hours when we left on a trek that would take us 115 kilometers with 19 vehicles, including the communications, mess hall, and supply sections as well as a team from B-6 FA (our MLRS battery) and the 12th Chemical. "Be safe, XO. Keep me apprised of your movement," he counseled.

"Will do, sir," I responded as I gave him a farewell salute.

Beneath his no-nonsense approach to duty, Dodson's concern for all of us was genuine. He knew that death, one of the Four Horsemen of the Apocalypse, was an ever-present threat. But he also knew that good training and an adherence to our well-tested procedures—our tactics, techniques, and procedures (TTPs), as we called them—was the surest way to mitigate injury and death alike.

Like the recon I had led three days earlier, this one was also long and bumpy. But we were upbeat and looking forward to getting into our fighting positions. We arrived safely and in good order in the early afternoon. Fortunately, our movement was not slowed by having to conduct survey operations along the way, since we had done that when we first explored the route a few days prior.

When we occupied our new field position, our priority was to establish communications with the DIVARTY TOC back in TAA Roosevelt. When we did, I called Dodson to report that we had arrived and were digging in. But I also learned from him on that same call that we would need to move to a more forward position farther north in the morning, requiring yet another jump toward the Iraqi border. Even though we would be staying in our current position only one night, McGary immediately began digging a fighting position beside our tent. He had not forgotten how a US aircraft had dropped an AIM9 on us days earlier and wasn't taking any chances, not even from "not-so-friendly" friendly fire. Besides, this TTP was standard practice for us, because if the enemy chose to drop some rounds on us, our best hope for survival was a well-prepared hole nearby. In this case, that hole was just outside the tent where we would sleep that evening, so we didn't have far to dive in the middle of the night.

McGary wasn't the only soldier hard at work in the recon party. Every soldier in the unit had been well prepared during our time at Fort Riley the previous autumn. I had issued clear guidance that I gleaned from units that had preceded us to the desert, like the 82ABN.[1] That detailed guidance highlighted a range of issues that needed special attention. These included noise and light discipline to enhance our operational security; the use of camouflage nets and vehicle dispersion to bolster our survivability; detailed route reconnaissance from one position to another to ensure we didn't unwittingly stumble into danger; proper nutrition and water hydration, particularly when the temperature climbed in the desert; and, of course, properly dug fighting positions, among many other things. We were doing all of this faithfully. There is no substitute for operational discipline in combat, and units that did the small things right were inclined to do the big ones right also. And we had some very big challenges in front of us that would require that level of devotion to discipline.

As I went about checking the progress of the quartering party and verifying that our communications had been established with the DIVARTY TOC back in TAA Roosevelt, McGary finished setting up our field quarters, completed our foxhole, and camouflaged our tent. When he was done, we hopped in HQ-5 and drove to the DTAC and Combat Command Carter to coordinate artillery positioning in the FAA. While he was very busy, MAJ Cuff was glad to see us for a second time that week. If things had been jumpy three days earlier when we conducted our initial reconnaissance there, they were about to get even more so in the coming hours. The entire 1ID would make its way northwestwardly like a juggernaut marching toward us from TAA Roosevelt. That included MAJ Cardenas's DIVARTY TOC, the remainder of B-6 FA, D-25 TAB and its counterbattery radars, and 12th Chemical as well as the newly arrived 2nd Chemical Battalion that had been assigned to us. Cuff took me to the DTAC operations map and gave me an overview of the division's deployment plans and a look at the mission given to us by VII Corps, our higher headquarters.

The map was covered with a transparent overlay of the division's operational graphics. It included the boundaries and other "control measures" that ground forces would use to control the positioning, movement, and activities of units in their respective sectors of operation. These "graphics," as we called them, were hand drawn with a black marker on a clear plastic sheet that was then overlaid on the map, so planners and operators could see how units would be positioned and would move about the battlefield, and what objectives they would be ordered to take. The battle schematic also pictured an assortment of ground-control measures, including boundaries between divisional units in the VII Corps's initial plan of attack and our role in making the initial breach in the Iraqi 26ID lines to facilitate the assault of other divisions deeper into Iraq. There was also a more detailed map of the division plan with symbols showing the present locations of both friendly and enemy units, phase lines (PL) that were used to control and limit the movement of units on the battlefield, and assembly areas for units to occupy during the course of the operation. Also pictured—and critically so—were the fire support coordination measures (FSCM) designed to permit or restrict the use of artillery or air-delivered ordnance on the battlefield. These "permissive and restrictive" FSCMs were especially important because they were used by ground and artillery units alike to ensure that our cannons, rocket launchers, helicopters, and Air Force CAS assets delivered their deadly fires on the enemy, and not on friendly forces.

The VII Corps graphics that hung on the map in front of us were impressive not only for their specificity but for the sheer expanse and boldness of the operational plan we would undertake (see map 8.1).[2]

They depicted VII Corps assembly areas (where TAA Roosevelt was situated) southeast of where we stood in the DTAC, "Danger Forward". Arrayed in front of me was the path the BRO would take. It was a vast 120-kilometer west-northwest motion from the TAA to forward positions we would occupy for the assault into Iraq. The graphics also showed the breach approach we would use to cross the Saudi-Iraqi border as well as the enemy objectives we would seize as we advanced into Iraq and eventually to Kuwait. It was, simply put, an enormous sweeping operational arc beginning in the Saudi Desert at the town of Hafar al-Batin and, like a huge left hook thrown by an imposing boxer, culminating in the far northeast in eastern Kuwait. The size and scope of this operation left me wondering if we could actually pull it off and live to tell our grandkids about it. It was breathtaking. But Cuff and I had little time to marvel at the size of the task. We both had work to do since the main body of the division would leave TAA Roosevelt within hours to deploy to our location short of the Iraqi border to take up positions in what was, up until then, the sector where Combat Command Carter had conducted reconnaissance and counterreconnaissance operations.

The plan for the rest of the division to deploy to the FAA was basic. The 3rd Brigade, designated Task Force (TF) Iron, would relieve Combat Command Carter of its forward security mission, including the conduct of reconnaissance and counterreconnaissance of the enemy. Specifically, TF Iron would take up a security zone opposite the Iraqi 26ID in the northernmost portion of the division sector. The 1st Brigade would move into the division sector behind TF Iron and occupy positions on the left side, while the 2nd Brigade would move in and situate itself on the right. The 4th Brigade with its helicopter battalions would establish itself in the division's rear area behind the 1st Brigade, while the DISCOM would take up a position southeast of the 4th Brigade in DSA Junction City. Meanwhile, the DIVARTY would occupy positions throughout the entire division sector—40 kilometers wide—in support of the forward-deployed brigades. It was an enormous area and a challenging endeavor. The updated mission of the BRO, taken from the division's Operational Order (OPORD) and codenamed "Operation Scorpion Danger," had a straightforward directive: "On order, 1st Infantry Division (M) attacks as the

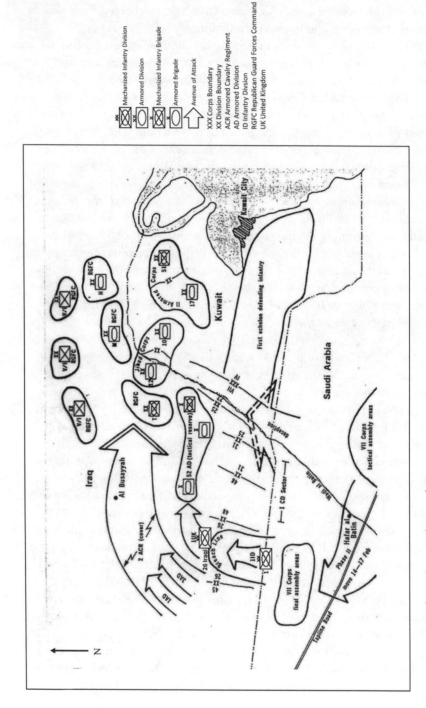

Map 8.1. Initial VII Corps Scheme of Maneuver

VII Corps main effort to penetrate IRAQI defensive positions; defeat enemy first echelon forces and conduct the forward passage of lines of VII (US) Corps forces. On order, follow VII Corps' main attack in zone to destroy the RGFC."[3] It was, as combat mission statements are, a short and doctrinaire "who, what, when, why, and how" approach to getting things done. But what caught my eye was the reference to the RGFC, the Republican Guards Forces Command. These were the best troops Saddam had, and they would be held in reserve; and unlike the less capable Iraqi 26ID deployed to our immediate front, the RGFC would put up a stiff fight. The question in my mind was whether the Republican Guards would have any fight left in them after we had facilitated the movement of other attacking infantry and armored divisions of the VII Corps through the breach to assault the RGFC deeper inside Iraq and Kuwait. But I had little time to think about that. There were artillery raids and preparation fires to plan and execute, both of which would require major logistical support that demanded my personal attention in the days ahead.

That afternoon, after I left Cuff at the DTAC, I prepared my advance party for the jump forward to new positions at 0900 hours the next day. As I examined my map for a likely position farther forward, I watched A Battery 6–27 FA (MLRS) with the 75th FA Brigade, now part of our force artillery, launch an ATACMS missile into Iraq from an adjacent division sector. The ATACMS had 950 M74 antipersonnel/antimateriel (APAM) submunitions in each missile with a range of 128 kilometers (80 miles). It was an ideal weapon for soft targets deep in the enemy's rear area, particularly thin-skinned vehicles and structures, like ammunition carriers, fuel transporters, and supply points, all tempting targets. It was also very deadly when targeted against radars or missile systems like SCUDs, which had been fired at coalition forces since the war began. With A-6–27 FA's launch of this missile, there was no doubt that we were now conducting ground warfare, and I knew that we would soon deliver deadly destruction from our cannons and MLRS launchers on the men of the Iraqi 26ID. As I noted in my diary that evening, "Soon they will taste our firepower. Iraqis are firing flares at our positions. They would be shocked to realize what's in front of them." No sooner had I selected a position for the DIVARTY TOC on my map, than I received an updated FRAGO from Cardenas. We were ordered that evening to jump to a position in the morning even farther northward, just south of Phase Line (PL) Cherry, a graphic battlefield-control measure on my map that delineated the limits of our movement forward.

When I awoke early on February 14 to a bright and sunny day, I was eager to get to our next location. The small mess hall unit we had brought with us prepared some coffee, and that, with an MRE, was my quick breakfast. McGary rose early, packed up the Humvee, filled in the foxhole he had dutifully dug the previous day, and prepared for our jump forward. At 0900, I took the quartering party forward to the new position to prepare for the arrival of the separates, the DIVARTY TOC, HHB, B-6 FA, D-25 TAB, and 12th Chemical. While we were busy at work reconnoitering this latest "new" position for the DIVARTY TOC and the separates, the powerful BRO was on the road from TAA Roosevelt along two major avenues of approach within the 1ID's set boundaries, Zone Red on the right and Zone Green on the left. The division's units began their nearly 120-kilometer march at PL Cantigny, then crossed PL Somme, PL Meuse, PL Argonne, ending at PL St Mihiel in the vicinity of PL North Carolina in the forward battle area. Zone Red, on the right side of the division's sector, was the route taken by the 3rd and 2nd Brigades to the FAA. The 1st Brigade would travel on the left side of the division sector in Zone Green, while other divisional units would travel in either zone as directed. Dodson managed to secure a helicopter that day and observed much of the division's massive and very orderly movement from the air and was impressed—something that didn't frequently occur in the mind of this very disciplined officer who had very high standards when it came to operational precision. He noted his pithy approval in his journal that day: "Seeing those convoys spread out across the desert is an awesome sight."[4]

Later that afternoon everyone arrived in "good order" as I noted in my journal, and we quickly settled in for combat operations in the center of the division's sector just beyond PL North Carolina and short of PL Cherry, but not without a close call. The trailing end of the HHB was led by First Sergeant (1SG) David Sislo. He had taken a route along the dangerous Tapline Road to drop off excess equipment at a storage area designated for us in what was called Log Base Echo, located southwest of the FAA. While passing the town of Hafar al-Batin, at the base of the Wadi al-Batin—the streambed that many thought would be an avenue of approach for attacking Iraqi forces into Saudi Arabia—an Iraqi SCUD missile broke apart in flight and exploded near Sislo's convoy. As the HHB commander, CPT Hymel, noted, "Things were heating up" when the rear area was under Iraqi attack.[5] It was also a major indicator to us that the Iraqis were beginning to detect the movement of US forces westward.

Later that night we would drop two BLU-82 (Bomb Live Unit) 15,000-pound bombs—nicknamed "Daisy Cutters" for the obliterating effect these blockbusters had—on enemy positions of the Iraqi 26ID. This would not only impact frontline enemy troops but would further reduce the threat to our division's forward-deployed units. Two of those units that would benefit were the 1st Squadron, 4th Cavalry Regiment (1–4 CAV) and the 1st Battalion 41st Infantry (1–41 IN), which would provide protection to the division's 1st Engineer Battalion (1-EN) as they bulldozed 20 attack lanes the next day in the sand berms that separated Saudi Arabia and Iraq, to facilitate our eventual invasion. Those BLU-82 bombs created an overpressure of 1,000 pounds per square inch near ground zero and would flatten everything out to 5,000 feet. If you were the unlucky person to be at ground zero, there would be no trace of your existence afterward.

In the meantime, we had much work to do. Our maintenance operations had been very good despite my worry about repair parts, which were not yet in the supply line to us. As I noted to myself that day, "Sooner or later, things will break. No parts won't help." On top of our equipment maintenance, the long hours we worked, the tough terrain we traversed, the pressure we all felt as combat operations got underway, fatigue took its toll on all of us. And fatigue can be deadly. I noted as much in my diary that evening: "1–4 CAV managed to get its guys shot by each other. They continue to jump at shadows. Relax is the message we need. The soldiers are well trained. The leaders must remain calm. I have encouraged the CDR [Commander] to rest. Spoke to 1st BDE CDR, COL Bert Maggart, 5–16 INF CDR, Skip Baker, and his S-3 my neighbor Brian Zahn. I pray all will be OK. I told Brian to keep his head down." Dodson was nonstop 24 hours a day. He had the weight of the world on him as the person charged with putting together the largest battlefield artillery force since World War II. Among my many duties, I took it upon myself to gently prod him to look after his own need for rest. "Boss, you need to get some rest. You can't fight this war on adrenaline alone," I would caution.

"XO, I'm fine, now how's the prepositioning of ammunition going?" His question back to me was his way of saying, "Don't worry about me, worry about shooting artillery." I smiled back knowingly as I shared with him the latest ammunition status, but I'm also just as certain that my face transmitted a lingering concern that he needed some rest. He was my boss, and I was just as responsible for him personally as his XO as I was for the other soldiers of the TOC and the separate batteries under my charge. But Dodson had the rank to say, "No," while others didn't.

Later that day when I ran into my Riley Place neighbor and friend MAJ Brian Zahn, a superb infantryman serving as a battalion S-3 in the

5th Battalion, 16th Infantry (5–16 IN), I felt compelled to offer him similar advice to take care of himself. It occurred to me that Brian and I both shared a common concern; how our wives and kids were doing as we busied ourselves opposite the Iraqi 26ID. No doubt our families worried, particularly our wives who didn't have the ever-present distraction of combat operations to occupy their minds. Theirs was a waiting war. Ours was to plan and prosecute the shooting one. As I drove back to the DIVARTY after my encounter with Zahn, I chased the somber thoughts out of my head that we might not be coming back. How would those who survived look at the wives and kids who lost a husband and a father? Zahn and I were both well trained. Our soldiers were too. But fatigue kills when leaders make bad judgment calls on the battlefield because they are dead tired. And we saw that nearly happen with our division's 1–4 CAV that very day when one of its soldiers was seriously wounded by one of its own in the near-fratricide shooting incident.

Meanwhile, Dodson was juggling several balls in the air simultaneously. MG Rhame had issued new planning timelines that day, and Dodson saw his challenge as twofold. First, G-Day, the day the ground assault would commence, had not been firmly set. So the backward planning that would lead up to the execution of the artillery raids to soften up the enemy, and the artillery preparation to destroy as much of the Iraqi 26ID as possible before our tanks and infantry fighting vehicles moved forward, was complicated, to say the least. All of this had to be accomplished sequentially and with precision. To get things in the right sequence, we needed to know when the ground assault would begin. And this was in doubt as late as February 14 even as elements of the division were moving across the Iraqi border to put eyes on the enemy in a counterreconnaissance mission. Additionally, because the timeline could compress significantly if G-Day was moved up precipitously, there was the distinct possibility that we would have precious little time to get the necessary cannon and rocket ammunition in place to support the raids and the preparatory fires we were expected to deliver. This problem fell directly on me and our very able DIVARTY S-4, MAJ Brooks, to resolve. It would demand our detailed attention and considerable time and effort in the coming days.

On February 15, the ammunition challenge came to a head. Dodson and I stood disbelievingly in the DIVARTY TOC as we were briefed by Brooks on how the Division Ammunition Officer (DAO) in Log Base Echo, the VII Corps logistics base well behind our lines, could give us "no assurance" that we would receive the ammunition we needed to execute the raids and the preparation fires. Dodson was disgusted and hardly able to disguise his disapprobation of the ammunition-supply operation. He made clear to me that we had to resolve the situation as soon as possible— "ASAP," he said pointedly. I told him that the only way to ensure that our needs were truly understood by the logisticians we dealt with was for Brooks and me to "get in someone's face." That meant a long ride over rough terrain 80 kilometers to our rear. I captured this in my diary that day: "MAJ Barry Brooks and I leap bureaucratic walls today to get the ammo we need for the Arty raids and counter recon fight. The G-4 planners and DAO have fallen short again. If we had not made the 80 kilometers trip back to Log Base E, we would have been stuck with only 1/3 of what we needed. There is no substitute for energy and initiative. The CDR was very tired last night. He must rest."

The trip to Log Base Echo was long and lasted well into the night. When we arrived under the cover of darkness, we made our way to the DAO, who seemed oblivious to the actual amount of ammunition we would need to conduct both the raids and the preparation fires. After some heated and frank discussion, I made clear to the DAO that the issue was not debatable. They had to deliver. I emphasized that the DIVARTY's raid missions and planned preparatory fires were the top priorities for the entire VII Corps. Brooks then whipped out the fire plan he had brought with him to illustrate the point. If we didn't get what we needed, the targets would not be softened, and that meant our ground troops would have to take them on. Lives would be lost unnecessarily. Convinced after our appeal, the DAO signed the DA Form 581 (Request for Issue and Turn-In of Ammunition) that Brooks had brought along and issued the order to have the ammunition prepositioned in our sector. At that moment, we took a big step toward ensuring our battalions could draw the projectiles, propellants, fuzes, and rockets we would fire in the hours and days to come. Had we not made the trip in pitch-black darkness that night, preferring instead to "fix" the problem over unreliable radio and field telephones, I'm sure we would have been unsuccessful. Sometimes there's no substitute for the "personal touch," and the 160 kilometers Brooks and I endured was worth the effort. But it took a toll on both of us as we bumped across the Saudi desert under black-out driving conditions with no lights except the useless "cat eye" lamps of my Humvee. Honestly, I found these lights as worthless for night navigation in the pitch black as an umbrella in a raging hurricane. Nevertheless, that trip, which was absolutely necessary, was also a big achievement.

When we arrived back at the DIVARTY TOC late that night, Cardenas was visibly relieved that we had resolved the issue. When Dodson

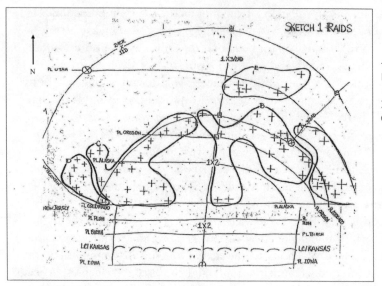

Map 8.2.   DIVARTY Raid Sketch Map of Enemy Targets, February 16, 1991

popped into the TOC to get our update, he was also pleased but made clear to us to "stay on top of those ammo guys," fearing that, yet again, they would fall short, a persistent problem indeed. When I crawled into my sleeping bag that night, I needed the rest badly and hoped the boss would also sleep better knowing that we had made incremental progress in getting ourselves lined up to begin the raids.

When we awoke on February 16, the DIVARTY TOC was busy building fire plans for the units we had under our control, including 5–18 FA (203mm) and A Battery 1–158th FA (an Oklahoma National Guard MLRS unit), both elements of the 75th FA Brigade, and B-6 FA, our own MLRS battery. Our mission, derived from the division's, was equally short and concise: "1ID (M) Artillery along with TACAIR, Attack Helicopters and all fire support resources provides fires to support Division attack and penetration of enemy forward positions with massive preparation, continuous suppression and destruction of enemy indirect fire systems, coordinate support coverage for all Division moves and on order support VII (US) Corps's attack in zone."[6] Phase I of this operation, building our combat power to that point, was accomplished, including the ammunition supplies Brooks and I had struggled to arrange. We were now entering Phase II, which would include artillery, and tactical air strikes by the Air Force and Army attack helicopters from our division directed at enemy positions in front of us prior to the invasion. We were eager to get this phase underway.

The first raids were scheduled for 1545 on February 16 and would focus on high-payoff targets along the front lines of the Iraqi 26ID, including an area on the left side of the division sector we called "the fishhook," an arrangement of enemy units comprised of infantry and artillery units. These included deadly D-30 (122mm) howitzers we would need to destroy to reduce the enemy's ability to conduct their own artillery fire.

The targets were arrayed in groups labeled "A" through "E" (see map 8.2).[7] Group "C," which was the largest, contained 22 individual Iraqi targets, whose configurations were shaped like a "fishhook." The "fishhook" (situated opposite our 1st Brigade) and Group B (opposite our 2nd Brigade) were just beyond PL Wisconsin, approximately ten kilometers north of the Saudi-Iraqi border. Both were loaded with important targets including command-and-control facilities used by the Iraqis, as well as their artillery and other enemy fire support assets. Indeed, these Iraqi units could be used against us in a very effective manner, including raining deadly fire down on our advancing troops once the breach operation began. Our mission was clear. Kill them. Kill them all.

The raids that day went off like clockwork, in large measure due to the concept the DIVARTY had developed, and the skill of the artillerymen who executed them. I noted this significant day in my journal: "We fired our first raid against the enemy. B/6 FA launched 72 rockets on enemy positions in a glorious fire storm. I escorted an AP photographer and a Washington Times pool reporter to the front to see the action. They were impressed." Given the range we would need to reach targets in Groups B and C (the fishhook), B-6 FA's MLRS rockets, which could achieve a range of 32 kilometers, was an obvious choice. Before the raid, Dodson dispatched me to accompany a *Washington Times* reporter and an Associated Press (AP) photographer who had been sent out by the press pool to cover the action. Dodson wanted me to make sure they were kept safe and had a chance to see our soldiers in action, unfiltered. On my way to the position, I briefed the reporter, Michael Hedges, about our raid concept without exposing any classified components. As we traversed the sand dunes en route to B-6 FA's firing positions in HQ-5 packed with combat equipment and several radios, Hedges asked me from his cramped back seat if I thought Saddam would back down. I turned around, looked at him, and said bluntly, "No." I then shared with him my background as a Middle East FAO who had covered the Iran-Iraq War as a current intelligence analyst with the DIA. Too much had transpired, I said, for him to back off now, and "cutting and running" at this point might well accelerate his downfall—which nevertheless I felt was an eventuality for the megalomaniac.

As we wound our way around sand dunes toward B-6 FA, Hedges asked me why Saddam thought he could win in the first place. It was a good question. Surely Saddam knew he was overmatched militarily. I looked down at a baseball bat I kept at my left knee, that McGary and I had retrieved from the desert floor just days before. It had likely bounced out of a unit's recreation kit in the back of a supply truck, and we joked that, aside from using it to swat rocks in our spare time, it was also our weapon of last resort. I paused for a moment, thinking about Hedges's question, and then motioning to the bat at my side I responded, "It's curious to me why any country would take on a nation whose national pastime is swinging a bat." We both laughed as we rolled up to B-6 FA's firing position just in time to see them launch several rockets downrange.

It was a sobering sight, displacing our light-hearted exchange moments earlier. After we exited my Humvee, we both stood there in riveted silence, witnessing the first artillery raids conducted by the BRO DIVARTY. "VAH-ROOOMMMM, VAH-ROOOMMMM, VAH-ROOOMMMM" was the sequential ear-splitting sound erupting from M270A1 launchers that, since being built, had never fired a round in anger. It was truly deafening, creating an excruciatingly loud whooshing and rushing roar that, if you got too close without ear protection, could shatter your hearing in a split second. As a dozen rockets ripple-fired from individual launchers, 3.3 seconds apart, each rocket left a long white contrail behind its bright yellow and orange exhaust plume, which was prominently set against a brilliant blue desert sky. Streaking toward unsuspecting Iraqi soldiers of the Iraqi 26ID at Mach 2, twice the speed of sound, they were awe inspiring in their destructive power. This was truly the most lethal artillery system ever conceived by any army in history, and we were witnessing it in action.

In less than a minute, an Iraqi soldier would hear an explosion high above and in front of him. It would be the last sound he would hear as 644 DPICM (Dual-Purpose Improved Conventional Munitions) from each rocket dispersed in a deadly elliptical pattern in the sky to fall on their intended targets below. Capable of destroying both personnel and armored vehicles, the individual bomblets would explode all around his position, peppering him and his fellow soldiers with a multitude of fragments that would produce certain death. Once dispersed, 12 rockets would cover a footprint of 12 acres. For a crew member on a D-30 122mm howitzer, even a well-dug defensive position would not prove effective in combatting what Iraqis who survived the war would later call "steel rain." Death would come almost instantly for the lucky ones, while the wounded would be riddled with the DPICM's small steel fragments. Without medical care, they would die painfully, probably alone, wishing they were home in their villages with their families, not languishing in the desert fighting a war Saddam Hussein had brought upon them.

Hedges, like a boy at his first baseball game, excitedly asked for a closer look, and I had the battery commander, CPT Nichols, take him to one of the three launchers in the platoon nearest us. There he would sit next to the gunner inside the launcher cab as the crew fired the next mission. Being in a launcher as it fires is an unforgettable moment. With a driver on the left, the gunner in the middle, and the crew chief on the right side, it's cramped quarters for sure. I know because I had occupied an observer's seat in a launcher on training missions at Fort Riley and in Germany. As the rockets leave the launcher cage, where two rocket pods of six rockets each were loaded side-by-side, the mighty tracked vehicle would rock ever so slightly back and forth in response to the recoil effect caused by the launch of each round. The crew chief and his gunner would monitor the status of each rocket displayed on the gunner's control panel as it fired. Once all had been launched, they would report to the platoon fire direction center (FDC), "Rounds complete." Hedges, escorted by Nichols, climbed into the launcher for the mission. When the next firing order came down via the digital signal over tactical radios from the FDC, the launcher swung into action as its launch cage rose and began to orient toward the target. When the firing order was given to the launcher by the FDC, once again the roar of deadly ordnance headed for the enemy rumbled across the desert floor. But as Lady Luck would have it, one rocket's exhaust plume caused an exterior fire on the ablative heat-resistant coating on the front of the launcher cage. While the fire was quickly extinguished by the crew after reporting, "Rounds complete," this extracurricular and unplanned event added more excitement to what was an already engaging moment. When Hedges returned to my Humvee, he asked of the on-board fire, "Is that normal?" I seem to recall making a smartass comment along the lines of "No, we normally save that part for reporters only."

On that historic first day of the raids, the 75th FA Brigade's 1–17 FA (155mm), 5–18 FA (203mm), A-1–158 (MLRS), and A-6–27 FA (ATACMS) and B-6 FA (MLRS) would account for themselves well, pouring devastating fire on the enemy's positions, particularly those located in the "fishhook." Things went well because Dodson and his team of fire planners had planned well. The overarching concept of the raids had been thought through carefully by Dodson and the VII Corps Artillery. As Dodson would later note in an interview with the Center for Military History,

> These raids had several purposes. One was, most obviously, to destroy the enemy. The other one was to test his response. The other one was to practice counter fire if any came about and then to train our units and our headquarters in tactical movement, fire control, give our soldiers experience firing in near combat conditions, and to kind of test our mettle. And so, between the 16th and I think, let's see, the 23rd, each day we sent out three cannon battalions and the equivalent of an MLRS battalion to fire these raids. We gave each one of the headquarters an opportunity to lead one of these, so they could exercise their own command and control."[8]

Dodson's sagacity was on full display here. He understood that the raids, while vital in taking down targets of opportunity in advance of our ground assault, also offered us an opportunity to exercise the full range of our artillery TTPs. Cannon and rocket units would be firing live rounds in combat. FDCs would be calculating technical firing solutions and transmitting firing data from their computers and manual systems to the guns and rocket launchers that would then send their lethal ordnance downrange. Brigade and battalion headquarters under our control would be given the opportunity to control raid operations day-in and day-out to hone their tactical and technical fire control skills, including unit movement, positioning, and fire planning.

Dodson was particularly concerned that the brigade-level organizations—like the 75th FA Brigade—had a chance to control actual missions during the raids. He knew that when the ground assault began, the fast pace of the maneuver units we supported would require that the DIVARTY and field artillery brigades hand off fire support control between artillery headquarters as they leapfrogged forward to keep up. Otherwise, effective control would be impossible as the artillery attempted to bound ahead to maintain constant fire support for our maneuver forces, who would rapidly pursue the enemy like hounds on a fox hunt. It was a brilliant strategy, and the field artillery brigades and battalions performed in spectacular fashion during the raids. Of these field artillery brigades and their role and efforts in the raids, Dodson noted the impressive results: "[The field artillery Brigades were] all under our control but we allowed them to command and control their own units. We expended over 9,200 rounds of cannon and 1,600 rounds of MLRS."[9] We would fire a lot of ammunition during the raids, and Brooks and I felt as if we had paternity over each round and rocket. We had fought the ammunition-supply bureaucracy tooth and nail to secure this precious commodity for our firing units, but as it turned out, that was only half the fight. We also had to supervise getting the ammunition on the ground as close to the firing units as feasible. This would allow them to travel shorter resupply distances, pick up ammunition, reload quickly, and then shoot it at the enemy, which was our fundamental mission.

One challenge, however, was getting engineer units with the bulldozers we needed to dig ammunition transfer points (ATPs). These ATPs, located in forward positions, would house the projectiles (the rounds), powders (the propellants put behind the rounds), fuzes (that are screwed into the tip of the round to set it off on impact), and rockets (propellant and fuze already contained in each rocket) that we required. All of it would be delivered to us from rear-area ammunition supply points (ASPs) and corps ammunition resupply points (CARPs) to the ATPs we needed to construct. ATPs were simple in design, essentially a large square or rectangular structure with about a ten-foot-high surrounding berm to protect troops and ammunition from direct fire or observation by the enemy. Unfortunately, most of the engineer assets we would need to do the digging were already committed to the pre-assault clearing of obstacles at the front, where maneuver units would launch the ground attack.

Fortuitously, Brooks and I intercepted a VII Corps engineer platoon wandering around the desert that had been separated from its unit. We "took operational control" of them and plied them with food, water, and fuel, provided they stay with us to dig the ATPs we badly needed for the ammunition en route from Log Base Echo. Happy to have a temporary "home" and supplies in the desert, they cooperated fully, and Brooks and I were delighted they did. At that moment, VII Corps ammunition trucks were showing up in our sector at long last. The one thing we didn't want was to have the supply trucks turn around and leave us because they had no designated place to download their precious cargo. Neither of us wanted to go back to Dodson and try to explain that ammunition had been sent back to the rear area because we couldn't dig some holes in the ground. The only suitable holes that would have mattered in that case would have been two field graves for Brooks and me!

On the morning of February 17, I arose to a mess made in our HHB area by a huge windstorm the previous night that had blown several of our tents to the ground, including Cardenas's. McGary and I had managed to hold ours down during the night, largely due to his diligence in deploying the canvas structure correctly in the first place with deeply driven stakes and reinforced trenches around the base. Cardenas and his driver were not so lucky, but in short order he directed his driver to get with McGary and find out what he had done to make the difference. The whole incident provoked much laughter, except for the troops who were covered with sand when their tents collapsed, leaving them to search for personal equipment blown about our position throughout the night and early morning hours.

Other events of the day were far less humorous. I went by the DIVARTY TOC to check in and was informed that B-6 FA was on tap for more raid activity. The focus would be, once again, on targets near and short of Groups B and C. B-6 FA would be joined by LTC Gingrich's 4–5 FA (155mm) and the 75th FA Brigade's 1–17 FA (155mm), 5–18 FA (203mm), A-1–158 (MLRS), and A-6–27 FA (ATACMS) capable of firing longer-range APAM missiles deep behind enemy lines; as noted earlier, these missiles were particularly effective on radar locations and supply depots.

It would be a busy day, and Dodson wanted me out supervising raid activities. After some morning chow and much needed coffee, McGary and I prepared and loaded HQ-5 with the gear we would need for the day. That included topping off the fuel tank and checking the engine oil and water levels, loading up MRE rations and drinking water, and inventorying our basic load of small-arms ammunition, hand grenades, and an M72 LAW (Light Anti-Tank Weapon) that we always carried with us. I dutifully verified the artillery positions I would visit, plotted them on my map, and entered them in our GPS. I had grown to trust the GPS, but not as much as the fully gimbaled marine compass on my dashboard. With more than 2,000 years of accuracy behind the concept, the compass had proven itself, and I knew it would that day also.

However, before we departed and much to my distress, there was a major problem with ammunition, again. When I was summoned to the TOC, I learned from Cardenas that the ammunition flow had stopped abruptly. Shaking my head in disgust, I spent the rest of the morning and the better part of the afternoon on the phone with ammunition authorities, trying to fix the problem. From my diary that day: "When I arrived at the TOC this AM, I was greeted with the news that the flow of ammo to the ASP and CARPS had stopped! I spent the rest of the morning sorting this out. Apparently, the Corps G-3 pulled the plug in a panic to assess whether there was enough ammunition to support a 7-day or 28-day war. The SOB doesn't realize we are executing now and it's too late for such foolishness. By 1500, we had the flow back under way." Such is the way of war, in which "combat" is not just with the enemy. If soldiers think they are immune to bureaucratic SNAFUs (a World War II soldier term meaning "situation normal, all fouled up") simply because they're in a war, they would be wrong. Fortunately, Brooks and I were able to get the problem resolved quickly, much to Dodson's satisfaction. Pulling the plug on ammunition resupply in the middle of the operation would have been a disaster. Dodson was right. We had to constantly keep our eyes on the ammunition issue.

Freed from the latest ammunition crisis, McGary and I headed to B-6 FA, located almost due north of the DIVARTY TOC. On the way to the firing point where one of their three firing platoons would launch a raid, I stopped at their battery headquarters to check their target list and review their preparations. They were in good order when I arrived. I conferred with the battery fire direction officer (FDO), 1LT Jeff Fishback, about their success on the first day of the raids. Morale was high, and I was proud of them. Fishback told me where I could rendezvous with Nichols, and I left immediately, not wanting to miss the action. I rolled into the firing position of B-6 FA's 2nd Platoon just in the nick of time. Nichols met me as I exited HQ-5 and told me they were about to execute a raid mission. We then chatted a bit about his launchers' maintenance status. The operational readiness of the MLRS launchers was always on my mind since they were critical fire-support assets that we needed to be ready to operate at a moment's notice. As Nichols and I conferred, my attention was interrupted. What happened next was the most frightening thing I had ever witnessed in my, then, 18 years of military service.

As I stood with Nichols by my Humvee about 100 meters from the launchers, I saw that the crew closest to us—which was the left flank of the platoon—had aimed their launcher not north toward the enemy, but south toward our rear area and friendly forces! I immediately turned to Nichols and abruptly declared, "This isn't right! Tell him to 'check-fire' now!"—the command that artillerymen use to halt a fire mission immediately. Nichols rushed to the microphone of his radio in his Humvee and yelled the order, "CHECK-FIRE, CHECK-FIRE, CHECK-FIRE!" to the platoon's FDC to halt this potentially deadly mission, but it was too late. The first rocket left the launcher on a path directly over McGary and me.

Stunned, we stood helplessly by our Humvee as the rockets headed toward the DVARTY TOC and other 1ID units. Moments later, in an act of unmitigated desperation, I tore my Kevlar helmet from my head and broke into a dead sprint toward the errant launcher with the intent of slamming my helmet on the cab's armored door to get the attention of the unaware crew inside. But after running about 10 meters, the shockwave, overblast, and toxic exhaust caused by the rockets flying less than 50 meters above my head was too great. I immediately realized it was a hopeless effort. The six rockets programed to fire on this mission would be expended by the launcher in 20 seconds. Futilely racing toward the launcher to physically intervene would waste precious seconds better spent sending a warning to the DIVARTY TOC as this deadly ordnance was speeding toward them at the other end of a mission gone horribly wrong. I now had—maybe—30 seconds at my disposal as the rockets flew southward. It was vital that I warn them that certain death was headed their way, so they could possibly take shelter in the foxholes that were dug outside of the DIVARTY TOC and throughout the HHB area.

I ran back to HQ-5, lunged toward my AN/VRC-46 FM radio, grabbed the hand mic, and yelled across the DIVARTY command fire (CF) frequency, "INCOMING, INCOMING, INCOMING!"—the standard emergency warning to take immediate cover from inbound artillery fire. To my horror, I heard nothing back from the DIVARTY TOC, and with my heart in my throat, I feared the worst as the final rockets left on a mistaken azimuth (direction) certain to fall near soldiers of the BRO. I was heartsick as my spirit sank like a rock. I knew the deadliness of these MLRS rockets. The thought that they would rain down on friendly forces—my troops—was more than I could bear. I thought of them, their faces, their wives, their kids. It was nauseating.

After the rockets left the launcher, I ordered Nichols to suspend all missions until he determined what had happened to cause such a calamity. The reason was almost immediately determined. The crew had lost its digital radio signal with the FDC that was routinely used to transmit firing data from the FDC computer, which generated the firing solution, directly to the launcher's on-board computer. To continue his participation in the mission, the crew chief asked that the data be sent to him over a voice radio connection. When he received the data, he wrote it on a 3-by-5–inch paper index card, but in the process of transcribing the target location coordinates, he transposed the numbers he was given such that when the data was manually entered into the launcher's onboard computer, it traversed in an opposite direction from where it should have been aimed. This completely avoidable mistake, a deadly one, was directly due to a failure to follow the established procedures we routinely observed requiring the use of digital communications to transmit firing data. A digital transmission of the firing order from the FDC would have ensured that the target information sent to and received by the launcher was correct, thereby limiting the possibility of human error.

As soon as I put Nichols in "check-fire," I jumped in my Humvee to speed back with McGary to the DIVARTY TOC. While we were headed south, suddenly Cardenas's familiar voice popped across the CF frequency, inquiring what had happened. I felt my chest lighten a bit and gave him a short report. Several minutes later when I pulled into the DIVARTY's position, I fortunately observed there was no evidence of damage, and I made my way quickly to the TOC.

When I arrived, I told Cardenas I had been terrified that rocket fire had hit them since they didn't respond to my radio calls. He explained that they had all been very busy monitoring the progress of the ongoing raid when I called with my warning to take cover. When they recognized my alarmed voice over the radio giving the "incoming" warning, they all reflexively took cover, practically diving headfirst out of the five-ton "expand-o van" truck that housed their operations center into nearby foxholes. But as they did, Cardenas turned to one of team members, Staff Sergeant (SSG) Ernest Healey, who like others in the TOC was preparing to take cover in a foxhole outside. Cardenas realized that someone had to continue to monitor the command radios to assess "what the hell" was going on and directed Healey to remain and do so. Healey dutifully complied with what must have seemed at the time a "sacrificial lamb" mission. So too did MAJ Mike Madden, one of Cardenas's assistant operations officers, who took cover under one of the desks in the TOC. Understanding what was happening at the time was essential, and having experienced TOC personnel there to monitor the situation was critical. That said, Cardenas was skeptical that this was an enemy attack. After all, the DIVARTY TOC had just made a very long move, and there was, as he told me later, "no way" that the Iraqis had discovered our new position that quickly, much less directed long-range missiles or artillery toward us. Something else was happening.

Sure enough, the steadfast Healey, while inside the TOC, heard Nichols's voice come across the command radio net explaining that, indeed, his unit had fired the errant rockets to the rear and the explosions the TOC heard nearby were regrettably his. Cardenas was relieved to know that we had not been targeted by the enemy but was hopeful that no one was hurt by this grave mistake. After they heard the secondary explosions stop, just 2 kilometers away from the TOC, Cardenas thanked Healey for his performance and had him give everyone an "all clear." The TOC personnel promptly returned to their stations and then immediately tried to contact me. In short, they had been a bit preoccupied when I called en route to the DIVARTY TOC. It was, in retrospect, completely understandable. But for me, racing in their direction and wondering if they were still alive, it was also a bit unnerving. The HHB's Hymel later aptly recorded the response of his soldiers to my "incoming" warning, which spread rapidly by voice from members of the TOC as they bailed out of the expand-o van for the safety of a nearby foxhole: "We found that there were no problems with our reaction time or the location of our survivability positions, but many soldiers chose to dig them deeper that afternoon."[10] Experience is a great teacher in combat, particularly when it's a close call. I later learned that the rockets fell only 300 meters from one of D-25 TAB's radars. More ominously, the rockets also landed only 50 meters—164 feet—from the 1st Battalion, 34th Armor (1–34 AR) TOC. Not surprisingly, their battalion commander had very little nice to say about the DIVARTY after that. I couldn't blame him a bit if he never did. Later, much relieved that no one was killed in what could have been a catastrophic error, I penned a rather routine note about a day that was anything but routine:

> The big event, however, was when B/6 2nd PLT (B-223) [launcher bumper number] fired 6 rockets on the wrong TGT [target] grid and put them 50 M [meters] from 1–34 AR's TOC, 2 kilometers due east [in fact west][11] of our TOC. Thank God no one was hurt! I had just arrived at the firing point when it happened. Everyone on the point watched helplessly as 6 rockets went over our heads toward our forces. I prayed immediately that no one would be hurt. This was a near disaster which was caused when the gunner put the wrong grid in the computer. The incident was compounded when the section chief didn't check to see the launcher was aimed toward us. Unfortunately, this stuff happens in combat.

Written after I had absorbed the full impact of this potentially disastrous event, my matter-of-fact entry was in no small way an effort to put the whole thing behind me. In truth, I was shaken. The horrible memory of rockets flying just above my head that I could not stop disoriented me badly, so much so that in writing my diary entry that evening, I mistakenly recorded the rounds as landing to the east of the TOC when in fact they landed to the west. In truth, I can't imagine what I would have written that evening had the soldiers in my charge been casualties of this horrible incident. It unsettled me to my core, as it did others. To make matters worse that day, two soldiers in the 1–41 IN, part of the 1ID's 3rd Brigade deployed on a screening mission near the border with Iraq, were accidently engaged and killed by one of the division's AH-64 attack helicopters that put a Hellfire anti-armor missile into their M2 Bradley IFV. Six other soldiers were wounded in the same incident. The proximate cause was the misidentification of a friendly unit for an enemy one. We in the DIVARTY, however, were remarkably lucky—beyond belief—that our deadly errant rockets that day didn't inflict hideous losses on the DIVARTY TOC, the D-25 TAB radar section, and the 1–34 AR TOC.

After I crawled into my sleeping bag that night, I struggled to expel a nightmarish thought from my head. My DIVARTY TOC and D-25 TAB comrades, my friends, the husbands of families I knew back at Fort Riley, may have been—that day—the victims of the very rockets that we had planned to send toward the Iraqi 26ID. As I concluded my diary that evening, I penned this painfully obvious line: "We, however, dodged a big, big bullet. War is hell." I then drifted into a fitful sleep, grateful that my writing that night was just a diary entry, not letters to widows bearing my profound regret. The events of that day are seared into my memory and have caused me much distress ever since.

Despite this serious incident, the DIVARTY's raids continued on February 18, this time under the control of the 1(UK)FA, which had joined our ranks three days earlier with its three 155mm battalions, one 203mm howitzer battalion, as well as an MLRS battalion. The focus of the British cannoneers that day would be on pounding away at the targets in the vicinity of Groups B and C as well as others near the front. Unfortunately, my focus was on the regrettable matter of the previous day of raids.

Early that morning, Dodson and I met with VII Corps Artillery Commander, BG Abrams, to discuss the B-6 FA near disaster. By then the facts were clear, as they were from the inception of the incident. The crew chief was at fault for entering the wrong data, and the battery FDC was wrong to permit the launcher to stay in the fight when its digital radio equipment had failed. Had the data been passed over a digital signal—which was the standard procedure—it would have gone directly to the launcher's computer without error. I had already ordered the battery commander not to conduct any further fire missions without using digital data. However, the immediate question at hand was whether to leave Nichols in command or replace him in order to send a message that mistakes like this were unacceptable. I told Abrams directly, with Dodson's support, that if we relieved Nichols—who was highly respected by his subordinates—in the middle of a combat operation, it would devastate the unit's morale. The entire battery knew what went wrong, and, indeed, the other crews followed proper procedures. Besides, Nichols was one of my most competent commanders. I was impressed by him and trusted his judgment from the time I had first met him when he was a second lieutenant in the 3ID Artillery six years earlier. Abrams supported my recommendation. We agreed that the launcher chief who had entered the wrong data should be replaced. That was prudent and proper. Dodson stood behind my recommendation on that too but ordered me to sit the battery down and ensure they adhered to proper and established procedures. Like me, Dodson understood the worst thing a combat unit can do in the face of adversity is to hang their heads in despair. Dodson had made the same point to me when we took our first casualty in D-25 TAB in TAA Roosevelt. My diary entry captured our deliberations that day in the wake of this near-disastrous event:

> We met with BG Abrams this AM to discuss the firing incident. He advised us to find out what went wrong, hold the responsible accountable, and get on with business. This is essentially what we did prior to his visit. I spoke to the officers of B/6 tonight and told them adherence, rigidly, to established procedures is the standard. I told them that we can fire safely in combat without being untimely. Finally, I told them there are two things they can do with their heads after this incident; drag them on the ground or get them in the game. If they do the former, I will give them a new assignment immediately. If the latter, then get busy. They must pick themselves up and get in the fight.

With the arrival of February 19, I went back to B-6 FA to observe them conduct more raid missions on the target groups near the front, along with the 75th FA Brigade's 5–18 FA (203mm) and the 1–27 FA (MLRS) of the 42nd FA Brigade, now also in support of the DIVARTY. Nichols's unit was recovering from their brush with catastrophe and the infamy that would have been associated with a major fratricide. They were back in the fight with the renewed sense of discipline that I expected of them and their young leaders. They had made a huge mistake, and they knew it. However, I could tell they were still a bit shaken. It was, I supposed, unavoidable, given the enormity of the error. Who wouldn't be a bit more cautious in steering clear of a similar miscalculation? It unnerved everyone. But in combat, nervousness, hesitancy, uncertainty—indeed "jumpiness"—in a unit can be as pestilential to the morale and spirit of its soldiers as the spread of a deadly infectious disease.

When I arrived at B-6 FA, the division's chief of staff (CoS), COL Fred Hepler, was also there to watch, no doubt to make sure all was in order. After our incident and the fratricide that had killed two infantrymen with a Hellfire missile, it was clear that the leadership at division was also a bit jumpy. But my job was to project calm and assure B-6 FA that they had my confidence, and it was not misplaced. During the raid that very day, they blew up a major enemy logistics base. The sounds of secondary explosions north of the border berm—emanating from the enemy target as it continued to disintegrate—were heard shortly after B-6 FA launched their rockets on the final mission of the day. This good result couldn't have come at a better time for a unit that was—just two days earlier—reeling from a devastating and potentially deadly blunder. They had their heads back in the game. Of that I was confident.

As I rode back to the DIVARTY TOC, I was happy for Nichols and his troops, but soon the reality of maintenance and logistics was on my mind once again. Indeed, the previous day, February 18, COL Morris Boyd's 42nd FA Brigade, stationed in Germany, officially joined our team of burgeoning artillery units. The list of field artillery units tasked to support us had grown dramatically with the addition of two 155mm battalions and another powerful MLRS battalion (see table 8.1). Another field artillery brigade—while increasing our combat power—also meant more logistical support would be required to ensure they too had what was needed to conduct the ongoing artillery raids as well as the preparatory fires we would shoot prior to the breach operation.

Adding to our headaches, our communications systems were failing at a critical time. With the raids ongoing and G-Day approaching, we needed reliable logistics and communications, and we had neither. The normally cool and collected Dodson was at his wit's end with the pulse code modulation (PCM) tactical phone system that served our TOC. He needed to speak frequently and reliably to several other artillery commanders as he worked long hours to coordinate the enormous preparatory fires we would shoot in support of the ground assault. Jumping into HQ-6, the bumper number of his command Humvee, to drive long distances over difficult and expansive terrain to do face-to-face coordination was not a realistic option. In the compressed time that we had to develop fire plans and related operations, it would simply consume too much of his day. Planning time, like the paucity of repair parts we had, was not something in great supply as G-Day fast approached. I noted as much in my diary: "Commo [PCM phones] was awful. COL Dodson has had it. I am equally fed up with logistics. I can't even get the DMMC to return calls and keep

Table 8.1.   1st Infantry Division Artillery Organization for Combat (February 18, 1991)

1ID (Mechanized) DIVARTY: Force Artillery Headquarters (HQ)	
1-5 FA (155mm SP)	DS 1st Brigade
4-5 FA (155mm SP)	DS 2nd Brigade
4-3 FA (155mm SP)	GS
B-6 FA (MLRS)	GS
D-25 TAB	GS
75th Field Artillery Brigade: R 1ID (M) DIVARTY, Alternate FA HQ	
1-17 FA (155mm SP)	R 4-5 FA
5-18 FA (203mm SP)	R 1-5 FA
A-1-158 FA (MLRS)	GS
A-6-27 FA (ATACMS)	GS VII Corps Artillery
C-26 TAB	GS
1st (UK) Armored Division Artillery: R 1ID (M) DIVARTY	
2 FD (155mm SP)	GSR 4-5 FA
26 FD (155mm SP)	GSR 4-5 FA
40 FD (155mm SP)	GSR 4-5 FA
32 HV (203mm SP)	GSR 4-5 FA
39 HV (MLRS)	GS
42nd Field Artillery Brigade: R 1ID (M) DIVARTY	
3-20 FA (155mm SP)	GSR 1-5 FA O/O (on order), R 1-5 FA
2-29 FA (155mm SP)	GSR 1-5 FA
1-27 FA (MLRS)	GS

Key: Direct Support (DS); Reinforcing (R); General Support Reinforcing (GSR); General Support (GS)

me posted on what is in process for DIVARTY. We are running on the 'fumes' of our efforts at Ft. [Fort] Riley. These two areas, logistics and commo, have been utter failures during Operation Desert Shield."

On the morning of February 20, it was clear that G-Day was nearing. The artillery raids were in full swing. The battle-damage assessments we were getting back from intelligence sources, including a British unmanned aerial vehicle, pointed to the severe impact we had on the Iraqi 26ID and the second echelon of Iraqi divisional forces—including the Iraqi 52nd Armored Division (Iraqi 52AD)—positioned behind them.

On the logistical front, our ammunition supplies were at last beginning to flow slowly and with some regularity. We still had issues with repair parts and the maintenance of our PADS we used to conduct survey operations. Nine of the PADS systems we had in the DIVARTY were inoperative and backlogged for maintenance awaiting parts to be flown in from the US. My diary entry that day summed up our situation even as we were yet closer to launching the ground assault. The bright spot was that mail was finally arriving from home, a blessed logistical success: "Commo remains as awful as ever. Logistics is no better. The ammo is moving, albeit like a snail. We were given a 'heads up' to be prepared to attack on short notice. The S-4/S-3 and I worked ammo implications for the CDR [Commander] late into the night. Hopefully we will help him understand what we really have to do the job. You don't always get what you need. Mail arrived today, in several cases, a month old."

Indeed, communicating between families was important. Whenever a letter would arrive from a deployed soldier to families back at Fort Riley, it was shared widely within the support groups. Everyone was hungry for any tidbit of information. Besides the general news reported on Cable News Network (CNN) and information shared by the few rear-support officers at Fort Riley, letters were the best source of information and were extremely treasured. For security reasons, we were prohibited from sharing specifics, often communicating in generalities about life in the desert. While we were still in TAA Roosevelt, there were phones in the VII Corps rear area where soldiers—standing in line for up to 30 minutes—were permitted a short call home while under strict guidance not to compromise security. On one occasion, Cardenas, always the inquiring operations chief, asked his wife, "Tell me what is going on with the overall war." He was curious about what was being told to folks back home since the only "news" we had—aside from the British Broadcasting Corporation (BBC) reports we would pick up on our long-range AN/GRC-26 tactical AM (amplitude modulation) radio in the DIVARTY TOC—was what we knew ourselves but couldn't share. Mary Cardenas thought it a bit odd for her to share "news" on the war when Ed was in the middle of it. But she did her best to render a "report", which wasn't much. Nonetheless, families cherished the calls, which as a security precaution abruptly stopped once we jumped forward to the FAA.

Despite our other logistical problems, including the glacial-like movement of mail, the good news was that enemy activity had been light since the raids began. In fact, there were reports that some Iraqi positions had been abandoned. The previous week had been a busy if not eventful one for the BRO.[12] The division's engineers had been occupied preparing our movement forward into Iraq. Almost a week earlier, on February 15, our forward units cut 20 maneuver lanes through the border berms and marked them with ground-guide stakes to show our advancing forces how to proceed. Elements of the 1–4 CAV and the 1–41 IN had established positions 5 kilometers inside Iraq, but on February 16 they pulled back for fear we would "tip off" the enemy that the assault was near. On February 17 our division and corps planners finalized their approach to the attack. Later that same night, our forward maneuver forces engaged several enemy reconnaissance units without much effect, except the fratricide of two 1ID soldiers with Hellfire missiles launched from one of the 4th Brigades AH-64 helicopters, the same day that B-6 FA had its brush with disaster.

Notwithstanding our efforts to avoid giving the enemy advance warning, it was clear that the Iraqis knew that things were heating up. By February 18 both the 1st and 2nd Brigades had pushed their ground units north of PL Cherry and settled along PL Vermont, which coincided with the border between Iraq and Saudi Arabia. By then, both our division's and DIVARTY's intelligence teams had drawn some conclusions about how the Iraqi 26ID was responding to our forward movement and the punishing effect that our artillery and air strikes were having on them.[13]

First, the Iraqis kept their vehicles out of direct fire engagement from our maneuver units. Second, it was clear to us that the Iraqis did not coordinate their artillery fires with their own maneuver units. This didn't surprise me. As I had told Rhame in Dodson's office back at Fort Riley the previous August, the Iraqis did not orchestrate fire and maneuver tactics well, something I learned from watching them fight the Iranians. Third, the Iraqis were slow to make decisions on what to do. This lack of agility would hurt them badly in the days to come. Fourth, they had no counterfire capability to speak of. When our artillery shot, we frequently moved to new positions immediately after a fire mission to avoid possible counterfire from returning Iraqi artillery and rocket units. Virtually no such threat had materialized from the Iraqis. Fifth, and curiously, there were emerging signs that the Iraqi 26ID had given up its will to fight. Finally, the Iraqis were firing a fair amount of nighttime artillery illumination to help their reconnaissance forces keep an eye on us.[14]

With these observations in mind, on February 20 we continued our deadly fire with raids orchestrated by the 42nd FA Brigade TOC, which had only recently arrived in our sector to support the DIVARTY. As Dodson had done with the 75th FA Brigade TOC days earlier, he demonstrated the same sagacious focus in tasking the 42nd FA Brigade to control the raids that day. In the mix was the 2–29 FA (155mm) and the C-1–27 FA (MLRS) from the 42nd FA Brigade, our own LTC Smith's 4–3 FA (155mm), and A-1–158 FA (MLRS) and A-6–27 FA (MLRS), both from the 75th FA

Brigade. With that much MLRS firepower and the ability to shoot rockets 32 kilometers, it was clear to any observer that we were targeting deeper units on the battlefield, such as artillery and logistic units in the Iraqi 26ID and the forces, like the Iraqi 52AD, reinforcing them. Additionally, we treated the enemy to 2 BLU-82 15,000-pound "Daisy Cutter" bombs on their front-line defensive positions. No one could survive that, so I thought.

When February 21 arrived, things began to come to a head, but there was much to do that day. The raids proceeded on schedule with Gingrich's 4–5 FA (155mm), the 75th FA Brigade's 1–158 FA (MLRS), and the British 32nd Heavy Artillery (HV) (203mm) pounding away at enemy targets opposite the BRO. Meanwhile, the artillery force under us had grown further with the addition of the 142nd FA Brigade from the Arkansas National Guard. They brought with them two 203mm (8-inch) battalions and an MLRS battalion from the Oklahoma National Guard. Altogether, the force artillery now was an impressive assemblage of firepower. With nine 155mm howitzer battalions, four 203mm howitzer battalions, three MLRS battalions, two MLRS batteries, one ATACMS battery capable of shooting long-range tactical missiles, and two target acquisition batteries, this was likely the largest force artillery assembled by the US Army since World War II (see table 8.2). Like a hungry tiger, this nearly 11,000-man artillery force had to be fed with fuel and ammunition in the days to come, and I was keenly focused to ensure that happened.

That morning, Dodson dispatched me to the 142nd FA Brigade to ensure they were prepared to support operations. While they were a very competent National Guard unit, in Dodson's view, their cowboy swagger didn't inspire confidence, considering their conception of acceptable "military discipline." My mission was to ensure that their fire planning and command-and-control systems were in good order. I had a good conversation with their S-3 and his assistant and was confident that they were ready. Up until then, the 142nd FA Brigade had not participated in any of the raids, and under Dodson's concept, they would get that experience prior to G-Day. Cardenas had them teed up to shoot the next day, and based on my discussions with them, they were prepared and eager.

Later that same day, the senior artillery commanders, including the VII Corps Artillery's commander, Abrams, all the field artillery brigade commanders, and my boss, Dodson, assembled to review our plans for the employment of this huge artillery force during the ground-assault phase once the raids were completed. It was a good meeting, and I felt confident that these senior leaders understood the plan. After the meeting, I convened the DIVARTY staff and directed that they review

Table 8.2. 1st Infantry Division Artillery Organization for Combat
(February 21, 1991)

1ID (Mechanized) DIVARTY: Force Artillery Headquarters (HQ)

1-5 FA (155mm SP)	DS 1st Brigade
4-5 FA (155mm SP)	DS 2nd Brigade
4-3 FA (155mm SP)	GS
B-6 FA (MLRS)	GS
D-25 TAB	GS

75th Field Artillery Brigade: R 1ID (M) DIVARTY, Alternate FA HQ

1-17 FA (155mm SP)	R 4-5 FA
5-18 FA (203mm SP)	GSR 1-5 FA
A-1-158 FA (MLRS)	GS
A-6-27 FA (ATACMS)	GS VII Corps Artillery
C-26 TAB	GS

1st (UK) Armored Division Artillery: R 1ID (M) DIVARTY

2 FD (155mm SP)	GSR 4-5 FA
26 FD (155mm SP)	GSR 4-5 FA
40 FD (155mm SP)	GSR 4-5 FA
32 HV (203mm SP)	GSR 4-5 FA
39 HV (MLRS)	GS

42nd Field Artillery Brigade: R 1ID (M) DIVARTY

3-20 FA (155mm SP)	R 1-5 FA
2-29 FA (155mm SP)	GSR 1-5 FA
1-27 FA (MLRS)	GS

142nd Field Artillery Brigade: GSR 1ID (M) DIVARTY

1-142 FA (203mm SP)	GS
2-142 FA (203mm SP)	GS
1-158 (-) FA (MLRS)	GS

Key: Direct Support (DS); Reinforcing (R); General Support Reinforcing (GSR); General Support (GS)

their own plans and be prepared to "back brief" Dodson at 0900 the next morning, February 22.

Back briefs are essential in planning combat operations, not only to go over the specifics of the plan, but to assure the commander—in this case the detail-oriented Dodson—that all contingencies were covered. The regimen followed a formalized sequence beginning with an intelligence and weather update from the S-2 (Intelligence Officer), an operational plan update from the S-3 (Operations Officer), a logistics assessment from the S-4 (Supply and Logistics Officer), followed by the status of personnel from the S-1 (Personnel Officer), and a communication lay down from the CESO (Communications and Electronics Signal Officer). Then Dodson's top enlisted man, CSM Manning, would give his assessment of troop training and morale. As XO, I would conclude with observations that may have been overlooked. At the end, the commander would plow back into questions he might have and then issue final guidance to all of us on next steps to take. It was a disciplined and essential process since, once the operation began, we would be on the move and enveloped in the fog of war. At that point, we would have to rely on the plans we had crafted or fall back on our skills to derive and adopt new ones on the fly. When you're in the planning business, you want to make sure your plan is feasible and one you can actually execute. No one wants to be stuck trying to redesign a sinking battleship. That's why you must think through what might go wrong during the operation and discuss how to alter the plan quickly. In that regard, evaluating all of the courses of action we might face was part of the effort, and Dodson and his DIVARTY team were very good at this.

After I had spoken to the staff and given them guidance in preparation for the next day's brief back to Dodson, I headed out with McGary to check our ammunition ATPs and then view the raids conducted that day between 1200 and 1340 hours by our own 4–5 FA (155mm), the 75th FA Brigade's A-1–158 FA (MLRS), and the 1(UK)FA's 32 HV (203mm). Meanwhile, the division was reporting light contact with the enemy as darkness fell. That evening, I spent time reviewing the staff's plans in the DIVARTY TOC, when close to midnight a call came across our secure PMC telephone line from Rhame. I took the call for Dodson since he had retired to his tent for some much-needed rest. Rhame was short and to the point: we attack in two days. I noted this moment in my diary late that night: "The CG [Commanding General] ended my day with a call that G-Day was 24 February. I called the CDR [Commander] at 2330. The war is on. MG Rhame told me 'Scott you'll be able to tell your grandchildren about this one.' I pray so." When I called Dodson from the DIVARTY TOC, he answered the field phone we had installed in his tent and took the news matter-of-factly, as was his style. But as I headed to my tent to get some rest, my sense of expectation was also gripped by doubt. What would we confront? Had the raids done their job? Would Iraqi forces lash out in a last-minute chemical assault to kill as many of us as they could? Or would we roll over the Iraqi 26ID and its reinforcing Iraqi 52AD like an 18-wheeler over a discarded beer can on I-70 outside the main gate at Fort Riley?

The next morning, February 22, our other DIVARTY battalion, LTC Emerson's 1–5 FA (155mm), along with B-6 FA (MLRS), the 3–20 FA

(155mm) from the 42nd FA Brigade, the 1–142 FA (203mm) and the 2–142 (203mm) from the 142nd FA Brigade, the 5–18 FA (203mm) and A-158 (MLRS) from the 75th FA Brigade, and the 1(UK)FA's 40 HV (155mm) all participated in the largest raid we had yet fired. The targets engaged were at the center of the Iraqi 26ID to destroy what was left of their front-line forces. Additionally, Gingrich's 4–5 FA (155mm) orchestrated a cross-FLOT (Forward Line of Own Troops) mission in support of the division's AH-64 Apache attack helicopters to engage additional ground targets farther toward the enemy's rear area. It was a complex artillery mission designed to destroy and suppress enemy systems that could fire on the attacking Apache helicopters of the division's 4th Aviation Brigade, commanded by COL Jim Mowery. Requiring much coordination, 4–5 FA's Gingrich did so with his typical attention to detail and precision. Also participating in this difficult and dangerous operation were A-1–158 FA (MLRS) and A-6–27 FA (MLRS), which would fire specifically on Iraqi air defenses, obliterating them with their "steel rain," the term Iraqis gave the deadly DPICM bomblets each rocket contained.

Meanwhile, I conducted a forward reconnaissance to scout a new position for the DIVARTY TOC along PL Vermont south of the Iraqi border. As McGary and I went forward, we passed many of our armor and infantry units, which were chomping at the bit to mount an attack. It was impressive. The BRO, a mighty combat division of infantry, armor, artillery, aviation, and support troops—approaching 26,000 strong— was well postured to attack the Iraqi 26ID and lay waste to what was left of them after days of artillery raids that we hoped were having a punishing effect. I located a position that I thought would work for the DIVARTY TOC, radioed the grid location that was displayed on my GPS back to the TOC, and then returned.

When I arrived, I was again confronted with the familiar challenges of ammunition, logistics, maintenance, and the lack of repair parts. I was convinced that in a fast-paced operation, it would take days, maybe weeks, for our logistics support to catch up. Designed for a European scenario that envisioned support arranged in depth across a potential battlefield, our logistics support plan did not match the challenges posed by desert warfare, particularly the lack of transportation infrastructure to support a rapidly moving operation. My fear was that when we had major problems, scores of our vehicles, artillery pieces, and the PADS we used for survey would be broken down and strewn across the battlefield with nothing to fix them. Repairing them in such an environment, in combat, would be a nightmare—indeed, a Herculean task. My diary that day summed up my concerns: "I 'reconned' forward today to south of PL Vermont for a new position. We stopped to watch B/6 fire another raid. Very impressive. Ammo is still a problem. The Corps bean counters held up the process again until we unbroke the log jam tonight. We can't get our PADS fixed. Nine down at the 85th Maintenance (2 from me). Parts must come from St Louis. We'll be in Baghdad before a solution. Logistics will never keep up." When I awoke on February 23—with G-Day a day away—the DIVARTY TOC, along with the HHB, quickly packed up and moved to the forward positions I had selected the previous day. Meanwhile, VII Corps froze our radio frequencies in place; we normally changed them daily for operational security. We took this calculated risk to reduce potential confusion on the battlefield by sparing units the need to switch frequencies in the middle of a complex operation. That morning we were ready to fire our final raid with our 3rd Brigade direct support battalion, 4–3 FA (155mm), 1–17 FA (155mm) from the 75th FA Brigade, 1–142 FA (203mm) and 2–142 FA (203mm) from the 142nd FA Brigade, and the 1–27 FA (MLRS) from the 42nd FA Brigade. And as on the previous day, the DIVARTY assigned a cross-FLOT mission to one of our direct support battalions, this time Emerson's 1–5 FA (155mm), with support from B-6 FA (MLRS) and A-1–27 FA (MLRS) to suppress the threat to Mowery's attack helicopters from enemy air defenses.

Dodson assigned another reporter to me that morning, a CNN correspondent, to view the final artillery raid. He interviewed me with the 1–27 FA (MLRS) firing a huge raid mission in the background. Quite impressed, he asked me what I thought about how Saddam Hussein would respond to these raids. I said, "There's no hiding from artillery" and that if they were smart, "this will wake them up, so they can smell the coffee and go home." Then I added, "We're just going to duke it out." And that's precisely what we did through the raids.[15] I learned later that my sister Elaine saw the report later that day. A VMI classmate of mine who worked for the Chief of Staff of the Army saw the report and later told me an entire table of generals, including our former division commander, GEN Sullivan, exploded in laughter over my "wake up and smell the coffee" comment. I'm glad they found it humorous, but at the time, my focus was on getting this reporter back to where he came from and out of my hair.

When I returned to the DIVARTY TOC, I spent the rest of the day in chasing ammunition we would need for the next day's preparation fires. My diary that evening held a pithy conclusion: "Tomorrow we attack. May God be with us." Over an eight-day period, the artillery raids were highly successful, involving the efforts of superbly commanded and trained field artillery units. Virtually all of the battalions and batteries assigned to the DIVARTY brought devastating fire on the maneuver, artillery, air defense, command and control, and logistics of the Iraqi 26ID as well as targets in adjacent Iraqi divisions, including the Iraqi 48th Infantry Division (Iraqi 48ID) and the Iraqi 52AD (see table 8.3).[16] Despite the sterling results the raids achieved, their success has gone unnoticed in most accounts of this war. The artillery's contribution has been obscured by characterizations of the Gulf War as merely a 100-hour blitzkrieg executed by ground forces charging across the desert to defeat an incompetent enemy that the Air Force had pounded into submission. In fact, the maneuver brigades, battalions, companies, and platoons of the BRO performed magnificently and brought death and destruction to the enemy they encountered. But that's an incomplete story. Similarly, while the efforts of the Air Force in gaining air superiority to facilitate the destruction of many Iraqi targets deep behind enemy lines is entirely accurate, it's only part of a larger effort. The field artillery was a significant component in that larger endeavor. Indeed, the firepower of the BRO DIVARTY was on full display even before the breach operation commenced.

First credit must go to the soldiers who pushed rounds and rockets downrange every day for eight days of tough and dangerous fighting. Credit must also be given to the efforts of commanders and staff alike who worked tirelessly to develop technical and tactical fire plans amid shifting schedules, uncertain logistics, and ever-changing ammunition support expectations. But the success of the raids was, in a very profound way, due to the vision, focus, and determination of Mike Dodson. His expertise, tactical savvy, keen focus, and understanding of how to train, motivate, and command the force artillery was essential to the success of the raids. His plan for executing them demonstrated the perspicuity of this exceptional combat commander. He was both clear and resourceful: destroy the enemy we had targeted; test the enemy's response to our attacks; practice our own counterfire tactics if the enemy fires back at us; and finally, train our units, both field artillery brigades and battalions, in the operations, movements, fire planning, coordination, and execution we would need to execute the raid program successfully. He did. We did. And the results of this effort would be validated—or not—when the division made its breach of the Iraqi 26ID. Our magnum opus was scheduled to come when the preparation was fired on G-Day. But the artillery raids of the DIVARTY and its force artillery—the combat operation that has gone little noticed and hardly acknowledged, but for those of us who executed it, not forgotten—were a magnificent and resounding overture to precede our attack of Iraqi forces by the BRO.

Table 8.3.   1st Infantry Division Force Artillery Raid Results 16–13 February, 1991

Date	Firing Units	Enemy Targets
16 February 1991	5-18 FA (203MM), B-6 FA (MLRS), A 6-27 FA (MLRS), A 1-58 FA (MLRS)	122mm and 130mm Artillery Battalions/Batteries/Command Posts, Anti-Aircraft Platoons, Tank Platoons
17 February 1991	4-5 FA (155mm), 1-17 FA (155mm), 2-18 FA (203mm), B-6 FA (MLRS), A 6-27 FA (MLRS), A 1-158 (-) FA (MLRS)	122mm and 130mm Artillery Battalions/Batteries/Command Posts, FROG (Free Rock Over Ground) Systems, Anti-Aircraft Platoons, Tank Platoons
18 February 1991	2 FD (155mm), 26 FD (155mm), 40 FD (155mm), 32 HV (203mm), 39 HV (MLRS)	122mm and 130mm Artillery Battalions/Batteries/Command Posts, Unidentified Battalion Command Posts
19 February 1991	5-18 FA (203mm), B-6 FA (MLRS), 1-27 FA (MLRS)	122mm and 130mm Artillery Battalions/Batteries/Command Posts and Logistics, Anti-Aircraft Systems, Brigade Command Post
20 February 1991	2-29 FA (155mm), 4-3 FA (155mm), C 1-17 FA (MLRS), A 1-158 FA (MLRS), A 6-27 FA (MLRS)	122mm and 130mm Artillery Battalions/Batteries/Command Posts, Tank Platoons
21 February 1991	4-5 FA (155mm), 32 HV (203mm), A 1-158 FA (MLRS)	122mm and 130mm Artillery Battalions/Batteries/Command Posts, FROG (Free Rock Over Ground) Systems, Tank Platoons
22 February 1991	1-5 FA (155mm), 3-20 FA (155mm), 1-142 FA (203mm), 5-18 FA (203mm), B-6 FA (MLRS), A 39 FD (MLRS), A 1-158 (-) (MLRS)	Assorted Artillery, Maneuver, Command, and Logistics Targets
23 February 1991	4-3 FA (155mm), 1-17 FA (155mm), 1-142 FA (203mm), 2-142 FA (203mm), 1-27 FA (MLRS)	Assorted Artillery, Maneuver, Command, and Logistics Targets

In total, a force artillery of nine 155mm howitzer battalions, four 203mm howitzer battalions, three MLRS battalions, two MLRS batteries, one ATACMS battery, and two target acquisition batteries fell under the control of Dodson's DIVARTY. Altogether, they fired 9,208 cannon rounds and 1,606 MLRS rockets and, by our calculations, took a deadly toll on the Iraqi 26ID and nearby enemy divisions. That destruction included 50 tanks, 139 armored personnel carriers, 30 air defense systems, 152 artillery cannons, 27 missile launchers, 108 mortars, and 548 wheeled vehicles.[17]

It was an impressive kill count for the BRO DIVARTY whose motto "Drumfire" was validated in every sense of the word by the drumming we gave the Iraqi 26ID. It was a fight to remember. When the artillery raids of the 1ID were done, it would be proof positive that, as I had said to the *Washington Times*'s Michael Hedges on the first day of the raids, it's unwise to pick a fight with a nation that swings baseball bats for fun. Particularly so if the player at bat is the Big Red One DIVARTY.

9

Into the Breach

I awoke early on the Sunday morning of February 24, 1991, and was totally focused. But my senses were punctuated with a degree of anxiety and uncertainty about what we would face once we entered and passed through the breach that the BRO would create in the Iraqi defenses. Nonetheless, the 1ID would do its duty. It always had. The BRO had a tradition to uphold. The division's CPT Idus R. McLendon of C Battery, 6th US Field Artillery fired the first American shot in World War I on October 23, 1917, near Bethelemont, Lorraine, in France. The BRO in World War II led the invasion of French North Africa near Oran in Algeria on November 8, 1942. The division assaulted the beaches in the invasion of Sicily on July 10, 1943. And the BRO spearheaded the bloody attack of Normandy on June 6, 1944, when the 16th Infantry Regiment's COL George Taylor led his troops off a deadly Omaha beach. Consistent with that heritage, the BRO of my generation would lead the VII Corps into combat. As we were poised to invade Saddam Hussein's Iraq, it was impossible to avoid the significance of the moment, and where we stood on the desert floor in Saudi Arabia. It had to be this way. The 1ID was ready to attack first, again, just as we had in World Wars I and II.

There was a slight chill in the air as the sun rose, but the soldiers of the DIVARTY and the impressive artillery force COL Dodson had assembled required no "warm up" to get ready for the action that day. We all knew that in just a matter of hours the battle would enter a new phase. We had been engaged for over a week in an artillery fight to destroy as much of the Iraqi 26ID as we could. Our firepower would continue to give us the advantage for the impending attack. And that would include a huge artillery assault on remaining enemy targets across the breadth and depth of the battlefield when we fired the preparation.

Many of these targets were situated just a few kilometers north of the new location that HHB had occupied the previous day. From that position, just south of the international border along PL Vermont where we slept the previous night, was the "neutral zone." A disputed area of 7,044

136

square kilometers along the border between Saudi Arabia and Iraq, the zone formed a large diamond whose short axis projected north and south of the uncertain boundary between the two countries. It was created after the adoption of what is known as the Uqair Protocol of 1922, an agreement that defined the demarcation between Iraq and the Sultanate of Nejd, the polity that preceded Saudi Arabia's existence as a state. But that morning, this "neutral zone" would not be neutral. It would serve as the invasion launch point for the 1ID into Iraq.

PFC McGary had already started to disassemble our tent and pack up our gear in the Humvee that was both our mobile home and combat conveyance. "Sir, want a cup of coffee?" he asked.

"Sure," I responded. I loved coffee when I could get it, and McGary knew that my need for a cup of "Army Joe" to jump-start my day was as necessary for my alertness as it was for his mental health. McGary learned that my mood was far better when caffeine flowed readily through my veins, and that almost always made his day better too. That morning was no different, even as our natural adrenaline kindled both of us for what lay ahead: an invasion.

The mess hall crew had a limited offering that morning of MREs, juice, water, and coffee. Soon McGary returned, carefully balancing my coffee and an armful of MREs we would need in the days to come. "I hope you didn't get any of those tuna fish ones," I groused, referring to a particularly unpopular choice with a lot of us. We both preferred beef and chicken varieties.

"Nope, we lucked out, sir. All good ones," McGary said with a hint of accomplishment in his voice.

As I sat in our now loaded HQ-5, sipping my coffee, I read from my *Prayer Book for the Armed Forces*. My parish priest, Father Rob Sanders of Saint Paul's Episcopal Church in Manhattan, Kansas, had given it to me with a note penned on the inside cover: "May God go with you. You are always in our prayers." Each morning since I had arrived in Saudi Arabia, I had found some time, if even briefly, to read the daily office, a ritual of prayers and scripture readings. One such prayer seemed especially poignant that morning: "Lord God, almighty and everlasting Father, you have brought us in safety to this new day: Preserve us with your mighty power, that we may not fall into sin, nor be overcome by adversity; and in all we do, direct us to the fulfilling of your purpose; through Jesus Christ our Lord. Amen." I closed the book, took a sip from the cup of coffee McGary had brought to me, and said a prayer to God for His protection of me, Roger, and our troops. I then asked that He watch over Shelley, Amy, John, and Paul. They were most precious to me, and the thought of never seeing them again was a weighty one. It was best to put them in the hands of God. It was all I could do at that point.

That night some of the DIVARTY's wives and families had gathered to celebrate a late Valentine's Day. Shelley and Mary Cardenas were taken aside by Diane Dodson, who explained that the ground war would soon start and that she intended to share this somber news with the entire group at the end of their evening together. It was emotional for our loved ones who were there celebrating a belated Valentine's Day. Both Mary and Shelley struggled with how they would share the news with our children. Later that evening, the Cardenas kids, Adam, Emily, and Anne, would respond by walking into Mary's bedroom and silently donning the desert camo hats Ed had given them, showing solidarity with their dad in the only way they knew how. Shelley, as was her custom, would bring the kids together to pray. We, of course, were unaware of how our families were responding, but one thing was true. For families at home, as it was for soldiers in the desert, that day duty came first on both fronts.

I carefully placed my prayer book in the canvas bag where I kept personal items, including pictures of Shelley and the kids, and my diaries. I then turned my attention to immediate tasks, the first of which was to put on my chemical protective outer garments. Reaching for my duffle bag where I kept clothing, I retrieved my MOPP gear that consisted of a pair of heavy charcoal-lined trousers and a zip-up jacket. The charcoal in the inside liner of the MOPP pants and jacket was designed to neutralize some chemical agents but in short order would begin to wear off on your skin as a black dirty film, not a very pleasant side effect. By putting the MOPP suit on early, we were in a better posture to protect ourselves quickly, having only to don our gas masks, rubber gloves, and boot covers. I then swallowed one of the foul-tasting PB anti–nerve agent pills designed to slow the effect of the deadly agent and give me enough time during an attack to inject myself with an atropine autoinjector that we all kept in our gas mask carrying case. These autoinjectors, we were told, would fully counteract the nerve agent. But you had to act fast, and I had my doubts whether anyone would be fast enough. The injection procedure entailed taking the autoinjector and jamming it into your thigh muscle, which would cause a spring-loaded needle to penetrate your clothing and skin and then automatically dispense the atropine drug into your system. The thought of self-impalement, even for a good reason, was not a pleasant notion. But at least I was comforted that there was a chance it might work as advertised, provided I could get to it quickly enough.

After making all the necessary preparations to 'load up and then inspecting units throughout the morning, I eventually made my way to the DIVARTY TOC to check in on the status of operations and logistics. I entered the DIVARTY TOC and found the S-3 Plans and Operations team, along with the S-2 Intelligence section, abuzz with tasks and unusually busy. The short electronic bursts and bleeps of binary data, which were our fire plans transmitting over digital radio nets to firing units, filled the air with a sense of urgency. I felt as if I were in the middle of a fire drill as people scurried about. Our TACFIRE computer team, the soldiers who developed our computerized fire plans in a large computer truck connected to the TOC expand-o van, were working feverishly. Orders and directives flew about the TOC. "Hey, that fire plan ready yet?" someone shouted. "Where's the list of updated enemy positions?" another barked. Still another asked urgently, "Did anyone update the fire control measures on this overlay? Let's get this done, people." It was an exceptionally busy place that morning as the DIVARTY team updated enemy positions in our target lists and continuously revised status boards and unit positions on our operational map. No one looked up as I came into the TOC. They were riveted to their work.

Weaving among preoccupied soldiers, I made my way toward MAJ Cardenas, our very steady and focused S-3, and asked, "We ready to go?"

He looked up and past all the activity swirling around him and said to me with a slight hint of amusement in his voice, "As ready as we can be." Then he added, "Looks like the prep will be fired this afternoon, not tomorrow."

"Why the change?" I asked.

Cardenas motioned toward the situation map on the TOC wall and said, "Enemy resistance is light, and the maneuver guys think we can go now." It was then clear to me why the TOC was as busy as a beehive.

Dodson was preoccupied as well, assessing the impact of altering the attack. The previous day, he had met with all the field artillery brigade commanders who would support the preparation with fires from their subordinate battalions and batteries. That meeting went well, and everyone was ready to execute the preparation at dawn on G+1 or February 25. But early that morning, our senior Redleg had indications that the timeline of the attack was accelerating rapidly. Dodson learned that not only would the preparation be moved up sooner in the overall attack plan, but that the fire plan would need to be shortened to conform with the collapsed timeline. This meant that Dodson and the DIVARTY target team might need to make significant and complex changes in the fire plan on short notice, compute new technical firing data, and distribute it to units, which, in turn, would need to send that new firing data to their cannons and rocket launchers. Turning on a dime quickly would be no small feat, requiring much agility and focus by the DIVARTY TOC and the many subordinate headquarters we would orchestrate in firing the preparation. That morning, standing in the DIVARTY TOC consumed with activity, I could tell we were in a very fluid situation. Our planners, anticipating a change, were already adjusting the plan, not wanting to be caught flat-footed at the last minute.

Part of the challenge Dodson and the DIVARTY team faced with an accelerated timeline, however, was not only adjusting the preparation fire plan on the fly but verifying what would be attacked and when. Fire plans had several elements included in them: the target's location and type; how many rounds it would take to destroy, neutralize, or suppress it; the units that would engage the target; and the precise time that it was to be engaged. All of this would need to be updated by the DIVARTY's fire planners in a short span of time. Originally, the preparation had been planned for two hours to support a dawn ground assault. That ground attack was to begin on G+1, or the day after the division would create breach lanes through which our 1st and 2nd Brigades would advance to pre-assault positions in front of the Iraqi 26ID. But at 0538 on February 24, after those breach lanes were cleared, the 1st and 2nd Brigades determined—and then reported to the Division TOC—that enemy contact was light, and maybe the full attack could begin earlier. My immediate thought upon learning this was that the artillery raids had in fact been decisive in destroying and dramatically weakening the combat power of the enemy's frontline units.

As a result, it made complete sense to go early. In the eastern sectors of GEN Schwarzkopf's vast CENTCOM theater of operations, things were also rapidly proceeding, with coalition forces moving forward quickly. Both the Marine Corps and French forces were maneuvering north into Kuwait swiftly. Our VII Corps Commander, LTG Franks, was aware of this and asked MG Rhame—given the light resistance in the BRO's sector—if he was ready to launch the full attack now, an assault that was originally supposed to occur at dawn on the next day, G+1. Rhame told Franks we were ready. Rhame then hurriedly called Dodson on the radio at 1100 that morning to see when Dodson could be ready to fire an abbreviated preparation in support of an early ground assault by the division at 1500 that day. Dodson said he could update the plan and execute the preparation at 1230 since the force artillery was already in place with the necessary ammunition to execute a two-hour preparation. As soon as Franks obtained permission from CENTCOM for an accelerated attack on February 24, the BRO was ordered to begin the ground assault at 1500. The original two-hour preparation would now be truncated to one hour; 30 minutes of firing before the 1st and 2nd Brigades attacked the Iraqi 26ID, followed by 30 minutes of firing at deeper Iraqi targets as our maneuver units advanced farther into the enemy's rear area.[1]

With only 90 minutes to finalize the fire plan—consistent with what Dodson told Rhame he could accomplish—our DIVARTY TOC team swung into action. Our radios and PCM phones lit up with a flurry of notifications to all our many battalions and batteries. Cardenas and his team wasted no time in alerting the force artillery that the preparation would be shortened and executed at 1430 hours. That gave everyone about three hours to reprocess detailed and complex fire plans, plans that had taken days to develop.

With the raid targets we had attacked over the past eight days, the targeting processes our intelligence people had employed had been very disciplined, with plenty of time to plan them. Indeed, a good portion of that target analysis and planning for the raids had begun weeks earlier in TAA Roosevelt, well before we moved to our forward positions. During that process, we made logical assumptions using doctrinal templates about how Iraqi forces would array themselves on the battlefield. Following an initial assessment of what we thought we would see from the Iraqis, like a football coach scouting an opponent, we then looked at how the Iraqis had historically positioned their units for battle, which was similar, but not identical, to Soviet doctrine. After that, we reviewed intelligence information from photographic imagery intelligence (PHOTINT), signals intelligence (SIGINT), and electronic intelligence (ELINT), further refining the target locations based on real—not assumed—intelligence data. And again, just as a football coach adjusts his plan during a game once he sees his opponent get in formation to play, we too adjusted our target locations. This was a very agile and adaptive process that occurred daily throughout the raids and was at work as we hustled to alter the plan that morning. But Dodson faced a new challenge now. He didn't have weeks or days. He had 90 minutes.

In planning the original two-hour preparation, Dodson had wanted to hit every target three times to ensure its destruction. But with a preparation cut in half, he calculated we could attack targets half as many times, or about 1.5 times per target. Moreover, under the original fire plan, Dodson planned to attack targets from front to rear. This would

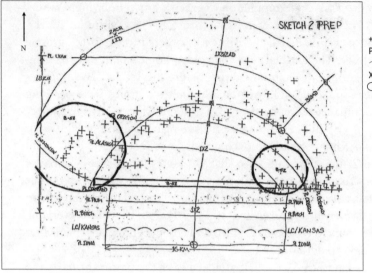

Map 9.1. DIVARTY Preparation Sketch Map of Enemy Targets, February 24, 1991

have the effect of a rolling barrage of cannon and rocket fire that would not only destroy the enemy's positions, but very likely impact retreating Iraqi troops as they headed north toward their rear area to avoid certain death. The revised plan would focus on attacking primary targets, like Iraqi artillery, heavy mortar, and surface-to-air missiles throughout the entire battle area, whether positioned near the front or deeper on the battlefield. As Dodson put it later, "So, all of those primary targets were covered in the first 30 minutes . . .there was a lot of work done and fire planning that morning too. It was a busy, busy time."[2] Part of that "busy time" was the rearrangement of not only how many targets would be covered, but the way they would be attacked. Under the original planning for the preparation, Dodson instructed the DIVARTY to develop target sets, or groups of enemy units, throughout the division's sector (see map 9.1).[3] He also had the DIVARTY planners formulate targets that would be triggered for engagement as advancing friendly units reached certain phase lines, the graphic depictions drawn on our operations map that we used to coordinate the phases of the operation as it progressed. Using them as a trip wire to control our fires would permit the engagement of enemy targets in front of the 1st and 2nd Brigades while avoiding friendly units as they moved forward from one phase line to another.

However, under the new plan Dodson rapidly conceived that morn-ing, many of the target or group sets would now be attacked in the first 30 minutes of the preparation. The targets developed by phase line, how-ever, would now be engaged in the second 30-minute timeframe, along with deeper targets like long-range guns, rocket launchers, and missile systems, which could threaten our maneuver forces as they advanced northward.[4] This altered plan was accomplished in the span of just an hour and a half and was a major realignment of our fire planning that had gone on for weeks. Fortunately, we had more than enough cannon and rocket ammunition positioned on the ground with the battalions and their firing batteries to service the new preparation fire plan. Brooks and I had the scars and bruises to show for it too.

Cardenas and his team were also busy with other details, including making sure that updated fire support coordinating measures (FSCM) were in place. These measures were designed to facilitate the expedited engage-ment of targets while concurrently providing our rapidly advancing friendly forces with safeguards against accidental engagement by our own artillery and attack aircraft. Once established, graphic representations of these mea-sures were displayed on maps, firing charts, and overlays. These FSCMs were also stored digitally in our TACFIRE computers so that every firing battery, battalion, and field artillery brigade in the fire planning computer network had access to this critical data. The day before, the VII Corps repo-sitioned the fire support coordination line (FSCL) farther north to the 50-grid line, a place on the map 40 kilometers north of our TOC position. This FSCL was a line on the map beyond which US forces could expedi-tiously attack targets without the need to coordinate with ground forces. Since our ground assault would be well south of the FSCL, shifting the FSCL northward was added assurance that those same ground forces would not be hit with friendly fire from air or artillery. The goal was to kill the enemy, not commit fratricide. Our near miss with B-6 FA's rockets days ear-lier was a searing reminder that units must adhere to doctrinal procedures to ensure fires land where they are supposed to: on top of the enemy. And the DIVARTY TOC had become quite expert at employing FSCMs, even hastily. A week earlier when the 1(UK)FA was orchestrating one of the raids, the DIVARTY TOC received a report from the US Air Force team assigned to the 1ID that one of their A-10 "Warthogs" providing CAS sup-port in front of us was "having a field day" on one of the enemy targets and wanted to continue their attack. The pilot asked if we could delay by 15 minutes a time-on-target (TOT) mission that the 1(UK)FA was moments from firing! Unfortunately, during that raid, all of the firing units were on radio silence for security reasons, and the DIVARTY had no way to stop the mission, now only seconds away. The DIVARTY TOC swung into action, quickly established a hasty ACM (airspace coordinating measure), passed it to CPT Rick Radice, our British LNO, and moved the aircraft out of danger from being hit by rounds flying through the air. It was just in the nick of time, and moments later, the A-10 pilot—now observing the 1(UK)FA's fires for us—excitedly reported "great shooting—targets destroyed!" Skilled then, our operations team was doing the same that morning as they reshaped fire plans "on the fly" and the vital FSCMs associated with them.

Amid the hastened activity that characterized the reprograming of the preparation, I checked with Cardenas's team to verify the location of "Danger Forward," the DTAC, a few kilometers west of our position. The DTAC would act as the Crossing Force Center (CFC), monitoring the division's units as they crossed through the breach to engage the enemy. This is where I planned to station myself—along with my fellow maneuver brigade executive officers in the division—throughout the now accelerated preparation and the subsequent movement of field artillery units forward into enemy territory. My job there was to be a liaison between the DTAC and the DIVARTY TOC to ensure that force artillery unit movements were in sync with the advancing infantry and armor units they supported. The last thing we wanted was to get some stray artillery unit out in front of our direct fire forces and mistaken for the enemy. After my duties were complete at the CFC, I would then rejoin the DIVARTY TOC and move forward. But for now, my focus was on getting into position before the preparation began at 1430.

When I left the DIVARTY shortly before noon, as everyone scrambled to finalize fire plans, I wondered if this very complex operation and our support for it would come off as we wanted? Last-minute changes of the magnitude we witnessed that morning come with pronounced risks in combat. True enough, plans are just that, what you intend to do. But in combat, "when the shit hits the fan"—or as one old sergeant used to say to me, "When the feces collide with the electronic oscillating and rotating mechanism"—any plan can fall apart rapidly. I was worried about this one. Not only did we need to execute this preparation with precision, and do so flawlessly, we also had to expedite the return of the field artillery brigades with us to support our sister divisions to the left and right of the BRO. Indeed, those divisions would continue to attack after we had broken through and destroyed the Iraqi 26ID. For the DIVARTY that meant, after the preparation, successfully moving the 75th FA Brigade and 42nd FA Brigade to the west to support the 1st Armored Division (1AD) and

3rd Armored Division (3AD), respectively, and the 142nd FA Brigade and the 1(UK)FA to the east to support the 1(UK)AD maneuver units. All of this would support the strategic and dramatic "left hook" Schwarzkopf had designed to knock Iraqi forces off their feet and sweep them from Kuwait. As I pulled into "Danger Forward" where the CFC was located, my worries were unabated.

The DTAC, composed of four M577 tracked command-post vehicles parked side-by-side, like the DIVARTY TOC, was a busy place too. Each of the M577 tracks had a rectangular canvas tent extension connected to the back of the vehicle that, when further connected with adjoining track extensions, formed a larger rectangular enclosed workspace that housed operations, intelligence, fire support, air defense, engineer, transportation, signal, and logistics personnel. Together these sections would monitor the battle and, in this case, the flow of units through the breach. Everyone there was scurrying about, checking unit positions on maps hung on the side of the canvas walls, monitoring radio nets of every sort, and taking note of developments in the battle as they bubbled up from subordinates. That included three maneuver brigades, an aviation brigade, the DIVARTY and its four brigades of artillery, and the DISCOM. Together, this amounted to ten armor and infantry maneuver battalions, 16 field artillery battalions (including three separate MLRS/ATACMS batteries that approximated a battalion's worth of rocket launchers), two aviation battalions, and seven support battalions across the BRO. It was a hectic time, yet an orderly environment punctuated by the subline nature of what we were doing: engaging in combat in which our mission and the lives of our soldiers hung in the balance.

McGary followed me into the DTAC to set up our AN-GRC 39 radio remote set that was connected by wire to the radio mounted in HQ-5 parked nearby. This remote would allow me to communicate with the DIVARTY on the CF frequency, the channel on which we would coordinate the actual movement of artillery units toward and through the breach, without interfering with other operations inside the DTAC. There was enough going on without my contributing to the confusion. I put the remote set on a small olive-green 2-by-3–foot field table—that would be my workstation that day—positioned in front of a map displaying our artillery positions. As I looked at the fire support map hanging in front of me, I could not help but be impressed with the huge number of artillery units that were arrayed on it. They were ready to unleash the largest artillery preparation fired since World War II: nine 155mm battalions, four 203mm battalions, three MLRS battalions, one ATACMS battery, two

Table 9.1. 1st Infantry Division Artillery Organization for Combat (February 24, 1991)

1ID (Mechanized) DIVARTY: Force Artillery Headquarters (HQ)	
1-5 FA (155mm SP)	DS 1st Brigade
4-5 FA (155mm SP)	DS 2nd Brigade
4-3 FA (155mm SP)	GS
B-6 FA (MLRS)	GS
D-25 TAB	GS
75th Field Artillery Brigade: R 1ID (M) DIVARTY, Alternate FA HQ	
1-17 FA (155mm SP)	R 4-5 FA
5-18 FA (203mm SP)	GSR 1-5 FA
A-1-158 FA (MLRS)	GS
A-6-27 FA (ATACMS)	GS VII Corps Artillery
C-26 TAB	GS
1st (UK) Armored Division Artillery: R 1ID (M) DIVARTY	
2 FD (155mm SP)	GSR 4-5 FA
26 FD (155mm SP)	GSR 4-5 FA
40 FD (155mm SP)	GSR 4-5 FA
32 HV (203mm SP)	GSR 4-5 FA
39 HV (MLRS)	GS
42nd Field Artillery Brigade: R 1ID (M) DIVARTY	
3-20 FA (155mm SP)	R 1-5 FA
2-29 FA (155mm SP)	GSR 1-5 FA
1-27 FA (MLRS)	GS
142nd Field Artillery Brigade: GSR 1ID (M) DIVARTY	
1-142 FA (203mm SP)	GS
2-142 FA (203mm SP)	GS
1-158 (-) FA (MLRS)	GS

Key: Direct Support (DS); Reinforcing (R); General Support Reinforcing (GSR); General Support (GS)

MLRS batteries, and two target acquisition batteries (see table 9.1). It was an enormous assemblage of lethal firepower like nothing I had seen in my then 18 years of service, and certainly nothing our maneuver brethren had witnessed either.

In fact, many infantry and armor officers I had served with to that point had little appreciation of the destructive capability of the field artillery. This was due in part to the less-than-adequate replication of artillery effects in peacetime training. Given the limited nature of maneuver exercises at Fort Riley and even at the sprawling NTC in California, artillery effects were frequently "simulated" with smoke grenades and pyrotechnic devices. While they made a large flash and booming sound, they weren't artillery rounds exploding near and among troops. Moreover, the cost of firing expensive rounds and rockets in training would be exorbitant, to say nothing of the danger to our soldiers. But this day there would be no simulators or white smoke to signify the effects of the artillery. Nor would there be green-eye-shaded auditors worried about firing too much training ammunition. This would be "the genuine article."

Our fire support planners in the DTAC, MAJs Cuff and Birdseye, shared thoughts with me over what was about to happen. Excitement and urgency filled the DTAC. This was it, G-Day. We were going to invade Iraq and finish off what was left of the Iraqi 26ID. We hoped our casualties would be light despite dire warnings to the contrary by our war planners, particularly those at the VII Corps. We worried about the land mines our forces would encounter too. And, of course, we wondered if Saddam would unleash chemicals in a last desperate effort to halt us in our tracks. To be sure we were well trained, and we were confident. Moreover, CPT Visser's 12th Chemical, which was under my supervision, had established a fully equipped and manned decontamination site to handle chemically contaminated soldiers and vehicles. We were prepared for the worst. But buried deep in all of us there was an uncertainty that gnawed at our guts. "Let's get on with it," I thought to myself. I was ready. Every Redleg in the DIVARTY was ready. The BRO was ready. At 1300 hours, the official order came down from division headquarters that, in fact, we would fire the preparation at 1430 to support a 1500 ground assault. Game on.

When I had departed the DIVARTY TOC earlier that morning, I had synchronized my watch with Cardenas. But after I arrived at the DTAC we had a follow-up "time hack" to mark, or verify, the actual time to ensure that everyone was on the same timeline for the preparation and movement forward. This "time hack" involved a controlling station, the DIVARTY in this case, announcing on the radio, "Stand by for time hack in one minute." This was an alert to everyone to pull out their watches and get ready to set them. The controlling station would then announce, "At my mark, the time will be 1400 hours." After that a countdown would proceed "five, four, three, two, one, mark!" at which time everyone would set their watches precisely at 1400 hours. It was an important procedure, because the preparation would begin sharply at 1430, and it was essential for everyone to be on the same sheet of music, as we said. This would be the "mother" of all scheduled fires, and we wanted to get it right. For artillerymen like us, it was all about precision.

As we approached preparation time, I looked at my watch. It was 1428 with two minutes to go when I heard the unmistakable sound of an 8-inch howitzer battalion fire its powerful 203mm rounds. KAH-BOOM, KAH-BOOM, KAH-BOOM, BOOM . . . BOOM-BOOM-BOOM! The sound of firing echoed across the desert floor. My first battery assignment as a second lieutenant was in an 8-inch battery, and the sound those big cannons made was forever etched in my mind. I knew for certain it was the thunderous sound of those 200-pound rounds as they flew down-range toward the enemy. But these rounds were fired early and not on schedule! I reached for the radio microphone and called Cardenas in the DIVARTY TOC to report what I heard. He responded, with a hint of res-ignation in his voice, "Yeah, I think that came from our Arkansas guys."

"Roger that," I said, shaking my head.

Cuff then asked me, "Did someone fire early?"

I responded blandly, "Don't worry, there're all headed in the right direction." To be sure, we all knew the National Guard gunners in the 142 FA Brigade battalions were a bit trigger-happy. Cardenas had wor-ried about their eagerness earlier that morning when we were conversing in the DIVARTY TOC. The 142nd had shot well during the raids, but they were anxious to get in the fight. And that day, I suspect they may have decided that they would push the first rounds downrange for brag-ging rights, notwithstanding the schedule of fires.

But soon those early rounds were a distant memory as a tremendous cacophony of more KAH-BOOMS and the ear-penetrating roar of rock-ets filled the air and rumbled across the desert like nothing we had ever heard. Rockets flew downrange, leaving white contrails behind them as their crews processed thousands of digital signals over their fire direction system. Simultaneously, cannon rounds arched toward the enemy, pre-ceded by the standard fire commands that were called out repeatedly by 258 howitzer crews in the force artillery above the booming sounds of projectiles sent on their way toward the Iraqi 26ID.

"FIRE MISSION!" a cannon section chief would "sound off" to alert his crew.

"BATTERY ADJUST; 6 ROUNDS!" was the command that focused the units on the mission and the number of rounds to be fired. On that day, cannons firing six rounds, one after the other, in a single mission—of many—would have been routine to service most targets.

"SHELL HE, LOT XY!" signaling the type of round to be fired, in this case "high explosive," and the production lot from the factory. We had varying lots of ammunition, and it was important to keep track of them as we calculated our computational adjustments to compensate for the variances among lots.

"CHARGE 6 WHITE BAG!" would declare the size of the propellant the mission required to hit the target at the designated range. A charge 6 would push a cannon round farther than, say, a charge 3, 4, or 5.

"FUZE, VT!" or "FUZE TIME; TIME 21.5!" or "FUZE PD!" revealed the type of fuze to detonate the projectile on or above the heads of the enemy. A variable-time (VT) fuze had an embedded radio transmitter to emit a signal that, when bounced back from the ground, would explode the shell exactly 20 meters—65.6 feet—above the target, raining hot metal fragments in a downward cone on the enemy with deadly effect. A regular mechanical time fuze required the crew to manually set the time on the fuze with a tool to rotate the fuze timer until it aligned with the right increment number etched on the fuze to reflect the time called out by the section chief. When exploding, it achieved a similar deadly result. And a point-detonating (PD) fuze exploded when it struck the target or the ground nearby, spitting hot steel upward and outward in a 360-degree circle of death.

"DEFLECTION 3207!" was the order establishing the direction the gunner, seated on the left side of the howitzer, would traverse, or aim, the cannon tube in order to point the howitzer in the right direction.

"QUADRANT 302!" indicated the height the assistant gunner on the opposite side of the cannon would raise the tube to achieve the correct elevation to fire the round.

While all of this was going on, the rest of the crew, the numbers 1, 2, and 3 men, would hustle to load the rounds they would fire. Each round was placed on the howitzer's automatic loading tray that would cradle the round until it was rammed into the tube. Before ramming, the section chief would lean over to ensure that the fuze, now screwed firmly on the front end of the projectile, was set with the right time of flight so that the projectile would explode precisely when over its intended target. When the chief verified the time was set correctly, the next command was given.

"RAM!" would come the command as the number 1 man firmly lodged the projectile in the breech of the cannon, using the howitzer's automatic rammer and producing a discernible "THUMP" as it did.

"CHARGE 6 WHITE BAG, I SEE RED!" the number 1 man would sound off to ensure that the right powder charge was being loaded in the breech behind the round and that the red ignition pad on the end of the charge would face to the rear to be ignited by the primer once the breech was closed.

"CLOSE!" would then ring out as the heavy steel breechblock slammed shut on the combination of death that had been loaded into the howitzer.

"PRIME!" the section chief then would command, alerting the crew that the primer, a brasslike shotgun shell, had been inserted in the firing mechanism at the back of the breechblock; the primer would produce the flash of fire to ignite the chain of events sending the projectile downrange.

"HOOK UP!" was then commanded by the section chief as the number 1 man, who would fire the cannon, attached his green rope lanyard with a hook on the end to the firing mechanism.

"SET!" would be declared by the gunner, who confirmed the howitzer was pointed to the right azimuth.

"READY!" the assistant gunner would confirm, signaling that the howitzer was at the right elevation to fire the round.

"FIRE!" would then be commanded by the section chief. The number 1 man would then put a strong, steady pull on the lanyard, which would ignite the charge and instantly fire the cannon. The cannon tube would then violently recoil to the rear of the howitzer as the projectile was expended forward through the cannon tube, expelling a cloud of white cordite smoke that would shroud the entire crew until carried away by a breeze. Crews had to take particular care during the firing of the round not to be in the recoil path. A recoiling cannon tube packed a lot of raw energy that could seriously injure or kill a man on the spot if it hit him on the head or upper body.

Then, with the same speed and determination, the tube would return "to battery"—forward to its origination position—ready to accept another round with the command of "RELOAD!" by the section chief. This combat litany of fire commands—just seconds in duration and varying only with different deflections, quadrants, and shell, powder, and fuze combinations—would reoccur and ring out thousands of times from gun crews that afternoon as the force artillery of the BRO massed its preparation fires on the enemy in a deadly punctuation mark to the raids that preceded it. The process, down to the individual artilleryman on a cannon or launcher, was precise, orderly, disciplined, and deadly accurate.

I stepped out of the DTAC to take it all in while the earth rumbled under my feet. It sounded as if all hell had broken loose and continued unabated. Indeed, that very morning, Rhame was heard to declare over the division command radio net, "We should look to our front, it is a grand and glorious day for the field artillery."[5] Viewing the preparation from

The 1st Infantry Division Artillery (DIVARTY) Command and Staff on March 19, 1991, after the conclusion of hostilities, standing by an Iraqi 122mm D-30 howitzer captured by the soldiers of Headquarters and Headquarters Battery (HHB) of the DIVARTY on March 2, 1991. The photo was taken west of the "Highway of Death" near oil-field fires in the vicinity of Ar Rawdatayn, Kuwait, approximately 25 kilometers south of Safwan, Iraq.

First Row (left to right): CPT Phil Thurston (Reconnaissance Survey Officer), MAJ Don Mathews (S-1), LTC Scott Lingamfelter (XO), COL Mike Dodson (DIVARTY Commander), MAJ Ed Cardenas (S-3), MAJ Barry Brooks (S-4). Second Row: MAJ Tom Conneran (Assistant S-3), *CPT Chris Hubbard (Assistant S-3), CPT Sandy Artman (S-2), CPT Ralph Nieves (Liaison Officer to 1st UK), CPT Bill Turner (Battle CPT-Day), *MAJ Charlie Wise (Assistant S-4), MAJ Jim Stoverink (Operations Duty Officer-Night), MAJ Mike Madden (Operations Duty Officer-Day). Third Row: 1LT Tim Bizoukas (Counterfire Officer) (atop cannon), *MAJ Rich Kirsch (Fire Direction Officer-Day), *MAJ Dave Denhal (Fire Direction Officer-Night), *MAJ Oscar Judd (Fire Direction Officer-Night). Shadow taking the photograph: CPT Joe Willis (Chemical Officer). Not Pictured: CPT Cherie Wallace (Assistant S-2), CPT Tom Martin (Assistant Communications and Electronic Signal Officer), *MAJ Luis Rodriguez (Communications and Electronic Signal Officer). (*Personnel attached temporarily for duty [TDY] to 1st Infantry DIVARTY during the war.)

1st Infantry Division Artillery (DIVARTY) encampment with tents and foxholes in TAA Roosevelt (January 1991).

HMMWV (High Mobility Multi-Purpose Wheeled Vehicle), "Humvee," in forward assembly area (FAA) (February 1991).

B Battery 6th Field Artillery MLRS position in TAA Roosevelt (January 1991).

Armored Combat Earthmover (ACE) digging a survivability position for an M109A2 155mm howitzer of B Battery 1st Battalion, 5th Field Artillery (February 1991). (Courtesy of David Fowles)

B Battery 6th Field Artillery MLRS convoy from TAA Roosevelt to the FAA (February 1991).

Soldiers using an M-2 aiming circle to orient M109A2 155mm howitzer of B Battery 1st Battalion, 5th Field Artillery on the direction of fire (February 1991). (Courtesy of David Fowles)

1st Infantry Division Artillery (DIVARTY) Tactical Operations Center (TOC) position near Ar Rawdatayn, Kuwait, approximately 25 kilometers south of Safwan Iraq (March 1991).

Laundry Day at the 1st Infantry Division Artillery (DIVARTY) position near Ar Rawdatayn, Kuwait (March 1991).

1st Infantry Division Artillery (DIVARTY) Tactical Operations Center (TOC) position in FAA behind protective berm prior to preparation (February 1991).

1st Infantry Division Artillery (DIVARTY) Tactical Fire Direction System (TAC-FIRE) vehicles in convoy (February 1991).

1st Infantry Division Artillery (DIVARTY) mobile kitchen trailer (MKT) (February 1991).

LTC Scott Lingamfelter (DIVARTY XO) (left) and MAJ Tom Conneran (DIVARTY Assistant S-3) removing chemical protective clothing (February 28, 1991). (Courtesy of Ed Cardenas)

LTC Scott Lingamfelter reunites with his family: (from right to left) nephew Evan, Shelley holding Paul, John in the center, and Amy in the foreground, July 6, 1991.

1st Infantry Division vehicles ready for loading on the *Nosac Rover* in Dammam, Saudi Arabia, June 8, 1991.

Big Red One Port Support Activity (PSA) loads an M2 Bradley Infantry Fighting Vehicle (IFV), June 8, 1991.

Big Red One Port Support Activity (PSA) lifts MILVANS (Military Container Vans) into the *Ville de Havre,* May 20, 1991.

1st Infantry Division Port Support Activity (PSA) Commander LTC Scott Lingam-felter, PSA XO MAJ Charlie Wise, and PSA Transportation Officer CPT Renee "The Hammer" Miller supervising the loading of the *Nosac Rover* (June 9, 1991).

Soldier approaching a "Wolf Burger" for a lunch break while working in the port of Dammam, Saudi Arabia (May 1991).

Soldiers from B Battery 6th Field Artillery MLRS observing a fire mission during artillery raids (February 17–23, 1991).

Close up of a Multiple Launch Rocket System (MLRS) rocket headed downrange during artillery raids (February 17–23, 1991).

M109A2 155mm howitzer firing on enemy positions (February 1991).

A pair of M109A2 155mm howitzers firing during artillery raids (February 17–23, 1991).

Howitzer from B Battery 1st Battalion, 5th Field Artillery firing on enemy positions (February 1991). (Courtesy of David Fowles)

Burning oil wells with destroyed Iraqi equipment in the foreground (February–March 1991).

Destroyed Iraqi supply truck (February 28, 1991). (Courtesy of Ed Cardenas)

Destroyed Iraqi tank in the vicinity of Objective Norfolk in Iraq (February 27, 1991).

Destroyed Iraqi howitzer and truck in the vicinity of the "Highway of Death" in eastern Kuwait (February 28, 1991).

Numerous destroyed Iraqi vehicles and equipment in the vicinity of the "Highway of Death" in eastern Kuwait as they attempted to escape (February 28, 1991).

Iraqi prisoners of war (POWs) captured and escorted by soldiers of the 1st Infantry Division (February 1991).

their position near the breach sight, the 12th Chemical's CPT Phil Visser and his "top sergeant," 1SG Silas Darden, candidly admitted to each other that "we were thankful that we were not on the receiving end of the predatory barrages"[6] that the BRO was delivering to the unfortunate Iraqi 26ID. Likewise, CPT Dave Fowles, who commanded B Battery of Emerson's 1–5 FA, made this observation: "We saw an incredible demonstration of indirect firepower as we watched the firing of thousands of artillery rounds as far as we could see in both directions. The experience was far beyond anything that I had ever imagined during my previous years of schooling and training."[7] I echoed this sentiment in my diary later that night: "Today we attacked. We pounded the enemy with a 30-minute preparation which was awesome. Everyone who saw it was speechless except the CG [Commanding General] who was excited beyond words." Indeed, Rhame was very enthused as his aide-de-camp, CPT Payne, related to me later. As hundreds of exploding artillery shells, filled with TNT and the explosive mixture called Composition B, landed on their frontline enemy targets, a huge wall of black-grey smoke rose from the desert floor in front of the BRO. Payne, an artilleryman himself, recalled that Rhame "was jumping" like a head coach witnessing his team score the winning touchdown. It was easy to understand his excitement as 258 cannon tubes and 85 MLRS launchers created a cloud of death and destruction in front of him.[8] Many other infantry and armor soldiers who witnessed the preparation fires that day, which were certainly more impressive than the "simulations" they had seen during their training, would be equally impressed and in awe. As Dodson would later remark of the preparation, "I am confident that we've convinced every senior commander as well as commanders down to company level of the value of artillery again."[9] The artillery had always been known as the "King of Battle," and that day, G-Day, the title was irrevocably confirmed for all who witnessed the Desert Redlegs in action. When the preparation concluded, 6,136 cannon rounds and 414 MLRS rockets had landed on top of the Iraqi 26ID in the largest preparatory fire since World War II.[10] For them, it would be a living hell. For the soldiers of the 1ID DIVARTY and its supporting brigades, battalions, and batteries, it would be—as Rhame had so aptly put it earlier that morning—a "glorious day" of accomplishment.

At 1500, the maneuver units of the 1st and 2nd Brigades began moving forward, as the DIVARTY directed its fire toward deeper targets on the battlefield. As I monitored the fight with Cuff and others in the DTAC that afternoon, it was clear that the artillery raids and the preparatory fires had done their job. Both the 1st and 2nd Brigades were advancing rapidly through the remnant of the Iraqi 26ID toward their objectives along PL Colorado, which was depicted on our maps as a large arching line well into enemy territory (see map 9.2).[11] In the process of moving forward, the brigades captured between 500 and 800 POWs who were described as "broken in spirit" and ready to surrender.[12] But some of the enemy resisted and refused to come out of their fighting positions to surrender. Cuff and I listened intently as the 1st Brigade commander reported on the enemy situation. After conferring with the division's leadership, the decision was made that if enemy forces would not come out of their fighting positions and surrender, we would plow them under in their trenches with our tanks and engineer equipment.

Mine plows had been mounted on the front of many of our tanks, designed to till up explosive devices, pushing them to the left and right of advancing armor, thereby avoiding detonation under the vehicles. The brigades also had M9 ACEs (Armored Combat Earthmovers), highly mobile armored tracked vehicles that provided combat engineer capability to frontline forces. Both our tank mine plows and the ACE vehicles were most suitable for the grisly task of dealing with resisting enemy forces who refused to surrender. This was not a day to get in the path of the BRO.

As the afternoon wore on and we concluded most of our supporting fires, Dodson made the decision to pass control of the force artillery to the COL "Gunner" Law's 75th FA Brigade while the DIVARTY TOC moved through the lanes cut in the berms on PL Vermont that coincided with the border between Saudi Arabia and Iraq. The DIVARTY TOC moved in one convoy, and the HHB followed in a second. It was not completely smooth. Although the lanes in the berm were well marked, as the sun went down, visibility worsened significantly. Cardenas had the DIVARTY TOC in position north of PL Vermont before sundown. But the remaining elements of the HHB moved more slowly and didn't arrive in the new location until after dark. In the process, some of the HHB elements became "disoriented"—Army-speak for "lost." The HHB's CPT Hymel put it aptly later: "We lost two vehicles on the convoy; the ambulance lost a generator, and the CESO (Communications and Electronic Signals Officer) was just plain lost. The ambulance was repaired with a smaller generator and the CESO found us at dawn."[13] Once the DIVARTY TOC arrived in position, I remained at the DTAC, monitoring the final force artillery movements as they transited the lanes cut in the border to their new locations north of PL Vermont. When the units successfully cleared their lanes, we packed up to rejoin the DIVARTY. McGary and I

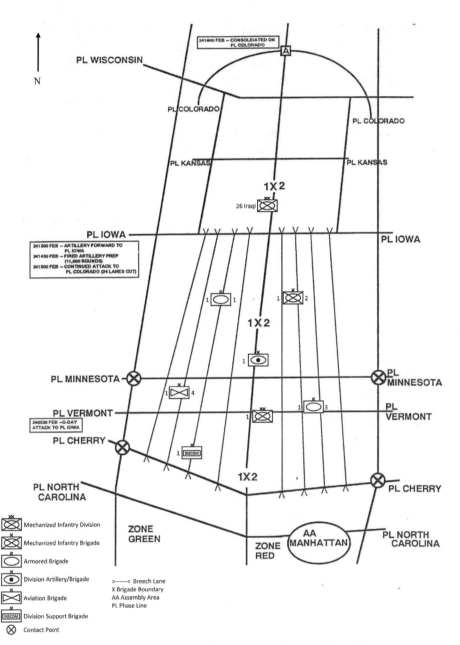

Map 9.2. 1st Infantry Division Assault Positions, February 24, 1991

were both anxious to hit the road since moving in a thin-skinned Humvee at night in combat was a bit risky, particularly if we took fire from anyone, including our own forces. I called Cardenas to get the grid location of the TOC's new position and plotted it on my map. We then headed north and, along the way, recovered some of the lost HHB elements and led them into position. I noted all of this in my diary that evening: "I joined the TOC at 1900 or so after policing up several elements of the HHB that were lost (including the 1SG). Over 800 POWs were captured by our forces (1ID) today. Tomorrow will be different, I suspect." For sure, it had been a hell of a day, and I wondered if the next day would be as adventurous. As the division advanced, we captured many worn-out and defeated soldiers of the Iraqi 26ID. Those that survived, no doubt, were glad their part of this war was over. Meanwhile, 7,500 miles to the west and nine hours behind us, the morning edition of the *Wichita Eagle* led with "Land War Erupts" along with an item entitled "Fort Riley families worry—and wait," noting that for us in the BRO, the waiting was over. But for our families the war was not over yet. In fact, it was high anxiety for many of our loved ones. One prominent Manhattan citizen said it well: "There's probably a lot of wives putting their kids to bed and trying very hard not to watch TV. They're doing whatever they can to keep their minds off what's happening," said Chris Heavey, general manager of the Manhattan Town Center Mall.[14] As McGary and I rolled out our sleeping bags on the upper deck that we had constructed in the rear of HQ-5 outside of my quarters on Riley Place months earlier, at least we knew what was "happening." I did wonder how Shelley was handling all of this. By now she knew we had invaded Iraq. I wished I could tell her all would be fine. But it wasn't clear to me that it would be. My worries soon gave way to fatigue. McGary and I were both bone-tired, and we were looking forward to some rest because we knew a lot lay ahead of us before this battle concluded. The question in my mind was "What's next?" Would we really continue our push into Iraq, or would we hold fast where we were as the other divisions, like determined football running backs who had slid off our left and right shoulders, did their jobs and made their way forward to engage Iraqi forces? The answer would come soon enough.

Before we moved from TAA Roosevelt to our forward positions, Rhame had lobbied the VII Corps diligently to have a "follow-on" mission after the breach was secured. It made no sense to him to occupy the destroyed position of the Iraqi 26ID when we could be moving forward to engage the enemy deeper in Iraq. For example, we could target the vaunted Iraqi Republican Guard. But Rhame's request had been a "hard sell" to the VII Corps planners. Maybe they thought we would be too combat depleted, with lots of casualties, and would need to recover after the breach operation. But rest was not something well-suited for a division whose motto was "No Mission Too Difficult, No Sacrifice Too Great, Duty First!" VII Corps relented to Rhame's desire to have a follow-on objective and indeed gave the BRO an on-order mission to continue the attack into Iraq. But as I drifted to sleep that night, we were not certain if we would be conducting a follow-on attack.

When we awoke early on the morning of February 25, we had a busy day ahead of us. First the 1st, 2nd, and now 3rd Brigades of the division, following a short artillery preparation, attacked at 0600 that morning to rapidly overwhelm any remaining Iraqi resistance and seize objectives along PL New Jersey, the northernmost limit of the division's sector of operation. As the forward brigades cleared enemy bunkers and trench lines, they captured two brigade command posts, as well as the command post of the Iraqi 26ID. Among the captured was one brigade commander, several battalion commanders, and numerous company commanders and platoon leaders. It was a big haul. By 1200 hours that day, the division was in position to pass the 1(UK)AD, including its 2,500 tracked vehicles and 5,000 wheeled vehicles, off our right shoulder northeastward to attack Iraqi positions beyond our sector.[15]

As we transitioned the 1(UK)FA to its division, Dodson began the effort to untether the other supporting field artillery brigades and send them back to the combat divisions they would support as those divisions advanced off the left shoulder of the breach we were making in the enemy's lines. The 42nd FA Brigade was cut free first and headed west to link up with the 3AD as it advanced north and northeast into Iraq. The 75th FA Brigade then departed our sector to link up with the 1AD, which would make a similar north and northeast advance, also sliding off the left shoulder of the 1ID.

Both field artillery brigades had to make 20- to 40-kilometer lateral moves westward for their linkups, which would be no easy task. Getting them on the road was a priority for Dodson. Finally, the 142nd FA Brigade would link up with the 1(UK)AD on the BRO's right shoulder and attack forces northeast of our sector. Remarkably, it all went rather smoothly, but with a twist. Dodson made the decision to move the 1(UK) FA through the breach ahead of their British maneuver forces. The BRO's 2nd Brigade had secured that area of our sector, so pushing the royal Redlegs up early was a safe and prudent move. But more importantly,

Dodson wanted to make sure that the British artillery was far enough forward and set to provide firing support for the 1(UK)AD maneuver units as their infantry and armor units advanced beyond the 1ID's forward lines to attack Iraqi units to the northeast. As it turned out, it was a brilliant stroke because the movement of the British maneuver units continued slowly until 0100 the next day. Had their artillery been in the rear of the pack, so to speak, it would have been very hard for them to get into position to provide fires in support of a fast-paced move northeastward by the British division once their maneuver units broke out.

The separate units, for which I was responsible, were also busy with the arrival of dawn. HHB was fully engaged in supporting the DIVARTY TOC, among a plethora of other tasks. B-6 FA (MLRS) was busy getting in position for additional missions to support the division's advance. D-25 TAB was focused on maneuvering its Q-36 and Q-37 radar sections into position to provide counterfire support to accurately locate surviving enemy firing batteries that might fire their guns. During the initial ground assault, the radars had acquired a few enemy artillery units shooting at us. But as it turned out, following the raids and the preparation, the enemy's ability to fire artillery had been largely neutralized. Nevertheless, these radars were critical assets, and positioning them to support the forward movement of the division was important. Meanwhile, 12th Chemical had packed up their decontamination site on the south side of the breach and began moving northward, happy that there were no chemical attacks to deal with. As they did, they were taken aback by the carnage they saw: "Many dead and wounded enemy lay strewn about the area. Survivors shell-shocked by the horrific pounding they endured appeared desperate to surrender. Truth be told they informed us they knew they would be treated better by the US military as prisoners than they were treated by their own regime. By close of the 24th, over 1000 prisoners had been collected and there were hundreds more waiting their turn to give up."[16] On the morning of February 25, HHB, B-6 FA, and D-25 TAB reported unexploded US ordnance everywhere, including artillery shells and bomblets from MLRS and Air Force submunitions. The Army expected a dud rate for the M77 MLRS submunitions, 644 in every rocket, to be about 5 percent, a figure that had been validated in operational testing years earlier. But it was clearly higher now, maybe as much as 23 percent.[17] That would not have been enough to make it easier on the enemy, given the thousands of rockets we fired at them. Even a rocket with just 500 properly functioning bomblets was almost as deadly as one with 644. But for our troops traversing the battlefield once occupied by the enemy, deadly unexploded ordnance lying about was no small threat. It was a profoundly real threat if someone drove over one and accidentally detonated it. We were surprised to see so many and took extra care to avoid them. Farther north of us, 12th Chemical was very busy too. Its smoke platoon was engaged in providing hasty smoke screens in the form of thick white vapor to obscure the movement of our advancing armor units making assaults on Iraqi units that had miraculously survived the deadly artillery preparation.

McGary and I were also preoccupied and had been since we arose early to take on another mission. We would scout forward for a new position for the DIVARTY TOC north of the breach lane's exit, and just south of PL Colorado. I checked with the TOC, which had given me a location to orient my reconnaissance as well as the numbered breach lane we should use to make our way forward. The Iraqis had laid mines in front of us, and we needed to proceed carefully. One antitank mine would make our Humvee a smoking pile of junk, not to mention what it would do to us. Each of the several lanes the division had cleared had numbered guide stakes emplaced on either side of the lane to indicate a safe path forward for vehicles. This would help us make our passage through the cleared lane—at least that was our hope.

We diligently checked our gear, including our weapons, to ensure we were ready. With chambered rounds in our weapons, we mounted up and headed north to our assigned lane. When we entered it, both McGary and I were keenly diligent to stay between the guide stakes and keep a keen eye for unexploded ordnance. We hadn't come this far to get ourselves blown sky-high by either an enemy land mine or a "friendly" unexploded submunition. When we exited the lane and began to move north of the breach, everywhere we looked we could see evidence of the enormous destruction our artillery had wreaked upon the enemy. The devastation was complete, so much so that it was hard to imagine that Iraqis—or any other living being—had ever been there in the first place.

When we arrived at the position I was first given, I was advised by the DIVARTY TOC to move farther north again to continue our reconnaissance. We found a new site and remained there until the DIVARTY TOC and the HHB arrived just before dark, occupied the position, and established tight security against any Iraqi elements that might still be in the area. On top of that threat, the weather seemed to be getting worse, and soon we found ourselves being battered by a rainstorm making a muddy mess of our new position. We were also short on vehicle repair parts and fuel, which confirmed my fear from weeks earlier that logistic support

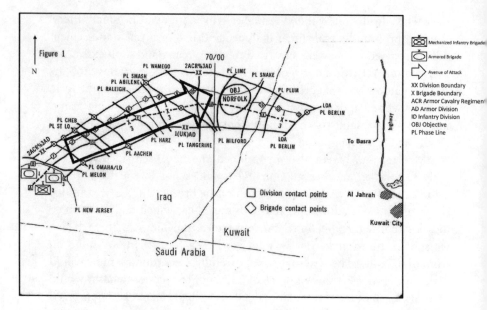

Map 9.3.   1st Infantry Division Assault toward Objective Norfolk, February 26, 1991

couldn't and wouldn't keep up with us in a fast-moving operation. If we were ordered to jump forward soon, I wondered if we would have enough diesel and gasoline fuel to do so. In the days to come, my worries would be justified. At 1600 hours that afternoon, the division learned that we would indeed resume the attack. We were to move from our positions short of PL New Jersey northeastward toward Republican Guard positions near Objective Norfolk just west of the Kuwaiti-Iraqi border (see map 9.3).[18] It would be a very long march preceding our attack.

Shortly after the DIVARTY TOC was set in place at the new location, Cardenas asked that I pop in for an update. There he briefed me that at dawn, we would depart to positions some 70 kilometers to the northeast to support the attack on Iraqi Republican Guard divisions. We had heard rumors that Schwarzkopf has been "furious" that the VII Corps planned to keep the 1ID in reserve where we were. But Stormin' Norman had other plans for the BRO. With respect to our division's role, he ordered the VII Corps's commanding general to "get them in the fight now." So the VII Corps wasted no time in alerting us that we would bound forward at dawn the next day. Just as Rhame had been prescient about ordering the division to get ready to deploy to the Middle East in the early fall of 1990, even before we had been alerted to go, so too were his efforts to secure a follow-on mission for the division from the VII Corps planners weeks earlier. His foresight and grit enabled both the corps and the division to quickly launch us toward Iraq's Republican Guards on short notice. Besides, this was no time to test Schwarzkopf's patience. It was time to get our ass in gear and get moving.

Our former division commander, Sullivan, was fond of reminding soldiers of the BRO, "If you're looking for a fight, you've come to the right place." But Rhame had doggedly sought that fight out, and we were, once again, headed for a big one. It was time, as William Shakespeare penned in his *Julius Caesar,* to "cry havoc, and let slip the dogs of war." It would surely be so as the 1ID prepared that night to pursue the enemy deep into Iraq. We were made for it.

10

A Relentless Pursuit

The early morning fog hung heavily over the DIVARTY TOC on February 26, 1991, as my driver, PFC McGary, and I crawled out of our fabricated sleeping loft in the back of our Humvee. I quickly made my way to the TOC to get an update on the plan for the day and to find a hot cup of coffee. When I entered, everyone was making final arrangements to pack up equipment and begin a long cross-desert road march—possibly in excess of 70 kilometers before we were done—to a position deep inside Iraq. Traveling that distance guaranteed that we would consume a lot of fuel that day. MAJ Cardenas then informed me that, given the fast pace we would experience in the coming days, COL Dodson determined that we might need to split the DIVARTY TOC in two, with Cardenas taking one half and myself the other. The idea was that we would leapfrog forward, taking turns getting into position to control the artillery battle, as we bounded toward the enemy to keep up with our fast-moving maneuver brigades. The concept made sense to me, but what wasn't clear at the time was how far we would go into Iraq before we would begin this "jump TOC" procedure.

The division had issued FRAGO 96–91 codenamed "Jeremiah III" for the follow-on offensive the previous evening. At 0430 that morning, the order came down that we would indeed resume the offensive. But there was a problem with the available maneuver space the division had to operate within. The 1(UK)AD's logistical units, to the rear of the British maneuver forces, were situated on terrain the BRO would need if our maneuver brigades were to advance abreast in what would be a movement-to-contact mission toward the enemy well inside Iraq. Since the area the division occupied was now compacted with all manner of supply activity supporting the British, our division made the decision to initially deploy the brigades forward in a narrow single column. The 1–4 CAV would lead the way and screen the BRO from enemy observation, followed by the 1st Brigade, the 3rd Brigade, and the 2nd Brigade, which was then in reserve.

That meant that the DIVARTY TOC, following the maneuver brigades and their supporting units, would be well to the rear, raising our concern that we might get trapped so far back that our ability to keep up would be in jeopardy and maybe impair our ability to support our maneuver brethren racing far ahead of us. Dodson anticipated this problem with his "jump TOC" idea of splitting the DIVARTY TOC so that we could bound forward. This envisioned one TOC element assuming control in a stationary position while the other would jump ahead to establish a new location to take control, thereby allowing the trailing element to leap forward and repeat the procedure. However, initially, the first leg of the division's movement would be in column until we reached the assembly area some 40 kilometers in front of us (see map 10.1).[1] At that point, it was contemplated that the brigades would attack abreast, greatly shortening the length of the division's march column while quickening the pace forward. But our first order of business was to get deep enough into Iraq to transition to that combat formation with the maneuver brigades side-by-side. That's when the "jump TOC" operation would make sense, and we could stay tucked up and close to the battle to support the maneuver brigades with artillery fire as they advanced toward the enemy.

When we moved out early that morning, we made the decision that the HHB would travel in two columns abreast to reduce the length of our convoy since, not being the size of a brigade, we had the lateral maneuver space to do so. This would help us on the first long leg of our movement into Iraq to maintain good order and control over our troops and equipment. Cardenas would take the lead position in the column, and I would follow at the end, keeping a watchful eye for any elements that fell out of the march along the way that would need repair or assistance. Cardenas and I would also stay in radio contact, he reporting what was ahead, while I shared the status of vehicles that fell out as well as how we were keeping up. Vehicles moving in convoys—whether on a hard surface road or in the sand—tended to vary in speed while seeking to maintain a proper interval. It was our practice to keep vehicles dispersed—about 100 meters apart—to mitigate the effect of any attack on the convoy as it moved. But the slowing-up, speeding-up that occurred as the convoys encountered varying terrain created an accordionlike effect. This often resulted in the rear elements of the formation having to go very fast to close the intervals that opened up between vehicles. This road march would be no exception. In short order, McGary and I—positioned at the rear of the convoy—found we were flying across the desert at high speed, sometimes upward of 50 miles an hour to keep up. When we hit a rising

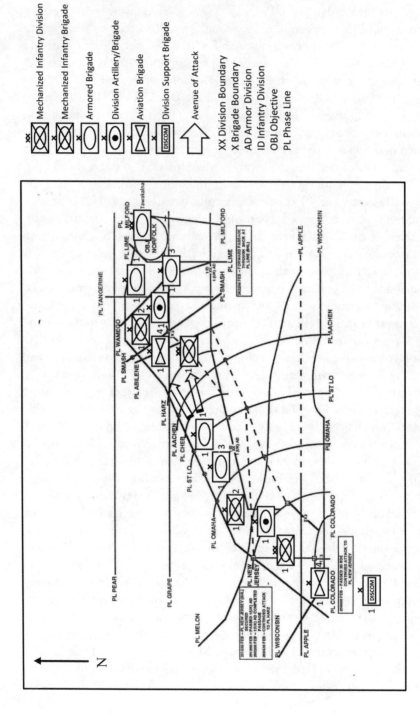

Legend

⊠⊠ Mechanized Infantry Division
⊠ Mechanized Infantry Brigade
◯ Armored Brigade
⊙ Division Artillery/Brigade
⊠ Aviation Brigade
DISCOM Division Support Brigade

⬆ Avenue of Attack

XX Division Boundary
X Brigade Boundary
AD Armor Division
ID Infantry Division
OBJ Objective
PL Phase Line

Map 10.1. 1st Infantry Division Scheme of Maneuver, February 26, 1991 sand dune at this speed and immediately fell off the other side, it felt as if we had left the ground. It reminded me of a television show I watched in the late 1960s, *The Rat Patrol,* which chronicled the tales of jeep-borne Allied commandoes chasing and dodging the German Wehrmacht around the sand dunes of Africa's Sahara Desert. Now we were doing the same, except we weren't dodging anybody. We were looking to close rapidly with the Iraqis in a classic movement-to-contact, engage them in a fight, and defeat them.

By 1030, after five hours of marching, the lead elements of the division had still not made contact with enemy forces, encountering only long lines of aimless Iraqis done with battle along the way as they walked unescorted across the desert in an effort to avoid more combat. As we continued deeper into Iraq, radio communications became a distinct challenge given our division's elongated road march. If we didn't close up, maintaining situational awareness of where friendly and enemy forces were on the battlefield would become more and more difficult. When the division reached PL Hartz around midafternoon, some 60 kilometers from where we had started earlier that morning, the DIVARTY TOC arrived at a position we thought would be our location for a while. But no sooner had we stopped and begun to set up than we received orders to continue the march deeper into Iraq. Had we remained there, it was Dodson's intent to initiate our "jump TOC" drill, but he decided to move us forward in unison at least another 10 kilometers, where we thought we would situate ourselves for the assault. Meanwhile, fuel was a problem. I spoke to MAJ Brooks, our S-4, who was also very concerned about whether the fuel supply units would be able to keep up with us. We were running low—very low—on that precious commodity. The irony was inescapable. Here we were in the oil-rich Arabian Desert and virtually out of fuel. Nonetheless, we quickly got back in formation and continued our march forward. This time we would travel in single file, not abreast, since we would lose daylight soon, and moving in darkness in columns abreast would be harder to control.

As we continued our trek deeper into Iraq, the sun slowly dipped toward the horizon, and I wondered when and where we would arrive in position to begin the attack. Then, as darkness fell like a blanket on our convoy, we stopped to visit the tactical headquarters of VII Corps Artillery that had bounded forward in tracked vehicles to maintain situational awareness of the artillery fight. There we encountered BG Abrams, the VII Corps Artillery commander, whom I had not seen since the firing incident with B-6 FA ten days earlier.

Table 10.1.   1st Infantry Division Artillery Organization for Combat (February 26, 1991)

1ID (Mechanized) DIVARTY: Force Artillery Headquarters (HQ)	
1-5 FA (155mm SP)	DS 1st Brigade
4-5 FA (155mm SP)	GS
4-3 FA (155mm SP)	DS 3rd Brigade (2nd Armored Division)
B-6 FA (MLRS)	GS
D-25 TAB	GS
210th Field Artillery Brigade: GSR 1ID (M) DIVARTY, Alternate FA HQ	
3-17 FA (155mm SP)	R 4-3 FA
6-41 FA (155mm SP)	R 1-5 FA
C-4-27 FA (MLRS)	GS

Key: Direct Support (DS); Reinforcing (R); General Support Reinforcing (GSR); General Support (GS)

I went inside with Cardenas to coordinate our newly assigned artillery support, the 210th Field Artillery (FA) Brigade (210th FA Brigade) under the command of COL Gary Bourne. They were supporting the 2nd Armored Cavalry Regiment (2ACR) that had battled Iraqi forces in and around Objective Norfolk all day. Now the 210th FA Brigade would transition to our control prior to the 1ID's forward passage of lines that evening to assume the battle from the 2ACR. The 210th FA Brigade brought with them 3rd Battalion, 17th Field Artillery (3–17 FA) and 6th Battalion, 41st Field Artillery (6–41 FA), both 155mm battalions, and an MLRS battery, C Battery, 4th Battalion, 27th Field Artillery (C-4–27 FA). Dodson placed 6–41 FA and 3–17 FA, respectively, in a reinforcing mission to 1–5 FA, which was in direct support of the 1st Brigade, and to 4–3 FA, in direct support of the 3rd Brigade. The 210th FA Brigade's MLRS battery, C-4–27 FA, would join our B-6 FA and 4–5 FA in a general support mission for the entire division. Dodson then instructed the 210th FA Brigade to take charge of the artillery fight for our division, until we completed the last leg of our move into assault positions that evening (see table 10.1). After that, the DIVARTY TOC would resume control of the battle.

When we finished our short visit with the VII Corps Artillery, we got our bearings and headed toward the location near where the BRO's brigades and battalions would begin their assault on enemy forces on Objective Norfolk (see map 10.2).[2] That attack would be one for the books. It is generally accepted among military tacticians that the toughest

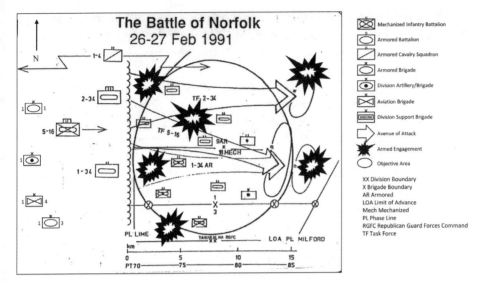

The Battle of Norfolk
26-27 Feb 1991

Mechanized Infantry Battalion
Armored Battalion
Armored Cavalry Squadron
Armored Brigade
Division Artillery/Brigade
Aviation Brigade
Division Support Brigade
Avenue of Attack
Armed Engagement
Objective Area
XX Division Boundary
X Brigade Boundary
AR Armored
LOA Limit of Advance
Mech Mechanized
PL Phase Line
RGFC Republican Guard Forces Command
TF Task Force

Map 10.2.   1st Infantry Division Positions during the Battle of Norfolk, February 26–27, 1991

mission a combat unit can execute is a forward passage of lines, in which one friendly unit passes through another friendly unit to assume the fight. But this forward passage of lines would be further complicated—and more dangerous—because not only was the 2ACR engaged in fighting the enemy that we would confront once we assumed the fight, but the forward passage of lines would be accomplished under the cover of darkness, at a division level with two brigades abreast. It was very complex, with the potential for significant fratricide if things went awry. It had all the makings of a potential disaster, but our maneuver planners had managed to coordinate this precarious mission against all odds—odds no betting man in his right mind would take with a London bookie.

The scheme of maneuver, despite its intricacy, was straightforward. The 1st Brigade would attack the Iraqi 9th Armored and 18th Mechanized Brigades of the Tawakalna Republican Guards Division on the northern (left) part of Objective Norfolk, and the 3rd Brigade would attack the 37th Brigade of the Iraqi 12th Armored Division (Iraqi 12AD) in the southern (right) sector. Supporting this attack at 2100 hours, the division's 1st Battalion, 1st Aviation Battalion (1–1 AV)—with its deadly accurate Apache AH-64 attack helicopters and antitank Hellfire missiles—would conduct deep attacks in the division's sector against Iraqi armor targets. Prior to this attack, the 210th FA Brigade, on orders from Dodson, organized and conducted preparation fires on enemy positions. At 2200 hours, the brigades began their forward passage of lines, and in less than 500 meters—a third of a mile from where the attack began—they were in direct contact with Iraqi forces.

As this was underway, our DIVARTY TOC convoy raced to our new position to resume control of the artillery fight. It was significantly farther than the 10 kilometers we estimated from the last position where we had halted earlier in the day near PL Hartz. As we moved forward in the dark, we passed burning tank hulks that had been the targets of the 2ACR earlier in the day. They, in part, lit our way forward, but it occurred to me that we, in our unarmored vehicles, could be easily mistaken by our own troops for fleeing enemy vehicles as we moved through the darkness of the desert near the Iraqi-Kuwaiti border. Overhead, the unmistakable "whop-whop" of the 4th Brigade's 1–1 AVN attack helicopters' blades cutting through the crisp night air left me in awe of the combat power we had assembled. As we snaked forward, passing numerous burning vehicles to the left and right of our thin-skinned convoy, I called Cardenas on the radio and asked, "Are we supporting this fight or leading the attack?" Cardenas was sure we were behind the front lines, but no sooner had he said so, than the high-pitched roar and clanking of M2 Bradley IFVs materialized on either side of our convoy. As they raced past and ahead of us, I was left with the thought, "Well, if we're not leading this damn attack, why the hell are all of these infantry armored vehicles flying past us like bats out of hell?" At that point, I was beginning to appreciate what Clausewitz meant when he wrote of the "clouds of great uncertainty" or "the fog of war": "War is the province of uncertainty: three-fourths of those things upon which action in war must be calculated, are hidden more or less in the clouds of great uncertainty. Here, then, above all a fine and penetrating mind is called for, to grope out the truth by the tact of its judgment."[3] We were in the middle of that "fog," and I was acutely aware of it, with burning tanks, armored vehicles flying by, and the rolling sound of battle ahead of us. This was not a drill. It was war. Accordingly, I mustered all my senses to keep focused, while relying on my own judgment and faith—yes faith—that we would survive this ordeal.

Cardenas and I were not the only ones shrouded in that "fog." Our own LTC Emerson—commanding the 1–5 FA in direct support (DS) of the 1st Brigade that was spearheading the division's attack just kilometers ahead—was keenly aware of the danger. The 1st Brigade, like other units of the division, had hastily prepared for a movement to contact mission the previous day. Much of that planning focused on the ground scheme of maneuver, more so than fire-support planning. Nevertheless, Emerson took steps then to address the challenges he foresaw in providing artillery fires to such a fast-paced operation.

First, like Dodson who planned to split and leapfrog the DIVARTY TOC to ensure we kept up with the division, Emerson was also concerned that his battalion would remain close to his supported maneuver forces to provide fire support. As a result, his S-3 operations officer, MAJ Jim Holt—who had been my assistant S-3 when I was the DIVARTY's S-3—conferred with Emerson and decided to tuck two of 1–5 FA's firing batteries close behind the advancing maneuver battalions of the 1st Brigade as they marched toward Objective Norfolk. Meanwhile, Emerson would use LTC Larry Adair's 6–41 FA, which was reinforcing 1–5 FA, to initially support 2–34 AR, the brigade's battalion that would be the main effort. This was a wise move, because 6–41 FA was already positioned well forward, supporting the 2ACR that would hand the battle to the BRO later that night. That would ensure that the lead elements of the 1st Brigade would have fire support from a unit that was already familiar with the sector and in forward positions to fire.

Second, Emerson was very concerned about the potential for fratricide from artillery fire in a rapid movement forward—through friendly forces—to engage enemy units. He expressed his concern to the 1st Brigade commander, COL Maggart, about the use of Dual-Purpose Improved Conventional Munition (DPICM) projectiles, which had the same sort of submunition used by our MLRS units. The higher-than-normal failure rate of DPICM came as a surprise to all of us, particularly the problem that unexploded ordnance posed for our troops moving about the battlefield. Emerson planned to use high-explosive (HE) projectiles that blew up on impact and didn't leave bomblet hazards for friendly forces to stumble upon. The only problem was that he had far more DPICM projectiles on hand in his ammunition trains than HE rounds and would need to exchange the DPICM for HE, quickly. Unfortunately, what he also lacked was enough time to do the swap. As luck would have it, Emerson's ammunition supply team fell upon an unmanned AHA filled with HE rounds and immediately made the necessary—and unauthorized—exchange in an act of bold battlefield initiative. Years later, Emerson would learn that one of his Industrial College of the Armed Forces (ICAF) classmates had commanded the supply battalion responsible for that AHA. But for the life of him, that supply battalion commander couldn't figure out how he suddenly had so much DPICM in the storage facility just a day later. Alas, the "fog of war."

Finally, Emerson reasoned that—with a fast-paced night operation as envisioned—illumination fires would be needed to assist the ground units in engaging enemy targets under darkness. His battalion carried a fair amount of 155mm illumination rounds in their basic load, a projectile that—when fired—ejected a bright flare under a slowly falling parachute to light the battlefield for friendly forces. But he decided that employment—even of this capability—would reside with the ground commanders that Emerson's batteries would support. That was an added safety feature to ensure that there was positive control of indirect fires as the division made its nighttime forward passage of lines through the 2ACR to attack the Tawakalnas.

As darkness approached and 1–5 FA took up positions on the division's left flank behind the 1st Brigade near the FLOT (forward line of own troops), Holt was anxious to contact his designated reinforcing-fires unit, 6–41 FA. But when he tried to contact 210th FA Brigade, which was acting as the force artillery headquarters for the BRO until the DIVARTY TOC was in position to assume control of the artillery fight, he was greeted with dead silence on the radio net. He then called the 6–41 FA directly and contacted the unit's commander. In short order, 6–41 FA's Adair popped into Holt's operations center, where they exchanged plans and graphic overlays for their maps. Holt quickly arranged a scheme to leapfrog his batteries with those of 6–41 FA, which they did throughout the night, so fire support would be available to the ground commanders as they advanced on Objective Norfolk. It was the kind of quick and efficient battlefield coordination between a direct support battalion and its reinforcing unit that both men had been trained to do, despite poor communications and accompanying battlefield confusion. To be sure, Emerson's plan to use illumination also proved very useful as volleys were fired in support of attacking maneuver forces. Holt succinctly recalled the hectic nature of that night: "We heard and saw main battle tank and Bradley rapid fire. We fired an occasional illumination volley. I recall chaotic calls on the command net. With the wind, sand, fog, all of it was surreal, with the added factor of sleep deprivation."[4]

To the south, my close friend LTC Smith's 4–3 FA was supporting COL Dave Weisman's 3rd Brigade. Like 1–5 FA, they too were also racing to the front to get in range to support the 3rd Brigade's rapid movement forward. The 3–17 FA, commanded by LTC Jeff McCausland, was assigned by Dodson to reinforce Smith. Unfortunately, McCausland—like Smith—could barely range the front line where Wiseman's brigade would conduct their assault. The good news was that 3–17 FA, like 6–41

FA to the north, was at least in a forward position—having supported the 2ACR hours earlier—to provide support to the 3rd Brigade. Like Emerson had, Smith also decided to keep his batteries tucked up behind the 3rd Brigade's units, speeding ahead so they would be in position to fire. Again, having reinforcing artillery already in the forward area gave both direct support battalions a "breather" until they were able to arrive at their forward firing positions to resume support for their respective maneuver brigades. Unquestionably, the rapid pace of the division's movement to contact over a wide and expansive desert at high speed, posed serious challenges to supporting artillery trying to keep up, particularly our M109A2 howitzers with their decades-old propulsion system. They simply could not match the speed of the newly developed M1 Abrams tanks and M2 Bradley IFVs.

The "fog of war" and poor communications also bedeviled Smith's battalion. His XO, MAJ Joe Riojas, was very concerned when he discovered, while attempting to coordinate the movement of 4–3 FA batteries, that two of the battalion's firing units found themselves forward of their supported maneuver forces. Not only could this subject them to direct fire from the enemy, it could also expose them to potential fratricide by our own maneuver units that might mistake them for Iraqi combatants. This was in no small part a result of overstretched lines of communication that made it very difficult to communicate by radio. Indeed, Riojas learned from a signal unit that he had stumbled across, that limestone in the desert subsurface could attenuate radio signals, further degrading communications and creating more confusion. Not only were units like 4–3 FA and 1–5 FA dealing with the vicissitudes of human error, they were also confronting obstacles naturally occurring in a desert environment. Nevertheless, both direct support artillery battalions, their reinforcing battalions, and the DIVARTY proved equal to the task in overcoming the challenges of poor communications, outdated propulsion, and the uncooperative nature of the desert. The determination and ingenuity of these Desert Redlegs to stay in the fight was undeniable.

While Emerson's 1–5 FA and Smith's 4–3 FA were rapidly maneuvering into position to support their respective maneuver brigade's assault, Cardenas and I continued to rush headlong into this maelstrom. As we approached our new position (see map 10.2) around 2230 hours, the DIVARTY had traveled almost 100 kilometers, 30 more than we expected. There we witnessed the flashing lights of battle and heard the loud report of tank fire. The sky was aglow intermittently with an eerie orange light show, not unlike the lightning storms at home on the plains of Kansas.

Indeed, the heavens above told the hellish story below. There could be no doubt by anyone that the BRO was bringing the full force and violence of its combat power on the Iraqis, particularly the vaunted Tawakalna Division.

These Republican Guard Forces Command (RGFC) troops were the best that Baghdad had. They were composed of the most loyal and trustworthy members of the Iraqi armed forces. The elite of the Iraqi Army, they reported directly to Saddam Hussein and were well treated by the Iraqi dictator, who depended on their allegiance to ward off challenges to his rule. They were also well trained and equipped with the best Soviet equipment, including the modern T-72 tank with its 125mm high-velocity smoothbore gun. Moreover, the RGFC troops were better compensated than the run-of-the-mill Iraqi soldier. Essentially, they were like mercenaries ready to inflict great mayhem and death at their leader's command. They could trace their history back to 1969 when they were created as a presidential guard, and their fundamental mission then was to protect Saddam from being overthrown—which was why they were well cared for. They were also mostly Sunni Muslims, like Saddam himself, as opposed to Shia Iraqis who were less loyal to the regime. The RGFC had been content in Saddam's Iraq, which required loyal troops to keep both the masses in their place and Hussein steadily atop the political structure that was his dictatorship.

During the Iran-Iraq War, the RGFC underwent an expansion. But when deployed on the battlefield where massive Iranian human wave attacks confronted regular Iraqi troops, the RGFC were often kept in reserve. There they were positioned to remind less loyal Iraqi units, often partially composed of Shia Iraqis, that retreat in the face of advancing Iranian forces would invite a fate far worse than anything Iran would inflict upon them. In any case, Saddam kept the RGFC on a short string and protected them. And in this war, he had positioned them as a final line of defense. He knew it. They knew it. And we knew it. As I had told MG Rhame when he had visited Dodson's office to quiz me about how the Iraqis would perform, the RGFC would stand and fight, but our superior firepower and training would overwhelm them. We were in the process of doing just that on February 26 at a place we called Objective Norfolk. That night, the Tawakalnas stood in the way of Kuwait's liberation. Their defeat would not only be a victory for us but a direct affront to Saddam, their supremely malevolent patron.

Once the DIVARTY TOC arrived in position at 2330 hours, we took control of artillery forces from the 210th FA Brigade and resumed monitoring operations as the maneuver brigades battled with the Iraqis throughout the night. The "KAH-WOP" and reverberant "BOOMING" of tank fire, the careening echoes of ricocheting rounds, all accompanied by ripple bursts of machine-gun fire, filled the chilly night air. The battle was joined. When I pulled in with the last vehicles of the HHB, I exited HQ-5 and headed to the DIVARTY TOC. As I did, I observed how my own shadow—like a phantom in the night—appeared, disappeared, and then reappeared in front of me as the sky lit up with the nearby flashes of battle to our east. When I entered the TOC, I found Cardenas and his weary team attempting to get a clear picture of the fight, and Dodson was practically dead asleep on his feet. As the sounds of battle continued outside, one of the TOC operations officers motioned toward Dodson and then, placing his index finger across his lips, signaled to me not to wake him. Dodson hadn't rested in days, and it had finally caught up with him. But he was not about to leave his place in the TOC, even if asleep upright.

To my delight, someone was already brewing a pot of coffee, and I helped myself to a cup. Cardenas and I talked a bit and determined that when morning came, we would start our jump TOC operations as we plunged deeper into Kuwait. But for now, after a very long cross-desert march deep into Iraq, we needed to rest. I returned to my Humvee where McGary waited for the go-ahead to bed down. We crawled into the upper half of our sleeping platform in the back of the vehicle, our weapons at arm's reach, where I managed to muster enough energy to pen an optimistic entry in my diary: "We advanced deep into Iraq today, over 100Ks. The enemy is retreating as we advance and giving up in droves. We have overwhelmed him with our combat power. Tonight we had a major battle with the Republican Guard (Tawakalna). They have been defeated in detail. We are all worn out, but we retain the spirit of the hunt. Onward!" As I tucked my diary in my canvas bag, I could feel the irresistible need to sleep. Before drifting off, I couldn't help but think, as the sounds of war echoed around us, that the only thing separating me from a stray round was the thin plastic olive-green cover that was the top of our Humvee. But that worry wasn't enough to ward off the fatigue that drove me to unconsciousness.

When dawn arrived on February 27, we awoke to a smattering of secondary explosions from damaged or destroyed Iraqi tanks and armored vehicles, which the night before had been attacked by our M1 Abrams tanks and their 120mm smoothbore cannons, and M2 Bradley IFVs with their 25mm guns firing 200 rounds per minute. This deadly combination of direct fire weapons had set the enemy's tanks and other armored vehicles ablaze, including the modern Soviet T-72 tanks that the

Russians had built to oppose NATO troops in Europe. As the Iraqi equipment continued to burn, the intense heat ignited any remaining ammunition or fuel in them, creating an impressive fireworks display of subsequent explosions that served as a battlefield punctuation mark that the enemy had been set upon by the BRO. When I crawled from my Humvee, somewhat rested, I headed for the DIVARTY TOC to check in. The people who had managed to get some rest were energized as they planned artillery support to continue the attack through Objective Norfolk and deeper into Kuwait.

Cardenas briefed me that at 0600 the 2nd Brigade, which had been in reserve, was ordered to move forward and pass through the 1st Brigade on our left to continue the attack. At this point, the nature of the fight had shifted from a deliberate attack of the enemy on Objective Norfolk to an exploitation, an offensive operation that takes advantage of a successful attack and is designed to further disorganize the enemy throughout the depth of the battlefield. The division would move out that morning to attack an objective inside Kuwait, Objective Denver, to intercept Iraq's retreating army heading northward (see map 10.3).[5] That meant we could expect to move swiftly all day, pausing only when we needed to confront the enemy.

The plan was for me to take the jump TOC forward to a position and hold there until the HHB joined me with elements of the 210th FA Brigade TOC. CPT Hymel set about organizing the HHB, but our fuel supplies were critically low just as we were about to move deeper into Iraq and across the Kuwaiti border. Fortunately, as we were about to leave, Brooks, our diligent S-4, arrived with 400 gallons of diesel, not enough to top off each of our vehicles, but enough to get us going. After fueling the neediest vehicles, we started our movement through the battlefield that earlier had been the scene of a violent conflagration. I checked my map to ensure I had the next location plotted correctly and entered the map coordinates into our GPS. Once again, we chambered rounds and ensured we had ready access to our basic load of small-arms ammunition, hand grenades, and an anti-armor M72 LAW we always carried with us. I was hoping we would not have to use it against any Iraqi armor that had managed to miraculously escape death the previous night—because if we missed with it, the only defense we would have was for McGary to floor the accelerator on HQ-5 and pray we could outrun any returning fire.

When we left, we found our path largely unmarked except for tank tracks that were made hours before. I hoped they were our tracks, because if they were, our path was likely cleared of any unexploded ordnance or

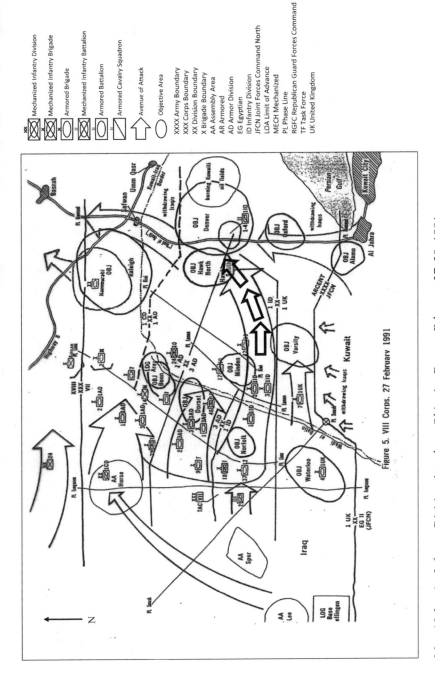

Legend:

Mechanized Infantry Division
Mechanized Infantry Brigade
Armored Brigade
Mechanized Infantry Battalion
Armored Battalion
Armored Cavalry Squadron
Avenue of Attack
Objective Area

XXXX Army Boundary
XXX Corps Boundary
XX Division Boundary
X Brigade Boundary
AA Assembly Area
AR Armored
AD Armor Division
ID Infantry Division
JFCN Joint Forces Command North
LOA Limit of Advance
MECH Mechanized
PL Phase Line
RGFC Republican Guard Forces Command
TF Task Force
UK United Kingdom

Figure 5. VIII Corps, 27 February 1991

Map 10.3.   1st Infantry Division Attack on Objective Denver, February 27–28, 1991 land mines. Shortly, within five minutes of departing, we encountered the first signs of Iraqi soldiers moving about the battlefield. I drew my 9mm pistol and rested it on my thigh in case any of the wandering Iraqis moved toward us with hostile intent. Then more Iraqis showed up to the right at about 100 meters from our vehicle. McGary reached for his M16 and—in one quick and fluid motion—took his hands off the steering wheel, flipped his rifle safety to the "fire" position, pointed it across my lap toward the enemy, and was ready to drop these Iraqis on the spot. I smacked him hard on the top of his helmet and angrily snapped, "Roger, drive the damn vehicle! I'll watch out for the damn bogies," referring to the Iraqis as fighter pilots refer to unidentified aircraft. Frankly, I was more concerned about hitting unexploded ordnance in the path of our Humvee than panicked Iraqis—even armed ones—scurrying about the battlefield a football field away. Besides, McGary's excellent driving skills were more important to both of us than his marksmanship, which was damn good too.

We continued to move forward though a nightmarish landscape populated with scores of destroyed and burning armored hulks smoldering all around us. Iraqis, in their drab-green uniforms, could be seen on either side of us, either running away in fear or wandering aimlessly in search of somewhere safe to flee. As we neared our designated location closer to the Kuwaiti border, pausing to await remaining HHB elements, we found that the position—only hours earlier—had served as an Iraqi headquarters. It had extensive fortifications and, ominously, a deep underground bunker that appeared to house the command-and-control elements of the unit. One of the "jump TOC" sergeants, SSG Ernest Healey, volunteered to enter the bunker to see if any Iraqis remained there. I held him back. I didn't want to risk his life over some frightened and armed Iraqi hunkered down deep in an abandoned bunker who would willingly remain there until we left. I took my 9mm pistol out, fired a round into the bunker's inside wall, and waited to see if there was any response. When none was forthcoming, I told Healey, "Keep an eye on it. If someone comes out, you'll know what to do." He smiled knowingly, and we continued to secure the position from disoriented Iraqis moving peripatetically about the battlefield.

Soon Hymel caught up to us with the rest of the HHB. We compared notes to ensure that we were ready to move forward, but as soon as we closed our pocket notebooks and moved toward our vehicles to depart, six armed Iraqi soldiers walked right into our position to surrender. Immediately greeted by 60 HHB soldiers armed to the teeth, the Iraqis unhesitatingly threw down their weapons and stretched their arms skyward, removing any doubt about their hostility. They had no fight left. Hymel and his security force searched them, sat them down in a line front to back, and then offered them both food and water. Once they were processed, Hymel stood them in a line, pointed to the southwest, and said, "Shadley, Shadley." That was the name of the rear-area commander, COL Bob Shadley, whose DISCOM had established holding areas for POWs shortly after the BRO had conducted the breach operation days earlier, taking its first prisoners. The Iraqis dutifully responded, "Shadley, Shadley!" and then marched off. When units behind us encountered these POWs, no doubt, they also employed the "Shadley" drill repeatedly. These poor Iraqis had no idea who or what "Shadley" was. But they would learn—as they made their way to the rear—that 1ID troops would give them food and water and repeat "Shadley!" pointing them southwest and away from danger. I suspect that after experiencing several iterations of this routine every place they stopped, that many POWs may have eventually reasoned that this "Shadley" thing might not be such a bad idea. At least they wouldn't be killed. So many of them marched toward the DISCOM, having mastered exactly one English word: "Shadley."

As the Iraqis marched out of our security perimeter, I returned to my vehicle and started to spread my battle map on the hood of HQ-5 to verify the route we would take into Kuwait. But suddenly, one of my men called out to me, "Hey, sir, take a look at this!" Just over one of the berms in front of us, more Iraqis walked up, this time no less than 400 of them![6] Tossing my map back in the Humvee, we quickly deployed our security perimeter again and confronted this huge force. They too were tired and hungry, and about a third of them were barefooted. They were ready to surrender and follow our instructions without hesitation. Our troops took their weapons and piled them on a nearby tar-surfaced desert road that had, no doubt, been constructed to support oil-exploration activities years earlier. We then put the POWs in two columns inside our security cordon, sitting them down front to back as we had with the first batch.

As they were arranged and searched by our security force, I noted with some pride the focused and calm seriousness of our troops, including the small cadre of women, about ten, we had in the HHB intelligence and administrative sections. Male and female soldiers alike stood patiently, weapons at the ready and aimed for the first sign of hostility. The Iraqis may have been too tired to notice the presence of armed women standing guard over them, but for the observant ones, it must have been a true culture shock. Yet in the same moment, those same US troops were passing MREs and bottles of water to these famished and thirsty POWs who appeared somewhat stunned with the generosity of their captors.

SGM Vann, the DIVARTY TOC's senior enlisted man, stood beside me and said, "Ain't this a picture, sir, or what?" as he too was proud of the compassion of the troops he had trained for this day. I cautioned Vann, who had worked for me when I was the S-3, that we needed to be careful not to give away too many rations or the limited water we had for ourselves. Vann chuckled and said in response to my concern, "Sir, don't worry, the MREs they're giving up are the tuna fish ones." I recalled my dislike of that particular selection and thought to myself, "No wonder the troops are so generous."

Just as we began to organize this latest group of POWs, Dodson called to inform us that he and his driver were surrounded by 50 POWs, which in short order grew to 100 in number. Like McGary and me, Dodson and his driver had little more than a 9mm pistol and one M16 to handle this challenge. Hymel immediately dispatched a smaller security team to help him deal with the problem, after which Dodson headed for our position. Later the same day, Dodson would shift from traveling in his Humvee to an M2 Bradley IFV that the division provided him. As a senior commander, he needed to move in a more protected manner. As luck would have it, later that afternoon, his Bradley popped over a berm and almost ran headlong into a T-62 tank. Quickly turning and driving rearward to then swing into a position to engage it with his heavy 25mm turret gun, he hesitated when he saw an Iraqi hop out and flee the tank on foot.[7] No doubt this Iraqi had learned what a Bradley gunner can do to you. But for now, having just rolled into our position after his first close encounter with POWs in his Humvee, Dodson—like us—wanted to see these prisoners quickly processed so that we could resume our movement forward to Objective Denver.

Just then, our unit surgeon, CPT (Doctor) Jon M. Sullivan, walked up to inform me that one of the POWs would surely die on the spot if he didn't get urgent help. Sullivan, a pediatrician by trade, was good, and I trusted his judgment. "Sir, there's a fellow over there who, ironically, is a doctor, and he's severely dehydrated," Sullivan said with profundity in his voice.

"What do you recommend?" I asked.

Sullivan responded, "We have to bag him right now," referring to the soldier's need for at least one bag of saline solution to rehydrate him. I looked at my watch and asked how long it would take, and Sullivan noted, "20 minutes." I gave him the go-ahead but warned him we needed to get moving as soon as possible. Water was a problem. Like fuel, we did not have an unlimited amount of it, and 400 POWs would consume a lot of water. The idea that we could be there all day treating thirsty and dehydrated POWs just wouldn't work. We needed to get moving. It was a hard decision to make. The humanity question alone was pressing. But we were there to fight a war, and my job was to keep us moving to the objective.

While Sullivan administered the saline to the near-dead Iraqi doctor, I discovered to my surprise that one of the POWs spoke almost perfect English. I had him brought forward and told him to translate for me. I then proceeded to inform these 400 tattered, tired, and defeated POWs that they were under the custody of the allied coalition and that they were expected to strictly follow our instructions or, if they failed to do so, would be dealt with accordingly. My Iraqi translator dutifully translated my words, including the now standard "Shadley" pitch. Hymel asked if they should be given a compass to keep them headed in the right direction, but I was sure that if we did that, the prisoners would use it immediately to veer off to the north as soon as we were out of sight. Sending them back to potentially fight another day was ill advised.

Sullivan finished his work with the moribund Iraqi doctor and was discouraged. "Sir, he really needs a second bag, or he'll die today. Can I give him one with an IV to take with him?" Sullivan thought that with a little help, the doctor could use the intravenous needle still plugged into him and have his comrades help him administer the second bag. I approved his request. "Doc," the nickname all of us used for him, really wanted to help this fellow. His Hippocratic Oath must have had a special meaning that day as he contemplated the fate of his medical comrade. I suppose the pediatrician in him was also at work, stimulating some big-hearted compassion for an Iraqi "Doc."

As we stood the POWs up to march them off, many were repeating, "Shadley, Shadley!" as if to assure us of their compliance. I did all I could to resist cracking a smile as they sounded off "Shadley!" not wanting to betray the seriousness of the moment. But none of my training had prepared me for a situation calling for POWs to march away of their own volition into the waiting arms of a colonel named "Shadley," many kilometers to the rear. In a word, it was hilarious.

As these POWs disappeared, I was more eager than ever to get on the road, and so was Hymel for fear that even more Iraqis would come our way and further delay us. We didn't want to become a POW welcome center. After processing about 406 of them over the last hour, we felt we had done our part. Besides, they had been cooperative to that point, but we didn't

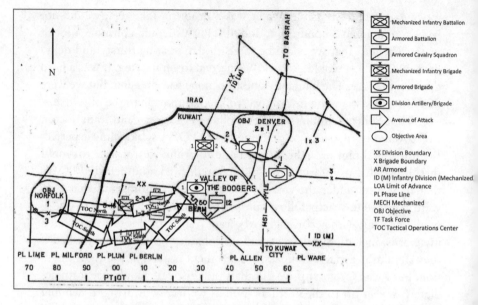

Map 10.4.   1st Infantry DIVARTY Movement from Iraq to Kuwait, February 27, 1991

want to tempt fate. As we prepared to depart, Hymel's heavy-maintenance team finalized their destruction of the Iraqi weapons we had seized. Weighing in at 50 tons, HHB's M88 armored recovery vehicle, normally used for retrieving and towing damaged or overturned armored vehicles on the battlefield, churned the weapons into a crushed and twisted heap of steel. Once that was accomplished, we were ready to be on our way.

I returned to HQ-5 and put my map on the hood. By then, the other half of the DIVARTY TOC had pulled into position. There Hymel, Cardenas, and I conferred on the locations we were given to jump to, about 50 kilometers altogether, which would place us 24 kilometers inside Kuwait. Both TOC elements would take routes in the southern half of the division's sector from our position east of Objective Norfolk, across PL Milford, PL Plum—closely paralleling the Kuwaiti western border, which was congruent with the Wadi al-Batin—and then across PL Berlin, which lay inside Kuwait (see map 10.4).[8] My half of the TOC would take a south-southeastern route (TOC South). Cardenas's portion would take a route north of us (TOC North) in the same easterly direction. When we both arrived, we would be within 15 kilometers of each other and ready, on order, to take the next jump northeast or reunite as the situation dictated.

I looked at my map, and there were no prominent terrain features to orient us, aside from the Wadi al-Batin that ran northeast to southwest tracing the western Kuwaiti border with Iraq. Beyond this one feature there were old and unreliable desert trails that, while appearing to be roads, were largely undiscernible on the ground, except for rudimentary tar ones that were often covered with blowing sand. What really worried me was the network of wadis and washboard terrain that sat between us and our destination. I hoped the sand would be firm enough to handle the weight of our wheeled vehicles and not slow us down, but I couldn't be certain.

I took note of a border police station that appeared as a small black square on my map at an intersection of some trails to the southeast on the Kuwaiti side of the border. I used that police station—about 20 kilometers southwest of where we were—as the point we would initially head toward along what appeared on the map to be a reliable road. Then we would travel another 12 kilometers on that same road, hoping it would be firm enough to handle our heavy vehicles. We would then turn north-northeast and head to our destination. I put the grid location of our future position in my GPS, briefed the convoy leadership, conducted radio checks to ensure our communications were working, and started a long trip that could take many hours. As I put my map away, I thought to myself, "This might be a challenging march." That would turn out to be both prophetic and wildly understated.

The 210th FA Brigade TOC would also accompany us in our convoy. To retain good order and reduce the length of the convoy—particularly our exposure to detection by lingering enemy forces nearby—I consulted with their S-3, MAJ Bill Siegert, who was an accomplished artilleryman, on whether we should march in column or abreast. We elected to travel in two columns side-by-side as the DIVARTY had done a day earlier. The previous day the 210th FA Brigade had had a close call involving ten enemy armored personnel carriers and a T-62 tank that attacked their brigade support area (BSA) containing the logistical elements that supported them. Fortunately, the Iraqi threat was destroyed by a 2ACR security team accompanying the BSA.[9] I could tell that this had really shaken some of them. They were very concerned about our lack of heavy armament to accompany the DIVARTY TOC forward into Kuwait. There was nothing that I could do to fix that, as we had just what we had: thin-skinned vehicles, small arms, hand grenades, a few M72 LAW, as well as 50-caliber machine guns mounted on our heavier trucks and Hymel's M88 armored recovery vehicle. Like it or not, I told them we would have to rely on a swift movement forward to get us where we needed to be, and we should get moving immediately.

By the time we finally left, we were well into the afternoon. I started off by pushing us as fast as we could travel in the hope we could close on our positions before sunset. POWs were still evident as we departed the Objective Norfolk area. CPT Seefeldt, whose D-25 TAB was traveling with us, heard one of them call out, "See you in Baghdad!"[10] But for now, my concern was not getting to Baghdad; it was getting to our next position.

Unfortunately, while the southern route I took looked fine on a map—giving some evidence of a desert road—it soon gave way to a desert surface that was hard sand about one inch deep and, as Hymel would later comment, "nearly fluid for the next six feet."[11] Making our way over this terrain was like driving on a dune-covered beach. The going was slow, and the heavier trucks often sank in the very soft sand, exactly what I feared. Beyond that hazard, our parallel convoy columns with the 210th FA Brigade frequently came dangerously close and nearly entangled as vehicles maneuvered to remain under control in the sandy sealike surface on which we navigated toward Kuwait.

Making our way eastward, we kept watch for enemy activity. At one point, the 210th FA Brigade, which was in the right column of our convoy, spotted a lone Iraqi tank moving to our south and immediately reported it to me on the radio. The enemy tank commander's intentions weren't known, and it wasn't clear that he had observed our convoy and even if he had, that he would even bother with us. It was more than likely that he was just scared and trying to escape the fate he had witnessed with the destruction of the rest of his unit. We stopped briefly while I used my binoculars to take a closer look at the target. I conferred with Siegert to see if there might be any reason to attempt to engage the enemy in the event he would circle back and become a threat to the rear elements of our convoy. We both agreed that our best course of action was to evade him and continue on our way. Even a lone tank can pack a punch against thin-skinned convoys like ours, but in this case, we decided to let sleeping dogs lie.

As we continued moving, the sun set rapidly, and dusk turned to darkness. McGary and I broke out our NODs so that we could see where we were headed. I calculated that if we continued to make progress, even slowly, we could be in our position by 2000 that evening. But the soft sand and our maneuvers to contend with it had caused us to travel farther south than I had intended. I adjusted our route in a more northeasterly track, but that decision put us in even more challenging terrain dominated by large and unstable sand dunes. None of these hazards appeared on the map. Moreover, our NODs, which used the ambient light of heavenly bodies to generate a grainy-green image in the device, were ineffective in helping us navigate; the full moon that evening was obscured by cloud cover. Repeatedly, our convoy columns came perilously close. At one time I could have reached out my door and touched the driver of the 210th FA Brigade Humvee traveling beside us.

Suddenly, everything came to a full stop when I received a radio call from Hymel informing me that several of our trucks had become helplessly sunken in the sand. I stopped and walked back to inspect the problem. In the process of negotiating the sand dunes in the dark of night, the two convoy columns—in a very short span of time and distance—had crisscrossed at the low point where two large sand dunes converged. This intertwined and unplanned entanglement turned the convoy into a Gordian knot. For the next hour, officers and troops alike struggled in the pitch black to restore order and continue our march. While assessing things, I found myself very tired and realized I was casting aside good sense when I was almost crushed to death between two vehicles that were inches apart. Instead of taking a route in front of one of the two vehicles, I tried to slip quickly between the two, and just as I did, one of the vehicles shifted forward and closed the gap on the other. I was seconds from being crushed like an eggshell, a death that would have been completely my fault. As I realized what had happened, I stopped, shook my head, and reminded myself of how fatigue was a killer on the battlefield. That near miss did get my adrenaline moving again, and I worked faster, if not smarter, to get us back on the road.

Once we had the two columns back in order, we continued our movement forward. It was then that Hymel called me from the rear of the convoy to ask why we weren't moving. I replied that we had been traveling for about ten minutes and that he should be underway too. I stopped while Hymel investigated the situation, only to have him report back to me that his section of the convoy had managed to form a circle around the crown of one large sand dune. When it came to an eventual stop, each vehicle was waiting in the dark for the vehicle in front of it to resume movement. As a result, the rear element of our convoy was frozen in circular indecision. The road march we had begun that afternoon was becoming "the road march from hell" as we later called it. I paused for another 30 minutes as Hymel set things straight and rejoined us. Once together, we resumed our march northeastward toward our final position.

It was now nearing 2200 hours when we ran headlong into a large and extended berm of sand that was clearly man-made, and not by anyone from Kansas. I exited my vehicle to investigate, along with Siegert of the 210th FA Brigade, making sure not to make too much noise. We both determined that the berm ran generally east and west, but we were not sure how far the obstacle extended. We were also keenly aware that at some point in time, enemy forces had occupied the other side of the berm, maybe remnants of the 50th Brigade of the Iraqi 12AD. The question in my mind was "Were they there now?" Then Siegert confided to me that his commander, Bourne, thought we should stop at our present location in front of this massive berm and remain there until first light. I found that idea a risky proposition at best as we had no idea what was on the other side of the berm. But Bourne, who outranked me, was insistent. I went over to confer with him. I told him then that I thought the best option was to continue movement to our destination, but that I would check with Dodson, my boss, to get his assessment.

I knew Dodson as well as any XO in the Army could know his commander. We thought alike and sometimes with a unity of purpose that even surprised us. So I was very confident what his guidance would be when I reached him on the radio. I picked up the mic and called him.

"Drumfire 6," Dodson's call sign, "this is Drumfire 5, over."

"This is Drumfire 6, over," Dodson answered.

"Roger, this is Drumfire 5, the brigade commander I'm traveling with feels we should remain here overnight. It's my judgment that we should continue with our mission. What's your guidance, over?"

"This is Drumfire 6, continue with your mission," he said with the predictability of London's Big Ben striking on the hour.

With Dodson's backing, I returned to the 210th FA Brigade commander and shared the brief conversation I had had with my boss and said, "Sir, I'm taking my part of the convoy and moving to the position according to plan. You can continue to accompany us or remain here tonight and see what's on the other side of that berm when the sun rises. But I won't be here to see it with you." I had no interest in waiting to find out if there were remaining elements of the Iraqi 12AD on the other side of the earthen structure. After a brief discussion with his staff, his S-3, Siegert, came to me and said, "We'll be coming with you."

At that point, I made the determination that we would do a sharp left turn, travel westward until we came to the end of the berm, and then race north. As we left, we traveled just a short distance before we arrived at the corner of the berm, and then we turned north, paralleling the western side of the structure until we were in the open desert again. Fortunately, the sand was firmer as we moved north, and we maintained a good clip for the rest of our seemingly endless journey. Finally, we arrived at our position marked on the map as hill 532 about 24 kilometers east of Kuwait's western border with Iraq.

I was glad that we had arrived safely and very grateful that God had watched over us, as well as spared me from being flattened between two heavy vehicles due to my own stupidity. Hymel reported that everyone was accounted for and in position. We then deployed the TOC and informed Dodson we were finally in position. I looked at my watch, and it was almost midnight when McGary and I finally contemplated crawling into the back loft of HQ-5 to get some much-needed rest. I was struck by how long ago it seemed that we had fired the preparation and how far we had traveled: moving through the breach, then across the Iraqi desert into the face of the RGFC; confronting hundreds of POWs; and then enduring what truly was the "road march from hell."

Exhausted after the challenges and mental stress of the previous 18 hours, I visited the TOC to ensure that the folks there were in good order and had established communications with Cardenas and the other half of the TOC 17 kilometers northwest of us. I then checked to see if we had a new location for the next day, where we would link up with Cardenas in the morning. Planning ahead was essential. You never close your eyes to rest before you understand the next mission, particularly in a fast-moving operation. I wanted all of us to be ready to move out smartly in the morning, maybe even before first light.

An immediate concern, however, was fuel. It had been our persistent worry since departing the breach area. Then, we were just low on fuel. Now, we were running on fumes. Virtually every vehicle in my half of the TOC and HHB was nearly empty, with less than an eighth of a tank in most cases, and we had no idea when we would be resupplied. Hymel thought we would have to sit where we were until fuel found us. We conferred and decided—for now—that the only practical option we had was to syphon what little diesel we had in our two 15-kilowatt electric generators that powered the TOC complex and use it in the vehicles. I instructed McGary to take HQ-5 over to the TOC, where we would transfer some of the diesel for our use in the morning. "Sir, I'm not sure I can drive this damn thing 20 feet before we're out of fuel!" he complained, his voice betraying his fatigue. Nonetheless, he coaxed our Humvee to the generator behind the TOC that, for now, was the closest thing we had to a gas station in the desert. There, like a thief in the night, McGary used a rubber hose to syphon about five gallons, bringing us to about a quarter of a tank, when we decided that was enough. At about seven miles to the gallon that our Humvee would get, we had maybe another 35 miles, or 55 kilometers, we could travel. When McGary was done, it was time for both of us to get some rest. As I got in my sleeping bag, my brain was preoccupied with logistics. It was clear that we had defeated this enemy and that the war would soon end. But ending it on an empty tank of fuel was at once inglorious and dangerous. There were still bands of roving Iraqis, and we needed the ability to maneuver. So my first task in the morning would be to locate fuel. I scribbled a diary entry before I fell asleep. The last line summed up the saga that was February 27: "When we arrived, we were all beat, but I was glad we accomplished the mission."

At first light on February 28, I found that the mess hall had managed to brew some coffee on their cooking burners that used gasoline, not the precious diesel fuel we so desperately needed. That was some consolation, considering the challenge we faced with a shortage of diesel fuel for our vehicles. When I stopped by the TOC, MAJ Madden, the operation officer in my element, informed me that at 0400 hours the division had received orders to continue the attack to secure Objective Denver. Dodson, Madden told me, wanted us to move forward at 0600. The 2nd Brigade had already started advancing at 0530 hours. All this activity further inspired me to get on the road to find some fuel, fast. I checked my watch and told Madden and Hymel that I would go forward immediately to link up with fuel trains—somewhere—supporting some of the other forward units.

When McGary and I left at sunrise, we soon found ourselves on a road that ran through a labyrinth of dried-up wadis—streambeds—and rocky outcrops on either side of us. It had the appearance of a canyon scene in a Hollywood western, in which one side traveled unsuspectingly on the road below, while hostiles waited to ambush them from positions above or just around the next bend. That terrain would forever be known to us as "the valley of the boogers," the not-so-affectionate term we used for the remnant of Iraqi soldiers in the area who were armed, scared, and maybe trigger-happy, as they evaded US forces. As McGary maneuvered HQ-5 along a meandering valley floor, we watched keenly for enemy movement in the area. After about 30 minutes, we rounded a corner that spilled out into a large flat canyon. There, to our utter amazement, sat MAJ Jim Boyle, the XO of 4–5 FA, with a 2,500-gallon tanker truck filled with diesel fuel. Exiting my Humvee, I declared, "Jim if you weren't so damn ugly, I'd kiss you!" I called Madden, gave him the map coordinates where he could find us, and then ordered the HHB to meet us there for refuel operations "ASAP."

I was glad to exit "the valley of the boogers." While we knew a cease-fire would soon occur, as the sun rose on the desert that morning, Kuwait remained a very dangerous place, especially for our division commander. Rhame's call sign, "Danger 6," took on a special significance in an incident vividly recalled by his aide-de-camp, CPT Payne. Rhame, his CSM Fred Davenport, and G-3 operations officer LTC Bullington were traveling in their Humvees along with a security detachment of two M-1 tanks. In one of those tanks was MAJ Don Osterberg, the division G-3 plans officer, whom Rhame had directed to travel with him and Bullington in case they needed to put together a hasty plan. While stopped near a destroyed Iraqi T-72 to get a better look at it, suddenly, machine gun bullets began to impact all around them, spitting the sand upward. Rhame immediately ordered everyone to jump in their vehicles to evacuate. But there was no time for that. Bullington yelled for all of them to jump into a nearby Iraqi earthen fortification to escape the hostile fire. After a few seconds, they peeked over the top of the revetment to see what was happening, and there before their eyes, Osterberg was standing atop his tank's turret, arms horizontally extended, palms down, signaling an Apache AH-64 helicopter to come to a hover. Exposing himself to certain danger, Osterberg wasn't conceiving detailed plans, he was executing one to prevent a bad situation from becoming much worse. His infantry instincts were on full display as he climbed out onto the turret, even as his anxious gunner called to him, "Sir, this is kill or be killed, request permission to fire!" Osterberg responded, "Negative!" knowing the aircraft had to be ours, since Iraqi air capability at that point was nonexistent. Observing this from the Iraqi defensive position, Payne was amazed at Osterberg's audacity, which worked. The helicopter, that had flown closer to observe its "target," came to a hover, then sat down, and Osterberg went out to confer with the pilot. Soon the aircraft departed, and Rhame and his team, no worse for the incident, coolly went about their business. To be sure, in the closing hours of this conflict, everyone faced danger amid the "fog of war," even the fellow who went by the call sign "Danger 6."[12]

Meanwhile, my part of the DIVARTY TOC made its way forward, and we promptly refueled, followed by the HHB two hours later. In the process, Cardenas radioed me and gave us a rendezvous grid to meet up north of "the valley of the boogers" along a road that ran northwest to the position we would eventually occupy (see map 10.5).[13] As soon as we were fueled, we proceeded as fast as we could. On the way, Cardenas called and informed me that at 0723 LTG John Yeosock, the Commanding General of ARCENT, had ordered a cessation of hostilities. We ren-

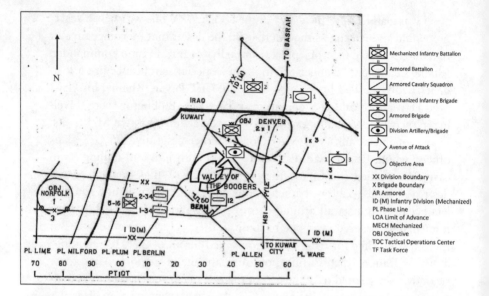

Map 10.5.   1st Infantry DIVARTY Rendezvous in Kuwait, February 28, 1991

dezvoused and reunited atop a knoll that rose above the Kuwaiti desert and revealed the stunning vastness and destruction before us. The sun was up, but in the distance to the east we could see, rising on the horizon, ominous pillars of smoke coming from oil wells that the retreating Iraqis had set aflame. Cardenas pulled up in his HQ-3 by my Humvee and said with a pleasant resignation, "Well, it looks like it's over." I was glad it was, glad to see him, and very glad to learn that we were permitted to remove the uncomfortable chemical defense MOPP gear that we had been wearing since the morning we fired the preparation four days earlier.

When I removed my MOPP suit, first the jacket and then the baggy pants, the temperature seemed to drop 20 degrees in an instant. I broke out one of the cigars my sister's husband, Hank Miller, had sent me weeks earlier with a note to "smoke one for me on victory day." He had acquired them from a tobacconist in Richmond, Virginia, who knew Hank didn't smoke cigars, so he asked him whom he was buying them for? "They're for Gayle's brother fighting in Iraq."

The vendor handed Hank a full box of premium cigars, saying, "Here, these are on the house. Tell him to kick some ass."

Standing on the knoll and observing the destruction before us, we had kept that promise to the fullest. I had no cigar cutter, so I bit the end off of one, lit it up, and let the smoke waft over me like incense in a celebratory liturgical ceremony. Shortly, I was joined by our Assistant S-3, MAJ Conneran, whom I offered to join me with a victory stogie. If nothing else, the aroma of cigar smoke covered my unpleasant body odor after four days in the MOPP outfit that retained every ounce of my sweat.

After conferring with Cardenas, we were given new map coordinates that took us northeast to our final position near Ar Rawdatayn, a site just west of the coastal road that stretched from Basra in the north to Kuwait City farther south (see map 10.6).[14] That stretch of road would be referred to as the "Highway of Death," and deservedly so. As we made our way toward it, we passed more destroyed Iraqi units. Along the route, we encountered the charred remains of Iraqi soldiers who had died while trying to drag themselves away from the deadly fires of their incinerated vehicles. McGary stopped the Humvee at one destroyed vehicle to take it in. "Damn, sir," was the only comment he could muster. While it was a gruesome sight, I was emotionless. Iraq had brought this on itself. Every mile that passed under the wheels of our Humvee revealed how complete the destruction was. By the time we arrived at our final position within sight of the coastal road, the rape of Kuwait by Saddam Hussein was apparent everywhere.

Equally evident was the brutal price that coalition aircraft had exacted on retreating Iraqi vehicles strewn helter-skelter on both sides of the six-lane "Highway of Death." We passed numerous vehicles that held the near-cremated bodies of Iraqi invaders, burned alive as they attempted to escape a fiery agony. The mercy they had denied the Kuwaitis had been repaid with interest by coalition airpower all along that road. Unfortunately for Kuwait, and those of us now encamped near the coastal road, the Iraqis had levied a costly environmental and economic vengeance by setting scores of Kuwaiti oil fields and fuel-storage facilities ablaze east of us. In their demented minds, the Iraqis had decided that if they couldn't have the oil, neither would the tiny oil-rich sheikdom of Kuwait. It was a final slap in the face by cowardly invaders led by a vile tyrant whose megalomania had brought great devastation, not only to Kuwait but to the Iraqi people, including the widows and orphans of dead or dying Iraqi soldiers.

After arriving at our new position bordering the "Highway of Death" and erecting our tents, I was looking forward to sleeping on my cot that night as opposed to the back of my Humvee. But this was an inhospitable place. The low and steady roar of the burning oil fields and the smoke that belched from them filled the sky with inky black clouds heavy with the scent of crude oil. After McGary set up our tent, I walked around our new position to check on the soldiers, all of whom were happy we were

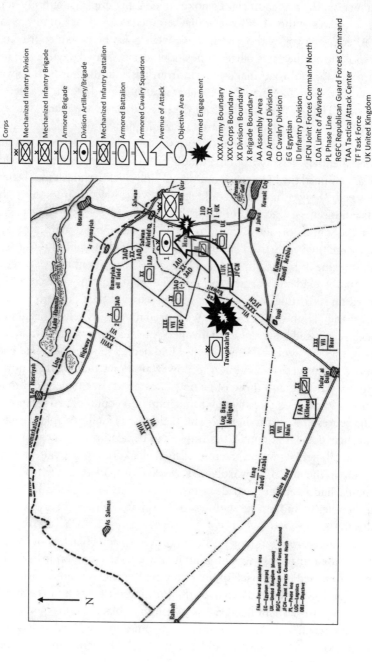

Map 10.6. 1st Infantry DIVARTY Advance from Objective Norfolk to Objective Denver in Kuwait, February 27–28, 1991

settling in for a few days of rest and recovery. There was plenty to do: maintenance on the vehicles, refueling, and even some personal hygiene. Meanwhile, the DIVARTY TOC was busy trying to understand our next move. Dodson spent most of the day at the division headquarters, meeting with Rhame to glean some understanding for what was ahead for us. I was also curious and headed for the DTAC to check in with MAJ Cuff to see if he had any news.

When I arrived at "Danger Forward" a few kilometers north of our new DIVARTY position in Kuwait, BG Carter, ADC-M, was there along with intelligence personnel who were debriefing a captured Iraqi general. Carter was a superb officer with a keen sense of both tactics and history. I went in and greeted him. I also knew he was a cigar lover and took a few with me wrapped in a sheet of paper and handed them to him. "Congratulations, sir. Looks like we did it," I said.

He accepted the cigars and remarked with a chuckle, "I hope no war plans are written on the paper you wrapped these in," referring to the famous Confederate soldier who at the Battle of Antietam lost his cigars that were wrapped with the Confederate battle plan, Special Order 191, detailing Robert E. Lee's unit movements for the Army of Northern Virginia. We both laughed at the idea, and then he introduced me to his captive. The fellow spoke broken English and was very pleasant. But he was also "spilling his guts," as one of our intelligence officers put it, about the location of every Iraqi troop unit in the area and, not surprisingly, demonizing Saddam Hussein, a predictable response by a senior officer looking for sympathy.

After my visit to the DTAC, I learned from Cuff that we would probably have a central role in setting up the peace-talk site north of us just inside Iraq at a 10,000-foot-long airfield the Soviets had constructed, named Safwan. After discussing the size and scope of that mission with Cuff, I headed back to the DIVARTY TOC, and once again, the evidence of destruction along the coastal road was both unmistakable and riveting. It truly was a "Highway of Death." When I arrived at the DIVARTY TOC, I told McGary to take some personal time to clean up and do some maintenance on HQ-5. I then walked the DIVARTY area, made small talk with the troops, and found some water, warmed it, and cleaned up a bit myself. It was great, for once, not to be in such a rush to get somewhere.

As I settled in for the evening to recount the hectic days that had preceded us, stretching back almost two weeks when we had begun firing the artillery raids, everything seemed like a blur to me. Reflecting on this, I thought of Shelley and the kids. I wondered how they would greet the news that the Iraqis were defeated? Did they have a clue if we were even alive, beyond the absence of an Army chaplain knocking at our door at 535A Riley Place? That night, I lay in my cot with the tympanic rumble of distant oil-well fires in the background. McGary and I quietly read or caught up with some personal tasks. He was in his cot, penning a letter home and, like me, hoping mail would come our way in the days to come. I made an entry in my diary that Thursday, February 28, 1991: "We continued our push into Kuwait today. We arrived at the coastal road to learn [that] Saddam will accept peace. Nevertheless, we are planning to continue offensive operations on the 2 remaining Republican Guard Divisions. We saw first-hand the rape of Kuwait. Everywhere you look, destruction fills your eyes. We observe several dead Iraqis, killed by our USAF bombs. I found myself unmoved for them given what had happened to Kuwait. We are located 3–4 kilometers from a burning Kuwaiti gas tank farm. The Iraqis torched this facility, so we are witnessing an enormous inferno tonight. The entire sky is lit up. A constant rumble comes from the fire several Ks [kilometers] from us. I have never seen anything like this. Saddam has been fully spiteful in these acts." War is a spiteful thing. For one, it spites peace. But there is a glory to it, that's for certain. A glory, however, that must be taken in stride. A brilliant military tactician, Lee put the nature of war in a timeless context after the Battle of Fredericksburg, December 11–15, 1862, which, likewise, had lasted a bit over four days. Speaking to James Longstreet as they both surveyed the slaughter of Union forces at Fredericksburg, he observed, "It is well that war is so terrible, or we should grow too fond of it."

Honestly, I felt no fondness for what had transpired, even as I held little pity for the Iraqis themselves after the slaughter they had visited upon Kuwait. But I did nurse a quiet pride in the troops I served with, including the young man who had drifted off to sleep on the other side of our tent. McGary had dutifully and faithfully piloted HQ-5 every inch of the campaign and did all that I asked of him. We, along with the BRO, had engaged in a relentless pursuit of the enemy. The 1ID was credited with destroying in part or in whole enemy formations from the 25th, 26th, 27th, 30th, 31st, and 48th Infantry Divisions, the Tawakalna Mechanized Infantry Division, and the 6th, 10th, 12th, and 52nd Armored Divisions. In the process, the BRO destroyed 558 tanks, 468 armored personnel carriers, 212 artillery pieces, and 268 air defense weapons and captured 11,425 prisoners of war.[15]

The results attributed to the DIVARTY were no less impressive, including 50 tanks, 139 armored personnel carriers, 30 air defense weap-

Table 10.2. Ammunition Expenditures by the 1st Infantry Division Artillery (DIVARTY) and Supporting Artillery, February 1991

	Ammunition Expenditures												
	Raids				Preparation Fires				Breach to Liberation of Kuwait				
Units	HE	DPICM	RAP	Rockets	HE	DPICM	RAP	Rockets	HE	DPICM	RAP	Rockets	Total
DIVARTY													
1-5 FA	1512		288		613	223			1093	1584			5313
4-5 FA	1064	212			672				1962	54			3964
4-3 FA	644		648			416			533	98			2339
B/6 FA				264				6					270
75 FA BDE													
1-17 FA		576	432		288	36							1332
6-18 FA	720	648			240	336							1944
A/6-27 FA				108								66	174
42 FA BDE													
2-29 FA			216		240	192							648
3-20 FA			288		336	192							816
1-27 FA				384				156					540
1 UK ARTY													
2 FD	360				480				548				1388
26 FD	180				634				159				973
32 HV	628				240				422				1290
40 FD	360				662				159				1181
39 FA				384				96					480
142 FA BDE													
1-142 FA	108		108			96							312
2-142 FA	216				216	24							456
1-158 FA				430				156					586
A/40 FA				36									36
210 FA BDE													
3-17 FA									518	573	154		1245
6-41 FA									220	1748	136		2104
C/4-27 FA												474	474
Total	5792	1436	1980	1606	4621	1515	0	414	5614	4057	290	540	27865
Total by Type	HE 16027				DPICM 7008				RAP 2270			Rockets 2560	

ons, 152 artillery systems, 27 missile launchers, 108 mortars, and 548 wheeled vehicles of various types. Additionally, Desert Redlegs destroyed 61 trench lines and bunker positions, 92 infantry targets (both dug-in and in-the-open), and 34 logistical sites.[16] As a measure of that achievement, the 1st Infantry DIVARTY's three 155mm battalions fired fully 25.7 percent (11,752 rounds) of all of the 155mm artillery rounds expended by all 28 of the 155mm battalions deployed across CENTCOM (45,641 rounds). Of that number, a single battalion, our own 1–5 FA, fired 12 percent (5,313 rounds). Our 4–5 FA shot 4,100 projectiles, while 4–3 FA expended 2,339 (see table 10.2).[17] It was a hell of an effort, and a hell of a haul, by a hell of a damn fine division and its DIVARTY.

We had done our job. Now what we all wanted was to go home, back to our families, back to our friends, back to the luxuriant plains of Fort Riley, far from an arid and death-filled desert. But that was not to be, not yet anyway, as we would find out when the sun rose in Kuwait the next morning. There was much work to do. More than I could fathom.

11

An Uncertain Peace

On March 1, just 48 days since we had arrived in Saudi Arabia, I awoke wondering what the day would bring. Once I was dressed, I stepped from our tent and looked eastward into what seemed to be Dante's inferno on the far side of the coastal road, the "Highway of Death." The smoke and fire from sabotaged oil wells to the east of us continued unabated. The atmosphere surrounding us was malodorous from burning oil, and I wondered if we would stay there for long or look for a more hospitable location, where the air was breathable. In a moment of good news, word filtered down that we could stop taking the vile anti–nerve agent PB pills, which were worse, in my mind, than the tuna fish MREs I despised. I went by the mess hall, which was now fully deployed and providing not only hot coffee but hot water for shaving and cleaning. It was a luxury. On top of that, the cooks were about to break into their B Rats, the dehydrated rations they could use to fix powdered eggs and grits, a refreshing break from MREs.

All around us, the Iraqis had abandoned vehicles and equipment as they fled the battlefield. Some of that equipment was put to immediate use by the 12th Chemical, which had latched onto an Iraqi command-and-control van that was probably used to house the Iraqi version of a TOC. It was a wheeled vehicle with an expansive interior that our chemical warriors quickly reconfigured with their decontamination equipment. Using the heaters and shower gear that were part of the decontamination apparatus, they created a shower room inside of the appropriated Iraqi van. It was a "field expedient" solution by enterprising soldiers. After weeks of toiling in the desert, it was greatly appreciated by soldiers covered in grime.

After breakfast, I sat in my Humvee next to our tent and pulled out a cigar, lit it up, and reflected on the last two weeks of combat operations. It had been a remarkable saga. We had fired on Iraqi targets relentlessly during artillery raids and the preparation—the largest by a US field artillery force since World War II—"set the preconditions for a deliberate attack," in the words of a division chronology of events.[1] The same report continued: "These fires were planned based upon detailed all-source intelligence efforts which combined imagery, RPV [Remotely Piloted Vehicles], recon [reconnaissance], and SIGINT [Signal Intelligence]. Massive firepower, precision ground maneuver and breaching battle drills were used to penetrate enemy front line defenses followed by rapid maneuver and massed direct and indirect fires to exploit success."[2] This was a precise and accurate account of a tremendous effort but left me wondering how we had managed to pull it off so quickly and with so few casualties. After I finished the cigar, I walked a short distance from my tent, now covered with a dingy soot from the oil fires, toward the DIVARTY TOC. As I did, I couldn't stop thinking about how much had transpired over the past two weeks. Just in the last 100 hours, the division had attacked over 260 kilometers; passed the British 1(UK)AD through our lines; conducted a long movement to contact across the desert, followed by the forward passage of lines, at night, under enemy contact; and then continued to spearhead the VII Corps's attack into Kuwait to cut off retreating Iraqi forces (see map 11.1).[3] It was a lot to contemplate, even in a short span of time. I again thought about Shelley and the kids and was comforted that, by now, they were aware that the war had ended. No doubt they had read the headlines in the *Wichita Eagle* boldly declaring "VICTORY" and were aware that we had thoroughly defeated the Iraqis.[4] Shelley would be relieved and would happily share the news with the kids that "Daddy will be home soon." Unfortunately, "Daddy" had no clue when he would be home as I strode toward the TOC to see what was ahead of us.

When I went in, I thought to myself, "Good grief, what more is there to do?" But our operations team was already busy trying to get a handle on the follow-on mission that had emerged in the wee hours of March 1. COL Dodson got a call at 0300, alerting us that the 1ID would push north to secure Safwan Airfield in southern Iraq near the northern border of Kuwait and just 35 kilometers from us. By 0615 the division had 1–4 CAV on the move to conduct a zone reconnaissance to secure the airfield. Safwan, with its massive 10,000-foot runway built by the Soviets as an airpower-projection facility, could handle just about any heavy transport the Russians had. But on March 1, 1991, there were no unarmed transport aircraft there. It was occupied by a dug-in Iraqi tank brigade.

This came as a surprise to GEN Schwarzkopf, who thought that Safwan was already secured by the VII Corps, based on a report from the corps's headquarters, a report that turned out to be wrong. When the CENTCOM commander-in-chief (CINC) was told it was in Iraqi hands,

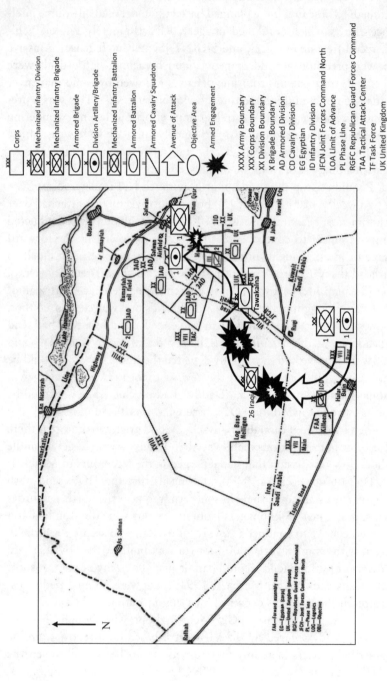

Map 11.1. 1st Infantry DIVARTY Advance from Saudi Arabia to Kuwait

Corps
Mechanized Infantry Division
Mechanized Infantry Brigade
Armored Brigade
Division Artillery/Brigade
Mechanized Infantry Battalion
Armored Battalion
Armored Cavalry Squadron
Avenue of Attack
Objective Area
Armed Engagement

XXXX Army Boundary
XXX Corps Boundary
XX Division Boundary
X Brigade Boundary
AD Armored Division
CD Cavalry Division
EG Egyptian
ID Infantry Division
JFCN Joint Forces Command North
LOA Limit of Advance
PL Phase Line
RGFC Republican Guard Forces Command
TAA Tactical Attack Center
TF Task Force
UK United Kingdom

FAA—Forward assembly area
EG—Egyptian (corps)
UK—United Kingdom (division)
RGFC—Republican Guard Forces Command
JFCN—Joint Forces Command North
PL—Phase line
LOG—Logistics
OBJ—Objective

he was, we were told, "hopping mad." Schwarzkopf later confessed that he became "unglued" when he learned that his orders to the VII Corps commander to seize the road junction east of Safwan had not been accomplished.[5] To be sure, the BRO was in position to do the job, but since the mission hadn't been given to us previously to do so, the airfield remained in Iraqi hands.

The confusion around Safwan's status and who controlled it, as Greg Fontenot noted in his exhaustive history of the BRO in Iraq, was a case in which higher headquarters simply miscommunicated with one another: "This incident occurred because of muddled orders and inaccurate or misunderstood reports."[6] No question that it caused tempers to flare among senior officers, but in the end, according to Schwarzkopf, his intent was clear. "I want Safwan airfield and Safwan Mountain occupied and thoroughly reconned . . . and I want all enemy equipment destroyed," Schwarzkopf demanded.[7] After he reissued his order, the VII Corps immediately turned to the BRO to get the job done. For "Stormin' Norman," his nom de guerre, having the surrender site on Iraqi soil was necessary to make clear to both Saddam and the world that the Iraqis had been completely ejected from Kuwait, that coalition forces were victorious, and that Iraq was vanquished. That made sense to me, particularly since I knew, having watched Saddam Hussein for years in my time at DIA, that the Iraqi dictator would undoubtedly try to discredit the terms of any surrender before the ink was dry on the parchment. Requiring that the surrender take place on Iraqi terra firma would make it more difficult for Saddam to fashion a false narrative to explain his defeat to the world. Saddam could be expected to engage in revisionist history to create an alternative reality within Iraq. He routinely lied to his people. But with a detailed photographic and media record of the proceedings at a prominent airfield on Iraqi territory, the world would know the truth. Nevertheless, the CINC had his reasons for selecting Safwan, and the 1ID now had its orders to seize it. Unfortunately, having dug-in Iraqi tanks there posed a complicating issue.

To support the operation, Dodson dispatched LTC Gingrich's 4–5 FA to provide fire support to COL Tony Moreno's 2nd Brigade. Dodson also sent the 6–41 FA from the 210th FA Brigade to provide reinforcing fire to Gingrich along with a Q-37 counterbattery radar from D-25 TAB in case the Iraqis were crazy enough to return artillery or mortar fire.

Dodson also tasked CPT Nichols's B-6 FA (MLRS) to be ready to fire its deadly rockets at any artillery threat that popped up. If that was not enough, the VII Corps Artillery placed our Arkansas friends of the 142nd FA Brigade in support of the DIVARTY. To be sure, we considerably

Table 11.1. 1st Infantry Division Artillery Organization for Combat
(March 2–5, 1991)

1ID (Mechanized) DIVARTY: Force Artillery Headquarters (HQ)	
1-5 FA (155mm SP)	DS 1st Brigade
4-5 FA (155mm SP)	DS 2nd Brigade
4-3 FA (155mm SP)	DS 3rd Brigade (2nd Armored Division)
B-6 FA (MLRS)	GS
D-25 TAB	GS
210th Field Artillery Brigade: R 1ID (M) DIVARTY	
3-17 FA (155mm SP)	R-4-3 FA
6-41 FA (155mm SP)	R 4-5 FA
C-4-27 FA (MLRS)	GS
E-333 TAB	GS
142nd Field Artillery Brigade: GSR 1ID (M) DIVARTY	
1-142 FA (203mm SP)	GS
2-142 FA (203mm SP)	GS
A-1-158 (-) FA (MLRS)	GS

Key: Direct Support (DS); Reinforcing (R); General Support Reinforcing (GSR); General
Support (GS)

overmatched the enemy with artillery fire support to secure Safwan. There
was no shortage of firepower for Moreno's brigade of tankers and infantrymen who, moving into position south and west of Safwan behind the
1–4 CAV, would certainly force the Iraqis out of their holes around the
airfield.

Moreno's brigade moved northeast toward Safwan at 1015 hours. It
proved to be a rather interesting encounter. When the lead elements of
the 1–4 CAV reached the airfield at about 0715, there was no evidence
that the Iraqis were ready to engage in a fight. In fact, according to the B
Troop commander of the 1–4 CAV, CPT Ken Pope, the Iraqis appeared
"demoralized, starving, and ragged."[8] As our DIVARTY troops had done
for hundreds of POWs that we had captured days earlier, Pope's troops
started handing out MREs, a generosity that angered an Iraqi colonel
who came forward to demand that the Americans leave the airfield.[9]
Pope wasn't about to leave, nor were other troops of the 1–4 CAV, who
were having similar encounters with the Iraqis. The Iraqis refused to
leave also. Something had to give.

As MG Rhame monitored the "negotiations," he was not satisfied.
On top of that, as Dodson would later observe, Rhame was "getting much

help from higher headquarters."[10] That was a polite way of noting that Stormin' Norman and other general officers who outranked Rhame in the chain of command were in "man-to-man coverage," ensuring that this time, Schwarzkopf's concept of operations to secure Safwan for the cease-fire talks would not go awry. Rhame didn't miss either Schwarzkopf's emphasis or his personal interest in getting the job done expeditiously.

Earlier that morning Gingrich had maneuvered his battalion into position to support Moreno's impending assault of the airfield. When Gingrich moved forward and closer to the airfield to personally assess the situation, he managed to become involved in a rather delicate "negotiation" of his own with an Iraqi major, on the perimeter of the airfield, who didn't seem ready to back down. Gingrich was a trained warrior who was blunt and to the point when it came to command. He wasn't a diplomat. Nonetheless, he acted with the cool aplomb of a pinstriped ambassador as he tried to defuse the situation. At one point, before he approached the Iraqis, he even removed his M9 9mm sidearm, openly handing it to his driver as a signal to the Iraqi major and his troops that he had no hostile intent since technically we were in a ceasefire. Eventually, after an extended conversation, Gingrich, on instructions from Moreno—whom he had been updating—told his Iraqi interloper, "I regret to inform you that if you do not leave by 1600 hours, I will be forced to kill your soldiers."[11] While the Iraqi major was disinclined to fight, and said as much to Gingrich, soon the major was joined by higher-ranking Iraqis who were far more intransigent and assertive.[12]

For Rhame, the process wasn't moving fast enough, and he ordered Moreno to advance his brigade forward to finish the job. Moreno maneuvered onto the airfield and took charge. After Moreno exchanged concise views with a couple of Iraqi colonels, who had now shown up on the site and were hastily exchanging messages with their superiors, Rhame finally told Moreno, "Tell the Iraqis to move or die."[13]

Moreno then unceremoniously cut the Iraqis short as they were reading from an officious statement and said pointedly to them, "If you don't leave by 1600 hours, we will kill you."[14] The Iraqis then asked for permission to leave some of their equipment in the area to also "secure" the site. Gingrich recorded Moreno's terse response to that Iraqi "face-saving" idea: "Colonel Moreno snapped back, 'Absolutely not!' He abruptly grasped a map and drew his finger across it to indicate to the colonels that they had to clear everything outside of that area. Colonel Moreno said, 'Anything in this area tomorrow, and we will kill it. The sun will not rise on your equipment being here.'"[15] In short order the Iraqis departed, pious statement in hand, and Moreno's 2nd Brigade occupied the airfield and began preparations to set up the surrender site. Not a shot was fired, but ultimately a combination of sheer determination by BRO leaders and overwhelming combat power were all the persuasion the Iraqis ultimately needed to convince them to withdraw. Gingrich, who witnessed this entire incident from beginning to end, appropriately observed that it was "a strange battle" indeed.[16] But Schwarzkopf was satisfied. Rhame was happy that he was. So was LTG Yeosock, the commanding general of ARCENT.

Shortly after Safwan was secured by the BRO, Yeosock flew north in his helicopter and met Rhame on the tarmac at the Kuwait City airport. Yeosock had absorbed the brunt of Schwarzkopf's disapprobation concerning the Safwan affair and was glad to see Rhame, who had set things straight. Rhame's aide-de-camp, CPT Payne, took note of the reunion of the two old friends: "Yeosock and Rhame met behind the helicopters. As Rhame approached Yeosock, a huge smile came across Yeosock's face. . . . he gave Rhame a huge bear hug and lifted him off the ground. Yeosock, with a huge grin, set Rhame down, and said, 'We did it Tommy, we did it!'"[17] The young Payne was amused by this expression of emotion from two straight-laced general officers. No doubt both were happy Safwan was resolved. But I suspect—as Payne did in witnessing this moment of ebullient expression—that both were very proud of the post-Vietnam Army that they had helped rebuild that had just thoroughly vanquished Iraqi forces.

Schwarzkopf had more for Rhame to do. He wanted the ceasefire site to be set up in a fashion that would create the right atmosphere for the defeated Iraqis, who would surely show up with a chip on their shoulder. According to Schwarzkopf, his guidance was both precise and specific to the 1ID: "I'd like to make sure they come in the proper frame of mind. Therefore, I want you to position a great deal of combat equipment along the airfield access road. Don't just park it—put it in fighting positions—but make sure it is clearly visible. I want the Iraqis to see fresh, undamaged, first-rate U.S. tanks and armored personnel carriers all over the place."[18] Rhame understood Schwarzkopf's concept—as it was related to him through the chain of command—and was eager to demonstrate the BRO's combat muscle to the Iraqis when they arrived at Safwan. In his autobiography after the war, Schwarzkopf wrote that he was sure Rhame understood what was required, noting, "I could almost hear him grinning over the phone."[19] However, Rhame later insisted "that conversation never occurred." Nevertheless, as Fontenot related in his history of the war, Rhame did get "plenty of guidance and understood the intent," but—in this case—not directly from Schwarzkopf.[20]

In short order, Rhame swung into action and handed the ball to BG Carter, his ADC-M, to supervise the security arrangements at Safwan. Schwarzkopf wanted the 1ID to meet the Iraqi delegation at a road junction six kilometers east of the airfield where the highways from Kuwait City to the south, Basra to the north, and Umm Qasr to the east intersected, the latter two inside Iraqi territory. From there, Carter would have the Iraqis escorted to the ceasefire talks through an impressive gauntlet of combat power composed of tanks and other armored vehicles, just in case the Iraqis were nursing any ideas that they had fared better in the conflict than they really did.

The next day, March 2, Schwarzkopf dispatched LTG Gus Pagonis, his top logistics officer, to Safwan with instructions to set up the site where the talks would take place. No detail was spared, down to the table where Schwarzkopf and the Iraqis would sit opposite one another. Carter directed the DTAC to redeploy to Safwan to coordinate the setup and keep Rhame apprised of the security operations to protect the site that the division would oversee.

While the collective attention of the division's leadership was focused on Safwan, I spent that day visiting DIVARTY battalions, assessing their actions to locate equipment that had either fallen out of unit formations while racing across the desert or simply gotten lost in the confusion. Both 1–5 FA and 4–5 FA were working hard to repair and recover their equipment. But 4–5 FA's mission to support the Safwan operation had interrupted any recovery operations. B-6 FA, our MLRS battery, was in good order and ready to return fire if the Iraqis were crazy enough to attack the site during the negotiations, while D-25 TAB's radars were up and running to detect hostile fire. The HHB, not involved with the Safwan operation directly, used the time to recover from our exhaustive road march.

On my way back from B-6 FA's positions south of Safwan, I came across a deserted D-30 122mm howitzer that the Iraqis had left behind in their hasty retreat. There I found the DIVARTY TOC's resourceful SSG Healey busy hooking it to an M35A2 2 ½-ton supply truck from HHB to tow the howitzer back to our position as a war trophy. It seemed entirely appropriate that an artillery outfit like ours take an enemy howitzer as a prize for our work. We had destroyed a number of them, and having one to show folks back home would be justified.

When March 3 arrived, it would prove to be both a memorable and historic day. I rose early, grabbed some chow, and went by the DIVARTY

TOC to check the current situation. The place was abuzz, monitoring the show of force we had assembled to support the ceasefire talks at Safwan. I verified the location of the airfield and told MAJ Cardenas that I was headed there to observe the activities. PFC McGary had HQ-5 in good shape. After several weeks of riding the old Humvee hard, he had spent recent days going over it with a fine-tooth comb. Checking the fluid levels, hitting all the lubrication points with a fresh load of grease, and making sure the communications equipment was in top-notch condition, McGary didn't miss a single detail. He was as proud of that vehicle as I was of him. "You ready to go see some history made?" I asked him.

"You bet, sir, let's do it!" he said as he jumped into the driver's seat like a teenager on his first date.

As we headed northward to Safwan along the now-silent "Highway of Death," I couldn't get over the amount of carnage and destruction that we had brought down on the Iraqi Army and wondered who was left to negotiate anything with us. Passing to the west side of Ar Rawdatayn, a rural community of small farms and related agricultural activities, we continued north to the border. As we drove through the once-again-manned Kuwaiti police station on the southern side of the border with Iraq, we entered the Iraqi town of Safwan, which like its neighbor to the south, Ar Rawdatayn, was a farming village. Making our way to the airfield, we turned northwest on a poorly maintained highway. Along the route, we were greeted by young Iraqi boys seeking food. They were poorly clad, dirty, and aggressive. We had been forewarned about them. "Don't stop to talk to them," we were told by others who had passed that way. "What they want is food, so toss them an MRE, because if you stop, they will try to enter your vehicle and take anything they can get their hands on," as one of our noncommissioned officers sternly warned before we left the DIVARTY TOC. True enough, the young scavengers raced toward us as HQ-5 slowed to make a turn. McGary was prepared. He had several MREs piled beside him. With the alacrity of a newspaper boy on a paper route, in one steady motion he reached to his prepositioned stack and tossed one into the waiting hands of a grateful Iraqi kid. Then in rapid-fire sequence he tossed out several more to others eager for a meal. Throughout the process, he didn't miss a beat, then stepped hard on the accelerator, and we rumbled off toward Safwan airfield in a cloud of dust. I didn't ask him what kind of MRE he was pitching—there were twelve choices you could get—but I wouldn't have been surprised if they were the tuna fish ones.

When we approached Safwan, I took notice of 4–5 FA's howitzers deployed to the southwest of the airfield and in firing positions. As we weaved through the US checkpoints that guarded the southeast entrance of the airfield, I noticed a Patriot missile battery deployed and ready to fire if there were any SCUD attacks, an unlikely event. On the airfield proper, deployed on the small hills surrounding the airstrip were M1 Abrams tanks and M2 Bradley IFVs with the main gun tubes pointed inward in an ominous manner that would surely impress anyone traveling down this corridor of firepower. As I approached the northwestern end of the runway, it was clear that a lot of work had been accomplished there in the short time since Moreno and the 1–4 CAV had enticed the Iraqi tank brigade to leave the premises two days earlier. I dismounted my Humvee and found MAJ Cuff, who had deployed to Safwan with "Danger Forward" to assist with coordination activities.

"Well, XO, what do you think of this?" Cuff said with a broad grin. He knew how disgusted we all were with the paltry logistics support we had grown accustomed to in recent weeks.

"Disgusting," I muttered. The setup had everything: food, water, tents, communications, you name it, it was there. It was as if the place, with all its bounty, had sprung from the ground like an artesian well conjured up by a desert jinn. It was an impressive, if not a somewhat opulent, arrangement (see figure 11.1).[21] Clearly, having Schwarzkopf's logistical pied piper, Pagonis, on site was the key to success. I wondered sarcastically to myself if I could convince the general to travel back to the DIVARTY and hang out with us for a few days after the ceasefire talks. Maybe I could get some spare parts for our equipment.

My cynicism was quickly replaced by attention to all the activity that swirled about the site. At the center of this incredible arrangement was a large general-purpose tent, 18 feet wide, 52 feet long, and 12 feet high, that had been outfitted with tables and chairs to accommodate the negotiations. To the right and left of this main structure was a series of smaller tents that housed operations personnel, communications, security teams to search attendees participating in the talks, and a VIP tent. A large complement of officers from the BRO was there along with other observers from CENTCOM and VII Corps to get a peek at this history-making event. As Cuff and I were bantering back and forth, our attention was diverted by an inbound UH-60 Blackhawk helicopter that was landing nearby. Carter made his way in the direction of the aircraft that was bearing none other than the four-star general who had selected me to be his aide-de-camp three years earlier, only to find myself stranded at the AFSC and leaving Schwarzkopf to select another candidate.

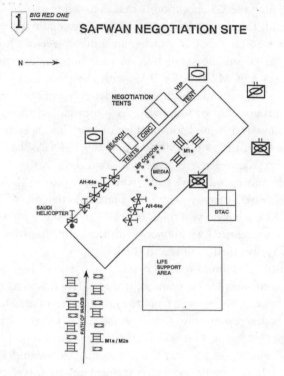

Figure 11.1.   Safwan Negotiation Site, March 3, 1991

As Schwarzkopf emerged from the helicopter to be shown about by Carter, his 6-foot-3-inch frame towered above the crowd, leaving me to imagine what it would have been like to be at his side throughout this remarkable operation. Wearing his camouflaged soft-billed cap, unlike the rest of us with our Kevlar helmets, Stormin' Norman struck an impressive figure. As 1100 hours approached, the time we had been told the talks were to begin, a large, regal, white helicopter bearing the golden crown of the Saudi Royal family landed and taxied down the airstrip. Soon Prince Khalid bin Sultan al-Saud, Schwarzkopf's senior military partner, exited the aircraft and joined the general as they prepared to receive the Iraqi representatives.

The arrival of the Iraqis had been personally planned by Schwarzkopf. Carter had arranged to meet the Iraqis at a transfer point, a road junction southeast of Safwan, and transfer the Iraqis into Humvees driven by 1ID soldiers. They would then enter the area from the southeastern end of the runway and drive down the center of the runway, flanked by the impressive array of BRO combat power Carter had assembled. On either side of the Humvees that carried the Iraqis were two M1 Abrams tanks and two M2 Bradley IFVs that served as escorts. Additionally, two imposing Apache AH-64 attack helicopters hovered directly above the Humvees. Together with the armored escort, they provided a thunderous cacophony that could not be ignored. As soon as the convoy transporting the Iraqis stopped, LTG Sultan Hashim Ahmad, the deputy chief-of-staff of the Iraqi Ministry of Defense, and LTG Salah Abud Mahmud, the commander of what by then was the defeated III Iraqi Corps, emerged and almost immediately disappeared with Schwarzkopf and Khalid inside the large meeting tent Pagonis had plopped down in the middle of the desert airfield.

It was impressive, and I found myself milling around outside the tent with Cuff while wishing I could be a fly on its wall. As a Middle East foreign area officer (FAO) in previous assignments, I was fascinated by what must be transpiring inside. Soon Cuff and I were joined by the BRO's Division Operations Officer, LTC Bullington, and we mused about all that had happened to that point. Bullington was instrumental in designing the follow-on mission after the breach operation that sent us hurtling toward the Tawakalnas days earlier, and I knew he was glad to have a moment to relax. To our surprise, our group was soon joined by none other than NBC correspondent Tom Brokaw, who immediately engaged us in some edgy small talk.

Outfitted in lightly colored tennis shoes, khaki pants, and the ubiquitous tan pocketed vest made famous by foreign correspondents, Brokaw said, "Wow, you guys really pulled this one off impressively. No one ever thought it would go as smoothly as it did." I looked at Cuff who smirked at the comment as if to say, "What a smart ass." It was so typical of the media. Arrogant too. Here we were, the most awesome combat force in the world, fully trained to battle and defeat the Soviet Union on the plains of central Europe, equipped with the deadliest combat systems on the planet, manned by the most capable soldiers I had ever served with, and facing an Iraqi Army that was nowhere near as capable as we were; and this condescending media luminary professes that no one thought we could get the work done as rapidly and decisively as we did? His suggestion unambiguously illustrated a post-Vietnam sense of low expectations for the military that the media had nursed for decades. Operation Desert Storm dispelled this ridiculous notion completely, but that didn't stop Brokaw from revealing an antimilitary news-media bias that was prevalent at the time. It pissed me off. Seeking to "set the record straight," as the saying goes, I told him that I had been a DIA analyst who had watched these same Iraqis fight the Iranians, and anyone with any knowledge of the region would have had to know that in the end we would win decisively. So much for an informed press. To be sure, we had not suffered the casualties some—including myself—feared were possible. But our performance and victory were never in doubt. The discussion then trailed away with Brokaw's characterization of the extracurricular and lurid social activities of correspondents now occupying the recently liberated Kuwait City, as if those salacious tidbits were important to us. They weren't. Cuff and I lost interest in the conversation at that point, and thankfully Brokaw, who shared his opinion with us that the coverage of the war was poor because it took so long to get stories out, went on to other things and drifted away to gather more "news."

We maintained our vigil outside the negotiation tent, and about an hour into the process, Schwarzkopf emerged at what appeared to be a break in the action. Rhame also stepped outside, where he was greeted by his aide-de-camp Payne with a cold bottle of water. Payne asked how things were going, and Rhame mentioned that it was tense. Apparently, the Iraqis couldn't account for one of our POWs they were holding. Schwarzkopf wasn't about to proceed until the whereabouts of our serviceman was known. But a few minutes later, things seemed to be resolved to his satisfaction when he reentered the negotiation.[22]

Then, a little more than an hour and a half after the talks began, the Iraqis emerged. Having been disabused of their invincibility, they were whisked away to report to Saddam, no doubt worried for their own necks, I suppose. *The New York Times* chronicled the 90-minute tête-à-tête this way: "Within two hours, the obviously humbled Iraqi delegation had accepted all the demands that were presented for a permanent cease-fire in the Persian Gulf war. In effect, the Iraqis had surrendered and the coalition's victory over the Government of President Saddam Hussein appeared complete."[23] After the talks concluded, Schwarzkopf and Khalid held a brief press conference as the division colors of the BRO fluttered gently in the breeze behind them. Schwarzkopf declared in a steady tone that we were "well on our way to a lasting peace."

Khalid was equally sanguine, remarking, "Honestly, I think it's every Arab's dream to have unity, prosperity, and peace."[24]

Their comments, while appropriate, I thought were overly optimistic. As I headed back to the DIVARTY TOC, I wondered if Saddam would really accept the terms that had been presented to the Iraqi delegation. I was hopeful he would, but I also knew how deceitful he was, and I had my doubts, thinking that unless Saddam was removed from power once and for all, it was unlikely Iraq could be trusted to keep any agreement.

McGary and I ran the gauntlet of Iraqi kids once again before crossing the border back into Kuwait and south along the "Highway of Death." When I arrived back at the DIVARTY TOC, I reported in and related my experience. The TOC team seemed a bit disinterested in my report of the significant activities of the day, and I further sensed that many of them were in a bit of a postbattle letdown. There wasn't much I could do about that except to make clear to all of them that we were there to soldier on, however long we would remain in the desert. Exhausted, I retired to my tent, where I settled down that evening and read some mail from Shelley and the kids postmarked February 4. In it were handmade Valentine cards from the kids. Amy made a point to include "XOs" in hers, a cute double entendre for hugs and kisses for the "DIVARTY XO." Paul, our youngest, who directed Shelley sign the card "Paulie," made his best effort to make a heart with glitter that filled the envelope and now covered my desert uniform. John had Shelley draw a picture—supposedly of me—in front of my tent with these instructions about his card dictated by him verbatim: "Dear Daddy, Have a nice day. Do not open until you are awake and don't send it to the bad guys because he will tear it up." Mail like this puts a lot of things in focus. That's why it's so important to the morale of soldiers. As I tucked these keepsakes in my rucksack, I longed for the day when I would hold these precious ones in my arms again. Later, before I fell asleep, I tried to capture the full scope of the day. It was an historic one, and I made some detailed notes. But despite all the energy of the day, my diary would end with a somewhat sour entry as we waited for what was next: "The negotiations, as they were, lasted 90 minutes with the Iraqis accepting all of our ultimatums. The Iraqis then left escorted in the same manner in which they arrived, a defeated Army of a defeated dictator. The D/A [DIVARTY] TOC is in a bit of a post action depression. After all of the action, now nothing but to sit and wait for instructions. Mail is flowing at long last. Support, however, is still awful. I've made some hard calls on awards. Folks aren't very happy. Tough, but it falls on me."

When the morning of March 4 arrived, I arose upbeat. I looked forward to a day when we could catch up on paperwork, record some details of our operation, and make some tough decisions on service awards for our soldiers. Sometimes that last matter can be emotional, but Dodson put this in my lap to do, and I did it as best I could. Meanwhile, Dodson was told that we needed to retrace our route back to Saudi Arabia to ensure we picked up all unspent artillery ammunition and abandoned equipment we had left in the wake of our operation. Locating that ammunition, so it could be collected and put back into the logistics system, was no small feat. We had stockpiled tons of the stuff, MLRS rockets and cannon projectiles alike, in anticipation of a two-hour preparation that would precede the breach nine days earlier. Since we had fired an abbreviated preparation, there were lots of projectiles and rockets to recover, and leaving them behind to the Iraqis or anyone else was not an option.

I coordinated with MAJ Brooks, our S-4, to take a helicopter and fly the route we had used to verify the location of our AHAs, so we could develop a recovery plan. We were lucky to get an aircraft for him as they were hard to come by. The desert sand had taken a toll on helicopter blades and the engine turbines that powered the aircraft, and many of our aviation brigade's assets were down for maintenance. But without air reconnaissance, Brooks could not have completed this task effectively and efficiently. As he took off, I watched and hoped he would succeed. No one wanted to wander around the desert looking for all this stuff, a job that could take weeks. Brooks returned later that evening with the news that he had not only found all the ammunition dumps but had also located an abandoned enemy artillery battery that we could attempt to recover on our way back to Saudi Arabia. While the Iraqi artillery battery find was intriguing, I was more pleased that we had our hands around the ammunition-recovery challenge.

We awoke to rain the next morning, March 5, with smoke from oil fires drifting over us. It was foul, and the sky looked as black as the Kansas horizon before a tornado. As it turned out, the Iraqis had blown up 535 Kuwaiti oil wells.[25] These oil fires were taking a toll on morale as we breathed the noxious air they produced. This reinforced my judgment that it would be good to get on the move again, anywhere other than where we were. The pernicious smoke combined with the lousy weather was so bad that Dodson canceled a helicopter we had scheduled to get him around to visit the subordinate units. To be sure, we were all looking forward to getting away from this miasmic environment, and a tactical move would be a refreshing alternative to sitting around waiting for the next mission. To that end, we were getting hints we would soon move south to KKMC, a large facility in Saudi Arabia southeast of the redeployment assembly area (RAA) we would occupy. The RAA would be close to the town of Hafar al-Batin, south of the now infamous Tapline Road that had claimed many in accidental vehicular deaths, including

PFC Kirk from D-25 TAB, our first casualty of this war. That sad memory notwithstanding, we would be happy to move there soon. A bright prospect emerged later in the morning when we learned that elements of the DIVARTY would be sent home to plan the division's homecoming celebration. CPT Hymel had the novel idea to use HHB soldiers we would send in the advance party to carry notes, messages, and the like to families who were all waiting anxiously for our return. It was a good idea and helped many of us think fondly of that eventuality.

Meanwhile, we faced persistent logistics challenges. It was like a severe cold that you just couldn't shake. Our issues ran the gamut from vehicle repair parts, to water supply, to radio repair support. It was now more than just an annoyance. If Dodson ordered us to get ready to move on short notice, I was concerned that we would have to tow as many vehicles as we were driving. Things had deteriorated so badly that Hymel had to "cannibalize" vehicles in the HHB, the term we used to describe removing a working part from one inoperative vehicle and putting that part into another vehicle to get it up and running. Unfortunately, once a vehicle was cannibalized for one part, like a helpless carcass in the wild, it was soon stripped of yet another part. In time, such a vehicle would become a shadow of its former self, making eventual repair of the devoured vehicle a long-term project, particularly when parts weren't flowing, and they weren't. I had worn myself emotionally thin in complaining to our support personnel in the DISCOM. And they were equally fed up with hearing from me and others too. After a while we all just grew numb to the frustration. Unfortunately for me, Dodson expected that I stay engaged like a "gnat in the ear" of the logistical system, even if they brushed me off as one would shoo away a sand fly. I did, as unproductive as it was, and despite having worn out my welcome with just about every logistician in the division.

Another tough day behind me, I concluded it on a high note. One of my favorite soldiers, Specialist Fourth Class (SP4) Donna A. Jefferies, was to be promoted that evening. The orders elevating her to sergeant (SGT) had come down, and she wanted me to do the honor. I was happy to be asked. Jefferies had worked for me as my administrative specialist when I was the DIVARTY's S-3. She was one of 17 female soldiers assigned to administrative and support functions in the HHB, whose assigned strength was 235 soldiers. These female soldiers—including two officers, four noncommissioned officers, and 11 enlisted—had been with us the whole way, throughout our march into the desert, our movement forward to positions where we would conduct artillery raids, our fierce artillery preparation, our breach of the Iraqi 26ID, our exploitation through the desert to slam into the Tawakalnas, our capture of hundreds of Iraqi POWs, our passage through the "valley of the boogers," and our liberation of Kuwait up to the "Highway of Death." I was proud of her and the other female soldiers. But initially, some of them may not have been as eager for this adventure as they turned out to be.

When Jefferies decided she wanted me to promote her, she had SGM Vann, who had been with me when I was the DIVARTY S-3, approach me to see if I would do the honors. Vann encountered me outside of the DIVARTY TOC earlier in the day and said, "Hey, sir, Jefferies is getting promoted this evening, and she would like you to promote her."

"Sounds good to me," I responded, "She was a real warrior with us, wasn't she?"

Vann chuckled and said, "Well, I got to tell you a story," he said, as if hiding a dark secret he had yet to share. Vann and I were close. He had been my right arm in the S-3 shop. This African-American sergeant major was a soldier's soldier. He had risen through the ranks from his Southern upbringing and knew how to make things operate by the book. He also could smell bullshit 5,000 meters away. Likewise, he knew how to deal with soldiers, male or female. If you stepped out of line, Vann had a way of getting you back in order without much delay in your step. So when he shared the "rest of the story," as the famous reporter and commentator Paul Harvey used to say, I was taken aback.

"Sir, did you know that a few of these gals thought you weren't going to take them through the breach?" Vann said with a hint of laughter.

I was shocked. "You gotta be kidding me," I said in stunned amazement. The thought had never crossed my mind. Not for a second.

"Yep, some of them were rumoring among themselves—they didn't know I overheard them—that you wouldn't take them through the breach but have some of the male soldiers remain behind with them and pick all of them up after we came back through!" Vann said.

"How did they arrive at that idea?" I asked disbelievingly.

Vann then told me that the women knew I was a straightlaced officer, Old Army, as they say, and that they "just knew" I would leave them behind to keep them safe. And moreover, they were fine if I did! When I stood there shaking my head in utter disbelief and holding back my laughter, Vann punctuated my reaction with "Yep, I laughed too," as he then bent over backward in a barrel-chested guffaw. I joined him in the levity, but honestly, I had no intention of leaving anyone behind, much less these female soldiers.

I then asked, "How did they respond when we loaded up to go through the breach?"

Vann looked at me through the tears of his laughter, grabbed my shoulder, and said, "Sir, like me, their eyes were as big as silver dollars!" making an oval by joining his index finger and thumb. The two of us then erupted in a duet of hysterical belly laughing, because we both knew that anyone—male or female—with an honest bone in their body was scared to be heading into mined enemy territory, even when we were facing a worn-down Iraqi force we had punished with deadly cannon and rocket fire for over a week.

Nevertheless, these warrior women had taken the same oath Vann and I had, to "defend the Constitution of the United States against all enemies, foreign and domestic." It was their sworn duty. And they hadn't disappointed me or anyone else in doing that, not for a single second. They were superb. That evening, when Vann read the promotion orders as many in the HHB stood at attention in the solemn and traditional ceremony, I recalled how these women had joined with their male counterparts in capturing POWs in the recent weeks, and how they were exposed to the same threats and dangers we all were. The thought made me swell with pride for, now, SGT Jefferies and the other women who had gathered for her special moment. My Army had changed since 1973 when I took my own oath on the plateau where the all-male VMI had stood since November 11, 1839. And as I pinned the sergeant strips on Jefferies's DCU collars, I couldn't have been prouder of a young woman serving in the BRO. She was every bit the soldier any of us were, and that evening she earned her place among NCOs in the same division that had a heroic reputation built by those who had gone before us. Now she was part of that. It was a special moment for me, as I knew it was for Jefferies, Vann, and the others in attendance that evening. We were brothers and sisters in arms and damn proud of it.

By March 6, the division was busy destroying enemy equipment that was left behind or tagging it for return to the US as war trophies or for training purposes for future conflicts. Many units, including the DIVARTY, were also busy repatriating Kuwaiti civilians who were headed south on the "Highway of Death." I recall making a visit with MAJ John Smith, our S-5 (civil affairs officer), who was working to acquire food and water for Kuwaiti refugees held in Iraq who were moving southward through our area of operations. As McGary and I pulled off the "Highway of Death," which had been cleared of many destroyed Iraqi vehicles to open the way for normal traffic, we were greeted by Smith. He took me over to a group of Kuwaiti women and children, where a translator shared some of their horrific experiences. One lady had her arm in a sling. The children were eerily quiet, mostly out of exhaustion, hunger, and thirst. All were headed home to an uncertain future, made more so because many of the women had no idea where their husbands were, the fathers of their children. One of the women related how her husband had had his arm severed by the Iraqi thugs who had invaded their country. She wept. I held my own tears back even as I thought about my wife, Shelley, and my own kids. These refugees were all exhausted, but we tried as best we could to supply them with food and water as they headed home, whatever was left of it. It was desperately hard not to feel their pain and suffering. I felt my anger rise and thought what justice it would be if Saddam were summarily executed by the people he had tormented. But that would be no justice at all, and I quickly chased the thought from my head. It's what Saddam would do, but we would need to rise above that sort of behavior if we were to restore true peace to the region.

Indeed, Saddam's inhumanity toward people in general stood in sharp contrast to the humanity Americans showed in the war, particularly in our treatment of Iraqi POWs. The handling of Iraqi prisoners by CPT Visser's 12th Chemical was instructive. His 3rd Platoon leader, 1LT Byler, had hauled, secured, and fed approximately 90 Iraqi POWs for two days following the breach until finally dropping them off at the VII Corps POW holding area near Safwan. In that group was an Iraqi captain who, before the war, had attended Wisconsin Parkside University. In the course of transporting these POWs, this officer expressed the concern of some of his men who thought they would be executed. Byler recalled that the officer "feared that we were hauling them off to kill them." Consequently, the Iraqis—who had relatives in the unit, such as brothers and cousins—wanted to ride in the same vehicles where their family members were seated, so that if they were to be shot to death, they would at least die together. Byler assured them no harm would come to them, but modified the seating arrangements in the transport trucks to accommodate their concerns until they were handed over to the POW camp authorities.[26] Saddam had not only horribly traumatized the Kuwaiti people by invading them, but he had induced in his own people an expectation of violence that would lead them to believe the US Army would summarily execute them on the battlefield. Fortunately for this Iraqi officer and his frightened men, they were prisoners of 1LT Bradley R. Byler, US Army, 1st Infantry Division, not the "Butcher of Baghdad."

What Saddam Hussein had wrought on Kuwaitis and Iraqis alike was disgusting to me, but not surprising. It would take much work to address the trauma that Saddam had visited on the Kuwaitis as well as his own population. I was glad that a robust Arab coalition had joined the US and Western allies to liberate Kuwait. They would be essential if we were to restore peace to this war-torn corner of the world. But in war—and the politics associated with it—there are always contradictions. Only days earlier, our B-6 FA had captured four Jordanian arms dealers and five Iraqi soldiers who were hiding in a bunker near a position the MLRS battery had occupied. These Arab traders had in their possession brand-new weapons and a briefcase chock-full of Iraqi and Kuwaiti money. B-6 FA handed them over to our MPs.[27]

This incident highlighted for me the profound challenge we would face in realizing the dream of Arab "unity, prosperity, and peace" that Prince Khalid Bin Sultan al-Saud had declared only three days earlier. To be sure, the coalition President Bush had assembled was remarkable. But Arab unity was not a certain outcome either during the war or after it. Had Israel gotten in, the coalition would have disintegrated. Had Jordan sent forces, which it didn't, the Palestinian population in that country—who were sympathetic to Iraq—might have revolted. Jordan had been a close ally of the US for years. Its leader, King Hussein bin Talal, was a major partner in the peace process. But even he was unable to stop his own citizens from helping the Iraqis with illicit arms. It made me ponder how the delicate ceasefire we had just arranged would hold up in the days and weeks to come. Would there be enough "stick-to-itiveness" by the Arabs to put Saddam Hussein in his place once and for all? I had my doubts and wondered if anything short of going to Baghdad to take him out forcefully would be enough to complete our work. Hope for Arab "unity, prosperity, and peace" seemed to me a fleeting notion at best and unattainable at worst.

In any case, there were some emerging indications that things might be winding down, notwithstanding my concern about Saddam's final status. Units that were supporting us were receiving redeployment orders. The 210th FA Brigade, which had reinforced us in the attack on Objective Norfolk, had been ordered to return to the 2ACR, and A Battery 1–158 FA (MLRS) was also being sent back to the 1CD. These pending redeployments added to our own expectations that this war was finally over and that soon we would all be headed for Saudi Arabia to pack up and leave for the US. When I returned to the DIVARTY TOC later in the day, I learned that several of the DIVARTY soldiers who had deployed to the region in December would be headed back to Fort Riley, loaded with the letters and messages from those who were, for now, remaining behind.

It was bittersweet. We were delighted that some were headed home, but for the rest of us, there was much work to do.

Our immediate task was getting sufficient trucking to transport the large amount of cannon and rocket ammunition we had with us, including the stockpiles Brooks had located during his air reconnaissance. Dodson had warned the division that this was going to be a challenge, and everyone seemed now to be aware of it. Then there was the issue of launching our reconnaissance party to scout out and set up positions in Saudi Arabia where we would happily head once we got the order. And, of course, what war would be complete without at least one unbelievable incident?

The 4–5 FA had a soldier who, during the attack, decided that he had had enough and deserted his position, winding up in a POW camp with thousands of Iraqis. While he was being held at a facility in KKMC, we still had a responsibility to take custody of him. I recorded the challenge in my diary that evening. Not surprisingly, even getting air support for a critical mission like this was difficult: "Had the devil of a time getting an aircraft to fly 4–5 FA personnel to KKMC to ferry a deserter they had to a confinement center. The SOB deserted, wound up in an allied POW camp with the Iraqis!"

As my day ended, I learned that I would lead an air-reconnaissance mission to RAA Huebner in Saudi Arabia, named after the main road at Fort Riley in front of the division headquarters that honored LTG Clarence Ralph Huebner, who commanded the BRO during World War II. Cardenas decided to name the DIVARTY sector in the RAA "Custer Hill," where our headquarters was located at Fort Riley, which seemed appropriate.

When I awoke well before dawn on the morning of March 7 for my flight, I headed for the DIVARTY TOC to verify the map coordinates of the RAA and the location of "Custer Hill" in it. When I entered the TOC, the operations team on duty had tuned our AN/GRC-26 tactical AM radio to the Armed Forces Network to listen to President Bush's address to Congress, declaring an end of the war. At 5:30 a.m. (0530 hours military time) on March 7, it was 9:30 p.m. (2130 hours) on March 6 in Washington, D.C. when the president addressed a joint session of Congress. We all listened carefully as he declared that with this war now over, a "new world order" had emerged: "From the moment Operation Desert Storm commenced on January 16th until the time the guns fell silent at midnight one week ago, this nation has watched its sons and daughters with pride, watched over them with prayer. As Commander-in-Chief, I can report to you our armed forces fought with honor and valor. And as

President, I can report to the Nation aggression is defeated. The war is over."[28] For those present in the TOC early that morning, it was encouraging to hear praise from our commander-in-chief. As he spoke, the only other sounds that competed with his voice were the humming of the generators outside of our TOC that ran our communications gear and the occasional interruption from a radio call from one of our units. Otherwise, Bush had our complete and undivided attention. He continued:

Now, we can see a new world coming into view. A world in which there is the very real prospect of a new world order. In the words of Winston Churchill, a world order in which "the principles of justice and fair play protect the weak against the strong." A world where the United Nations, freed from cold war stalemate, is poised to fulfill the historic vision of its founders. A world in which freedom and respect for human rights find a home among all nations. The Gulf War put this new world to its first test. And my fellow Americans, we passed that test.[29]

It was a moving speech, and as he finished, it was clear that it was very well received by the congressional cheers we heard over the crackling AM radio. We too were encouraged by the president's words as we listened from our position near the "Highway of Death," which only a week earlier had been the scene of fiery fury leading to the defeat of Saddam's invading army.

As I headed to my waiting helicopter to fly south to RAA Huebner, so much ran through my mind. My knowledge of the Middle East, of Arabs in general, and of the Iraqi dictator in particular, left me with a hollow feeling in my stomach. From my days of watching the Iran-Iraq War from a privileged perch inside the DIA, I knew how Saddam operated. I knew how he would very likely do all in his power to stay in control and rebuild his evil dictatorship after the US and the coalition departed. I knew how he would viciously suppress any opposition to his regime. I knew how he would summarily execute many of his subordinates to make examples of them to those lucky or crafty enough to survive. Saddam could be relied upon to do one thing for certain. He would reapply a fresh coat of intimidation to the xenophobic mural that told the story of his repressive and demonic regime. Indeed, it would be a deceitful panorama portraying his rise to power and his personal triumph over the latest effort by Western "Crusaders" to subjugate Arabs. If he were to stay in power, there would be more stories by more people like the sad

Kuwaiti refugees who were making their way down the "Highway of Death" back to an uncertain peace in postwar Kuwait.

As our helicopter wound up its turbine engine, filling my nose with the smell of jet fuel, my pilot went through his preflight checks. Before we lifted off, I found myself less assured by the president's speech than others who may have heard it. As we started to hover, the OH-58 Kiowa helicopter carrying us kicked up a wall of dust that obscured everything. Nosing forward and upward to regain our visibility, we emerged into the clear. But as we did, I had an equally clear sense that we, as a coalition, had more to do, a lot more. We, like the helicopter that carried me, would have to rise above the clouded geopolitical picture in front of us to secure the peace the president assured us was now in our possession.

When we arrived in RAA Huebner, it was what I expected it to be: flat and sandy with no features to speak of. My sense was that we needed to get an advance party from the DIVARTY south to the location as soon as possible, because there was much work to do to get the place ready. On the return flight northeast, we flew over a scene of complete destruction. I recorded in my journal that night: "The Iraqis lost tons of equipment, much appears intact, much destroyed. Saw the wire and mine field along the SA/KU [Saudi-Kuwaiti] border. This was the scene of a rout. I was worn out when I returned. Everyone is in better spirits. The advance party that was to go today was delayed until tomorrow. We are still waiting on a peace treaty. Until then, we are postured to continue operations." We dispatched an advance party the next morning, March 8, with D-25 TAB's CPT Seefeldt in command. Seefeldt was a "go-getter," and I trusted him to pull together whatever was needed to get "Custer Hill" ready for occupation. I recalled how he—or some enterprising person in his unit—had "requisitioned" a bus in the port to make up for the lack of transportation vehicles we had to get people to the desert, that West Point quarterback CPT Bill Turner chauffeured. I had no doubt that when we arrived at "Custer Hill," Seefeldt would have it ready, possibly with its own bus service.

But even as Seefeldt's advance party headed south, we were getting all manner of mixed messages. First, the peace treaty was not final. That alone did not bode well for our departure from Kuwait. Additionally, Dodson was getting on-again, off-again indications from the division headquarters about when the BRO would head south too. Adding to the mixed signals, Dodson relayed an order to me early that morning to have a DIVARTY-wide "shakedown" of troops by 1130 for unauthorized ammunition or other contraband that soldiers might have picked up and placed in their duffle bags. A shakedown for prohibited "war prizes," like Iraqi bayonets and pistols or other items, could be expected before we moved back to Saudi Arabia. But it was nearly impossible to complete a mission like this in just a few hours. In fact, we didn't finish until 1730 that day, but the importance of the exercise was accentuated when a soldier from another unit thought it would be "cool" to take an unexploded CBU-87 home in his duffle bag. This ultimately proved to be a very bad idea when the CBU exploded on a military bus, badly wounding him. As I often repeated to my troops, "Life is hard, but when you're stupid, it's really hard." Unfortunately, that stern aphorism didn't always work with soldiers bent on taking interesting but dangerous items back to the United States, including ones that might blow up in their laps.

Coincidently, I also learned that day that one of the casualties we had in the 12th Chemical as they moved northeast toward Kuwait may have been a reckless homicide, and not a fratricide incident as was initially reported to me by Visser. Visser was an outstanding officer, but as we all learned in combat, the first report isn't always correct. This one wasn't. Once Visser had reassembled his entire unit in Kuwait, he learned the facts. The soldier who died in this incident, SP4 Kenneth J. Perry, had been in a foxhole when one of his buddies picked up an unexploded CBU and playfully tossed it in his direction, where it exploded behind his head in a moment of tragic teasing. Visser knew as I did that this senseless act put an entirely different face on the incident. It may have been a practical joke simply gone bad, but it was also a homicide.

I prepared my notes and sought out Dodson to make sure he was aware of the situation that we had first thought was a fratricide. "I think we need to press charges, sir," I recall saying to him.

I could see in his face the gravity of the situation. Death in combat was not new to him. He had seen it before. I could tell he wished this was not something that would wind up in a general court-martial with all the emotion that would come with it, both for the family of the dead soldier and for the perpetrator. But Dodson's inner compass always pointed to "do the right thing." He looked at me and said simply, "Scott, we both know what needs to be done here." At that point, I reached out for a legal opinion from the division's top lawyer. Retreating to a small communication shelter I used for work away from the noise of the TOC, I called the staff judge advocate (SJA), LTC Warren Hall, our very able military lawyer at division headquarters, to advise him of the situation. When the SJA picked up the phone, I related the updated facts, and Hall readily agreed with me that the right course of action was to charge the offending soldier with homicide. It wasn't a pleasant task. But it was a necessary one. That soldier would eventually go to trial when we returned to Fort Riley, a decision both Dodson and I knew was right. Justice must never be denied, even in the fog of war. It was a hard way to end the day.

But even without this difficult decision, the day would have nonetheless been hard because of the multitude of support issues we faced just to keep the troops in food, water, spare parts, and fuel. As I went to bed that night I lamented in my diary about logistics, the lack of supplies, and how we would be back in Saudi Arabia before we would see a single repair part: "Everything is 'just too hard.' Thank God the Iraqis weren't."

March 9 was dominated by yet more issues with support. Frustrated, we knew we would need to take matters into our own hands if we were to get what we needed. I sent one of my officers to the division's logistics base, where our support battalion drew resupply parts. There he found a huge number of items we had requisitioned weeks earlier. Dodson was equally concerned, particularly about inventory control of spare parts as they moved through the system. That day, the "system" was a bunch of parts randomly tossed in a large cardboard box marked "DIVARTY."

Despite the never-ending trouble with support, at least the troops were getting some rest, even as we were anxious to get on with redeployment. In that regard, we were all cheered to learn Seefeldt and his advance party had made it safely to "Custer Hill" and were busy setting things up. As I expected, he dove into the mission headfirst. But no sooner had we entertained the idea of heading back to Saudi Arabia than there were rumors that the Iraqis might be violating the line of demarcation (LoD) that they were required to remain behind in accordance with the ceasefire agreement.

Sure enough, when we arose on March 10, Dodson informed me that the division was planning to mount an operation against the Iraqi Army near Umm Qasr, northeast of our position. Apparently, the Iraqi Army was trying to recover military equipment south of the LoD in our territory near the Iraqi port of Umm Qasr at the head of the Persian Gulf. Ominously, we also had indications that the Iraqis were using chemicals on their own civilians who might be ready to revolt against Saddam's regime. Dodson informed the DIVARTY TOC that the 210th FA Brigade, which had departed our sector days earlier, would be delayed and remain in place with an on-order mission to support us, a move clearly in response to the Iraqi mischief at Umm Qasr. The TOC spun into action. Dodson had them develop fire support graphics to prepare him to meet with the division planners at 0700 the next morning (see table 11.2). We

Table 11.2. 1st Infantry Division Artillery Organization for Combat (March 11, 1991)

1ID (Mechanized) DIVARTY: Force Artillery Headquarters (HQ)	
1-5 FA (155mm SP)	DS 1st Brigade
4-5 FA (155mm SP)	DS 2nd Brigade
4-3 FA (155mm SP)	DS 3rd Brigade (2nd Armored Division)
B-6 FA (MLRS)	GS
D-25 TAB	GS
210th Field Artillery Brigade: DS 2ACR, O/O (on order) R 1ID (M) DIVARTY	
3-17 FA (155mm SP)	GS
6-41 FA (155mm SP)	GS
C-4-27 FA (MLRS)	GS
E-333 TAB	GS
142nd Field Artillery Brigade: GSR 1ID (M) DIVARTY	
1-142 FA (203mm SP)	GS
2-142 FA (203mm SP)	GS

Key: Direct Support (DS); Reinforcing (R); General Support Reinforcing (GSR); General Support (GS)

also ordered up a helicopter for him so that he could move around the sector to ensure our units understood the emerging concept of operations. I was happy we were getting back in the swing of things, focusing on a combat mission. I recorded in my diary that evening what appeared to us to be the emerging mission: "The Iraqis are trying to recover equipment near Umm Qasr. We are planning to smack them if they keep it up."

Early on March 11, we received a warning order from the division to be prepared to support the BRO units as they conducted a screening mission northeast in the direction of Umm Qasr to interdict the Iraqis as they tried to recover more equipment from the area. When we awoke, McGary prepared HQ-5, and we moved out to visit B-6 FA, our MLRS battery. I told them that it appeared we might have to take action and to prepare their rocket launchers to provide supporting fire. It seemed to stir them from the doldrums of recent days. A clear and renewed mission focus was a good thing, because when I first arrived in their position, I was disappointed with their state of readiness and had to remind them bluntly that the war may not be over just yet.

The next day, March 12, we moved B-6 FA north along with the 142nd FA Brigade to support the screening mission forward, as it appeared that we might need to confront the Iraqis. At 2000 hours that night, the division ordered the operation to begin at 0700 the next morning. Once again, the DIVARTY assembled a robust artillery team to back up the operation in the event fire support was needed. Satisfied that the supporting artillery was in good order, I spent some time catching up on administrative tasks. But I was glad we had a combat task in front of us to escape our depressing preoccupation with logistics. When I went to bed that evening, I was upbeat and particularly glad the Division's CoS, COL Fred Hepler, had given me the go-ahead to draft a recommendation for Dodson to receive a Distinguished Service Medal (DSM), one of the highest decorations for achievement a soldier can receive. There were also officer efficiency reports (OERs) that I had to render for my subordinates along with AARs on the operations we had conducted to that date. Those AARs were very important as they would be used to capture things we had done well or poorly, something all units did because those very lessons might save lives in a future battle. It was a productive day, and one that brightened my mood: "A good day. Visited the COS today to seek guidance for an award for my boss. I wanted to ensure he is recognized for his efforts. COS says go with a DSM as COL D has been magnificent. Worked on OERs, awards, and AAR's. Late tonight we were given a warning order to move forward. I will recon in the AM. The move is to show the Iraqis that we are serious about signing the terms of peace as we want them to stop using chemicals on their people." Before evening arrived, I swung by the DIVARTY TOC to check in with Cardenas on the current situation. No doubt about it, Saddam was already doing what I thought he would: crushing any internal opposition to his regime in the wake of a devastating defeat. We were told he might use chemicals against revolting Shia Arabs in southern Iraq. He was. Cardenas also informed me to be prepared to lead a reconnaissance in the morning for a new forward position for the DIVARTY TOC. It was, by then, a task I was well familiar with, and McGary made our Humvee ready to move out early. As I drifted off to sleep that night, I knew the next day might bring some action. My hope was that whatever was before us, we would handle it in a "short and sweet" manner and that no one would get hurt in the process.

I rose with McGary early on March 13 to conduct the reconnaissance. We checked our gear, weapons, and ammunition, and did the necessary communications checks with the DIVARTY TOC. Departing for a position to the north near Al Qash' Ainyah, we managed to take a route that led us smack into an area "heavily concentrated," as I noted in my diary, with our own CBU-87 cluster bombs. The Air Force had dropped these on the Iraqis two weeks earlier, but now they were my problem. I saw the bomblets, yellow in color and about 7.8 inches long, scattered everywhere. "Stop, Roger!" I called out as he was about to roll over one. I opened my door and looked down, and sure enough we were surrounded with these things. I carefully stepped out, surveyed the area, and picked a path to lead HQ-5, with a very attentive McGary at the wheel, safely out of the area. Afterward, we took a circuitous route around the bombed area to the position we would need for the DIVARTY. I noted the dangerous location on my map and then proceeded to head home.

On the way, we stopped at what appeared to be a deserted chicken farm in Al Qash' Ainyah, an area noted on my map as "scattered cultivation" just south of the Iraqi-Kuwaiti border. Shelley had grown up on a farm, so I thought it might be nice to see what a Kuwaiti one looked like. As I approached what appeared to be a barn, it was eerily quiet. Just then I wondered if we were being watched. I slipped my hand closer to my sidearm and moved cautiously. No sense in getting shot by an unsuspecting adversary who might mistake my intentions. When I went in the barn, I could not believe my eyes. There before me were no less than 1,000 SS-30 (ASTROS II) rockets. The ASTROS II artillery system was built by the Brazilian Army in 1983 and had been purchased by Iraq during the war against the Iranians. With a range of 30 kilometers, the SS-30 could shoot its 127mm rockets deep into enemy territory with devastating effect. It was a lethal munition, and one that we surely didn't want the Iraqis to recapture. While McGary and I saw no SS-30 launchers nearby, we knew the Iraqi Army units operating in the area would be very keen to repossess this deadly ammunition cache. I then called Cardenas on my radio and informed him of our find. Better that our ammunition specialists take charge of this huge munitions stockpile than let it fall back into Iraqi hands.

While we were on our early-morning forward reconnaissance, the division's screening force moved forward along with 1–5 FA and 4–5 FA to support the maneuver forces. As the BRO closed in on Iraqi forces, our units continued to destroy enemy equipment along the way. Later, when the division's units closed on Umm Qasr, they found a large ammunition stockpile of their own, a cache of Silkworm missiles.[30] The Silkworm was made by the Chinese, modeled on a version of the 30-year-old Soviet Styx antiship missile. Despite its unsophisticated design, it had a range of 80 kilometers, gliding just 100 feet above the water, and could do serious damage to ships at sea. This was also a good find and one that would deny the Iraqis the opportunity to recover lethal ammunition that could do much harm to ships.

By the end of the day's operation, the Iraqis had withdrawn. When the entire issue shook out, it appeared that the Iraqis had misunderstood the limits of permissible movement on their side of the LoD as defined in the ceasefire conditions. Our show of force—including the movement forward of our forces along with a heavy attack-aircraft presence—got their attention. At any rate, the operation permitted the division to destroy and capture more Iraqi equipment.

When the sun rose on March 14, I could tell the warm season was approaching. It started getting hot quickly. After the action of the previous few days, it appeared we would slip back into a mundane existence. Now that the immediate danger of Iraq's violating the LoD had passed, the 210th FA Brigade and A-1–158 FA were once again ordered to move out of sector to link up with the 2ACR and the 1CD, respectively. After grabbing some breakfast and the required coffee to jump-start my day, I was called in by Dodson to let me know that our friends in the 142nd FA Brigade were once again "out of control." Dodson was in the middle of doing AARs, a high priority for him, when he was interrupted to take a call from some of our ground brigade commanders and our ADC-M, Carter, complaining about the behavior and military discipline of the Arkansas artillery battalions. Dodson was hot. Indiscipline had no place in the DIVARTY in his view of the world (mine either). Moreover, interrupting his serious-minded effort to record lessons learned was not a way to endear oneself to him.

Dodson mounted his Humvee and made a beeline for the 142nd FA Brigade's unsuspecting commander. When he returned, I couldn't wait to hear how the conversation had gone. When I asked him, all he could muster was, "Unbelievable." Apparently, some of the 8-inch cannon sections were riding around shirtless with Confederate flags flying high on their tracked howitzers. They thought that was patriotic. Dodson didn't. But when he related the story to me, it was all I could do to suppress my laughter. I'm glad I did, because it was clear these cowboys had "steamed" him badly. I noted the problem in my journal and my assessment of how the active Army utilizes the National Guard: "142nd FA BDE is out of control. They won't stay in uniform, they wander anywhere, across Iraqi lines having a good ol' time. Soon one will be a POW or KIA. The 'total' Army is not working as expected. We need to rethink this. The 142 shot well, but are undisciplined. Maybe there is no avoiding this, but I don't like it." Indeed, even though we weren't shooting at the Iraqis every day, all of us worried about accidents that could result from reckless behavior. It was enough that we had to watch carefully to avoid running over unexploded ordnance, much less have to call home to a wife or mother to tell them their soldier had been killed after being thrown shirtless from a howitzer bounding across the desert plains like a bronco-rider in a rodeo. Sure enough, that very day a Humvee from 4–5 FA ran over a bomblet, which exploded under the vehicle. By the grace of God, no one was hurt.

March 15 marked the end of two weeks of sitting under the burning stench and suffocating smoke of the oil fires that constituted Saddam's farewell to Kuwait. Despite this, we had settled into a routine of maintenance, vehicle repair, inventorying equipment, and trying to maintain morale while awaiting redeployment. We wanted a signal, any signal, that we would soon redeploy to Saudi Arabia to prepare for a return to Fort Riley and a long-awaited reunion with our families. As I headed for the DIVARTY TOC that morning, I learned that the Chairman of the Armed Services Committee, Congressman Les Aspin, and a congressional delegation were to visit a static display of our combat equipment at Safwan Airfield, where only 12 days earlier the ceasefire agreement had been negotiated. Dodson dispatched me to inspect our contribution to this show, which included radars and an MLRS launcher. After I had done so, I reported that everything looked fine, and I was sure the VIPs in attendance would be duly impressed.

On the way there, we encountered more desperately poor and begging Iraqi children who continued to be quite aggressive as we drove past them. McGary had perfected his MRE throwing technique, however, and we were spared from youngsters invading our vehicle. We also saw many Kuwaiti refugees headed south. They too were destitute. I noted this sad situation in my diary that evening: "The Iraqis beg along the road blocks to demand food. If you stop, they invade your vehicle. It's really sad, but you are forced to throw them an MRE on the run. Folks need water badly, particularly women with children for milk formula. So sad. Wars bring these things." Indeed, we felt that the war was over for us. As I drifted off to sleep amid the distant rumble of oil-well fires and the nearby generators that powered our TOC and communications equipment, I nevertheless wondered whether or not we would be headed south back to Saudi Arabia soon.

No sooner had I fallen asleep than McGary and I were suddenly awakened by a storm—a *shamal*—raging outside of our tent. We did our best to hold onto everything as the tent walls flapped in and out like a large-winged albatross trying to take flight. McGary had become adept at setting up our tent the right way. But that night Vann found his tent collapsing on top of him and his crew. McGary and I heard the commotion outside. Vann and the affected troops vented their frustration in a chain of uninterrupted vulgarities that would have made a seasoned sailor blush! It was hysterical, as the whole thing had the air of a Hollywood slapstick comedy. I spent most of the next day writing letters, catching up on odds and ends, and drying out clothes and equipment from the violent *shamal* that had upended Vann's tent and temperament.

March 17 was also a slow day, but, of course, there was always some logistical challenge to keep all of us from boredom. That morning I found myself struggling to secure a helicopter to fly to Al Qaysumah, a village near Hafar al-Batin in Saudi Arabia, to retrieve the 4–5 FA deserter, who had been held with Iraqi POWs for several weeks: "Another slow day. Wrote more letters. Worked a few logistic issues. Tried to get a UH60 to pick up the 4–5 deserter at Al Qaysumah in SA. It would be easier to straighten the coastline of Turkey than to get helo support. The losers in this war in order are, 1. logistics, 2. commo, 3. aviation, 4. mail, 5. the soldiers for all of the above reasons 1 through 4. On the bright side, we are able to fix one of our 5 tons that had a broken starter by taking a starter off of an Iraqi 5 ton, they [Iraqis] captured from Kuwait that we captured from Iraq. Let's hear it for battlefield logistics."

Later that day, Dodson learned from the division that we would finally be on the move soon, but not to Saudi Arabia. We were headed northwest back into the Iraqi desert. The final signing of the ceasefire was proceeding slowly, a predictable thing when dealing with the Iraqis. Dodson thought we would see the details "inked" between March 22 and 26, but I had my doubts. Saddam could be expected to delay if for no other reason than to demonstrate that he remained in the "driver's seat" concerning Iraq's destiny. He was a fox, and delaying things would show his people that he wouldn't be "pushed around," even by a conquering US Army sitting south of him. It made no sense at all, but for Saddam, making "sense" was not the objective. Saving his regime was his goal. And orchestrated delays were in keeping with the way he did business.

When March 18 arrived, it was a dark and overcast day, a bit cold too. Smoke and soot from the burning oil fires had settled on top of us like a wet blanket. We learned, thankfully, that we would make our initial move on March 20 to an intermediate location 15 kilometers south of our current position and then jump forward 100 kilometers northwest to and deeper into Iraq. There we would laager with other VII Corps forces in defensive positions as a show of force just in case Saddam thought we were leaving before the ceasefire agreement was final. We weren't.

By March 19, the wind had shifted, and the sky had cleared. Later that day we gathered the officers of the DIVARTY TOC and took a picture around and upon the 122mm D-30 howitzer we had commandeered weeks earlier. It was an iconic image, one that would remind all of us that we had been in combat as soldiers with the incomparably audacious DIVARTY of the Big Red One. That afternoon, we received word that we were now entitled to sew the patch of the 1ID on our right shoulder sleeve, a privilege granted only to those who had fought with the division in combat. I went back to my tent where I sat on my cot and removed a patch from a spare uniform shirt to transfer it to another. I would now display that patch on each shoulder, the left signifying my current assignment to the 1ID, the right my combat service with it. As I sat in my tent stitching that olive-drab shield, 2 ½ inches in width and 2 ¾ inches in height, flat at the top and with a ninety-degree angle at the base pointing downward and sporting a camouflage subdued black Arabic numeral "1" in the center, I was overcome with emotion.[31] As a tear ran down my face, I thought about all of the BRO soldiers who had gone before me. The ones who had fought and died, the ones who, having survived war, would silently reflect on their combat experience, not seeking any glory or special recognition, but only the simple company of a fellow veteran with whom they had stood shoulder-to-shoulder in combat. And I also thought about the ones who would not be coming home from this war, 27 from our division. I thought a lot.

When I drew the last stitch, tugged and knotted it, and cut the remaining thread with my bayonet, I felt undeserving. This was the province of others more deserving, like the 16th Infantry's 1LT Jimmie W. Monteith, a Virginian who died gallantly at Normandy, France, on June 6, 1944. There, on D-Day, while rallying and leading his troops and repeatedly exposing himself to grave danger, he gave the "last full measure of devotion," as President Abraham Lincoln said of Union soldiers at Gettysburg. We had not witnessed that level of sacrifice here. Nonetheless, we had lost 27 soldiers willing to give that last full measure of their devotion; other young soldiers like PFC McGary and SGT Jefferies were willing to do the same. I suppose that alone was reason enough for us to wear this honored olive-drab patch with a "1" on our right shoulder. But it was also humbling to be part of a band of brothers, and now sisters, who had gone before, selflessly serving in the 1ID.

When we arose on March 20, 1991, we began our movement out of Kuwait, having liberated it from Saddam Hussein. Now we would return to the Iraqi desert to await his final capitulation, not home to our waiting families and friends. To be sure, we were astride an uncertain peace, and I wondered, as we headed southwest across the Kuwaiti desert on the initial leg of our journey, if more than waiting was in our future. But wait, fight, or any other condition, we were the First Infantry Division, and our motto was clear. It wasn't "Duty when you feel like it," nor "Duty when it's easy," nor "Duty when you're happy," nor was it "Duty when you're ready." It was "Duty First." Period. And we weren't done.

12

An Unresolved Peace

We arose before sunrise on Thursday, March 21, at the intermediate position we had occupied the afternoon before. Our movement out of Kuwait
was in two phases. The first was a relatively short move, only 15 kilometers southwest. On the second leg, I would precede the convoy westward toward the Iraqi-Kuwaiti border, then swing northwest back into
southern Iraq. Our eventual destination that day would be TAA Allen,
named after MG Terry de la Mesa Allen Sr., who commanded the 1ID in
North Africa and Sicily during World War II. It seemed appropriate to
name it after him since the last time the BRO had fought in a desert, it
was under Allen's command. There we would wait until the ceasefire was
signed by Saddam Hussein. But as Greg Fontenot has also noted in his
history of the 1ID, our new location in southern Iraq would see "our
focus changed" from war fighting to "preparing equipment for the long
road march to the port."[1]

After verifying the route we would take, we expected to cover 135
kilometers during the second leg. Under the best conditions, that would
be taxing for any convoy of combat vehicles over improved roads. But we
would not have the benefit of good roads; rather, we could look forward
to the desert trails and soft sand that had vexed us weeks earlier when we
attacked into Kuwait. Before we left, I headed to the DIVARTY TOC to
check in, grabbing a cup of coffee on the way. "Well, here we go again,"
laughed MAJ Cardenas as he contemplated the idea of "reinvading"
Iraq. The day before, coalition forces shot down an Iraqi MIG fighter jet,
making us all keenly aware that while we were technically in a ceasefire,
albeit unsigned, the war wasn't completely over.[2]

"We've got a hell of a long march today, Ed," I observed as I headed
back to my Humvee to prepare for our 0900 departure.

"Yep," he responded, "what's new?"

When I got back to HQ-5, PFC McGary was ready and, as usual,
armed to the teeth. I was happy we were back at it. Sitting for weeks in
Kuwait was maddening, particularly since all we seemed to do was grouse

and complain incessantly about logistical anemia. A tactical move would take my mind off the frustration and stress of supply issues, awards, fratricide death investigations, and the lack of mail and news from home.

McGary was ready to move. "Damn, sir, I'm glad we're leaving Kuwait. I sure hope we don't have to come back anytime soon," he said. I agreed as our Humvee moved out precisely at 0900 to the first waypoint, a map location that I had plugged into the GPS to navigate our way back into Iraq. Waypoints were simply coordinates on the map that we plotted to follow a predetermined route. Cardenas carefully selected them and picked a route that, hopefully, would not take us through the soft sand that had characterized our initial movement into Kuwait, the infamous "convoy from hell." Nevertheless, I knew there would be ample opportunities for challenges to pop up.

It was a bright and clear day when we rolled out. As an added precaution, Cardenas had ordered up one of our OH-58-D observation helicopters to transport CPT Joe Willis, our DIVARTY Chemical Officer (CHEMO), so he could conduct air reconnaissance ahead of our convoy movement. I had him tuned on my radio to monitor what he was seeing ahead, including any trace of Iraqi elements that could be lingering about. It was unlikely we would see any at this point, but we didn't want to take any chances.

The initial trek departing Kuwait was uneventful, and I was pleased that we took a course that was north of the "valley of the boogers." Even though enemy elements had largely been cleared from that sector, I had no desire to retrace its canyons and blind bends in the road. The open desert, where we had a good line of sight and were able to observe possible activity for miles, was far preferable. At least we could react if something materialized on the horizon. It wasn't long until we had just such an opportunity.

McGary and I jumped five kilometers ahead of the HHB and DIVARTY TOC convoy to scout forward for any unexpected activity along our route of march. He was on course, as I helped him with our GPS and my compass affixed to our dashboard. That compass never failed us as a reliable backup to the GPS when the satellite signals went off-line, which happened frequently. As I alternated between scanning the featureless terrain, the GPS, the compass, and my map, I suddenly noticed on the path just ahead of us CBU-87 bomblets scattered about. I called out to McGary, "Bomblet ahead, veer left!" He did, but no sooner than he did, there was another. "Veer right!" I sounded as he lurched HQ-5 in my direction. Then there was another, and another. By then we knew that we had managed to speed smack dab into the middle of a field of unexploded ordnance. I said, "Stop, where you are. We need to see if we can walk this thing out of here." I got out of the Humvee, and as far as I could see, we were surrounded by the ominous presence of unexploded ordnance. The stuff was everywhere, and turning the Humvee around, since it didn't have a very tight turning radius, was not an inviting idea. Then I remembered Willis and the OH-58-D conducting reconnaissance ahead of us. I called Cardenas and asked him to send the CHEMO to our location. In short order, I could hear the familiar chop of helicopter blades cutting through the desert air, heading in our direction.

"Need some help, sir?" Willis cracked over the radio. I could "hear" him smiling mischievously.

"Yep, I guess we do," I said with a hint of embarrassment.

Willis and his pilot positioned the helicopter about 100 feet above HQ-5 and then radioed us instructions on a path to safety. He was in a perfect position to look down and see the ordnance clearly. We couldn't, unless I got out and carefully and slowly led the way on foot. "Drive 20 feet ahead and then turn 10 degrees left . . . now drive 15 feet and turn right 30 degrees . . . keep going, now turn left 15 degrees," he said in a continuous narrative that helped us escape this hazard more quickly than had we tried to walk ourselves out. After we had cleared the danger, Willis gave us a cheery, "Goodbye," offering to come to our assistance again if we managed to get ourselves tangled up in a minefield, or some other unfriendly obstacle. "Be careful, sir," he said with a hint of laughter as he and his pilot disappeared over the horizon. As I picked up the radio to call back to Cardenas to have him swing the convoy north of our projected path to avoid the same trouble I had encountered, I couldn't help but think that I had made Willis's day by having him rescue his XO from a self-inflicted mishap. Resuming our course westward, McGary grumbled, "I could have gotten us out of there, sir." His ego was wounded too. Maybe worse than mine.

When we approached the western Kuwaiti border with Iraq, we could see southwest of us a large assembly of vehicles that had belonged to an Iraqi unit that coalition forces had defeated weeks earlier. As we traveled westward, I detected the movement of several men scurrying about the abandoned vehicles. I suspected that they were Bedouin scavengers, but I wasn't sure. As we closed our distance with them, they appeared to take a more aggressive posture, racing to get in their vehicles. I radioed Cardenas and suggested that he get Willis and his OH-58-D in a position to see what he could observe. But as soon as I made that call, the small force hurriedly jumped in a truck and appeared to be heading our way, fast. McGary and I both went into action. He grabbed his M16 and chambered a round. I reflexively jacked a 9mm round into my pistol, when suddenly the truck veered away. As McGary was about to light them up with a magazine full of 5.56mm ball ammunition, I said, "Roger, stand down, I think they're headed away." As they sped off, I thought to myself, "You're lucky bastards, because expert marksman Roger Lee McGary was about to dispatch your ass to the afterlife."

We continued westward, crossing PL Plum and PL Milford. About 30 kilometers into Iraq, having skirted south and then west of what was Objective Norfolk where we had fought four weeks earlier, we began a northwesterly vector. As we did, we found the sand under our wheels to be far less firm. I radioed back to Cardenas to advise him because I knew the heavier vehicles in our convoy would likely get stuck, just as they had on the hellish march weeks earlier. Beyond that advice, there wasn't much I could do. We had our orders to head back into Iraq, and loose sand or not, we had to continue forward. The soft terrain coupled with rolling dunes around us couldn't be easily avoided. By late afternoon, the way-points I was following in my GPS took us on a northward path to our destination near a place on my map named Ghazlani.

When we arrived at the "RP" or release point, the final waypoint from where we would navigate the last few kilometers to our new position, I noticed a very large depression in the ground. Stopping, I got out and realized I was staring into a B-52 bomb crater. I slid down one side of it to the bottom, where I found a large metal bomb fragment, 16 inches long—jagged, twisted, and razor sharp on the sides where it had fractured away when the bomb exploded. I decided that I would keep it to show folks what death looks like when delivered from the bowels of a B-52 Stratofortress. Besides, it was just inert metal, incapable of blowing up, and not a threat to anyone unless you allowed your fingers to be cut by it.

Just as the sun was dipping below the horizon, McGary and I arrived at our position north of a large hill on the map marked "499," just 80 kilometers south of the Euphrates River. Without a doubt, we were "deep" inside southern Iraq, leaving me to wonder what was in store for us next. Shortly thereafter, COL Dodson rode up in his dust-covered Humvee, HQ-6, having taken his own path to check on the status of the main body of the convoy as it marched along the treacherous route to our new position.

We contacted Cardenas to get an update and learned he was just a few kilometers away. At 1840 the tired and dusty main body of the convoy that was the DIVARTY TOC and the HHB showed up in good order. But it was nonetheless eventful. At one point, Dodson had to untangle the 5th battalion, 18th Infantry (5–18 IN) of the 3AD that had cut across the tail end of the HHB convoy. It was no small problem, because when 5–18 IN split our convoy from its lead elements, the trailing vehicles became disoriented in the dust kicked up by other vehicles ahead or astride of them. It was a mess.

The desert surface also took a toll on our vehicles' tires, particularly our M35A2 2 ½-ton cargo trucks that carried supplies and equipment, the trailers they pulled, and the Humvees that transported many of us. You would think that "soft" sand would be easy on vehicle tires, but the rocky material and pumice from ancient volcanic events mixed into it was very abrasive, degrading the tires badly. Where the sand was soft underfoot, vehicles predictably sank and had to be pulled out, adding time to our march. Dodson had hopped back and forth along the entire convoy, which included not only HHB but B-6 FA (MLRS), D-25 TAB, and the 12th Chemical, composing six serials, each extending 11 kilometers from front to back. It was an amazement to me that Dodson could have actually beaten them all into position, but sure enough he had.

By 1930, most of the vehicles had arrived, and everyone worked feverishly to get set up. The DIVARTY TOC quickly deployed its equipment, and soldiers wasted no time digging in and setting up tents to get some rest. Everyone was flat exhausted, as I recorded in my diary that night: "Led the move back into Iraq today. Had to traverse the enormous destruction we visited on the Republican Guards. CBUs everywhere! Had to detour the convoy north then west. I don't want to get anyone hurt at this point. We came upon some scavengers we think were trying to move Iraqi trucks. We loaded our weapons and were ready to take them under fire. They seemed fairly scared and took off to the SW. Think they were Saudis. Our march today was 9 hours. We cleaned up and crashed in our cots."

When morning arrived on March 22, we got a better look at our position in TAA Allen and the area the division would call home for an undetermined period (see map 12.1).[3] Fortunately, no destroyed Iraqi positions or unexploded ordnance was nearby. Unfortunately, the sand was soft and loose, which meant we would be subject to its abrasive blasting effect when the wind got up. Dodson found me early that morning as I went on a desperate search for coffee and informed me that he was headed to the DTOC located just a few kilometers south of us in the vicinity of hill 499. After I located some coffee, I spent most of the morning in trying to account for a few vehicles that had not made it into position the previous

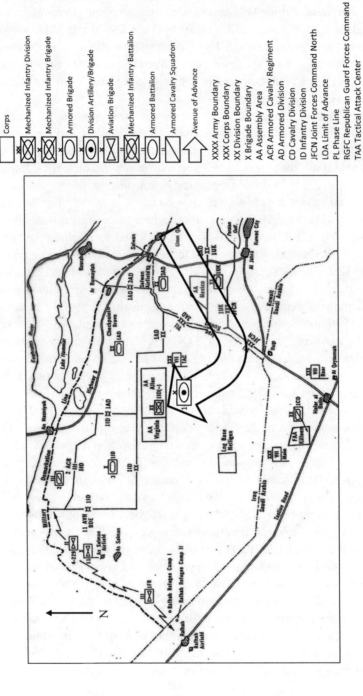

Map 12.1. 1st Infantry DIVARTY Movement from Kuwait to TAA Allen, March 21, 1991

XXX	Corps
XX	Mechanized Infantry Division
XX	Mechanized Infantry Brigade
X	Armored Brigade
•	Division Artillery/Brigade
•	Aviation Brigade
XX	Mechanized Infantry Battalion
XX	Armored Battalion
O	Armored Cavalry Squadron
⇧	Avenue of Advance

XXXX Army Boundary
XXX Corps Boundary
XX Division Boundary
X Brigade Boundary
AA Assembly Area
ACR Armored Cavalry Regiment
AD Armored Division
CD Cavalry Division
ID Infantry Division
JFCN Joint Forces Command North
LOA Limit of Advance
PL Phase Line
RGFC Republican Guard Forces Command
TAA Tactical Attack Center
TF Task Force

night. Later I visited B-6 FA, D-25 TAB, and the 12th Chemical to check on them. Everyone was in surprisingly high spirits, because at long last we had made a tactical move that helped everyone refocus on a mission instead of sitting around. Moreover, we were farther from the ill effects of the noxious oil-well fires that had created a filthy penumbralike shadow around us for three weeks.

When Dodson returned from the DTOC later, he pulled me aside and confessed he had no idea "what the plan was" in terms of our next steps, beyond noting the division's first flights back to the US were scheduled for May 16, almost two months away. As I thought about that schedule, it struck me that we couldn't remain in Iraq much longer if we would be expected to redeploy to Saudi Arabia, repair and clean vehicles, load them on ships back to the US, and get our troops on aircraft bound for Fort Riley. I knew Dodson shared my concern, but there was little either of us could do aside from keeping the troops engaged in the maintenance and repair of our vehicles. One thing was certain. We had the resourceful and dependable CPT Seefeldt back in Saudi Arabia, readying the positions where we would consolidate our units and prepare for our movement home. That piece of the puzzle was in place.

Among other things that had our attention was the need to set up an artillery range in the desert, so our units could conduct live fire training to keep our skills up if we were called on to continue to march northward into Iraq. Saddam still hadn't inked the ceasefire agreement, and our presence in the desert also served notice that we were postured to continue to fight, even as we prepared to return home. Moreover, live fire training would create a thunderous pounding that could be heard for miles, sending a clear signal that the BRO was still tuned up and ready to go.

My afternoon was consumed by the bête noire of my existence, namely supply and maintenance issues. The jump forward deep into Iraq did nothing to improve our maintenance posture, and the division's long supply trains continued their struggle to keep up. When I swung by our DISCOM supply unit that day, I didn't know what I would find. I felt like unloading my frustration on someone. But we were all—supporter and supported alike—so worn out with the challenges we faced in getting the parts, food, water, and fuel, that a degree of pessimistic fatalism had settled over us. I found myself in a state of resignation. Whenever I asked about a part, I was told that it was "inbound," or "on the way," or some other empty bromide designed to comfort, or defang, me, whichever was appropriate for the occasion. Abundant sarcasm found its way into my journal that day: "There is a town in Saudi somewhere named Route.

The place has everything, parts, personnel, mail, food, water, orders, administrative items. You name it, Route has it. Major assemblies are stacked 30 feet in the air. I can't wait to find this place. I know it exists because when I talk to the supply or admin guys, they tell me everything is 'in route.' I need a grid [location]."

On March 23, we awoke to an early spring rainstorm that lasted all day. It was dreary. But then MG Rhame showed up in our position to check on our status, and I perked up. Rhame was carrying an infectious optimism that was hard to ignore, much less avoid. He made clear to both Dodson and me that the role of the field artillery in this war had been decisive. "Never again will any infantryman or armor fellow ever doubt the power of mass fires like you guys delivered in this war," he said, leaning into both of us to add emphasis to his point. We knew. Nonetheless, his assertive comments stirred a quiet pride in both of us. Later, BG Abrams, the VII Corps Artillery commander, showed up, worrying that the field artillery might not get the credit it deserved. Apparently, he and Rhame had not crossed paths.

March 24 was my son John's fifth birthday, and I missed him, Amy, and Paul terribly. Later that day, I managed to speak to Shelley, and she told me the kids all had great fun at John's party. Mary Cardenas and her kids had joined in on the fun, and my heart was warmed by the thought that they had a reason to celebrate. In the meantime, I kept myself busy catching up on paperwork. When the lunch hour rolled around, I summoned McGary to get HQ-5 ready for a short ride to the "Wolf Burger," where pay phones had also been installed for calls home. The "Wolf Burger" was the creation of Chief Warrant Officer Fourth Class (CW4) Wesley Wolf, an aide to Stormin' Norman Schwarzkopf. Chief Wolf came up with the idea to dispatch lightweight food trailers, painted Kelly green and tan, to the field to cook hamburgers, cheeseburgers, and hotdogs for the troops. In addition to this ballpark fare, there was a small array of bagged chips and soft drinks. It wasn't McDonald's, but for the troops who had subsisted on MREs for months, the "Wolf Burger" was desert manna for sure. As McGary and I chowed down on the cheeseburgers the Wolf Burger had served up, the desert background and US combat vehicles all around us created a surreal backdrop to our lunch. Despite that, we immensely enjoyed a much-needed break from Army nourishment.

We had been in TAA Allen only a short while before we had our first official crisis. In the middle of one night, Cardenas was abruptly awakened by our surgeon, "Doc" Sullivan. Doc had called in a UH-60 medevac helicopter for one of our soldiers. Cardenas asked who was in trouble and the nature of the emergency. Sullivan then told him that one of our operations officers, CPT Ralph Nieves, required immediate surgery for life-threatening acute appendicitis. As Cardenas was asking if "everything was going to be okay," he could hear the chopper on its final approach to pick up the ailing Nieves. Cardenas learned the next morning that Nieves had undergone surgery and was recovering well in the division's field hospital. Later that day, a still-concerned Cardenas took his Humvee to check in on Nieves. It took a while to locate the facility. When he did and went in to visit the now-recovering officer, Nieves was very glad to see his boss, but also deeply concerned about his hospital situation. The facility was filled with Iraqi civilians, who had been injured during the war and were being served by our medical personnel. Nieves, like Cardenas, was of Hispanic heritage and shared his concern that because of his brown complexion, he would be mistaken by the nurses and doctors as "an Iraqi." He then quietly intoned to Cardenas, "Sir, will you talk to the doctors and make sure they know that I'm a US soldier with the DIVARTY?" Cardenas couldn't help himself as he burst out laughing in the hospital ward, shattering the solemnity of the place. He then composed himself enough to assure the now-recuperating and slightly paranoid Nieves that he would make sure he was not shipped off to some nearby Bedouin village by mistake and abandoned by us.

As the sun rose on that desert on March 26, we were greeted with bacon and eggs for breakfast, a welcome upgrade from the monotony of freeze-dried rations and MREs. The smell of fresh food cooking early that morning drifted past our tent and beckoned us to the mess hall with its assortment of equipment designed to cook a proper meal. Standing atop a trailer that folded out into a kitchen unit with burners and ovens, all fueled by gas, our cooks were busy delighting the troops with a true Army breakfast: bacon, eggs, grilled potatoes, grits, toast, and a wide array of jellies, butter, and other goodies. Somehow they had managed—at last—to get "real food," thereby encouraging us that the supply system had awakened that morning too.

When I finished breakfast, I collected my gear and headed for a waiting helicopter to transport me to DSA Junction City deep in the division's rear area to check on logistic support. CW4 John L. Brown had his OH-58-D ready to go at an idle—blades whopping slowly—as I approached the aircraft. I opened the cockpit door, crawled into the left seat, and donned the flight helmet he had waiting for me. "Hey, sir, ready to make this trip?" he asked through the aircraft's intercom.

I adjusted my helmet mic closely to my lower lip and said, "Yep, let's get in the air."

Brown was the consummate professional, and he loved to fly. He was a senior aviator, and I was glad to have him at the controls. Warrant officers (grades 1 through 5) were officers, meriting a hand salute from enlisted ranks as they were "warranted" as officers, although lower in rank than fully commissioned officers, second lieutenants through generals. Despite being oddly wedged between the enlisted ranks and the commissioned officer grades, warrant officers were regarded as highly professional, whether flying aircraft as Brown did, or doing other technical jobs in maintenance, supply, medical procedures, or administrative work. They were all good, very good.

When we took off and emerged from the dust storm the aircraft's rotors had created over the DIVARTY TOC, we quickly gained altitude into clear sky and headed south-southwest toward the logistics base that I was sure had a ton of parts earmarked for the DIVARTY. During the flight, we made small talk over the intercom about the war, and Brown told me a remarkable story. "You want to hear a good one, sir?" he said temptingly.

"Fire away," I responded, wondering if I was going to hear a dirty joke or a war story. At that point, everyone had a war tale of one sort or another. I had my share, including being trapped in the middle of unexploded ordnance. But Brown had a good one indeed. He related how he had personally caught an Iraqi brigadier general in the middle of the desert on day three of the ground phase. I asked him what he had done with the guy, and he said, "Sir, I couldn't find anyone to take him!" It made me think about how we had instructed numerous POWs to head toward "Shadley," our able DISCOM commander, who had established POW holding areas in the division's rear area. But then I wondered if that procedure would have been sufficient for an Iraqi general, particularly one having to march amid Iraqi privates who had been deserted by their officers on the front lines. So it was no surprise when Brown told me that the Iraqi general pleaded with him not to take him to either Kuwait or Iraq where he surely would encounter profound hostility.

"What did you do with him?" I inquired.

"Well finally I just flew him to the BRO DTOC and dropped him off there and let them deal with him!" Brown said with a burst of laughter. It occurred to me later that this Iraqi general may have been the one I encountered in the DTAC with our ADC-M, BG Carter, on February 28.

When we landed at DSA Junction City, I headed to the supply center. It was a mess. There were tons of parts everywhere, in excess of 50 large crates intended for DIVARTY units that had been dropped off by Corps-level support units now eager to leave Iraq. Not wanting to pass up the opportunity to secure this largess, I sent word back to the DIVARTY TOC to get a truck on the road to collect this treasure. On the way home with Brown, I had a chance to think about what was wrong with the logistics system. I knew that the Center for Army Lessons Learned (CALL) was waiting back at the DIVARTY TOC to interview MAJ Brooks, my very able S-4 logistics officer, and me on our experience dealing with supply and maintenance issues. I wanted to be sure not to come off as a whiner and complainer and tried to organize my thoughts rationally. But what we had been dealing with, the port, parts, fuel, water, food, and mail, was so illogical that I found it almost impossible to order my thinking.

We landed at dusk, and I got out of the aircraft, bent down to avoid the rotor wash, and trotted away to a safe distance. I turned to Brown, who gave me a smart salute, which I gratefully returned as he took off. I headed immediately to the DIVARTY TOC where I met the CALL team with Brooks. It was important work that CALL did in capturing what had transpired when it was fresh in the minds of those of us who had experienced the war. Our foremost memories were stories of the miserable resupply support we had experienced throughout the war. We spent hours with them, venting our spleens on everything from the dysfunctional port operations, to the disorganized on-again, off-again ammunition supply system, to the lack of spare parts, some of which we received that day from orders placed the previous October. When we were done, I was discouraged. I was sure that our "testimony" would be "explained away" with "fog of war" excuses. To be sure, there were enormous distances to travel to move things and people, but the dearth of support, both parts and major assemblies like engines and transmissions for vehicles, could not, in my mind, be alibied with arguments about how far things had to travel. Our logistics doctrine, based on our warfighting requirements for the north German plains of Europe, was an utter failure in the sands of the Middle East. Three hours later, around 2230, we concluded the interview, and I stumbled to my tent, where McGary was sound asleep, no doubt grateful I had not made him drive me 200 kilometers to the DSA and back. I had no dinner that night, and while hunger gnawed at my gut, I was too tired to tear open an MRE. Rest was more demanding. I crawled into my sleeping bag, opened my diary, and concluded with the events of what was a very long day: "Another late night. Spoke in depth to the Center for Army Lessons Learned (CALL) on the awful state of logistics. (CL I [food] thru CL IX [repair parts]). I doubt much will be done to fix anything."

When the sun rose on March 27, it was my 40th birthday. I walked out of my tent and stretched in the early-morning desert air and wondered how I would celebrate. The day before I had learned that the "Wolf Burger," which was under DIVARTY's supervision, had served 9,800 burgers in its four days of operation. Dodson was impressed with its production, and I wondered if my next task would be to erect a sign by the day's end declaring, "Over 10,000 Sold!" I thought maybe I would head there for lunch. But for now, I walked toward the mess hall for a cup of coffee. There I met up with Dodson, who had just returned from the morning meeting with the Division commander. Wolf Burgers weren't on his mind. Gratefully, neither were signs. But redeployment was.

He said plaintively, "XO, looks like we're waiting for the Iraqis to sign the peace agreement before we know what will happen to us." If a treaty were signed, Dodson thought we and the entire VII Corps would leave Iraq within 72 hours. If not, we would stage out of the area of operations, with the BRO leaving last on April 19. That sounded like an eternity to me, and I knew it would be a "bummer," as the troops would say, particularly as the 2ACR, the 1AD, and the 3AD would precede us back to Saudi Arabia and then home to waiting families. Moreover, if the 2ACR positioned to our northwest were to leave ahead of us, we might be required to move farther north toward the Euphrates to fill the void they would leave behind. Indeed, Dodson would fly north that day to get a view of the area. In the region south of the ancient river, he found flooded rice paddies and sabkhas, large salt flats. No doubt, that would mean mosquitoes, lots of them, and the idea of adding those beasts to the list of daily challenges we faced in the desert was not a welcome thought. Despite that possibility, Dodson was getting contraindications from Rhame that the division was also formulating plans for how to get out of the desert and back to Fort Riley, fast.

Later that evening I celebrated my birthday with the DIVARTY staff, sitting around a field table. Joined by MAJs Ed Cardenas, Barry Brooks, Tom Conneran, and Charlie Wise, we all enjoyed cans of "Near Beer," a nonalcoholic brew that had found its way to the Iraqi desert, amazingly through our supply system. It was little more than malt-tasting carbonated water, but when iced down, it at least gave you an excuse to enjoy company and some good humor with colleagues. Since alcohol was prohibited, "Near Beer" would have to suffice in celebrating four decades of life. Our entertainment that evening was provided by Wise, our assistant S-4, who was, without a doubt, one of the funniest men I have ever met. He had managed to memorize a full repertoire of Las Vegas comedy shticks and would act out renditions of them that kept us in stitches. It was better than watching the same act on TV, which we didn't have anyway. Wise filled that desert evening with side-splitting comic routines. After hours of laughter, punctuated by our own funny war stories from the past few weeks, including the episode where Willis had to lead me out of a field of cluster bombs, I headed for my tent. There I noted in my diary the events of my 40th birthday. While cheered by Wise's humor, I was so tired—physically and emotionally—that it felt as if it were my 60th.

The morning of March 28 started slowly as we prepared for a briefing later in the day on the procedures and measures we would need to follow in cleaning and returning our combat equipment to the US. Despite the uncertainty about how long we would remain in Iraq, we had little guidance from the division or the VII Corps. It was hard to imagine how we would get all of this work done in the desert. We needed to get into the port, where there would be sufficient water resources to hose down the mud and sand accumulated in every crevasse of our combat equipment. However, one thing was clear from the beginning. We were told the inspectors from the US Department of Agriculture would be tough to please and sticklers in avoiding the introduction of any alien microbe from the Iraqi desert to the plains of Kansas. While this was a threat hard to envision, we dutifully briefed our commanders and staffs across the DIVARTY on the mission, including the exhaustive steps required to comply with pest-conscious government bureaucrats.

March 29 and 30 blended together as we waited for more guidance on our move south. We occupied our time amid maintenance frustrations, staff work that had fallen behind schedule, and preparation for Easter Sunday services by our chaplain, MAJ Tom Jones. He organized a work group in HHB to construct an open-air chapel. Troops filled olive-drab plastic sandbags, 14 inches by 24 inches in size, with sand to construct pews, an altar, and other related "furniture" to give the chapel a proper setting. He then used 4-by-4-inch wooden posts that we had for building defensive bunkers to construct a ten-foot cross that he erected at the center of the worship area behind the altar. It was remarkable to see this thing rise from the desert floor. Moreover, it was a testament to a chaplain's inspiration and the soldiers' engineering. You couldn't help but be impressed as troops pitched in to create the structure. Without a doubt, it broke the monotony of waiting until we received orders to head home, while reminding us that even in the desert of Iraq, we could take time to thank God for seeing us through this ordeal.

When the sunrise service was held the morning of March 31, it was set against an eastern sky where the clouds of war, in the form of smoke from oil fires, rose above the horizon even as we celebrated the resurrection of Jesus. The contrast was inescapable. When the day concluded, I had a chance to speak with a journalist from the *Army Times*, Chris Donnelly, to give him my take on the war. I then retired to do some writing of my own for an article for the *Field Artillery* journal, a critique on the war and the role of the artillery in it, in which I addressed tactics, training, and equipment needs for future conflicts.[4] There was much, maybe too much, to write about, but I wanted to capture my observations when they were fresh in my mind.

April 1 through 6 were spent in wrestling with details on setting up and operating firing ranges for the cannon battalions to keep them up to snuff. It appeared increasingly unlikely that we would be headed north, but if we did, thunderous live fire training was a certain way to keep our artillery skills honed while reminding our enemies we were ready to resume combat. Dodson complained to me that, while the division staff was responsible for running the artillery range, it was a "zoo" with "no one in charge." Bedouins would wander in and out of the impact area. Unbelievably, there was a desert road—used by the US and Bedouins alike—that ran through the middle of the range. However, when the division's Master Gunner who ran the range would leave, no one remaining there had a clue how to orchestrate safety activities. For the detail-oriented Dodson, this was, as he would say, "unsat," and he turned to Cardenas and me to get things straight with the division. The very last thing Dodson wanted to deal with at that point was a caravan of dead Bedouins and camels strewn about the desert floor.

On top of all of this, the toxic clouds from the oil fires, as it turned out, were still a problem for us when the effects drifted westward. They were noxious—even while far away—and really took a toll on everyone. We did get some relief, however, on April 3 in the form of a brief but violent storm that blew the miasma somewhere else. Unfortunately, that same storm caused a lot of chaos. I noted this in my diary: "Night before last we had a big storm. S-2s female tent went down. A real scream. Major Charlie Wise did a stand-up routine as we all stood around in our shorts laughing silly." Wise, as he had in the past, sprang from the shambles of his collapsed tent in the middle of a raging storm and immediately broke into a spontaneous comic routine as improvised as it was hilarious. Pretending to be the Good Witch of the North in the 1939 movie *The Wizard of Oz*, he mocked the Wicked Witch of the West, saying, "Where did that bitch come from that knocked down my tent, dammit! Did you see her on that damn broom! Get her damn license number! Call the cops! Her ass must have been flying at Mach-2 through here! Damn that bitch!!!" Then he started mimicking the music used in the movie that accompanied the entry of the fictional wicked character who menaced Dorothy and her friends: "Do-ta-do-ta-doo, doo, Do-ta-do-ta-doo, doo." By then we were all crumpled over in laughter, even as we went about in the dark to recover articles of clothing, papers, and anything that was not nailed down. Fortuitously, McGary had, as the Bible said, "built his house on a rock" because, once again, our tent stayed in place. Still, even if it had blown down, you could hardly be angry while listening to Wise's slide-splitting antics. While we didn't have movies or a USO show to entertain us in the middle of the Iraqi desert, there was always the incomparable "Charlie Wise Show" playing at a tent near you.

When April 7 arrived, I fell very sick with what could only be termed "desert grunge." It was a horrible cross between flu and dysentery. There was very little I could do but lie in my cot and pray to get better. Doc Sullivan visited and gave me medication that didn't really help, but I took it dutifully in the hope that it would. Within the week both Doc and Dodson would have the same malady. And when you got it, you were flat out of action. As I lay in my cot, I wondered if this illness had roots in all the noxious oil-fire fumes we endured, or maybe the anti–nerve agent PB pills we choked down for weeks prior to our attack into Iraq. I wasn't sure of anything except that I was sick as a dog.

On April 9 we were enfolded in a major sandstorm and intermittent rain, and once again we were getting rumors that we would move south to Saudi Arabia soon. However, no sooner had the rumors appeared than, like a desert mirage, they disappeared. That morning Dodson told me we would be moving in "one day," then the warning order changed to "tomorrow." By the end of the day, the whole movement order was revoked. It was at that point that I decided to stop worrying about when we would move, preferring to focus on being prepared to move. At least that was a good use of my time instead of reacting to rumors.

On April 11, another rumor popped up that I would be the officer in charge (OIC) for the entire movement of the division from the port back to Fort Riley. It was a disquieting thought, even as I recovered from "the grunge." Like everyone else, I wanted to get home. I had spoken to Shelley on the phone a few times, and I knew that the war had taken a real toll on her and the kids. The idea of remaining in Saudi Arabia for months to pack up 6,000 combat vehicles, load them on ships, and send them back

to Fort Riley was daunting. I knew more about brain surgery than loading ships, and besides, that OIC job was ideal for a professional logistician, not an artilleryman. I put it out of my mind because if I had been in
charge of the division, I wouldn't have chosen me. I would have found
someone like a transportation officer who was trained in this specialty.
Besides, I had other things to worry about, like getting the DIVARTY
back to "Custer Hill" in RAA Huebner.

In fact, the next morning, April 12, I was scheduled to lead an
advance party to the RAA when I was summoned by Dodson to his tent.
"Scott, I'm sick to death," he mumbled. "You need to be here to repre-
sent me at the division and prepare us for movement south." I had never
seen Dodson so ill and asked him if he wanted me to get Doc Sullivan,
only to learn that Doc was suffering with the same thing. As I left the tent
to head to the division's morning meeting, Dodson called me back. "XO,
don't tell them how sick I am," he said. I understood. Dodson would not
sit still for being medically evacuated, and he knew that if Rhame feared
one of his brigade-level commanders was seriously sick, he would order
that evacuation immediately. I was uneasy with Dodson's request. But I
resolved for now to honor it, hoping, as I rode to the division headquarters, that no one would ask me how sick he really was. To my relief, no
one did, but I learned that we needed to be prepared to leave Iraq in two
days. That would mean my boss needed to get better soon. I thought the
news from division would cheer him up, but when I briefed him as he lay
in his cot, he acknowledged the message with a hushed, "OK." He might
have been cheered, but he was still a very sick man. After I left his tent, I
spent the rest of that day and the next two days preparing everyone to
leave Iraq.

Unbelievably, by the morning of April 14, we still didn't have a clear
"go" on the move south, despite having learned that the ceasefire had
taken effect three days earlier. Nevertheless, I ordered the DIVARTY and
HHB to prepare for movement. Down came the tents and camouflage
nets we had used to disguise our locations in the desert, a seemingly
meaningless exercise at that point, since we had destroyed any Iraqi
ground or air capability that would threaten us. But we had our combat
standards, and threat or not, we had, until my order, followed them faithfully. Then at 1930 that evening, Dodson got the call from the division
that we would move at 0800 in the morning.

We awoke early on the morning of April 15 with an exhilaration
that, at long last, we were leaving Iraq. We had not come here as occupi-
ers. We were liberators and always thought of ourselves that way. And

now we were finally prepared to make the first of two long convoy movements south to Saudi Arabia. McGary struck the tent, filled in the foxhole next to it, packed us up in record time, and readied HQ-5 for the long road march south. I managed to secure a cup of coffee before the mess hall closed its operation, then dutifully made the rounds through the DIVARTY TOC and the HHB area to ensure our officers and troops alike were packed up and ready to move out. The division had given us strict orders that we were to leave no equipment behind, not even a screwdriver. So I took great care to make certain that we complied. The troops were upbeat and so eager to leave Iraq, and if that meant turning over every grain of sand to ensure we had not forgotten anything, they gladly would have done so.

Personally, I was relieved that we were headed back to Saudi Arabia. The "separates," including HHB DIVARTY, B-6 FA, D-25 TAB, and the 12th Chemical, had been under my direct supervision. They comprised a total force of 621 soldiers and had performed remarkably well considering all that had transpired, both good and bad. I was looking forward to the next day when we would be headed for Saudi Arabia and I could focus on returning these very superb soldiers to Fort Riley to be reunited with family and friends. A death or serious injury at this point would have been needlessly tragic. It weighed on my mind.

As I made my way through the area, I took note of the field-expedient chapel our troops had constructed under the watchful supervision of Chaplain Jones to celebrate Easter two weeks earlier. It was still standing. Jones asked me if we should take it down. After all, it was built with US equipment, sandbags, and lumber. I thought momentarily and said, "No, leave it right where it is. God got us safely to this point. Maybe we should show our thanks. Besides, you never know who might have need of it," I said, half-joking since the only people who would likely come across it would be Bedouins who were Muslims. What harm would it do to leave a calling card behind to remind them that we came, we fought, and unlike the Christian Crusaders a thousand years earlier, we left of our own volition.

When 0800 arrived, Cardenas mounted HQ-3, called the division headquarters, and promptly reported our "Sierra Papa" or "SP," the term we used to inform higher headquarters that we were departing our "start point" in a convoy march. Then Cardenas proceeded to lead the DIVARTY TOC out of the position we had "reinvaded" three weeks earlier, with McGary and me bringing up the rear. As the last vehicle in the DIVARTY TOC and HHB column turned southwest, McGary started to move when I said abruptly, "Stop, Roger, I want to get out." Roger looked at me curiously as he hit the brakes, rocking the Humvee to a dead stop. I stepped out and walked behind the vehicle to look one last time at the makeshift open-air chapel we had constructed.

Standing there alone, I wondered if this latest "invasion" back into Iraq by US forces was actually an "evasion" of sorts, the evading that accompanies an unfinished job. My attention returned to our improvised worship facility. The structure we had used to celebrated Easter in the desert stood in marked contrast to the early-morning horizon behind it. I removed my Kevlar helmet, tucked it under my arm, and said a prayer that this abandoned place of worship would somehow have a positive impact on someone. Getting back in the Humvee, I motioned to McGary to move out. He gunned HQ-5, our reliable vehicle that had taken us so far—to that point over 1,825 kilometers of rugged terrain—and we too had Iraq in our rearview mirror. Soon our convoy would kick up a large cloud of dust that could be seen for miles and would obscure us as we headed southwest on the initial leg of a long road march ahead of us that day. The Bedouins, who had only recently moved back into the vicinity, must have been pleased to see us leave. Their simple and unencumbered life in the sands of Iraq could now return to the solitude and simplicity they once knew before we made war clouds of dust in their desert home.

Later that day around 1430, after traveling 70 kilometers southwest in the general direction of Hafar al-Batin, we stopped 15 kilometers short of the breach we had made in the Iraqi 26ID only two months earlier (see map 12.2).[5] There we camped just north of PL Colorado and south of a place on the map called Al Abtiyah, whose prominent feature was a small abandoned concrete building in the middle of a vast desert. The mess hall set up its mobile kitchen and made hot soup and coffee for everyone, which boosted morale after bumping across the desert for several hours. Fortunately, the convoy movement was uneventful, save for a few break-downs that we quickly repaired. McGary and I elected to sleep in the back of HQ-5 that night since we would be on the road early the next morning. Our second leg would begin with a short road march toward the breach site we had used to invade Iraq. After that, we would journey another 65 kilometers to a position just north of the dangerous "Tapline Road" in Saudi Arabia where, only months earlier, young PFC Kirk of D-25 TAB had become our first casualty.

My diary on the evening of April 15, 1991, reflected the feelings I had about all that had occurred in the recent months, not only to us but to the simple nomadic people of Iraq. For better or worse, they had witnessed a

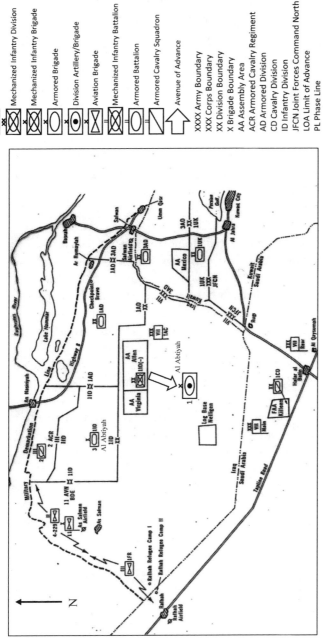

Corps · Mechanized Infantry Division · Mechanized Infantry Brigade · Armored Brigade · Division Artillery/Brigade · Aviation Brigade · Mechanized Infantry Battalion · Armored Battalion · Armored Cavalry Squadron · Avenue of Advance

XXXX Army Boundary
XXX Corps Boundary
XX Division Boundary
X Brigade Boundary
AA Assembly Area
ACR Armored Cavalry Regiment
AD Armored Division
CD Cavalry Division
ID Infantry Division
JFCN Joint Forces Command North
LOA Limit of Advance
PL Phase Line
RGFC Republican Guard Forces Command
TAA Tactical Attack Center
TF Task Force

Map 12.2. 1st Infantry DIVARTY Movement from TAA Allen to Iraqi Border, April 15, 1991 great conflict unfold in their otherwise peaceful desert, which, before our arrival, was disturbed only by the coming and going of the seasons. Yet they could not help but be changed by what had happened, what had been set in motion by the dictator Saddam Hussein and our violent blitzkrieg in response to it. Several questions ran through my mind. How were they changed? How would they respond in the years to come? How were we changed? How would we respond if the need arose in the future? I had no answers just then. Simply the reflections of a soldier—a Desert Redleg— who had helped bring so much destruction on the Iraqi Army; a soldier who had come to fight; a soldier who knew these nomadic people; and in the wake of Desert Storm, a soldier who wondered what would happen to all of us as we made our exit from Iraq. I composed my thoughts while sitting in my Humvee as the spring sun, which had warmed my face and hands as I wrote that afternoon, dipped slowly below the western horizon:

> This is our last night in Iraq. Tomorrow we will pass through the breach we made almost two months ago. All is quiet in the desert now. The Bedouins have reclaimed the silence that is the desert. As US forces headed south, these otherwise simple people seem to express in their faces that their lives are not so simple anymore. They understand that things are difficult but are not sure just how or where life leads now. We are the same. What will the future bring? As the Arab world struggles to understand how the latest defeat at Western hands will impact on their future, so must we strive to understand them. It seems we will forever speak different languages. Unfortunately for a moment, we spoke the common tongue of violence. Will we find equal understanding in the language of peace? Bukra, Inshallah.

As we left Iraq, this was—in my mind—every bit an unresolved peace. Exhausted and ready for some sleep, I placed my diary in the knapsack I kept near me. I then crawled into the narrow space at the back of HQ-5, the trusty Humvee that McGary and I had configured behind my quarters on Riley Place six months earlier. Lying there, I put my questions aside and slept peacefully in a now placid desert.

13

The Long March Home

The morning of April 16 was a red-letter day for the DIVARTY Redlegs. Soon we would depart Iraq. Unlike the Crusaders who sought to occupy the Middle East in the 12th to 14th centuries, we were ready to leave it behind. Our focus was riveted on returning to Fort Riley and the herculean work ahead. It was truly a remarkable effort that got us here in the first place, and it would be no less of a complicated, detailed, and maddening effort to retrace our steps back to Kansas. It would be a long march for sure, but we were ready to get on with it.

I awoke to the abrupt starting of the cold diesel engine of our Humvee that my driver, PFC McGary, mischievously cranked to roust me from my slumber. "Hey, sir, ready for some coffee?" he asked teasingly. If the engine wasn't enough to jump-start me into action, the invitation for some "joe" did the trick. I quickly dressed myself, grabbed my coffee and my gear, and headed to the DIVARTY TOC. There I checked in with MAJ Cardenas, who confirmed we would "SP," or begin, our 80-kilometer second-leg march at 0800 to a position just north of Tapline Road. Once there, we would remain overnight and make a third and final short march to RAA Huebner the next morning (see map 13.1).[1]

As the wind kicked up the desert sand—an extra incentive to get us moving—we were eager to get underway. After the HHB was packed up and ready to roll, Cardenas led us out of position at precisely 0800 on a planned all-day march south to a location east of tiny As Safayri north of Hafar al-Batin, an actual population center. We were familiar with our desert route, having used it from TAA Roosevelt to the FAA earlier in the war, from where we conducted the artillery raids, the preparation, and the attack into Iraq. Now we would backtrack through the same breach lanes with a largely different expectation, not a war ahead of us, but a homecoming.

As we approached the Iraqi-constructed defensive berm that we had cut through two months earlier, I was struck by how much had transpired in just four months. The evidence of destruction in and around the breach

245

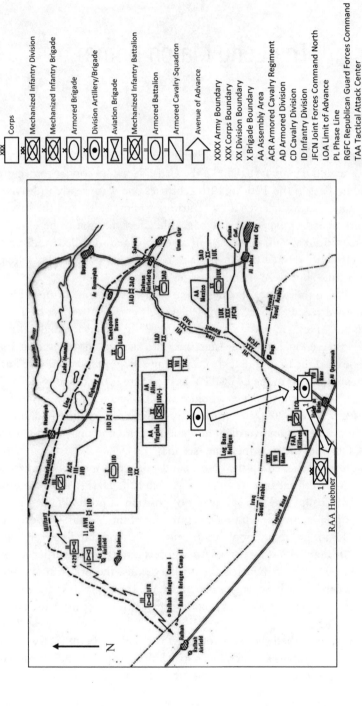

Key (legend):

XXXX (Corps)	Corps
XX	Mechanized Infantry Division
XX	Mechanized Infantry Brigade
X	Armored Brigade
O (dot)	Division Artillery/Brigade
X	Aviation Brigade
XX	Mechanized Infantry Battalion
O	Armored Battalion
Armored Cavalry Squadron	Armored Cavalry Squadron
Avenue of Advance (arrow)	Avenue of Advance

XXXX Army Boundary
XXX Corps Boundary
XX Division Boundary
X Brigade Boundary
AA Assembly Area
ACR Armored Cavalry Regiment
AD Armored Division
CD Cavalry Division
ID Infantry Division
JFCN Joint Forces Command North
LOA Limit of Advance
PL Phase Line
RGFC Republican Guard Forces Command
TAA Tactical Attack Center
TF Task Force

Map 13.1. 1st Infantry DIVARTY Movement from Iraqi Border to RAA Huebner, April 16–17, 1991 area was profound. As the sun poked through the overcast sky, in part cleared by the wind, I was optimistic and exhilarated. When we crossed into Saudi territory, both McGary and I let out a hoot! "Good-bye, Iraq," McGary yelled as he hit the accelerator to emphasize his glee—mine too. I pulled out one of my cigars and lit it up. It was reason to celebrate, even as I struggled to light it while bouncing across rough terrain.

In the process of crossing the Iraqi berm, the division's 2nd Brigade preceded us and managed to use the breach lanes designated for DIVARTY, not them. As COL Dodson later told me, that would have been fine, but they stopped immediately after exiting the breach area to account for all their vehicles. That caused a huge backup and bottleneck that compacted and complicated the DIVARTY's convoy as we moved through and out of our designated lanes. When McGary and I cleared the breach lane, I stopped to speak with Dodson, who was obviously intensely focused on getting the DIVARTY south of the breach and on its way. He was thoroughly perturbed with the traffic miscue and wasn't inclined to engage in small talk at that moment. "XO, we need to keep people moving, and make sure no one is left behind," he snapped. He noted his worry about vehicles that might break down before crossing back into Saudi Arabia. Since McGary and I had been near the rear of the column, I told him I was comfortable that all of our vehicles would get through in good order. I also reported that we had a recovery team from the HHB working to fix some broken trailers north of the berm, but aside from that, we were in good shape. Dodson didn't share my optimism one bit because he was required to certify to MG Rhame that absolutely everyone in the DIVARTY had crossed the breach area safely to Saudi Arabia. "Being comfortable" was not "absolutely sure." There was no room for error, particularly since Rhame was also "on the hook," as we would say, to report the entire division had crossed back into Saudi Arabia and was completely out of Iraq. Anyone left behind could become an "international incident" at that point, so for Dodson and his superiors, being "kind of sure" was like being "kind of pregnant." There could be no doubt in reporting.

After we cleared the traffic pileup, we moved several kilometers farther south and stopped at noon to refuel. There we gave the troops a break from marching over washboard desert terrain and rested from the bouncing that took an unforgiving toll on my back. Our Humvees didn't have the suspension of my BMW 320i waiting in my driveway at Fort Riley. When we hit a rough spot, the jolt would travel up and down my spine, reminding me that war, after all, was a young man's game. When we stopped, CPT Hymel reported to me that all his HHB vehicles were in fact safely across the berm and accounted for, a piece of news Dodson was glad to get. However, there were the other DIVARTY direct support battalions, 1–5 FA, 4–5 FA, and 4–3 FA (returning with the 2AD-F) that also had to report to Dodson. Those reports weren't in yet.

When we were fueled, fed, and rested, we resumed our desert road march to the next position north of Hafar al-Batin. By 1600, we had arrived. As the DIVARTY TOC set up to gather in the final crossing reports for Dodson, I ran into him, and I could tell he was still spun up. As I noted in my diary that evening, "He was all over us" and "involved in every aspect of the operation." It was understandable. He had tremendous pressure on him to certify that everyone was accounted for and safe. Plus, he was just then getting past his own bout with the "desert grunge" that had vexed many of us. Nevertheless, his intensity ramped up the pressure on all of us too. When we finally settled down for the evening, and all the reports were in, the pressure subsided. It was then that the always steady and focused Dodson I knew throughout the war was "accounted for" as well. I was glad. Despite my relief, I had a restless sleep that night—even as tired as I was—but I was more than willing to spend one more night in the back of HQ-5 if it would put me one day closer to home.

At 0600 the next morning, April 17, we made our final push across Tapline Road toward RAA Huebner. The division's military police teams showed up to escort us across the dangerous Tapline Road toward the RAA. We proceeded at 0630 in six parallel columns to shorten our convoy's exposure when crossing the deadly road. The 142nd FA Brigade from Arkansas was tucked in behind us, and I was hopeful they too would cross without incident, staying in uniform, with Confederate flags out of sight. As we traversed Tapline Road to the southwest, the huge ruts on either side of the road—caused by US tracked vehicles earlier—made crossing perpendicular to them very difficult. It was almost like negotiating enemy-made obstacles. We managed our way over the rugged shoulders of the main road, which—according to Dodson's watch—took about ten minutes for each of the six serials to cross. The 35-minute movement to our destination went smoothly. Cardenas's convoy serial went a bit too far south of Tapline Road before crossing into the RAA, but it all worked out fine.

When we arrived in the RAA, we discovered that CPT Seefeldt's preparation of the place was remarkable. He had arranged our DIVARTY site in a large semicircle with tents on the perimeter of a large parade field marked out with rocks with a US flag flying in the middle of it. Adjacent to that, he had constructed a soccer field with goals, and benches for opposing teams to sit and watch games. We were also surprised to learn that the

Saudis, in a moment of generosity I suppose, had stocked us with cases of Perrier water. I suspected they intended for it to be a proxy for the beer we wouldn't get any time soon in a Saudi Kingdom that prohibited alcohol. It wasn't, but it was a nice gesture. "Perrier in the desert," I thought, "Now that's one for the books." Seefeldt had outdone himself and was quite proud of his efforts as he gave me a tour of the area. However, my interest was neither on Saudi niceties nor soccer fields. It was on beginning the huge tasks we were told we would need to accomplish to get home.

That morning, I assembled the staff for a planning session on the numerous tasks we would need to address. That included movement schedules back to the port, wash-rack operations for the vehicles, staging requirements for loading the ships, and the aircraft schedule that would be involved to fly the troops back to the US. After we had assessed all of the reliable information we had gleaned from division planners, we gave Dodson an overview on what we knew. He took it all in, and then issued additional planning guidance to us. We spent the rest of the day, and into the evening, getting our revised redeployment briefing ready for the detail-oriented Dodson and scheduled a full presentation for him the next day.

At 1100 the next morning, April 18, the weather was decidedly warmer, and we briefed Dodson on the redeployment plan as we understood it. He was pleased with our work. I then had McGary fire up HQ-5, and we headed south to KKMC, the military facility about 70 kilometers from RAA Huebner, to check on some logistical matters and inspect the prewashing facilities. Along the way, we swung past the wash rack the division had constructed in the middle of the desert for units to do an initial cleaning of vehicles before transporting them back to the port in Dammam. The concept of washing our vehicles in the desert struck me as useless. There we were shrouded in dust storms, stirred by an unrelenting wind, and certain that we would have to wash them again once we were at the port. But those were the orders, and I wanted to be sure that I saw the facilities before we used them. Greg Fontenot in his account of the war captured the wash-rack scene aptly: "The division-built wash racks and hauled in water and pumps to permit at least a rough wash of equipment prior to heading back to the ports. Crews power-washing tanks with high-pressure wands miles from the nearest source of water provided grist for laughter among the soldiers. The sight must have puzzled those desert dwellers who saw it."[2] In truth, it was a waste of perfectly good water, but it gave the troops something to do, including getting wet under a hot desert sun. After inspecting this arrangement, I continued to KKMC, about

35 kilometers farther south of our position in RAA Huebner. It was a mess with no military discipline, and soldiers had seemingly forgotten the courtesy of saluting officers. I made several not-so-diplomatic corrections, reminding young soldiers that while hostilities were over, we were still in a US Army that observed certain military customs. After doing my part to restore some military discipline, McGary and I took advantage of the PX facilities there, including grabbing a real hamburger. The trip was worth the effort. While at KKMC, I also visited the division liaison element where someone mentioned, off-the-cuff, that they had heard I would command the Port Support Activity (PSA) that would bring the division home. Having heard this rumor back in Iraq, I didn't feel particularly "honored" with the task then, and wasn't now. But I was told that Rhame wanted a "strong-willed type to ensure things happen," and apparently, I fit his expectations despite my misgivings.

When April 19 arrived, all doubt was removed. Dodson came back from the morning meeting at the division and gave me the news. "Scott, Rhame wants you to command the Port Support Activity (PSA) and get the division home," he said. Dodson was surprised the decision had been made without consulting him first, but Rhame had his eye on me to get this job done. Dodson attempted to make the case to division planners that we split the duty between newly promoted LTC Mike Cuff and me, with Cuff doing the initial organizing while I took some rest and recuperation back at Fort Riley. I then would return to Saudi Arabia to execute the operation. Rhame rejected that idea the next day. He wanted a "junkyard dog" for this duty on "day one," and that would be me. And he wanted that leader in place full-time to ensure the division was not "elbowed out" when attempting to secure its fair share of transport and priority for vehicle shipment. Considering that other divisions and brigades from the continental US and the US Army in Europe (USAREUR) would be fighting hard to be first in line, Rhame wanted a hard-charger.

The news came as a real blow to my family, especially my daughter, Amy, who cried pitifully when she realized I would not be home to see her as a flower girl in my sister's wedding. But my disappointment and that of my little girl aside, this was a huge mission that had been placed on my shoulders, and to say that I was a bit intimidated is to understate my lack of confidence to do this job. Over 6,000 combat vehicles and related pieces of equipment had to be inventoried down to the last bumper number, cleaned to the smallest crevasse, loaded, secured, and transported with great care. Simple in concept, but a very difficult mission to accomplish, and one for which there was no room for error. As an artilleryman, I had a lot to learn. So on April 20, Dodson, Cardenas, MAJ Wise—who would be my PSA XO—and I boarded a UH-60 Blackhawk helicopter headed to the Port of Dammam to get the lay of the land. Dodson wanted to see things himself since the DIVARTY was to provide the leadership for the complex task that his XO would lead. Cardenas wanted to learn too so that he would have a jump on the detailed planning for the DIVARTY. When we arrived, we found that the ground transportation we thought we had arranged to transport us to and around the port for the day, had not arrived. Fortunately, I ran into one of my VMI classmates, LTC Yerry Kenneally, at the airfield who was working for LTG Gus Pagonis. Kenneally, who was in a position to "make things happen," came to our rescue and summoned up a vehicle for us, and we headed to the port. Later, I would learn that our mutual classmate, LTC Jimmy Chalkley, was the XO of the 7th Transportation Group. Thankfully, that was the very outfit that would orchestrate the support operations that the PSA would need to accomplish our mission. It was a bit of good news, indeed good luck, amid my thoughts about whether I was knowledgeable enough to make this operation happen successfully. At least I had two VMI "Brother Rats"—as we called ourselves—there to help me.

We then visited the division headquarters detachment that Rhame had sent ahead with BG Carter a few days earlier. Their job was to get the PSA established, as well as a host of other measures that would have to be put in place to receive the division's vehicles and units from the desert. To address this demanding task, the leadership of the division determined the best way to get the mission done was to form the PSA and assign men and women across the division's various units who possessed the proper skill sets that the PSA would need. That required some soldiers to stay behind in Saudi Arabia while others returned to their families, and for the leadership, that meant making tough choices.

After touring the port area, inspecting the wash racks, and getting at least a concept of the operation in our heads, we boarded our helicopter to return to the desert. The flight back gave me time to think about how to best organize the PSA, train it, and get it ready for a very challenging mission. When we landed in RAA Huebner, it was hot, and hot temperatures would be our constant companion in the port. I went to my tent, packed up my equipment, and made ready for another long trip in the morning back to the port to assume command and control of the PSA.

I arose early on April 21 with a lot on my mind. I thought about the past four months and the next several it would take to get the division home. I was deeply attached to the unit I had fought with in combat, and frankly I felt as if I were abandoning them. McGary helped me load my equipment in the vehicle that would take me to the port, since he wasn't driving me there. It was hard to leave him. He didn't have much to say. I could tell it was hard on him too. After all, we had been together through a hell of a lot in the recent months. I went to the DIVARTY TOC to say goodbye to Cardenas and the men who were so much at the center of the success we had enjoyed in this war. Then I ran into Dodson. It was awkward. Our relationship was professional, but we were now such friends that we almost knew what the other was thinking. He trusted me and let me do my job, and I admired his style of leadership, wisdom, and focus. So when I attempted to say "goodbye," I struggled for the right words.

As I did, he interjected, "What, XO?" knowing that I needed a friendly push to "get on with it."

I then said, "Well, I'm off, I'll report back when I arrive."

Dodson nodded approvingly, and we exchanged salutes. I then rode away from the DIVARTY, wondering what would be next. There would be a lot of "next" to keep me and the PSA busy.

It was a long trip in hot weather. By the time I arrived at Khobar Towers, our first home in January that we had irreverently named the "MGM" after the Las Vegas resort, the large facility of concrete high-rise buildings had been transformed into a fairly decent place to live. Carter had set up the division headquarters on the first floor of one of the buildings on the northern end of the complex, where I reported in. Cuff, who had done some initial planning of the staffing and manning of the PSA organization, greeted me in his normally cheerful manner, "Hey, XO, glad you're here!"

I struggled to replicate his enthusiasm without betraying how I really felt about being tapped for this job. "Yep, long ride and I'm bushed," I confessed.

"Don't worry Scott. Let me tell ya something. Tonight, you're gonna sleep the sleep of the dead," he said.

"Curious," I thought to myself, "that's precisely the kind of sleep I thought I was avoiding for the entire war."

Cuff went on, "Yep, after a hot shower, sleep will fall on you like a ton of bricks." As he explained it, the first night in a building that is quiet, air-conditioned, and comfortable—after months of living in the elements—would be completely relaxing. But more importantly, it would be a night when you didn't have to worry about whether you would make it to the next day.

Cuff and I then sat down and went over the organization of the PSA as it was envisioned. He had worked out many details, and I was pleased he had. After some chow, I reported to a room that had been assigned to me in the building, only to be told by a major, whom the division staff had appointed as the "Khobar Mayor," that I could stay there only for a while and would have to move later. After a brief but frank discussion, he agreed that I would remain exactly where I was and that my staff, including Wise, who was with me, would remain in their original rooms as well. Apparently, no one had briefed this "mayor" on the PSA and its space requirements, particularly since we would be there for a few months and hopping around from one spot to another was simply unnecessary. When I finally went to bed, Cuff was right, I slept the "sleep of the dead." The room was air-conditioned, the hot water worked, and the strange contraption in the bath area they called a toilet was a welcome luxury. I joked with Wise about how to "operate it." The comical Wise rose to the bait and cracked a joke that removed all doubt about what it was for and how to use it!

On the morning of April 22 I had breakfast at the contract dining facility near the division headquarters. It was much better than when we had first arrived in January, but it was still very different from a pancake restaurant back home. After breakfast, Cuff, the division team, and I sat down to dig into the details of how the PSA would come together and operate. Our first challenge was personnel. A search for "volunteers" seemed like the best approach, but in some cases, skill sets would drive the decision of who would be designated to be part of the PSA. To ensure the success of the operation, which was to return the division's equipment efficiently and quickly back to Fort Riley, we knew we would need strong leadership and capable soldiers. Despite my own hesitancy in embracing the PSA command, Rhame thought that I was the right "junkyard dog" the PSA needed at the top. To be sure, I was all too familiar with "logistics combat," having fought many battles on the desert floor to properly position artillery ammunition, get vehicles repaired, and move troops from one place to another, all amid confusion, changing orders, and danger at every turn. Those experiences would serve me and the men and women of the PSA well. So making the leap to commander of the PSA was a short step for me and my staff, but a giant leap in putting it together, training it, and getting the job done. I was more confident that it could be done, but in my wildest dreams, I had no appreciation for just how challenging this entire endeavor would be.[3]

The division's primary skills were in combined-arms war fighting and providing the support and logistic operations that fundamental mission required. Few if any in the BRO had the slightest idea of how to load-plan a Military Sealift Command (MSC) ship, much less some tramp break-bulk civilian freighter from Denmark. And few of us were trained to load ships that were designed primarily to carry Volvos around the world to waiting automobile consumers. But in this case, my consumer was the feisty, steel-jawed Rhame. And keeping that customer happy would take precision, a lot of training for soldiers unskilled at loading ships, and the discipline and determination to stay on track. Rhame made it clear to me to "have everyone home by the 4th of July, Independence Day," and made that point chest-thumpingly clear when I ran into him later that day. I got the message.

The first step was to organize the PSA. The division's staff made the decision to model the PSA on a typical battalion structure. That included a battalion commander, an executive officer (XO), and a typical S-1 though S-4 staff organization. Subordinate units would be organized as companies; a Headquarters Company, a Transport (Driver) Company, a Loader-Lasher Company, and a Maintenance Company.

The Headquarters Company and PSA staff were top notch. Wise, who had been assigned to Training and Doctrine Command (TRADOC) at Fort Monroe, Virginia, prior to the war and later functioned as our DIVARTY Assistant S-4, was designated as my XO. While affable and a bit of a "cutup," he was mission-focused and hard-nosed when it came to getting things done. He would be my right arm. He immediately went about organizing the staff functions and the initial housing and staffing of the PSA. The S-1, S-2, S-3, and S-4 were all skilled officers, along with our Transportation Support Officer (TSO) CPT Renee Miller. She was one of the few people in the entire PSA who had a clue about shipping operations, and she worked tirelessly to navigate the challenges of planning transport operations. My S-3, CPT Gene Malik, was also very competent and, along with Wise, worked to organize us as the soldiers assigned to the PSA reported for duty from across the division.

As the PSA staff came together, it became clear to me that they were top notch. They needed to be because they would be working in an environment that required lots of planning, liaison, and routine—but necessary—staff actions with other units in the port area once the 1ID headquarters left Saudi Arabia for Fort Riley. In that regard, daily situation reports alone were essential and required accurate input from across all PSA staff sections. Moreover, there were the daily requirements of soldier care, including personal fitness reports, physical training, medical needs, personnel actions, reenlistments, and, rarely, disciplinary action under the Uniform Code of

Military Justice (UCMJ). All of this would need to occur just as it would in the soldiers' parent units. As it turned out, it was a real testament to the entire selection process that I had but a handful of UCMJ disciplinary actions among the 567 soldiers of the PSA.

The PSA would first require the capability to move vehicles from one storage area to another to accommodate the positioning and loading of vehicles, both wheeled and tracked. That required a transport operation. While the Saudi port at Dammam was a large and well-equipped facility, parking space for thousands of combat vehicles among numerous divisions that would transit the port was limited, something we experienced in January when we first arrived. Our exit, however, would require that only the vehicles set to be next in line for loading would be parked in the port "staging areas." Initially, many of the division's wheeled and track vehicles would be parked 22 kilometers away from the port at KFIA, the airfield where our troops arrived in January. This required that the Transport Company be manned with drivers capable of moving many different classes of vehicles, including light-wheeled, heavy-wheeled, track, and specialized vehicles that had limited numbers of qualified operators in the division, like those required to move heavy engineer equipment. The challenge was to find the right folks to do the job. This operation dominated the PSA's early activities, even as the division's units shuffled vehicles from RAA Huebner in the Saudi desert to the port, then through the port's cleaning facility at the water-desalination plant near Dammam, and finally to "sanitized" outlying parking areas in and around the port. There the cleaned vehicles were quarantined in preparation for shipment home. The selection process for PSA drivers, who would position vehicles in the port to be loaded, was based first on the capabilities of the individual soldiers, and then on whether they were properly licensed to drive certain vehicles. By the time the mission concluded, these soldiers would have repositioned thousands of vehicles, often in complex traffic environments, and would do so safely without a single personal injury or major accident involving another vehicle.

The PSA would also require a Loader-Lasher Company whose mission would be to load and secure vehicles on ships of varying capacity and configuration, often in the oppressive heat of Dammam. The sun's unforgiving presence made the work of the loader-lashers miserable, requiring strong soldiers capable of working in a sweltering heat. Many of the soldiers were from combat units—infantrymen, tankers, or artillerymen. And while their mission would be somewhat delayed until ships were available to load, when the work began, they labored as hard as any group of soldiers I ever knew. The immediate challenge was to train the loader-lashers how to properly stow and secure vehicles on ships with varying configurations. Some of the ships would be massive roll-on/roll-off (RO/RO) vessels, which had huge ramps to drive equipment on board. Others were Maritime Prepositioning Ships (MPS) used by the Marine Corps to preposition equipment afloat in various locations around the world. Both ramps and onboard cranes were used to load them. Still others were break-bulk ships, which were classic freighters with large holds that use shore-positioned cranes to load each item of equipment painstakingly into the bowels of the vessel. Additionally, there were safety precautions that had to be learned, including dealing with cramped environments, overwhelming temperatures, fire drills, and, of course, the constant threat of being pinned between a steel vehicle and a steel bulkhead, not a place one wanted to be trapped. The 7th Transportation Group was tasked with training our soldiers.

The PSA would also require vehicular maintenance, lots of it. Therefore, a Maintenance Company was formed. Every vehicle had to be properly maintained even while they were waiting to be loaded. Engines would spring leaks, tracks would be thrown from their sprockets, and routine daily maintenance was a constant requirement for the more than 6,000 vehicles in our charge until they were safely loaded on ships. Division planners determined that a robust maintenance capability would be needed for the many different classes of vehicles that we were tasked to maintain and repair. Time was essential in ship loading, and units could ill afford to have a broken M1 tank blocking a narrow loading ramp when vessels were required to get underway at a specific time to meet exacting schedules. The personnel-selection process would require the identification of maintenance technicians capable of working on wheeled and tracked vehicles alike. The technicians would require the tools and equipment to replace or repair major components such as engines, transmissions, and drive assemblies, not to mention the performance of many other maintenance tasks. At the end of the PSA mission, it was rare when a vehicle had to be towed onto a ship, a difficult maneuver even for a fully operational vehicle. Moreover, heavy vehicle and track mechanics also had to move and assist in maintaining captured enemy vehicles that the division was returning to Fort Riley for display at the 1ID Museum. As a result, the M88 and M578 heavy-track vehicle-recovery operators had great sport in driving these objects of curiosity around, as did loader-lashers in stowing them.

Once the PSA was formed, we went to work almost immediately. Any homesickness that might have initially invaded the minds of our ranks, including mine, was quickly replaced with hard work and a keen focus to get the job done. Initially, the PSA was almost completely focused on positioning vehicles between the water-desalination site near Dammam, where washing took place, to remote quarantine sites, and then to staging areas in the port. Much of this work began even while the rest of the division was busy recovering and preparing to fly soldiers home. As space in staging areas at the port became available, it was essential that the division get its vehicles in those positions before they were taken by other units who were ready and willing to "get moving." When queuing up for loading a ship, the decision of "who was next" pivoted on who was staged and ready to load. A ship might be in port for only three days, so when it was time to load, it was no time to be caught flat-footed. I knew this. That's why I would, on the one hand, strategize with my team daily to take advantage of emerging opportunities to stage and load vehicles while, on the other, personally "lobbying" 7th Transportation Group for the next ship. In that regard, relationships in the port were everything, and having a VMI "Brother Rat" at the center of the 7th Transportation Group's operations was an advantage I appreciated. However, that also meant that the PSA had to perform, because when 7th Transportation Group said, "Go," that didn't translate to "Well, we'll think about it." I knew—always—that there was another aggressive PSA commander just like me eager to fill any void that might occur because we dragged our feet. Our PSA never did, and the "law firm" of Lingamfelter, Wise, Malik, and Miller saw to that.

Our PSA's transportation planners were busy every day, reviewing which ships were in port, who was at anchor ready to enter the port, whether they were headed to Houston or Beaumont, Texas—US ports easily connected by rail to Fort Riley—and working with 7th Transportation Group load planners. Without a doubt, building relationships and gaining insight was essential. Those relationships provided us vital feedback on what to do to better position the PSA to take advantage of emerging opportunities to acquire ships and load quickly. The indefatigable Miller, my highly capable Transportation Officer and master ship-loader, was the lynchpin of our organization. My PSA's acting sergeant major, Sergeant First Class (SFC) Doug Evans, nicknamed Miller "The Hammer." She was. When she got wind of a new ship possibility, she made sure the PSA's leadership set things in motion immediately. And if anyone slowed up or fell behind, she would let that hammer down. She was not someone to disappoint, and I admired her drive as well as seeing her in action.

Competition for available ships was pronounced. PSA commanders had their work cut out to keep the flow of their units moving. Those divisions ready to go, with vehicles positioned in a staging area in the port, proactive load planners, and loader-lashers standing by, were the ones who would get ships allocated to them. When a unit was informed that a ship was available to be loaded and was headed where that organization needed to go, a unit couldn't waste time warming up to the idea. They had to be ready, and our PSA was ready. I was glad I had "The Hammer" on my team in what could be a cutthroat environment maneuvering for vessels.

To keep Rhame and the division's staff informed, I sent daily situation reports (SITREPS) on the status of the PSA's activities. The PSA relied primarily on satellite communications (SATCOM) and intelligence-reporting platforms to transmit them. I was insistent that the SITREPS be comprehensive and accurate, so I organized a formal input process that I personally oversaw. I knew that with limited communication "pipes" to dialogue with the division's leadership, each SITREP needed to be clear and concise. In them I would characterize operations of the day, and what the PSA had accomplished along with (1) our personnel status, (2) the amount of equipment staged, loading, and loaded, (3) the ships we had allocated, and (4) the ships we had at sea and when and where they would arrive back in the US. Some days, completing the SITREP was simple; other days they were hectic, and many days it was just frustrating. But I made every effort to make the reports as accurate as possible.

Setting the priorities for how to stage vehicles and ship them back to Fort Riley was also a topic of considerable discussion. Many of the BRO brigade and battalion commanders had "reasons" why their equipment was especially critical and should return ahead of others'. Initially, Rhame had signaled his preference to ship vehicles in "unit sets," so commanders could more effectively get back on a combat-ready footing once home, an opinion rooted in the views of his subordinate commanders. They were anxious to reunite men and equipment so that they could return to the "normal" maintenance and training they needed to conduct back at Fort Riley. But shipping in "unit sets" would require that an entire unit's vehicles and equipment be loaded on one ship. This would have been a very inefficient way to get the entire division home as quickly as possible, which was Rhame's clear guidance. I had some tough decisions to make. I listened carefully to the load planners and the experts at 7th Transportation Group. I decided to prioritize the most critical vehicles that would be needed at Fort Riley first, and then those that would require special attention and maintenance. First, load planners explained that similar vehicles load best when configured together, since they are of similar profile and don't waste space between them in the load plan. Second, every ship needed ballast to maintain an even keel. That meant loading some heavier vehicles first—tanks and armored recovery vehicles—deep in the ship's hold to weight the vessel correctly. Since we would require several ships, we couldn't use all of our heavy vehicles too early in the process. Shipping in "unit sets" would not satisfy wise configuring and necessary ballast requirements. It fell on me to call my boss, Rhame, and convince him that the priority to get home fast should take precedence over a "unit set" approach. He readily agreed, and I breathed a sigh of relief. If he had not agreed, it would have been very likely that the mission would have taken weeks, if not months, longer.

Now armed with clear guidance on how to proceed, my planners and I set about securing ships. I reasoned that a top priority would be to get command vehicles, like Humvees and the Aviation Brigade's helicopters, shipped soon. First, Humvees are important in transporting leaders who supervise individual training, which would be a priority back at Fort Riley and provide a way to move supervisors from one training site to another, often many miles apart on the expansive post. Additionally, our helicopters would need major overhauling to deal with the wear and tear from continuous desert operations and the sand that had damaged their rotor blades. The sooner they were on the ground at Fort Riley, the earlier that restorative work could begin.

The opportunity to ship both types of equipment arrived when I got a call from my "Brother Rat" Jim Chalkley. He told me a Norwegian automobile-transport ship was inbound to Dammam and would be allocated to the BRO. "Scottie, this sucker is huge, so get every damn thing you can on it," he said with seriousness in his voice.

"Don't worry, Brother Rat, we'll cram her full," I said excitedly. It was a prefect ship for loading both Humvees and helicopters since it had hydraulic decks that could be raised or lowered to remove or increase the headspace to accommodate cargo. "The Hammer" and her PSA load planners went to work immediately, planning some heavy-tracked vehicles for the lower deck for ballast, allocating many of the division's Humvees for the other decks, along with the bulk of the division's helicopters. That ship, the *Nosac Rover,* was a huge roll-on/roll-off (RO/RO) that allowed for swift loading operations. PSA load planners were very optimistic and expected to put 1,344 items on her. 7th Transportation Group planners were not so sanguine. A day later my planners upped the ante, now planning to load the ship with 1,400 items. Everyone was wrong; at the end of the effort some 54 hours later, the *Nosac Rover* had gobbled up 1,516 items, including 62 vehicles from the 1CD based at Fort Hood, Texas. Indeed, she had swallowed many of the division's Humvees and helicopters. With every vehicle that exceeded the predictions of 7th Transportation Group planners, the BRO's PSA would utterly confound them by adding even more. I noted at the time that soon the transportation planners started referring to the *Nosac Rover* as the "No-shit Rover," which was their profanely incredulous reaction every time we exceeded their wildest expectations.[4] They were impressed. In short order, not only had the 1ID soldiers of the PSA established a new port record for loading a single ship, over 1,516 vehicles in just 54 hours, the performance established goodwill with 7th Transportation Group. That goodwill translated into a predisposition by transportation planners to get out of the way if they allocated a ship to the 1ID, particularly if that "Hammer" gal was nearby.

The planning for ships continued with great intensity even while the Loader-Lasher Company was establishing a record for hard work. I attended meetings every evening with 7th Transportation Group to argue, forcefully at times, for more ship bottoms. Ships would be allocated, then reallocated to other units for various reasons. There were some contentious discussions with our USAREUR-based VII Corps planners. They thought I was too aggressive in putting my case for the CONUS-based BRO. One time I was called in to the VII Corps headquarters to be advised to be "less aggressive." On June 24, I noted this in my diary: "I confronted by the Corps Rear Area CDR [commander] today, I am accused of putting the 1st ID above all else. Guilty! We however, pick up two more RO/ROs."

This was the environment the PSA lived in. However, the best argument our PSA had in its dealing with VII Corps, and other decision-makers, was the reputation we had earned with 7th Transportation Group. And in the port, hard work and performance were key ingredients in getting ship assignments to take the division home.

While the PSA's top challenge was to secure ships, things changed on a daily basis. Ships designated for the PSA changed; staging areas changed; loading plans changed; and arrival and departure times and dates changed. Uncertainty typified daily operations in the port. And my PSA's leadership team had to manage that change, not only to retain our reputation with decision-makers, but to keep the morale and spirit of our soldiers at a high level so performance wouldn't lag. And "change" was a consistent companion. On May 20, 1991, we were busy loading the huge *Ville de Havre*, a container vessel, with MILVANS, the 20-foot containers that would carry our smaller nonvehicular equipment back to Fort Riley. I recorded my frustration and amazement in my diary that evening.

Today was [a] typical day dealing with the Transportation Corps. Yesterday, late, we received a call that there was room for all 300 of our MILVANS on the Ville de Havre. We began loading. Our first 100 or so were priority MILVANS but as all would go, priority loading of these was no longer important. By 1400, we learned that only 160 would go. By 1700, the figure was 144 and 3 were being removed from the boat. At 2200, I stood by as the transporters argued among themselves as to what would be the best to ship in this "container" vessel; vehicles or containers. It was a real show. To no one's surprise, least of all mine, MILVAN containers, it was agreed, would be best and I was told maybe 225 would eventually go. We'll see. Maybe the number will be 100. It's a round figure anyway.

But the most pressing challenge for soldiers of the PSA was enduring the sweltering temperatures. The port was hot and humid day and night. And working conditions, while less stressful in the evening, were nonetheless dangerous. The loader-lashers and the drivers had to work in shifts as we loaded the ships, and there were few pauses for a break. Time was of the essence if we were to maintain our solid record and reputation with the transporters who were eager for units that put their shoulders to the wheel. And that work was hard and harsh. On June 22, 1991, I noted the miserable environment the PSA worked in each day as the soldiers were loading the *Hudson:* "I had a meeting at 24 Trans BN at 0800 to resolve the Hudson problem. They agreed to take our shortfall on the Saudi Tabuk. Later, Hudson loading went very well. We stowed HEMTTs [Heavy Expanded Mobility Tactical Trucks] in places the plan said they couldn't go. The temperature below deck is at least 115–20 degrees. Soldiers are soaking wet. We must drink bottle after bottle of water. When you walk out of the [hold] into 100-degree weather, it feels like it's 65 degrees. This must be like working in mines." As the PSA neared the end of our work, load planning and loading also became more difficult. Once the inventory of remaining vehicles to be shipped had dwindled to a few hundred, the PSA would have to use space in the holds of other ships headed back to the US that may not be fully loaded with equipment. And no ship would be permitted to leave until it was packed to the gills. But the last thing I wanted was to be stuck in the port with a skeleton crew of PSA soldiers and a handful of vehicles awaiting piecemeal for transport back to America. We couldn't imagine how long such a scenario might last. Concurrently, and with the frenetic pace of ship loading, my PSA transporters were also scheduling airflow for the PSA soldiers back to the US. That was further complicated because the PSA was not certain when it would complete ship loading. The challenge was to "lock in" aircraft and "bet" that all the vessel loading would be done when it was time to fly the troops home. I noted the challenge we faced on July 1, 1991: "We started loading Joseph Lykes late tonight. My MTO [Movement Transportation Officer] is unhappy because we are loading another break bulk when a RO/RO can finish us off. But I can't count on the ship schedules. I must maximize all ships. If the RO/RO is late (beyond 0300 3 July) I'm caught. I would lose a full day of loading. We fly on 6th of July. My back is against the wall. I asked God to help." While loading proceeded, airflow changes kept us guessing, trying to discern the intersection where the scheduling for airflow and the conclusion of ship loading would be in harmony. I noted the problem on July 2: "Ships loading is going well. Cape Diamond arrives early in the AM and we'll finish her quickly. The VII Corps fouled up our airflow (they wonder why I get in their business!). They took my requested departure time and backed it up 24 hours. Now I may have to leave on 5 July as opposed to 6 July. That may be too soon." Fortunately, things came together two days later, on July 4, and the PSA celebrated our own form of Independence Day. We finished our loading at noon that very day. Loading ships had consumed the PSA's collective energy. The conditions were harsh, the challenges many, and the frustrations abundant. I recorded how I dealt with a last-minute challenge to complete the PSA's work dockside as the last ship was finally loaded on July 4: "We finished our last ship at 1200 today. It was a struggle to the end. The 24th Trans BN wanted us to leave our last M88 recovery vehicle off until they had loaded some other unit's equipment in the space left over. We put the M88 on anyway as it was our mission to do. I pinned the NDSM [National Defense Service Medal] and SWA [Southwest Asia] medals on each of our soldiers. We will soon depart for the airport. It will be a long night." When the PSA was done, my VMI classmate and XO of 7th Transportation Group, Jim Chalkley, would confess to me that the soldiers of the BRO were the most accomplished loaders they had ever seen in any environment. Again, the division chose wisely when manning the 1ID's PSA. I must admit that I was a "reluctant warrior" when Rhame put me in command of it. However, years later, after I had retired as a colonel, having commanded the 6th Battalion, 37th Field Artillery in the 2nd Infantry Division (2ID), and after a second career as a member of Virginia's House of Delegates, my service with the PSA was one of the real highlights of my life. I noted this very sentiment on July 5, 1991, as I stepped on the aircraft with the distinction of being the last BRO soldier to leave Saudi soil:

> After a sleepless night, we loaded our two aircraft. The first half of my unit departed at 1015 on a 747. The second half at 1050 on a DC10. I was the last 1st Infantry Division soldier to depart Saudi Arabia at 1006 hours local on 5 July 1991. . . . I have had a wonderful opportunity to work with some of the finest people I have ever known. The officers, NCOs and soldiers of the PSA were superb in every respect. If any credit for what we accomplished is due, it is on their account. This is my final entry in this saga. Tonight I will be reunited with my family. At long last, I will again be complete.

The PSA represented everything that was—that is—good about the 1ID. The division's motto "No Mission Too Difficult, No Sacrifice Too Great, Duty First!" was the way the PSA approached the daunting task of shipping 6,524 combat vehicles and related equipment of the division, and other units, from the deserts of Arabia to the plains of Kansas. When done, the PSA had loaded 13 ships, seven of which were RO/ROs, two of which were MPSs, and four of which were break-bulks. Of the total number of ships, eight were US-flagged, and five, almost 40 percent, bore the flag of a foreign carrier, highlighting the international character of our coalition (see table 13.1).

On the day of our departure from Saudi Arabia, my final SITREP was transmitted to the division's headquarters at Fort Riley. It informed Rhame that his orders had been completed.

> At 1200 local Saudi Arabia time on 4 July 1991, the 1st Infantry Division Port Support Activity (PSA) completed its assigned mission to redeploy 6002[5] items of equipment to Fort Riley, Kansas. The men and women of this organization extend their congratulations to their fellow soldiers and officers of the Division as we celebrate together the independence of our great nation. We will depart Saudi Arabia on 5 July having held fast to the motto of the greatest Division in the Army; "No Mission Too Difficult, No Sacrifice Too Great, DUTY FIRST." The war is over, we're coming home.

Table 13.1.   1st Infantry Division Port Support Activity (PSA) Shipping Data, May-July 1991

	Ship	National Flag	Type	Departure	Arrival	Cargo
1	Ville Du Harve	Grenada	Roll-on/Roll-off	25 May 1991	15 June 1991	212 MILVANS
2	Saudi Hoffuf	Saudi Arabia	Roll-on/Roll-off	9 June 1991	1 July 1991	64 Vehicles/Aircraft
3	Nosak Rover	Norway	Roll-on/Roll-off	10 June 1991	1 July 1991	1516 Vehicles
4	Anne Gros	Norway	Breakbulk	13 June 1991	5 July 1991	278 Vehicles
5	PFC Obregon	US	MPS[1]	23 June 1991	14 July 1991	963 Vehicles/MILVANS
6	Lt Bobo	US	MPS[1]	23 June 1991	14 July 1991	818 Vehicles
7	Cape Hudson	US	Roll-on/Roll-off	25 June 1991	16 July 1991	569 Vehicles
9	Saudi Tabuk	Saudi Arabia	Roll-on/Roll-off	26 June 1991	17 July 1991	449 Vehicles
8	John Lykes	US	Breakbulk	28 June 1991	29 July 1991	249 Vehicles
10	Nancy Lykes	US	Breakbulk	1 July 1991	22 July 1991	325 Vehicles
11	Cape Inscription	US	Roll-on/Roll-off	3 July 1991`	24 July 1991	451 Vehicles
12	Joseph Lykes	US	Breakbulk	4 July 1991	27 July 1991	259 Vehicles
13	Cape Diamond	US	Roll-on/Roll-off	4 July 1991	26 July 1991	371 Vehicles

3101 Wheels; 1678 Trailers; 1114 Tracks; 87 Aircraft; 350 MILVANS; 3-17 FA 58 Tracks, 128 Wheels; 8 vehicles from 1st Cavalry Division. **Total: 6524**

Note: Records in the PSA vary slightly from the situation reports sent to Fort Riley by the PSA and the ship loading plans. This discrepancy may be the result of how individual vehicles were configured when loaded on the ship.

[1] Maritime Prepositioning Ship

The division's staff raced this SITREP to the parade ground where Rhame and US Senator Bob Dole of Kansas were taking a review of the division in honor of Independence Day and the division's return from combat. Rhame read the SITREP to the entire assembly, announcing we were finished loading and were headed home. For the PSA, it was truly "Duty First!"—the bold motto that every soldier who has ever served in the 1ID understands and takes to heart in all that they do.

As we took off on our way home, the aircraft cabin erupted into cheering. Soon many of the troops, dead tired, slipped into a deep sleep for the long ride home. After a refueling stop at the US Naval Air Station Sigonella, located in eastern Sicily, we flew to Shannon Airport in Dublin, Ireland, where we were greeted by the airport manager who announced, much to the delight of the troops, that to honor our great service in freeing Kuwait, the bars and restaurants were open to US soldiers at no cost. My acting sergeant major, Evans, and I exchanged horrified looks as we contemplated loading thoroughly inebriated soldiers back on the aircraft after they had consumed copious amounts of alcohol for the first time in six months. Evans took the initiative, jumped up, and said, as only a sergeant can, what his expectations were with respect to conduct. It was frank, and not the stuff of a Sunday-morning church service, but the troops got it. Two hours later, everyone—thoroughly relaxed by then—

was back aboard, and Evans and I, also having imbibed a bit, were relieved. It was the quietest aircraft ride I ever experienced, maybe the quietest in the history of manned flight.

As we flew over New York, we were able to see the Statue of Liberty. It was emotional. I then recalled watching the June 8, 1991, Desert Storm victory parade on the Armed Forces Television Network (AFTN) channel while sitting in PSA headquarters at Khobar. As I watched the broadcast, I was filled with pride to see our great division, the BRO in all its glory, march past the reviewing stand as President Bush and many national dignitaries looked on. At the end came a platoon of Vietnam veterans dressed in the green battle fatigues of that period. They didn't have the crisp uniformed step of their active-duty brethren who had marched ahead of them. But as they strode down Constitution Avenue in the nation's capital, the crowd on both sides rose to their feet in thunderous applause and cheering. It was as if this was their homecoming too, with healing in every stride. It was deeply moving for a veteran like me who had witnessed the unmitigated disrespect to their wartime service shown by antiwar protesters in the 1970s. And as the Statue of Liberty slipped under our wing as we made a turn to land for a brief stop in New York, I remembered those Vietnam veterans who had remained in the US Army, the generation of MG Tom Rhame, BGs Bill Carter and Jerry Rutherford, COL Mike Dodson, and my early mentors, COL Joe Monko and LTC Dean Phillips. It was their combat era that had rebuilt the US Army that had so recently and stunningly vanquished the army of Saddam Hussein. That parade—one I could witness only from afar—seemed to me to be a healing moment. And healing is a good thing after war.

Soon we departed on our last leg to Forbes Field in Topeka, Kansas. It was dark when we landed, and we quickly boarded busses to Fort Riley, arriving after midnight. There, to our amazement, was a huge reception staged in one of the hangars at the airfield. The division's band played as we entered, and Rhame greeted us with a hero's welcome. My boss, Dodson, was there too, beaming with pride that the final contingent of his command was home at long last. As I entered the hangar to be greeted by thousands of cheering families, I spotted Shelley on the other side of the expansive building, and our kids, Amy, John, and Paul, whom she had dressed in blue sailor suits. After all the ships we had loaded, it seemed appropriate to see my Army family wearing Navy blue. Following some remarks by Rhame, I stepped up to the microphone, thanked the PSA, and presented Rhame with one of the signature red hard hats the PSA had worn while loading thousands of vehicles on the ships bound for the US. On the front were the two silver stars of a major general and, on the side, a BRO patch. He loved receiving it as much as I did in presenting it to him.

Soon the ceremony broke up, and we all headed home. When I arrived at Riley Place, Shelley and I put the kids to bed. They were exhausted too. I opened a beer and stepped onto the back porch where my family had watched McGary and me struggle to build the loft in the back of HQ-5 nine months earlier. It was quiet, interrupted only by an occasional cricket in the forest behind our quarters. But my mind was wide awake. We had done so much in the past nine months that I could hardly process all of it. After a while, I went to bed, only to awaken early the next morning to find our son John downstairs watching Saturday-morning cartoons. I grabbed a cup of coffee and joined him, more to enjoy his presence than anything else. As he watched TV and played with some plastic toy blocks, he said without warning, "Daddy, were you a good guy, or a bad guy?" It was an uncomplicated binary question, and I sat there for a moment to contemplate the simplicity of it. It was as if the whole war flashed like a movie on fast forward before my eyes: the run-up to deployment, the preparations to deploy, the uncertainty, our arrival in Saudi Arabia, the beginning of the conflict, the artillery raids, the assault, the pursuit, the end. And the PSA. I thought about the guys we lost. The danger we faced. The exhilaration of victory, and yes, the Iraqis—men, women, and children—who were left behind to pick up the pieces of a war-torn nation. As John looked back at me for an answer, I said, "Son, we were the good guys," after which he went back to his toys, apparently satisfied with the answer. It wasn't really that simple. But it was the answer that came out. It was the answer that would have to suffice—for then—as I struggled to process all that had happened to me, our families, the DIVARTY, the Big Red One, and our nation.

We had engaged in a great adventure and did what we were trained to do, fight in a war better than anyone else in the world. And as I watched my little boy play in all his binary innocence, I was glad that war was over.

14

Retrospective and Reality

Did We Get the Job Done?

Much has transpired in the Middle East since the 1ID landed in Saudi Arabia and rolled across the Iraqi sands to defeat Saddam Hussein's army and his vaunted Republican Guards during Desert Shield/Desert Storm. In 2003, the US would again invade Iraq, even as we were simultaneously engaged in combat with the barbaric Taliban and Al Qaeda in Afghanistan. But the second war in Iraq was much costlier in blood and treasure for the US and its allies. From 2003 to 2018, the US experienced 4,493 killed and 32,292 wounded.[1] During Desert Storm, American casualties were considerably less with 382 deaths—147 from battle—and only 467 wounded.[2] In 2011, President Barack Obama ordered US troops home, pronouncing the latest war in Iraq was over. Unfortunately, the precipitous departure of the US before the Iraqi government was stable enough to govern effectively created a vacuum that gave rise to yet another insurgency. That uprising, led by the Islamic State in Iraq and Syria (ISIS), would be directed at the heart of the new Shia-majority government of Iraqi Prime Minister Nouri al-Maliki.

By 2014, ISIS would achieve remarkable success, driving Iraqi government forces out of western Iraq and capturing Mosul, a major population center in the north. Simply put, the Iraqi Army was not ready to assume the security mission of the country when the US made its quick exit. That was unfinished work. By 2014–2015, the US once again found it necessary to return to Iraq to restore order. President Donald Trump's redoubled effort to destroy ISIS in Iraq and Syria proved successful by the end of 2018. This unfinished work represented yet a third Iraqi War, even as the Obama administration was ending and the Trump administration began. When considering America's experience in Iraq, there is much to contemplate since the US-led coalition first landed in the Middle East in 1990—a lot to think about indeed.

In light of the US legacy in Iraq after Desert Storm, it is fitting that we ask ourselves three fundamental questions concerning our tactics,

267

strategy, and geopolitics. To be sure, we did many things well during Desert Storm and some things less well. Both the good and the bad deserve some analysis. First, how did we perform tactically with the doctrine we employed? Second, was the strategy we developed and implemented sufficient to accomplish the mission? And third, if we conducted the First Gulf War as we should have, why did we find it necessary to return to Iraq again in 2003 and 2014–2018?

Doctrinal and Tactical Lessons

The tactics, doctrine, training, and equipment employed during Desert Storm were crafted to fight a war against Soviet and Warsaw Pact forces on the plains of central Germany. However, in a twist of irony, they were ultimately used against a Soviet client state on the plains of the Iraqi desert. Interestingly, Vietnam War veterans were the warrior architects—having witnessed the shortcomings of our effort in Southeast Asia—who designed, built, and trained a force focused on defeating Soviet aggression in Europe that would prove to be victorious in Iraq. That included conceiving a joint warfighting doctrine across the armed services that would permit the application of all types of military force at the precise time and place on the battlefield to maximize combat power and crush any enemy as well as that enemy's will to resist.

In the Army, we embraced Air-Land Battle (ALB), a doctrine that called for the effective combining and massing of combat power. That included direct fire from the infantry, armor, and attack helicopters and indirect fire from the artillery, as well as air defense, electronic warfare, intelligence, communications, combat engineer, and logistics assets all focused at a key point and time on the battlefield to defeat the enemy. Combat power, however, involved more than strictly Army assets. We also contemplated the use of Air Force and Navy close air support and deep strikes against the enemy. All of this required a high level of training and a clear joint doctrine that could bring ground, air, and naval forces together in a more effective manner than had been done in Vietnam. By 1990, that joint doctrine in ALB was well developed and understood by US fighting forces like the BRO, albeit untested in combat. Desert Storm would be that ultimate test, and in large measure our joint and combined operations doctrine was validated. Yet there were "holes" in the fabric of our doctrine and warfighting systems to support combat operations. Chief among them was logistics.

Beans and Bullets

As Napoleon Bonaparte is credited with saying, "The amateurs discuss tactics; the professionals discuss logistics." Unfortunately, resupply in Desert Storm was a nightmare for those of us who had to struggle with it every day. In retrospect, I know now that the logisticians—particularly the professionals of the 1ID—were just as frustrated as those they supported, if not more so. No one wanted to fail, and they really tried to move mountains to support us. Unfortunately, the well-established and tested doctrine we had in place in 1991 to support battlefield logistics on the plains of Germany, or in the rice paddies, valleys, and canyons of South Korea, simply could not work in the desert. The infrastructure and framework to support logistics were completely lacking.

Indeed, the Army in Germany was served by a complex, mature, and highly resourced logistical support system. The one in South Korea was equally capable. But in both places, we had the luxury of roads, rail, and airfields, dependable telecommunications, and computer infrastructure to support supply operations. In Europe and Asia, we knew where the "beans and bullets" were, and when we could expect to get them. Moreover, Germany and South Korea had huge warehouses that permitted the stockpiling of parts and other supplies, thereby shortening the logistics tail. Little of that was in Saudi Arabia. There was certainly some infrastructure in the ports, but communications, warehouses, and road networks didn't extend much beyond them. This dramatically affected the critical area of vehicle maintenance and repair. Had it not been for that inventory of spare parts that combat units physically carried with them from Fort Riley, we would not have been able to function as well as we did. The robust supply doctrine that worked so well in Europe and Asia was completely absent in the desert, vexing logisticians and combat troops alike.

Many of us after Desert Storm saw the need to establish a logistics contingency operation in the Middle East similar to that developed by the US in Europe and Asia. In both regions we had POMCUS sites well stocked with military equipment and repair parts in the event of war. Soldiers, it was envisioned, would fly to the theater of operations with their "To Accompany Troops" (TAT) gear on military and commercial airliners and draw their warfighting equipment from these sites. Nothing like this was in the Middle East prior to the conflict, and it wasn't apparent to us that the US would establish any equipment stockpiles there after Desert Storm. Instead, we rushed to send everything back to the US from the Middle East as if we were packing up and heading home from a rented vacation beach cottage on the Outer Banks of North Carolina.

Creating robust POMCUS sites in the Middle East after Desert Storm would have better prepared us for potential conflicts in the future. Moreover, it would have been an overt sign to potential troublemakers in the region—like Iran and Iraq—that we were prepared to return on short notice. True enough, it would have been a diplomatic challenge to convince Saudi Arabia and others to support a large "stay behind" US military presence in the region. Radical Arab elements would predictably label them "Western bases" as the latest evidence of a new "colonialism." However, skilled diplomacy—like that used to build the 1990 coalition— could have successfully rebutted that charge. Unfortunately, that didn't occur. Having suffered from an unworkable logistics framework in Desert Storm, we then failed to take advantage of a postwar opportunity and the goodwill that existed with the Saudis to prepare for the next time we would need logistics support for such an operation. The worst logistics lesson, it turns out, was the failure to learn from our most recent experience.

Fire Support and Force Artillery Command and Control

This story was largely focused on the artillery, so it is fitting that we address some of the challenges and shortcomings Redlegs faced. Without a doubt, the tactical doctrine of the artillery was solid, particularly the use of standard tactical missions that were designed to support our maneuver units. The direct support (DS), reinforcing (R), general support reinforcing (GSR), and general support (GS) standard tactical missions have always provided a clear methodology to orchestrate artillery operations. This included not only how Redlegs supported infantry and armor formations, but how they mutually supported one another as they provided fires to maneuver units. We also validated time-tested fire planning procedures that were used to implement both the artillery raids and the huge preparatory fire program employed to destroy the enemy. However, tactical command and control of the artillery over the broad frontage we had in the desert—upwards of 40 kilometers—was difficult.

During Desert Storm, we discovered we were operating within an artillery command-and-control structure that was outdated for highly mobile desert warfare. At the corps level, the next-higher artillery headquarters for a division like ours was the corps artillery. That organization, in the European model, controlled the fires of field artillery brigades that were not under the operational control (OPCON) of the divisions. However, when the corps assigned one or more of these brigades to support a division like ours, then the DIVARTY commander would assume control of their fire planning, positioning, and tactical operations. Unfortunately, the implementation of this process in the desert was hamstrung in two ways.

First, there was uncertainty—up to and during the field artillery raids—about which specific field artillery brigades would eventually support the 1ID. Assignment orders were issued and then rescinded. Plans were made, and then unmade. All of this seemed to be rather odd to us at the DIVARTY level because there was never any doubt in our minds that we would be the main effort in making the breach for other VII Corps divisions to advance around and through us to invade Iraq. Yet the lack of clarity concerning which field artillery brigades we would have at our disposal made fire planning very challenging. This also contributed to uncertainty about the logistics support the VII Corps would allocate to those artillery brigades placed under OPCON to the DIVARTY. Their presence in our sector would most assuredly outstrip the 1ID's logistical capability. The earlier the corps planners decided who would support the BRO, the more time we would have not only to plan the firing, but also to ensure that the necessary logistics support, including ammunition and fuel, was in place to execute the mission.

Second, an early assignment decision by the corps artillery of which field artillery brigades would support the 1ID was necessary to facilitate critical terrain management decisions affecting the positioning of those units on the battlefield. The artillery brigades we would receive not only had to be positioned so they would not interfere with the movement of maneuver units on the ground, but also positioned where they were within range of the targets we needed to engage to execute our fire plans. Moreover, there were future operations to consider. We needed to wisely position them so that they would be able to quickly reconnect with the divisions that they would be supporting once they were finished supporting us. In every case, the brigades assigned to us had follow-on missions well beyond our sector, requiring long road marches to catch up with the maneuver units they would support in future phases of the war. Therefore, the sooner we knew (1) who would be supporting us in the raids and the preparation and (2) their follow-on assignments, the sooner we could determine logical positions for them. That early awareness would not only enable us to position them to engage targets we needed to attack, but also posture the brigades for a smooth and rapid exit of our sector to rejoin other divisions swiftly advancing into Iraq. Late or delayed decisions by the corps artillery, coupled with last-minute changes, affected our ability to do this. Tangentially, we also learned it was time to reevaluate the corps artillery's command-and-control structure and, when possible, place field artillery brigades during peacetime under the operational control of the divisions they would likely support during wartime. This would not only ensure the robust fire support a division requires in combat, but also create the training relationships during peacetime that make operations go smoothly during wartime.

Another significant lesson was the importance and role of the DIVARTY commander in the provision of fire support. The commander's presence in the division is indispensable in the successful orchestration and application of indirect firepower in fast-paced combat. In the planning, positioning, and supporting of fire support assets, the division commander and the DIVARTY commander were both essential in synchronizing combat power consistent with the maneuver plan to prosecute the battle. The orchestration of field artillery cannon, rocket, and missile units along with close air support from Army attack helicopters and tactical aircraft from the Air Force was no small task and required the focused expertise of a trained warrior-leader. In combat, successful planning demands that someone with command authority have primary responsibility as the synchronizing agent for critical tasks that must be accomplished flawlessly. The DIVARTY commander is that person. When you are tossing millions of pounds of ordnance through the air over friendly forces to bring death and destruction on the enemy, having several people taking different and uncoordinated approaches in the process is a recipe for disaster. As COL Mike Dodson noted with frustration several times during the war, just the development of fire support coordination measures (FSCM) was accomplished haphazardly.[3] FSCMs were our means of facilitating the planning, execution, and rapid engagement of targets with the appropriate weapon, or group of weapons, while simultaneously providing safeguards for everything else on the battlefield. This had to be done correctly. Fortunately, our division FSE under Dodson managed to orchestrate FSCMs to avoid serious issues on the battlefield, including the death of friendly forces. Indeed, Dodson was not a subscriber to the "big sky–little bullet" theory, nor the idea that you could aimlessly sling ordnance around the battlefield in an uncoordinated manner. In sum, there's simply no substitute for the presence of a DIVARTY commander in modern warfare to coordinate actions of this nature, vital measures and duties that cannot be left to chance. Incredulously, the

Army moved away from the DIVARTY structure during the insurgency-dominated years from 2005 to 2014 until realizing that DIVARTYs were indispensable in the orchestration of fire support within a maneuver division, particularly in conventional war. In 2015, these organizations were reestablished, a belated admission and reaffirmation by the Army's leadership of the DIVARTY's essentiality in orchestrating artillery combat power within the ground scheme of maneuver, including the DIVARTY commander's indispensable role as chief fire support officer.

In short, Desert Storm showed us the importance of the DIVARTY commander's acting as the force artillery commander, and it's a lesson that should be embraced in the future, when we must be prepared to fight a full spectrum of warfare, from insurgences to conventional wars like Desert Storm. To do otherwise is rank stupidity. But the Army's brief abandonment of the DIVARTY revealed that even clear lessons of success in full-scale conventional war can be easily discarded when the lessons of counterinsurgency are misapplied to the Army as a whole.

Joint and Combined Arms Operations

The joint and combined arms operations we employed during Operation Desert Storm known as Air-Land Battle (ALB) worked. A key lesson from Vietnam was that the Army must fight effectively and agilely as a combined arms team. Maneuver, artillery, attack air, engineers, logistics, communications, intelligence, and other elements of combat power must be employed in a focused and decisive manner at the right place and at the right time to crush enemy forces and their will to resist. It can't be done in a piecemeal manner, lest it become diffused and ineffective. Moreover, Vietnam highlighted that the Army, Air Force, Marine Corps, and Navy must fight jointly to take advantage of the various combat capabilities each service provides. For example, the modern Army has always benefited from the Air Force's ability to attack the enemy throughout the depth of their combat formations and logistic support centers with close air support and deep-strike missions. The Navy is also a vital partner for the Army, not only in moving Army units and supplies across the oceans, but in providing naval gunfire and air support from carrier strike forces deployed offshore in support of engaged ground troops. Of course, soldiers and Marines have always worked together, with the Marine Corps providing early assault waves that pave the way for a more robust ground capability by the Army to hold and gain ground. All of this is a testament to the need to fight jointly on the modern battlefield.

In what may be the irony of ironies in the modern history of US warfare, the captains, majors, and lieutenant colonels of the Vietnam War, a war that many outsiders saw as a failure, would create a modern joint and combined doctrine designed to fight the Soviet Union. However, it ultimately would be employed against Soviet surrogates—the Iraqis—in Desert Storm. There it would be validated by crushing Iraqi forces that were using the latest Soviet equipment and doctrine. Moreover, the joint and combined doctrine we used would serve to demonstrate to the USSR that an invasion of Europe would be ill-advised. In that regard, these demonstrative improvements may have hastened the demise of the Soviet Union as a Cold War superpower by revealing the futility of engaging forces like this in combat.

That said, US readiness for Desert Storm benefited from good timing, occurring as it did at the close of the Cold War. The US had robust, ready, and trained forces fully prepared to execute joint and combined operations to the fullest extent. That's a lesson worth remembering and sustaining. Unfortunately, during the years of counterinsurgency that followed in Afghanistan and Iraq, maintaining that capability and readiness to fight conventional wars was not a priority. Indeed, not only did those insurgencies consume much of our readiness capability, but our forces were downsized in the process. That further degraded our readiness. We must recover and rebuild our capacity to fight wars—not unlike the ability we had in Desert Storm—while rejecting further calls for reductions in forces and capabilities. Our warfighting doctrine worked in Desert Storm. It will continue to work and improve with new innovations. But if we expect that doctrine to remain successful, it must be backed up with capable and robust forces if we are to replicate our battlefield successes in the future.

Other "Holes" in the Operational Fabric: Equipping, Manning, and Deploying

We also had equipment and manning issues as well as a lack of doctrine for port operations. Gaps in how we were equipped were obvious. For example, the artillery needed an organic or embedded capability to perform simple combat-engineering tasks. These tasks included digging fighting positions for cannons and launchers, raising berms for TOCs and counterbattery radar sections, and bulldozing up earthen protection for field ammunition facilities. But there was insufficient engineering support to go around. The division's organic engineer capability, usually a battalion, to serve the entire division was simply not enough for all the engineering demands of a division, much less its artillery.

We also had a huge need for MHE equipment, like forklifts. We found that when it came to moving and repositioning ammunition, the organic capability we had—mostly five-ton wreckers and other heavy ammunition vehicles that had lifting equipment installed on them—was simply insufficient. Moreover, those same trucks were busy ferrying ammunition from holding areas to firing units and not routinely available to unload ammunition from division or corps delivery units.

Another gap was personnel manning. In the peacetime Army of the 1990s, manning was not up to par. The Army was already downsizing in the summer of 1990 at the same time Saddam was threatening the Gulf region with his aggression. At Fort Riley, we had weathered a series of manpower reductions and early retirements to pare down our numbers. In several cases, we let very fine soldiers go. Years earlier we would have been happy to retain those warfighters and keep them in important jobs where experience mattered. But as we ramped up for deployment to the Middle East, we knew we had holes in critical positions needed for 24-hour operations. Peacetime units stationed in the US—like ours—were barely staffed to do two shifts in a 24-hour period. And when we first showed up in the desert, the strain was obvious. Fortunately, the Army surged replacements to us to get us closer to manning our necessary three shifts, mornings (0600 to 1400), swings (1400 to 2200), and mids (2200 to 0600). It helped. But even as the Army poured troops into Saudi Arabia, the Army's personnel experts were more concerned with combat-loss replacements than with properly staffing units in peacetime. At least, that's the impression we had while standing on the desert floor in January 1991. In combat, you don't have the luxury of hanging a sign on your TOC declaring "Out for Lunch" or "Back in the Morning" or "Help Wanted." Nor is it a nine-to-five operation. Moreover, to be effective, TOC shifts need to be eight hours in duration, not 12. Combat is intense, and soldiers need downtime to rest, maintain their fighting equipment, and recover. This is particularly true of officers and senior NCOs who are making critical decisions during their shifts. "Leader rest," as we termed it, was essential for key personnel so that they would have the mental alertness and physical energy to make critical command-and-control decisions when life or death is in the balance.

I have detailed extensively the challenges we had in the port. In a Desert Storm scenario, the Army lacked a clear doctrine—beyond a very generalized one—for uniting arriving troops with their equipment for onward movement to positions in the desert. That's not to say that port operators didn't know what they were doing. Procedurally, they knew how to operate a port. But the operational skills and procedures they used were unknown to combat troops like us when we arrived to reunite with our combat equipment and move to the field. Ironically, those important procedural and operational skills existed in Europe where US units like the 1ID understood how to "fall in" on POMCUS sites stocked with large amounts of ready-to-use equipment and combat vehicles prepositioned in warehouses awaiting our arrival. Moreover, European ports were manned with host-nation civilian workers who were dedicated to offloading equipment efficiently. Not so in the port of Dammam, where we had to deal with disorganization in working through the difficulties. The Army—and soldiers in particular—are adept at taking bad situations and turning them around. But the port was painful. Virtually none of us in combat units were ready for the confusion and disorganization of port operations. We literally learned episodically, by the hour, and amid utter confusion that was further complicated when Iraq began dropping SCUD missiles around us. Despite all of this, when we left the port, we had learned some vital lessons. We—like old sailors handling the rigging of a ship—now "knew the ropes."

Indeed, port operations were more organized when we were leaving Saudi Arabia. When I was appointed to command the PSA, we organized ourselves based in part on what we had learned when exiting the port for the desert in January. One of those lessons was that each combat division needed such a PSA on both ends of a deployment operation. But in November of 1990 when we were deploying to Saudi Arabia, the last thing on our mind was needing to configure a specialized unit like a PSA composed of soldiers from units across the division to be on the ground to receive and organize our combat equipment for a quick and orderly linkup with arriving troops. We figured the "Army" would take care of that. We were wrong. That said, once we had our PSA set up to support our movement home, 7th Transportation Group in the port was very helpful in our success. Essential, I would say.

In sum, there were many tactical and doctrinal lessons from Desert Storm. These are but a few of them. If these and others are embraced in future conventional wars, the Army will benefit from some vital on-the-ground experience and the wisdom derived from it.

Strategic Lessons

The clear-eyed national leadership that President George H. W. Bush provided in developing a strategy to liberate Kuwait was brilliant. He understood that the US has a pivotal role in the Middle East and that international lawlessness of the type that Saddam Hussein had foisted on Kuwait was unacceptable. His skilled construction of a multination coalition to engage Iraq, defeat Saddam, and reestablish Kuwait's sovereignty was decisive. Additionally—and maybe the most vital aspect of the Bush strategy—he kept Israel out of the conflict. Had the Israelis entered the war, the coalition would have been shattered. Saudi Arabia and other Arab countries allied in the effort would have departed. They could never be regarded as having an alliance—even a de facto one—with the Jewish state attacking another Arab nation, even if it were Iraq. In short, Bush's adroit assembly of the coalition and his management of complex issues surrounding it was a textbook example of how to shape an alliance to do a very hard thing: engage in a land war in the Middle East and win.

To be sure, the coalition President Bush shaped was dominated by the US. With the exception of Saudi Arabia and other Gulf states that created access to the region for coalition fighting forces as well as financial support for them, Arab participation in combat was limited. Nonetheless, a US-led coalition was important in two ways. First, it would be an effective fighting force. This, in large measure, was the result of the NATO fighting standards observed by the US, Great Britain, and France that had been honed during the Cold War. They would prove to be lethally effective during Desert Storm. Our systems, fire support, maneuver, aviation, communications, and intelligence all worked in unison and validated the way we had planned to fight the Soviets in Europe. Moreover, it was all accomplished with a precision across an expansive desert that surprised many of us, particularly since several of those nations in the coalition had never actually fought in combined and joint operations with the US in recent history. And a lesson we all took from this was that if we were to be effective in combat in the future, the strong relationships we had with our allies during Desert Storm should be built upon and strengthened. Bush appreciated those relationships—enhanced through his uniquely personal diplomacy—and used them wisely.

Secondly and fortuitously, the coalition would highlight the dominance of American combat power, a fact not lost on the Russians as they stood by helplessly to observe events during Desert Storm, unable to influence them one iota. As the USSR teetered on demise in 1991, President Bush understood that our display of combat power against a Soviet surrogate would not go unnoticed. Besides, the Gulf War was a "good war," one with a clear victim—Kuwait—and a clear enemy—Iraq—and a just cause: the reestablishment of international peace, norms, and order.

And the US—not the USSR—was at the center of the coalition, and Moscow knew it.

While President Bush built an effective coalition and managed it, he also developed goals the coalition could readily embrace as it engaged in a major land war with Arab allies against Arab enemies, a predicament few Middle East experts foresaw: "Our objectives are clear: Saddam Hussein's forces will leave Kuwait. The legitimate government of Kuwait will be restored to its rightful place, and Kuwait will once again be free. Iraq will eventually comply with all relevant United Nations resolutions, and then, when peace is restored, it is our hope that Iraq will live as a peaceful and cooperative member of the family of nations, thus enhancing the security and stability of the Gulf."[4] These were straightforward goals and politically very palatable to Arab allies who were always uneasy about "US bases in the Middle East," particularly given our strong friendship with Israel. It was also palatable to the US Congress that recalled the quagmire Vietnam had become just two decades earlier. Clear and obtainable objectives were essential if the coalition were to survive and win. These objectives were well suited to the situation as it unfolded on January 17, 1991, when war began. The question to be resolved is this: Were these the most suitable objectives on March 1 of that same year when the conflict ended?

Geopolitical

Looking back on Desert Storm, we fought with the right tactics and doctrine. We crafted the right strategy to bring the coalition together and galvanize it to specific goals, including driving Iraq from Kuwait and reestablishing peace—albeit temporarily. However, did we succeed geopolitically? The initial strategy for winning the war and achieving the objectives of the coalition was sound. It worked within the coalition's established parameters to execute the mission. But were we successful in a larger sense? Did we advance regional and world peace among the "family of nations" and in this "new world order" that President Bush so boldly asserted? Or did we miss a major opportunity not only to completely defeat Saddam Hussein's military forces, but to remove him from power? Moreover, had he been removed in 1991, would we have been spared subsequent wars and the resultant expenditure of blood and treasure? If the world had seen clearly then that aggressor nations—and their leaders—would not be tolerated in this new epoch President Bush had proclaimed, would there be a more stable Middle East today with less opportunity for conflict? These are complex questions. To be sure, we were both agile—adaptive—tactically in fighting the war and strategically in building and sustaining the coalition to prosecute it. Yet did we demonstrate such an agility at the geopolitical level to decisively adapt our objectives to improve our geopolitical position after the war as conditions during the war presented themselves for exploitation?

The First Gulf War was the right war for the right reason. It was a just war fought justly, *jus ad bellum* and *jus in bello*. It was executed with great tactical and strategic fidelity and within its stated, albeit limited, objectives. Moreover, it showed the Middle East what real allies look like, how they can be dependable and effective, and that the US was a reliable partner in matters of world peace. Yet despite all of that, we failed to embrace the opportunity we had to bring the regime of Saddam Hussein to finality and thereby achieve a key objective that would advance our geopolitical goals in the region.

Consider what the president said in his speech to Congress on March 6, 1991.[5] Referring to "our uncommon coalition," he called us to a vision for the Middle East including the need for (1) shared security management in the region; (2) control over the proliferation of weapons of mass destruction (WMD); (3) the development of new opportunities for peace including peace between Arabs and Israelis; and (4) economic development.[6] All of these geopolitical objectives were a recipe for shaping an elusive peace in the Middle East. But they were also objectives that could be adapted to other hotspots in Bush's "new world order," vis-à-vis North Korea, Iran, and other pariah regimes that, like Iraq, were pursuing weapons of mass destruction that would further destabilize the world. President Bush's prescription for world stability could not have been better stated. Yet in the days and weeks when Saddam Hussein was most vulnerable to removal from power, we did not perceive the advantage of finishing him off, thereby displaying irresolution to dictators present and future.

This was made more poignant in Bush's remarks that same day when he said that "because the world did not look the other way," Kuwait was now free.[7] He concluded that we "lifted the yoke of aggression."[8] Unfortunately, we did look away from Saddam Hussein and failed to chop the head off the aggressive snake when it was there slithering helplessly in front of us. When Bush asserted that "we sacrificed nobly for what we believe to be right" during the war, he was correct.[9] But many of us on the ground saw the opportunity to finish the job, to remove from power the very person who had precipitated this war and caused so much destruction, death, and deprivation.

Here three lessons of statesmanship are instructive in evaluating the choices President Bush made in the culminating hours of Desert Storm. These lessons, developed by Larry P. Arnn of Hillsdale College, were drawn from his analysis of Winston Churchill's performance during World War II. They provide a suitable framework to examine whether Bush's choices and decisions were wisely taken.[10] The first lesson is "the profound significance of human choice, and the sublime responsibility of men."[11] The second is the "limits of war, of politics, indeed of all human action."[12] And the third, that "strategy must be rooted in the purposes of the nation; and its aims to preserve that nation in the pursuit of those purposes."[13]

Consider the first lesson: President Bush faced two major considerations when Desert Storm ended. The first was domestic political pressure to redeem a "peace dividend" at the close of a bipolar superpower confrontation by reducing military expenditures so they could be appropriated to bread-and-butter issues. Congress very much wanted to reduce military spending after the Cold War, which, oddly, was precisely the time we would need to fund a strong defense to thwart the very threats prevalent in the multipolar world of Bush's "new world order." The second condition was his own reelection effort, which would begin in 1992. His political advisors wanted to get out of Iraq as soon as possible and reap the political benefits of a stunning victory, thereby sustaining the president's approval ratings going into the election. In essence, Bush had to make a very "sublime" human choice: embrace the trends of the time or make the difficult decision to continue the war. Admittedly, it was a dilemma. But renewing the ground offensive—taking the fight directly to the doorstep of the Iraqi dictator—would have been a demonstrative, decisive, and proper action to end Saddam's despotic rule that had no place in any civilized world order, including Bush's. Saddam was ripe for the taking, and we were positioned to accomplish the mission. However, the choice Bush made, to remain galvanized to the initial goals of the coalition without attempting to adapt them to the exigencies of the moment, was a missed opportunity. In hindsight, it was a tragic failure by an otherwise brilliant man to exhibit the agility strategic leaders must retain to seize the initiative in securing a complete victory, not a partial one. Certainly, partial victories can be rationalized even when follow-on actions may be needed. But complete victory is necessitated when the threat can and likely will reemerge, thereby taking all that has been accomplished with blood and treasure and returning it to the status quo ante. When faced with a significant choice and a sublime responsibility to secure a complete victory, one that may have lasted, President Bush stumbled badly.

This brings us to the second point: a recognition of the "limits of war, of politics, indeed of all human action."[14] In other words, how do we recognize what the limits of both should be? To be sure, taking the war too far was a concern for President Bush and his advisors, particularly as the evening news suggested that, in the closing hours of the hostilities along the "Highway of Death," we were indeed "piling on." Arabs too were concerned about an apparent slaughter of Iraqi troops and how that would play out on "the Arab street," that is, publicly among Arabs viewing the war on satellite TV and in the print media. But when hostilities are truncated for whatever reason, there is a real risk that the necessary conditions for peace will elude victor and vanquished alike. In that regard, pursuing the Iraqis to Baghdad and deposing Saddam Hussein in 1991 could have brought a renaissance of rationality and reality to a region locked in a seventh-century worldview of Arab achievement and preeminence, a view little more than ancient history by then. Besides, nothing clears the air after war better than total capitulation by the vanquished and unambiguous victory for the winner. Anything less runs the risk of hampering the potential for peace with lingering doubts over the outcome of hostilities. Simply put, in understanding the limits to both war and peace, it's important that both are pursued to achieve an unambiguous result, so they work symbiotically in achieving and maintaining peace.

Finally, was our geopolitical strategy rooted in the purposes of our nation, and was the aim of our strategy focused on preserving US interests in the pursuit of those purposes?[15] In other words, was our geopolitical approach at the time sufficient to reinforce our own national interest? Our primary focus during Desert Storm was Iraq and its aggression against Kuwait. But this was not the single object of US interests in the Middle East then or in the past. For years our regional policy was dominated by support for Israel and its defense against Arab animus. We also concerned ourselves with the uninterrupted flow of oil from the Persian Gulf, not only to US markets but also to our NATO allies tasked with protecting Europe from Soviet aggression. But there were other concerns.

One of them was the rising threat of a militant Iran that followed the fall of the shah in 1979, a ruler who had been a faithful friend of the US in maintaining stability in the Gulf region, including the flow of oil to the world. The revolutionary Iran of 1979 was a growing threat to regional stability in 1991. When Desert Storm concluded, Tehran was spoiling for an opportunity to increase its influence in a postwar Iraq, destabilize it by inciting Iraq's Shia population, fill the void left by a rapidly departing coalition, and expand Iranian influence in the Gulf. By leaving Saddam's fate in doubt, the US put at risk its own regional interests to advance peace and keep Iran in check. Indeed, the removal of Saddam and his replacement with a free government—particularly with Arab participation—would have been a huge deterrent to Iran, which saw a weakened Iraq as an opportunity to advance its hegemonic goals to dominate the region, possibly displacing Saudi Arabia as the de facto leader of the Organization of Petroleum Exporting Countries (OPEC). Our failure to create that deterrence set the conditions later for a more influential and disruptive Iran, a result plainly not in US national interests then any more than it was years later.

There were other US missteps. GEN Schwarzkopf may have also inadvertently damaged our interests after the war with his decision to permit Iraqi Army helicopters to continue to overfly southern Iraq. He failed to anticipate that Saddam would use those aircraft to brutally suppress a nascent revolt against him by the Shia Marsh Arabs of southern Iraq, even as coalition forces looked on and did nothing. For the Marsh Arabs, who assumed that the coalition would never stand by idly while Saddam destroyed them, it was a bitter awakening. Frankly, it was a shameful moment, and one not lost on Arabs or others, like the Russians, that the US could not be depended on to follow through in the post–Cold War era, even when the choice was clear. Sadly, it also revealed dramatically that Bush's own words just days earlier about "not looking the other way" seemed to exclude Iraqis interested in overthrowing Saddam. Tragically, this error also played into the hands of Iran, which could remind Shia Arabs in Iraq that an unreliable US stood by and permitted them to be slaughtered after the war, weakening our credibility.

Our failure to remove Saddam also had negative implications for Israelis and Arabs alike, to say nothing of the damage to our efforts to broker peace between the parties. In the case of Israel, the US had skillfully kept the Jewish state out of the war. Iraq was defeated, and Israel had taken no part in that result, nor could it have been viewed as doing so. Similarly, had the coalition removed Saddam, Israel would have had no hand in that either. The net result would have demonstrated to Arabs that the US was a reliable partner in restraining Israel in a positive manner. Not capitalizing on the "good will" developed by keeping Israel out of the war was a major missed geopolitical opportunity by the US to achieve our interests in the region.

Finally, the failure to remove Saddam after the war was a missed chance to strengthen the hand of the Arabs, and Saudi Arabia in particular, as regional agents of peace. Saddam's postwar crackdown on the Marsh Arabs demonstrated that neighboring Arab states who stood by and did nothing were equally unreliable. For those unfortunate Iraqis, Arab "unity" was meaningless and, indeed, insincere rhetoric. Had Saudi Arabia taken the lead among Arabs in the coalition to remove Saddam, not only would it have served to further deter Iranian aggression, but it would have contributed to regional stability, including—possibly—the avoidance of subsequent combat in Iraq.

To be sure, redesigning the coalition's objectives after Kuwait was liberated would have been a daunting task, even for the diplomatically gifted World War II combat veteran residing at 1600 Pennsylvania Avenue in Washington, DC. But if there was anyone in the world capable of reshaping the coalition to take advantage of the emerging opportunity to bring finality to Saddam Hussein's regime, it was the sagacious and bold George Herbert Walker Bush. He would have been equal to the task, just as he was when he assembled the US-led coalition in the fall of 1990.

Unquestionably, it would have been hard. The Saudis would have been very hesitant. Other Arab states would have demurred. Indeed, some of our allies might have balked. The US Congress would have been taken aback and difficult to persuade. Yet this is what it means to make profound and significance human choices while embracing "the sublime responsibility of men." It would have been politically risky. Bush would have been second-guessed at every turn. Such is the price of leadership in the face of an opportunity that presented itself to secure lasting peace and avoid future conflicts.

All the right tactical parts were in place. We had assembled the most impressive military coalition since World War II, and it was sitting on the ground in Kuwait and southern Iraq. We were fully armed, capable, and ready to exploit the situation before us on March 1, 1991. Iraqi forces were largely defeated. The Iraqi people were disillusioned with Saddam's leadership and weary of his repression. Saddam was ripe to be overthrown or exiled. Yet we failed to act on the opportunity before us. We forewent *carpe diem* to establish *status quo ante bellum* in Iraq. We could have marched on Baghdad at a moment's notice. President Bush chose otherwise. It was a profoundly misguided choice that resulted in needless losses of US blood and treasure over a decade later.

Our lack of agility geopolitically—to be adaptive—in recognizing the opportunity and responsibility we had to secure a complete victory in the

First Gulf War by ending the regime of Saddam Hussein was a failure to finish our work. This failure set the conditions for further conflict that would become so very costly, more so than if we had gone to Baghdad in 1991 when the Iraqis themselves would have been willing allies in removing their dictator. Indeed, we won the war, but we lost the peace in what was a major geopolitical miscalculation.

Conclusion

The lessons of this conflict are of great value. When you combine solid war fighting doctrine with superior combat systems, quality training, and world-class officers, noncommissioned officers, and soldiers, they will be victorious. Desert Storm taught us that it is essential to maintain a military capable of fighting the full spectrum of warfare. Engaging in war is not always a choice. Sometimes it can be put off. Other times it is thrust upon a nation. When war does come, a nation must be prepared. The US fighting forces of Desert Storm were prepared to fight any war, anywhere, and at any time. As a nation, we must always ask ourselves if we can fight successfully today with the tactical forces we have at our disposal. We did then. Can we in the future? Equally important are the strategic lessons. President Bush's gifted leadership was essential in responding to the invasion of Kuwait. It was a textbook example of how to build and employ a coalition. But the final and most painful lesson was our failure to be agile in recognizing the geopolitical opportunities when they emerged. As a result, we have paid a costly price in the years of war that followed Desert Storm.

In the end, the one thing that never failed us was the American soldier. The BRO showed that to me in ways I will never forget. The one area where quality and professionalism mattered was in the performance of the officers, noncommissioned officers, and soldiers of the 1ID, particularly among the Desert Redlegs of the DIVARTY with whom I was so honored to serve. It is hard to overstate their excellence and devotion to duty. Their spirit was in keeping with that of their predecessors reaching back to World War I under the able leadership of GEN Charles P. Summerall, who was one of the most remarkable and beloved commanders in the history of the 1ID, himself a superb Redleg. His words then expressing his appreciation to the soldiers of the division he so deeply loved are suitable testimony to how many of us feel about the BRO today: "To the officers and soldiers of the First Division I owe my greatest measure of success. Their loyalty and devotion during World War I and in all the years since are more than any man could deserve. I believe that no one has ever been so much honored as I have by their admiration and confidence."[16] Truly, the men and women of the BRO never let us down, and they exhibited an esprit de corps that was at once exhilarating and humbling; exhilarating to behold them in battle, and humbling just to stand in their presence. They gave fulsome meaning to our division's motto "No Mission Too Difficult, No Sacrifice Too Great, Duty First!" Serving with and fighting alongside of them was the single highest honor of my Army career.

Duty First!

Glossary

Units Designations

1AD	1st Armored Division
1CD	1st Cavalry Division
1ID	1st Infantry Division
1 ID DIVARTY	1st Infantry Division Artillery
1(UK)AD	1st United Kingdom Armored Division
1(UK)FA	1st United Kingdom Division Artillery
1-34 AR	1st Battalion, 34th Armor
1-1 AVN	1st Battalion, 1st Aviation
1-4 CAV	1st Squadron, 4th Cavalry
1-5 FA	1st Battalion, 5th Field Artillery
1-17 FA	1st Battalion, 17th Field Artillery
1-142 FA	1st Battalion, 142nd Field Artillery
1-158 FA	1st Battalion, 158th Field Artillery
1-41 IN	1st Battalion, 41st Infantry
1-EN	1st Engineer Battalion
2ACR	2nd Armored Cavalry Regiment
2AD-F	2nd Armored Division-Forward
2-29 FA	2nd Battalion, 29th Field Artillery
2-142 FA	2nd Battalion, 142nd Field Artillery
2 Chem BN	2nd Chemical Battalion
2 FD	2nd Field Regiment
2ID	2nd Infantry Division
3AD	3rd Armored Division
3ID	3rd Infantry Division
3-17 FA	3rd Battalion, 17th Field Artillery
3-20 FA	3rd Battalion, 20th Field Artillery
4-3 FA	4th Battalion, 3rd Field Artillery
4-5 FA	4th Battalion, 5th Field Artillery

5-18 FA	5th Battalion, 18th Field Artillery
5-16 IN	5th Battalion, 16th Infantry
5-18 IN	5th Battalion, 18th Infantry
6-41 FA	6th Battalion, 41st Field Artillery
12 Chemical	12th Chemical Company
26 FD	26th Field Regiment
32 HV	32nd Heavy Regiment
39 HV	39th Heavy Regiment
40 HV	40th Heavy Regiment
42nd FA Brigade	42nd Field Artillery Brigade
75th FA Brigade	75th Field Artillery Brigade
82 ABD	82nd Airborne Division
142nd FA Brigade	142nd Field Artillery Brigade
210th FA Brigade	210th Field Artillery Brigade
A-1-158 FA	Alfa Battery, 1st Battalion, 158th Field Artillery
A-6-27 FA	Alfa Battery, 6th Battalion, 27th Field Artillery
B-6 FA	Bravo Battery, 6th Field Artillery
C-26 TAB	Charlie Battery, 26th Field Artillery (Target Acquisition)
C-4-27 FA	Charlie Battery, 4th Battalion, 27th Field Artillery
D-25 TAB	Delta Battery, 25th Field Artillery (Target Acquisition)
E-333 TAB	Echo Battery, 333rd Field Artillery
HHB DIVARTY	Headquarters and Headquarters Battery, 1st Infantry Division Artillery

Military and Other Terms

1LT	First Lieutenant
1SG	First Sergeant
2LT	Second Lieutenant
AAR	After-action Review/Report
AB	Airborne
ACE	Armored Combat Earthmover
ACR	Armored Cavalry Regiment
ADC-M	Assistant Division Commander-Maneuver
ADC-S	Assistant Division Commander-Support
AFN	Armed Forces Network
AFSC	Armed Forces Staff College

AFTN	Armed Forces Television Network
AGI	Annual General Inspection
AHA	Ammunition Holding Area
A-Hour	Alert Hour
ALB	Air-Land Battle
ACM	Airspace Coordinating Measure
AM	Amplitude Modulation
AMC	Army Materiel Command
AO	Area of Operation
AR	Armor
ARCENT	Army Central Command
ASP	Ammunition Supply Point
ATACMS	Army Tactical Missile System
ATP	Ammunition Transfer Point
BCTP	Battle Command Training Program
BDU	Battle Dress Uniform
BG	Brigadier General
BLU-82	Bomb Live Unit
BRO	Big Red One
BSA	Brigade Support Area
CALL	Center for Army Lessons Learned
CARP	Corps Ammunition Resupply Point
CAS	Close Air Support
CAV	Cavalry
CDR	Commander
CENTCOM	Central Command
CESO	Communications and Electronic Signals Officer
CF	Command Fire Net
CG	Commanding General
CHEMO	Chemical Officer
CINC	Commander-in-Chief
COL	Colonel
COMM-X	Communications Exercise
CONUS	Continental United States
CoS	Chief of Staff
CP	Command Post
CPT	Captain
CPX	Command Post Exercise
CSM	Command Sergeant Major
CWO	Chief Warrant Officer

DAO	Division Ammunition Officer
DCC	Deployment Control Center
DCU	Desert Camouflage Uniforms
Decon	Decontamination
DIA	Defense Intelligence Agency
DISCOM	Division Support Command
DIVARTY	Division Artillery
DMMC	Division Materiel Management Center
DSA	Division Support Area
DSM	Distinguished Service Medal
DTAC	Division Tactical Assault Center
DTOC	Division Tactical Operation Center
ELINT	Electronic Intelligence
EM	Enlisted Man
EOD	Explosive Ordnance Attachment
FA	Field Artillery
FAA	Forward Assembly Area
FAO	Foreign Area Officer
FDC	Fire Direction Center
FDO	Fire Direction Officer
FLOT	Forward Line of Own Troops
FM	Frequency Modulation
FRAGO	Fragmentary Order
FRG	Federal Republic of Germany
FSCL	Fire Support Coordination Line
FSCM	Fire Support Coordination Measurers
FSE	Division Fire Support Element
FSO	Fire Support Officer
GCM	General Court-martial
G-Day	Ground Day
GEN	General
HEMTT	Heavy Expanded Mobility Tactical Truck
HHB	Headquarters and Headquarters Battery
HMMWV	High Mobility Multi-Purpose Wheeled Vehicle (Humvee)
ICAF	Industrial College of the Armed Forces
IDF	Israeli Defense Force
IFV	Infantry Fighting Vehicle
IN	Infantry
INS	Inertial Position-Navigation System

Iraqi 12AD	Iraqi 12th Armored Division
Iraqi 26ID	Iraqi 26th Infantry Division
Iraqi 48ID	Iraqi 48th Infantry Division
Iraqi 52AD	Iraqi 52nd Armored Division
JP-4	Jet Propellant-4
KFAFB	King Fahd Air Force Base
KFIA	King Fahd International Airport
KKMC	King Khalid Military City
KSU	Kansas State University
LAW	Light Anti-Tank Weapon
LID	Lost in Desert
LNO	Liaison Officer
LoD	Line of Demarcation
LTC	Lieutenant Colonel
LTG	Lieutenant General
M1 Tank	Abrams Tank
M2 IFV	Bradley Infantry Fighting Vehicle
MAAF	Marshall Army Airfield
MAJ	Major
MG	Major General
MHE	Mechanical Handling Equipment
MILVAN	Military Container Vans
MKT	Mobile Kitchen Trailer
MLRS	Multiple Launch Rocket System
MOPP	Mission Oriented Protective Posture
MP	Military Police
MPRC	Multi-Purpose Range Complex
MPS	Maritime Prepositioning Ship
MRE	Meals Ready to Eat
MSC	Military Sealift Command
MSR	Main Supply Route
MTMC	Military Traffic Management Command
NATO	North Atlantic Treaty Organization
NBC	Nuclear, Biological, and Chemical
NCO	Noncommissioned Officers
NODs	Night Observation Devices
NTC	National Training Center
OC	Observer Controller
ODS/DS	Operation Desert Shield/Desert Strom
OER	Officer Efficiency Reports

OGD	Observer Group Damascus
OIC	Officer in Charge
OP	Observation Post
OPCON	Operational Control
OPEC	Organization of Petroleum Exporting Countries
OPFOR	Opposition Force
OPORD	Operations Order
O/O	On Order
ORR	Operational Readiness Rate
PADS	Position and Azimuth Determining Systems
PB	Pyridostigmine Bromide
PCM	Pulse Code Modulation
PHOTINT	Photographic Intelligence
PL	Phase Line
PLO	Palestine Liberation Organization
POMCUS	Prepositioning of Materiel Configured in Unit Sets
PSA	Port Support Activity
PX	Post Exchange
RAA	Redeployment Assembly Area
Recon	Reconnaissance
RGFC	Republican Guard Forces Command
RO/RO	Roll-On/Roll-Off
RP	Release Point
S-1 or G1	Personnel Officer/Section
S-2 or G2	Intelligence Officer/Section
S-3 or G3	Operations Officer/Section
S-4 or G4	Logistics/Supply Officer/Section
S-5	Civil Affairs Officer/Section
SATCOM	Satellite Communications
SCP	Survey Control Point
SGM	Sergeant Major
SGT	Sergeant
SFC	Sergeant First Class
SIGINT	Signals Intelligence
SITREP	Situation Reports
SJA	Staff Judge Advocate
SP	Start Point
SP4	Specialist Fourth Class
SPLL	Self-Propelled Loader Launcher
SSG	Staff Sergeant

TAA	Tactical Assembly Area
TAB	Target Acquisition Battery
TACAIR	Tactical Air Support
TACFIRE	Tactical Fire Direction System
Tapline	Trans-Arabian Pipeline
TAT	To Accompany Troops Gear
Tawakalna	Tawakalna Republican Guards Division
TDY	Temporary Duty
TRADOC	Training and Doctrine Command
TTP	Tactics, Techniques, and Procedures
TWT	Telewave Tube
UCMJ	Uniform Code of Military Justice
UNTSO	United Nations Truce Supervision Organization
USAREUR	US Army in Europe
WMD	Weapons of Mass Destruction
XO	Executive Officer

Notes

Introduction

1. The author's original map and reproduced original graphics now reside in the First Division Museum in Wheaton, Illinois. https://www.fdmuseum.org/.

2. Fort Riley

1. Directorate of Resource Management, Fort Riley, KS, "Economic Impact Summary, Fort Riley Kansas, 1 October 1990 to 30 September 1991," 1991.

3. The Convergence of Leaders

1. Colonel Michael Dodson, Commander, Division Artillery, 1st Infantry Division, interview by Major Thomas A, Popa, July 24–25, 1991, at Fort Riley, KS, U.S. Army Center for Military History, CMH Catalogue No. DSIT-C-068, July 24, 1991, 2.

2. 1–5 FA actually did not have a "C" Battery as most artillery battalions do. But they did have a "D" Battery that traced its lineage back to Alexander Hamilton's command of the battery, called "Hamilton's Own," during the Revolutionary War.

4. The Approaching Storm

1. Lieutenant Colonel Joseph P. Englehardt, "SSI Special Report Desert Shield and Desert Storm: A Chronology and Troop List for the 1990–1991 Persian Gulf Crisis" (Carlisle, PA: U.S. Army War College, 1991), 11.

2. Englehardt, "SSI Special Report," 12–13.

3. Colonel (Ret.) Greg Fontenot, "Operation Desert Storm: The 100 Hour War," *Bridgehead Sentinel,* Spring 2016, 16.

4. Fontenot, "Operation Desert Storm: The 100 Hour War," 16.

5. Colonel Michael Dodson, Commander, Division Artillery, 1st Infantry Division, interview by Major Thomas A, Popa, July 24–25, 1991, at Fort Riley, KS, U.S. Army Center for Military History, CMH Catalogue No. DSIT-C-068, July 24, 1991, 6–7.

6. 1st Infantry Division Warning Order, November 10, 1990.

7. Warning Order.

8. Major Ed Cardenas, "Expecting the Unexpected; My Experience with the 1st Infantry Division (Mech) during Operation Desert Storm" (lecture to the Rand Corporation, Santa Monica, CA, April 1993).

9. Cardenas, "Expecting the Unexpected."

10. Cardenas, "Expecting the Unexpected."

11. Fontenot, "Operation Desert Storm: The 100 Hour War," 17.

12. Fontenot, "Operation Desert Storm: The 100 Hour War," 16–17.

13. Captain Larry D. Seefeldt, "D Battery, 25th Artillery (TA) 'Wolfpack' Desert Shield/Desert Storm Historical Review 12 January–12 May 1991," July 19, 1991.

14. Dodson, interview by Popa, 10.

5. A First-Class Ride to Confusion

1. Lieutenant Colonel Joseph P. Englehardt, "SSI Special Report Desert Shield and Desert Storm: A Chronology and Troop List for the 1990–1991 Persian Gulf Crisis" (Carlisle, PA: U. S. Army War College, 1991), 5–10.

2. Colonel Michael Dodson, Commander, Division Artillery, 1st Infantry Division, interview by Major Thomas A, Popa, July 24–25, 1991, at Fort Riley, KS, U.S. Army Center for Military History, CMH Catalogue No. DSIT-C-068, July 24, 1991, 11.

3. Englehardt, "SSI Special Report," 48.

4. Englehardt, "SSI Special Report," 49.

6. War

1. Captain Murvin R. Hymel, "HHB 1st Infantry Division Artillery in Operation Desert Storm," 1991.

2. Colonel Ed Cardenas, US Army (Retired), email memorandum and message to the author, June 27, 2018.

3. Cardenas, email, June 27, 2018.

4. Colonel Vance P. Visser, US Army (Retired), email message to the author, February 6, 2018.

5. Cardenas, email, June 27, 2018.

6. Major General Thomas G. Rhame, "General Officer's Note for Soldiers of the First Division," January 17, 1991.

7. I spoke to Bill Turner, who would go on to become a brigadier general, about this incident years later. He informed me that he in fact returned the bus to the port the following day.

8. Lieutenant Colonel Joseph P. Englehardt, "SSI Special Report Desert Shield and Desert Storm: A Chronology and Troop List for the 1990–1991 Persian Gulf Crisis" (Carlisle, PA: U.S. Army War College, 1991), 50.

9. Englehardt, "SSI Special Report," 50.

10. Rhame, "General Officer's Note," January 17, 1991.

11. As evidence of my exhaustion late that night, my entry should have read "Saudis."

7. Preparing for the Fight

1. Major Ed Cardenas, "Expecting the Unexpected; My Experience with the 1st Infantry Division (Mech) during Operation Desert Storm" (lecture to the Rand Corporation, Santa Monica, CA, April 1993.)

2. Carl von Clausewitz, "Book 1, Chapter 7," in On War, translated by J. J. Graham (London: Nicholas Trübner, 1873; previously published Berlin: Dümmlers Verlag, 1832), under "Friction in War," https://www.clausewitz.com /readings/OnWar1873/BK1ch07.html.

3. Colonel Robert Land "Lanny" Smith, US Army (Retired), email message to the author, April 17, 2018.

4. Colonel Michael Dodson, Commander, Division Artillery, 1st Infantry Division, interview by Major Thomas A, Popa, July 24–25, 1991 at Fort Riley, KS, U.S. Army Center for Military History, CMH Catalogue No. DSIT-C-068, July 24, 1991, 17.

5. Colonel Vance P. Visser, US Army (Retired), email message to the author, February 6, 2018.

6. Cardenas, "Expecting the Unexpected."

7. Gregory Fontenot, The 1st Infantry Division and the US Army Transformed: Road to Victory in Desert Storm 1970–1991 (Columbia: University of Missouri Press, 2017), 168.

8. Lieutenant Colonel Joseph P. Englehardt, "SSI Special Report Desert Shield and Desert Storm: A Chronology and Troop List for the 1990–1991 Persian Gulf Crisis" (Carlisle, PA: U.S. Army War College, 1991), 61.

9. Fontenot, Road to Victory, 135.

10. Lieutenant Colonel Steve Payne, US Army (Retired), email message to the author, April 19, 2018.

11. Payne, email, April 19, 2018.

12. Payne, email, April 19, 2018.

8. A Fight to Remember

1. Lieutenant Colonel Lee S. Lingamfelter, "Operation Desert Shield Lessons-Learned," 1st Infantry Division Artillery Memorandum, October 15, 1990, 1–9.

2. Major Ed Cardenas, "Expecting the Unexpected; My Experience with the 1st Infantry Division (Mech) during Operation Desert Storm" (lecture to the Rand Corporation, Santa Monica, CA, April 1993).

3. 1st Infantry Division Memorandum for the Commanding General VII Corps, "Operation Desert Shield and Desert Storm Command Report," Annex A-E, (Chronology of Events, Desert Storm Overview, OPLAN/OPORD SCORPION DANGER, Staff Journal, Lessons Learned), April 19, 1991.

4. Colonel Michael L Dodson, Personal Journal, Saudi Arabia, February 14, 1991.

5. Captain Murvin R. Hymel, "HHB 1st Infantry Division Artillery in Operation Desert Storm," 1991.

6. ANNEX D (FIRE SUPPORT), Operation Order (OPORD 14–91 (OPERATION SCORPION DANGER), January 19, 1991.

7. 1st Infantry Division Artillery, Memorandum for the Commanding General VII Corps Artillery, "The actions of the 1 ID (M) Artillery during Operation Desert Storm, etc.," March 25, 1991.

8. Colonel Michael Dodson, Commander, Division Artillery, 1st Infantry Division, interview by Major Thomas A, Popa, July 24–25, 1991 at Fort Riley, KS, U.S. Army Center for Military History, CMH Catalogue No. DSIT-C-068, July 24, 1991, 18.

9. Dodson, interview by Popa, 19.

10. Captain Murvin R. Hymel, "HHB 1st Infantry Division Artillery," 1991.

11. In my diary, I incorrectly recorded that the rounds fell "east" of our TOC, when, in fact, they fell to the west.

12. 1st Infantry Division, Memorandum for the Commanding General VII Corps, "Operation Desert Shield and Desert Storm Command Report," Annex A-E, (Chronology of Events, Desert Storm Overview, OPLAN/OPORD SCORPION DANGER, Staff Journal, Lessons Learned), April 19, 1991.

13. 1st Infantry Division, Memorandum, "Operation Desert Shield and Desert Storm Chronology of Events" (Declassified), March 14, 1991.

14. 1st Infantry Division, "Chronology," March 14, 1991.

15. Leon Daniel, "Artillery Shots Greased Ground Surge," UPI, February 24, 1991. https://www.upi.com/Archives/1991/02/24/Artilley-shots-greased-ground-surge/5035667371600/.

16. 1st Infantry Division Artillery, Memorandum to VII Corps Artillery.

17. 1st Infantry Division Artillery, Memorandum to VII Corps Artillery.

9. Into the Breach

1. Colonel Michael Dodson, Commander, Division Artillery, 1st Infantry Division, interview by Major Thomas A. Popa, July 24–25, 1991, at Fort Riley, KS, U.S. Army Center for Military History, CMH Catalogue No. DSIT-C-068, July 24, 1991, 22.

2. Dodson, interview by Popa, 23.

3. 1st Infantry Division Artillery, Memorandum for the Commanding General VII Corps Artillery, "The actions of the 1 ID (M) Artillery during Operation Desert Storm, etc.," March 25, 1991.

4. Dodson, interview by Popa, 24.

5. Colonel Vance P. Visser, US Army (Retired), email message to the author, February 2, 2018.

6. Visser, email, February 2, 2018.

7. Lieutenant Colonel David Fowles, US Army (Retired), email message to the author, June 20, 2018.

8. 1st Infantry Division Artillery, Memorandum to VII Corps Artillery, March 25, 1991.

9. Dodson, interview by Popa, 42.

10. 1st Infantry Division Artillery, Memorandum to VII Corps Artillery.

11. 1st Infantry Division, Memorandum for the Commanding General VII Corps, "Operation Desert Shield and Desert Storm Command Report," Annex A-E, (Chronology of Events, Desert Storm Overview, OPLAN/OPORD SCORPION DANGER, Staff Journal, Lessons Learned), April 19, 1991.

12. 1st Infantry Division, Memorandum, "Operation Desert Shield and Desert Storm Chronology of Events" (Declassified), March 14, 1991.

13. Captain Murvin R. Hymel, "HHB 1st Infantry Division Artillery in Operation Desert Storm," 1991.

14. Stan Finger. "Fort Riley families worry—and wait," *Wichita Eagle*, February 24, 1991.

15. 1st Infantry Division, "Chronology," March 14, 1991.

16. Visser, email, February 2, 2018.

17. GAO Report to Congressional Requesters, OPERATION DESERT STORM Casualties Caused by Improper Handling of Unexploded U.S. Submunitions, (Washington, DC: General Accounting Office, August 1991), 3–4. https://www.gao.gov/assets/220/218254.pdf.

18. Major Ed Cardenas, "Expecting the Unexpected; My Experience with the 1st Infantry Division (Mech) during Operation Desert Storm" (lecture to the Rand Corporation, Santa Monica, CA, April 1993.)

10. A Relentless Pursuit

1. 1st Infantry Division, Memorandum for the Commanding General VII Corps, "Operation Desert Shield and Desert Storm Command Report," Annex A-E, (Chronology of Events, Desert Storm Overview, OPLAN/OPORD SCORPION DANGER, Staff Journal, Lessons Learned), April 19, 1991.

2. 1st Infantry Division Memorandum, "Command Report," April 19, 1991.

3. Carl von Clausewitz, "Book 1, Chapter 3," in *On War*, translated by J. J. Graham (London: Nicholas Trübner, 1873; previously published Berlin:

Dümmlers Verlag, 1832), under "The Genius for War," https://www.clausewitz
.com/readings/OnWar1873/BK1ch03.html#a.

4. Lieutenant Colonel James M. Holt, US Army (Retired), email message to
the author, May 31, 2018.

5. 1st Infantry Division, Memorandum, "Command Report," April 19,
1991.

6. Captain Murvin R. Hymel, "HHB 1st Infantry Division Artillery in Operation Desert Storm," 1991.

7. Colonel Michael L Dodson, Personal Journal, Iraq, February 27, 1991.

8. Major Ed Cardenas, "Expecting the Unexpected; My Experience with the
1st Infantry Division (Mech) during Operation Desert Storm" (lecture to the
Rand Corporation, Santa Monica, CA, April 1993).

9. 210th Field Artillery Brigade, Memorandum, "Summary of Significant
Events for the 210th Field Artillery Brigade during the Ground War in Operation
Desert Storm, 23–28 February 1991," March 12, 1991.

10. Captain Larry D. Seefeldt, "D Battery, 25th Artillery (TA) 'Wolfpack'
Desert Shield/Desert Storm Historical Review 12 January—12 May 1991," July
19, 1991.

11. Captain Murvin R. Hymel, "HHB 1st Infantry Division Artillery in Operation Desert Storm," 1991.

12. Lieutenant Colonel Steve Payne, US Army (Retired), email message to the
author, April 19, 2018; Colonel Donald A. Osterberg, US Army (Retired), memorandum to the author, August 8, 2019.

13. Cardenas, "Expecting the Unexpected."

14. Cardenas, "Expecting the Unexpected."

15. Cardenas, "Expecting the Unexpected."

16. 1st Infantry Division Artillery, Memorandum for the Commanding General VII Corps Artillery, "The Actions of the 1 ID (M) Artillery during Operation
Desert Storm, etc.," March 25, 1991.

17. Colonel Ralph G. Reece, Memorandum for Record, "155mm Ammunition and Fuze Use Southwest Asia," September 12. 1991.

11. An Uncertain Peace

1. 1st Infantry Division Chronology of Major Events, 1991.

2. 1st Infantry Division Chronology of Major Events, 1991.

3. Major Ed Cardenas, "Expecting the Unexpected; My Experience with the
1st Infantry Division (Mech) during Operation Desert Storm" (lecture to the
Rand Corporation, Santa Monica, CA, April 1993).

4. Robert S. Boyd. "Victory Iraq accepts all U. N. resolutions," Wichita Eagle,
February 28,1991.

5. General H. Norman Schwarzkopf and Peter Petre, It Doesn't Take a Hero
(New York: Bantam Books, 1992), 475.

6. Gregory Fontenot, *The 1st Infantry Division and the US Army Transformed: Road to Victory in Desert Storm 1970–1991* (Columbia: University of Missouri Press, 2017), 421.

7. Schwarzkopf and Petre, *It Doesn't Take a Hero,* 475.

8. Kevin Hymel, "Battle on the Basra Road," January 20, 2015. https://army history.org/battle-on-the-basra-road/.

9. Hymel, "Battle on the Basra Road."

10. Colonel Michael L. Dodson, Personal Journal, Kuwait, March 1, 1991.

11. Lieutenant Colonel John R. Gingrich, "The Battle of Safwan, Iraq," U.S. Army War College Study Project, June 8, 1992, 27.

12. Gingrich, "The Battle of Safwan, Iraq," 27.

13. Hymel, "Battle on the Basra Road."

14. Hymel, "Battle on the Basra Road."

15. Gingrich, "The Battle of Safwan, Iraq," 36.

16. Fontenot, *Road to Victory,* 421.

17. Lieutenant Colonel Steve Payne, US Army (Retired), email message to the author, April 19, 2018.

18. Schwarzkopf and Petre, *It Doesn't Take a Hero,* 478.

19. Schwarzkopf and Petre, *It Doesn't Take a Hero,* 478.

20. Fontenot, *Road to Victory,* 426.

21. 1st Infantry Division, Memorandum for the Commanding General VII Corps, "Operation Desert Shield and Desert Storm Command Report," Annex A-E (Chronology of Events, Desert Storm Overview, OPLAN/OPORD SCORPION DANGER, Staff Journal, Lessons Learned), April 19, 1991.

22. Payne, email, April 19, 2018.

23. Philip Shenon, "AFTER THE WAR: Cease-Fire Meeting; A Hard-Faced Schwarzkopf Sets Terms at Desert Meeting," *The New York Times,* March 4,1991. http://www.nytimes.com/1991/03/04/world/after-war-cease-fire-meeting -hard-faced-schwarzkopf-sets-terms-desert-meeting.html.

24. C-SPAN, General Norman Schwarzkopf Commander, Desert Storm and Lt. General Khalid bin Sultan, Commander, Joint Arab Forces, Safwan, Iraq, Cable Video, 12:18, posted by CSPAN, March 3, 1991, https://www.c-span.org /video/?16896–1/us-iraq-cease-fire-meeting.

25. Lieutenant Colonel Joseph P. Englehardt, "SSI Special Report Desert Shield and Desert Storm: A Chronology and Troop List for the 1990–1991 Persian Gulf Crisis" (Carlisle, PA: U.S. Army War College, 1991), 75.

26. Colonel Vance P. Visser, US Army (Retired), email message to the author, February 6, 2018.

27. Captain Richard E. Nichols Jr., "Bravo Battery, 6th Field Artillery Operation Desert Storm Historical Review," July 19, 1991.

28. President George H. W. Bush, "Address Before a Joint Session of Congress on the End of the Gulf War, March 6, 1991," https://millercenter.org/the-presidency /presidential-speeches/march-6–1991-address-joint-session-congress-end-gulf-war.

29. Bush, "Address to Congress," March 6, 1991.

30. 1st Infantry Division, Memorandum, "Operation Desert Shield and Desert Storm Chronology of Events" (Declassified), March 14, 1991, 10.

31. The combat uniform version of the 1st Infantry Division patch had a black or "subdued" numeral "1" in keeping with our camouflage scheme.

12. An Unresolved Peace

1. Gregory Fontenot, *The 1st Infantry Division and the US Army Transformed: Road to Victory in Desert Storm 1970–1991* (Columbia: University of Missouri Press, 2017), 437.

2. Lieutenant Colonel Joseph P. Englehardt, "SSI Special Report Desert Shield and Desert Storm: A Chronology and Troop List for the 1990–1991 Persian Gulf Crisis" (Carlisle, PA: U.S. Army War College, 1991), 82.

3. Major Ed Cardenas, "Expecting the Unexpected; My Experience with the 1st Infantry Division (Mech) during Operation Desert Storm" (lecture to the Rand Corporation, Santa Monica, CA, April 1993).

4. Lieutenant Colonel L. Scott Lingamfelter, "In the Wake of the Storm: Improving the FA after Operation Desert Storm," *Field Artillery,* August 1991, 27–29.

5. Cardenas, "Expecting the Unexpected."

13. The Long March Home

1. Major Ed Cardenas, "Expecting the Unexpected; My Experience with the 1st Infantry Division (Mech) during Operation Desert Storm" (lecture to the Rand Corporation, Santa Monica, CA, April 1993).

2. Gregory Fontenot, *The 1st Infantry Division and the US Army Transformed: Road to Victory in Desert Storm 1970–1991* (Columbia: University of Missouri Press, 2017), 438.

3. Two years later, when I was in command of the 6th Battalion, 37th Field Artillery in the 2nd Infantry Division in South Korea, I was grateful for my experience commanding the PSA and the lessons I learned.

4. As a footnote to this story, *Nosac Rover,* later named *Terrier,* was still in service in 2017 and flagged under Norway. Apparently, its construction was very sound as evidenced by this website, http://ship-photo-roster.com/ship/terrier, accessed April 13, 2018.

5. As noted in table 13–2, there were discrepancies in the total number of vehicles and trailers the PSA actually loaded in the port bound for the US and how we accounted for the total number. Moreover, the total number includes not only the division's vehicles and trailers, but a US field artillery battalion stationed in Europe as well as some vehicles from the 1st Cavalry Division at Fort Hood, Texas, that we also loaded on our ships. In sum, our total turned out to be 6,524, a figure I discovered after I reconciled my diaries with other PSA records.

14. Retrospective and Reality

1. Nese F. DeBruyne, American War and Military Operations Casualties: Lists and Statistics (Washington, DC: Congressional Research Service Updated September 14, 2018), 14–15, https://fas.org/sgp/crs/natsec/RL32492.pdf, accessed December 20, 2018.

2. DeBruyne, Casualties, 9–10.

3. Colonel Michael Dodson, Commander, Division Artillery, 1st Infantry Division, interview by Major Thomas A. Popa, July 24–25, 1991, at Fort Riley, KS, U.S. Army Center for Military History, CMH Catalogue No. DSIT-C-068, July 24, 1991, 16.

4. President George H. W. Bush, "Address to the Nation on the Invasion of Iraq, January 16, 1991." https://millercenter.org/the-presidency/presidential-speeches/january-16-1991-address-nation-invasion-iraq.

5. President George H. W. Bush, "Address Before a Joint Session of Congress on the End of the Gulf War, March 6, 1991," https://millercenter.org/the-presidency/presidential-speeches/march-6-1991-address-joint-session-congress-end-gulf-war.

6. Bush, "Address to Congress," March 6, 1991.

7. Bush, "Address to Congress," March 6, 1991.

8. Bush, "Address to Congress," March 6, 1991.

9. Bush, "Address to Congress," March 6, 1991.

10. Larry P. Arnn, "Three Lessons of Statesmanship," Imprimis 46, no. 12 (December 2017): 2–7.

11. Arnn, "Three Lessons of Statesmanship."

12. Arnn, "Three Lessons of Statesmanship."

13. Arnn, "Three Lessons of Statesmanship."

14. Arnn, "Three Lessons of Statesmanship."

15. Arnn, "Three Lessons of Statesmanship."

16. Charles Pelot Summerall, The Way of Duty, Honor, Country; The Memoir of General Charles Pelot Summerall, edited by Timothy K. Nenniger (Lexington: The University Press of Kentucky, 2010), 235.

Bibliography

Books

Englehardt, Joseph P., Lieutenant Colonel. *SSI Special Report Desert Shield and Desert Storm: A Chronology and Troop List for the 1990–1991 Persian Gulf Crisis*. Carlisle, PA: U.S. Army War College, 1991.

DeBruyne, Nese F. *American War and Military Operations Casualties: Lists and Statistics*. Washington, DC: Congressional Research Service, updated September 14, 2018. https://fas.org/sgp/crs/natsec/RL32492.pdf, accessed December 20, 2018.

Fontenot, Gregory. *The 1st Infantry Division and the US Army Transformed: Road to Victory in Desert Storm 1970–1991*. Columbia: University of Missouri Press, 2017.

GAO Report to Congressional Requesters. *OPERATION DESERT STORM Casualties Caused by Improper Handling of Unexploded U.S. Submunitions*. Washington, DC: General Accounting Office, 1991.

Schwarzkopf, H. Norman, and Peter Petre. *It Doesn't Take a Hero*. New York: Bantam Books, 1992.

Summerall, Charles Pelot. *The Way of Duty, Honor, Country; The Memoir of General Charles Pelot Summerall*. Edited by Timothy K. Nenniger. Lexington: The University Press of Kentucky, 2010.

Articles

Fontenot, Greg, Colonel (Ret). "Operation Desert Storm: The 100 Hour War." *Bridgehead Sentinel*, Spring 2016.

Lingamfelter, L. Scott, Lieutenant Colonel. "In the Wake of the Storm: Improving the FA after Operation Desert Storm." *Field Artillery*, August 1991.

Interviews

Dodson, Michael, Colonel, Commander, Division Artillery, 1st Infantry Division.
Interview by Major Thomas A. Popa, 24–25 July 1991. U. S. Army Center for
Military History, CMH Catalogue No. DSIT-C-068.

After-action Reports/Reviews

Cardenas, Ed, Major. "Expecting the Unexpected; My Experience with the 1st
Infantry Division (Mech) during Operation Desert Storm." Lecture to the
Rand Corporation, Santa Monica, CA, 1993.

Hymel, Murvin R., Captain. "HHB 1st Infantry Division Artillery in Operation
Desert Storm," 1991.

Nichols, Richard E. Jr., Captain. "Bravo Battery, 6th Field Artillery Operation
Desert Storm Historical Review," July 19, 1991.

Seefeldt, Larry D., Captain. "D Battery, 25th Artillery (TA) 'Wolfpack' Desert
Shield/Desert Storm Historical Review 12 January—12 May 1991," July 19,
1991.

1st Infantry Division and Division Artillery Documents, Reports, Plans, and Orders Division

1st Infantry Division Memorandum. "Operation Desert Shield and Desert Storm
Chronology of Events" (Declassified), 14 March 1991.

1st Infantry Division Memorandum for the Commanding General VII Corps.
"Operation Desert Shield and Desert Storm Command Report," Annex A-E
(Chronology of Events, Desert Storm Overview, OPLAN/OPORD SCOR-
PION DANGER, Staff Journal, Lessons Learned), April 19, 1991.

ANNEX D (FIRE SUPPORT), Operation Order (OPORD) 14–91 (OPERATION
SCORPION DANGER), January 19, 1991.

1st Infantry Division Timeline, 1991.

Division Artillery (DIVARTY)

1st Infantry Division Artillery Memorandum for the Commanding General VII
Corps Artillery. "The actions of the 1 ID (M) Artillery during Operation Desert Storm, etc.," March 25, 1991.

Index